Rational Analysis for a Problematic World Revisited

Rational Analysis for a Problematic World Revisited

Problem Structuring Methods for Complexity, Uncertainty and Conflict

Second Edition

Edited by

Jonathan Rosenhead & John Mingers

JOHN WILEY & SONS, LTD
Chichester · New York · Weinheim · Brisbane · Singapore · Toronto

Other Wiley Editorial Offices

John Wiley & Sons, Inc., 605 Third Avenue,
New York, NY 10158-0012, USA

Wiley-VCH Verlag GmbH, Pappelallee 3,
D-69469 Weinheim, Germany

John Wiley Australia, Ltd, 33 Park Road, Milton,
Queensland 4064, Australia

John Wiley & Sons (Asia) Pte Ltd, 2 Clementi Loop #02-01,
Jin Xing Distripark, Singapore 129809

John Wiley & Sons (Canada) Ltd, 22 Worcester Road,
Rexdale, Ontario M9W 1L1, Canada

British Library Cataloguing in Publication Data

A catalogue record for this book is available from the British Library

ISBN 0-471-49523-9

Typeset in 11/13pt Baskerville by Footnote Graphics, Warminster, Wiltshire
Printed and bound in Great Britain by Biddles Ltd, Guildford and King's Lynn.
This book is printed on acid-free paper responsibly manufactured from sustainable forestry, in which at least two trees are planted for each one used for paper production.

Contents

Contributors   vii

Preface   xiii

Acknowledgements   xvii

1   A New Paradigm of Analysis   1
    Jonathan Rosenhead and John Mingers

2   SODA – The Principles   21
    Colin Eden and Fran Ackermann

3   SODA – Journey Making and Mapping in Practice   43
    Fran Ackermann and Colin Eden

4   Soft Systems Methodology   61
    Peter Checkland

5   Soft Systems Methodology in Action: Participative Creation
    of an Information Strategy for an Acute Hospital   91
    Peter Checkland

6   The Strategic Choice Approach   115
    John Friend

7   Gambling with Frozen Fire?   151
    Allen Hickling

8   Robustness Analysis: Keeping Your Options Open   181
    Jonathan Rosenhead

9 Robustness to the First Degree   209
Jonathan Rosenhead

10 Drama Theory and Confrontation Analysis   225
Peter Bennett, Jim Bryant and Nigel Howard

11 The M&A Play: Using Drama Theory for Mergers and Acquisitions   249
Nigel Howard

12 An Overview of Related Methods: VSM, System Dynamics, and Decision Analysis   267
John Mingers and Jonathan Rosenhead

13 Multimethodology – Mixing and Matching Methods   289
John Mingers

14 Mixing Methods in Practice   311
Richard Ormerod

15 Diverse Unity: Looking Inward and Outward   337
John Mingers and Jonathan Rosenhead

Index   357

Contributors

Fran Ackermann

Professor at Strathclyde University

Fran Ackermann is a Professor in the Management Science Department at Strathclyde University, Scotland. She is interested in the role that Group Decision Support Systems and Cause Mapping can play in supporting the development and implementation of strategy and in risk assessment and forensic modelling. She has wide experience with both public and private organizations from a consultancy/action research basis and has written widely in the areas of operational research, strategy and information systems.

Dr Peter Bennett

Department of Health, London

Following a degree in Physics and PhD in Philosophy of Science, Peter joined the Operational Research Group at Sussex University, researching on decision-making in conflicts. This started a long-term interest in decisions involving risk, uncertainty, multiple objectives and conflict. Moving to Strathclyde University in 1987 as senior lecturer and then Reader in Management Science, he served as Postgraduate Course Director. He was also involved in consultancy and applied research work for organizations ranging from multinational companies to local community groups. In 1996 he joined the Economics and Operational Research Division of the Department of Health as Principal OR Analyst. His work has covered various policy areas, but with a particular focus on analysis of risks to public health, including issues of risk communication and governance. Meanwhile he has continued to collaborate with academic colleagues, particularly in the development of Drama Theory.

Jim Bryant

Professor at Sheffield Hallam University,

Jim Bryant is Professor of Operational Research and Strategy Sciences at Sheffield Hallam University. Over the past decade he has been centrally involved in the development and application of drama-based analysis and methods, notably for handling intra- and interorganizational relationships. Alongside his work on strategic partnerships and alliances, he has acted as a problem-structuring consultant and facilitator particularly to public sector and community clients. He is presently Chairman of the Conflict Research Society, a widely-based professional body concerned with the study of conflict and collaboration at all levels in society.

Peter Checkland

Professor at Lancaster University

Peter Checkland gained a first in Chemistry at Oxford in the 1950s. He joined ICI when it was developing a new industry: making synthetic fibres from nylon and polyester polymers. Working first as a technologist then as a manager, Peter remained with ICI for fifteen years. When he left to start a second career in university teaching and research, he was manager of a 100-strong research and development group.

Joining the postgraduate Department of Systems Engineering at Lancaster University, Peter Checkland led what became a thirty-year programme of action research in organizations outside the university. Initially the research theme was to examine the possibility of using the well-developed methods of systems engineering in management problem situations rather than in the technically defined problem situations in which the methods had been refined. The work finally established Soft Systems Methodology (SSM) as an approach to tackling the multi-faceted problems which managers face; in doing this, it also established the now well-recognized distinction between 'hard' and 'soft' systems thinking. SSM is now taught and used around the world. Its development through action research is described in many papers and in four books: *Systems Thinking, Systems Practice* (1981); *Soft Systems Methodology in Action* (with J Scholes, 1990); *Systems Information and Information Systems* (with Sue Holwell, 1998) and *SSM: A 30-Year Retrospective* (1999).

Peter Checkland's work has been recognized in a number of awards: he holds honorary doctorates from City University, the Open University and Erasmus University (The Netherlands), a Most Distinguished and Outstanding Award from the British Computer Society, and the Gold Medal of the UK Systems Society.

Colin Eden

Director at University of Strathclyde

Colin Eden is Director of the University of Stratchclyde Graduate School of Business, and is Professor of Management Science. He has written over 200 articles published in management, operational research, and strategy journals. His book, with Sue Jones and David Sims, *Messing About in Problems* (Pergamon, 1983) was the first version of the approach to problem structuring reported in this volume. He has published seven books in the field of management science, managerial and organizational cognition, group decision support, and strategy making. His most recent book, with Fran Ackermann entitled *Making Strategy: the Journey of Strategic Management*, introduces an attention to the strategy making process and the role of qualitative modelling to a strategic management audience. Recently he has been a consultant to the senior management teams of, for example, Scottish Natural Heritage, the Northern Ireland Office, Elsevier Science, the Royal Ulster Constabulary, and Bombardier. As well as a continuing interest in strategic problem solving and strategy making, he is currently conducting research into strategic risk and the behaviour of disrupted and delayed complex projects.

John Friend

Lincoln School of Management, University of Lincoln

John Friend, after graduating in mathematics from Cambridge, worked for ten years in management support roles in the steel, airline and chemical industries, before joining in 1964 the new Institute for Operational Research in the Tavistock Institute of Human Relations. Here, working alongside social scientists, he carried out research on policy making in city government and played a leading role in pioneering the Strategic Choice Approach to planning under uncertainty. This paved the way for several further action research projects in aspects of public planning, especially in inter-organisational policy domains. With Allen Hickling and other colleagues, he built up wide experience in facilitating strategic choice workshops, as reported in their joint book *Planning under Pressure: the Strategic Choice Approach* (second edition Butterworth-Heinemann 1997). Since leaving the Tavistock Institute in 1986, he has been developing software for strategic choice and also undertaking further development work in fields ranging from local community action to the participatory management of international development projects. He is currently a Vice-President of the Operational Research Society and a visiting professor at the new University of Lincoln.

Allen Hickling

Allen Hickling and Associates, Rugby

Allen Hickling qualified as an architect in Bristol after an early career which involved experience as a sailor, railway porter and semi-professional magician. Moving to North America, he worked as a planner, design consultant and racing driver before taking his Master's degree in Architecture and City Planning at the University of Pennsylvania. After joining the IOR Coventry office in 1971, he took responsibility for a wide range of action research projects, producing a handbook on the Strategic Choice Approach which was translated into French, Dutch and Portuguese. Since starting his own consultancy in 1980, he has become deeply involved in applying Strategic Choice principles and methods to policy-making, in collaboration with civil servants, industrialists and others, especially in The Netherlands.

Over the last decade he has worked more in the UK with groups of multi-organizational stakeholders concerned primarily with environmental issues.

Nigel Howard

MD and Chairman, ISCO Ltd

Visiting Professor at Sheffield Hallam University

His early work in game theory was applied to the first SALT agreement, nuclear proliferation and Vietnam; it has since been used on many business and government policy problems. In recent years he has been the chief developer of a new approach – 'drama theory'. He has taught at the LSE and the Universities of Pennsylvania, Waterloo, Ottawa and Aston. From 1987 to 1997 he published a bi-monthly research letter Co-operation or conflict, now an Internet site (www.nhoward.demon.co.uk/drama.htm).

He is the author or two books and numerous articles in books and scientific journals. From 1997 onwards he has applied a technique derived from drama theory – Confrontation Analysis – to defence problems. This has resulted in a new paradigm application to Peace Suppose Operations and a project for a Command and Control System for Confrontations. He is developing proposals for implementing this new paradigm through changes in military doctrine, training, organisation, methods and systems. A cognate system will provide integrated support, at all levels for companies that need to make a success of alliances.

John Mingers
Professor of OR and Systems, Warwick University
John Mingers is Professor of Operational Research and Systems at Warwick Business School, University of Warwick. He is Subject Leader for the OR and Systems Group and was Programme Director for the M.Sc. in Management Science and Operational Research. He is also a past Chair of the UK Systems Society and has been a member of the Council of the OR Society. John studied Management Sciences for his first degree at Warwick and later completed a Masters in Systems in Management at Lancaster University. In between he worked firstly as a systems analyst and then as an OR analyst for British Leyland, Miles Druce (a steel stockholding company) and Elida Gibbs (part of Unilever). His research interests include the use of systems methodologies in problem situations – particularly the mixing of different methodologies within an intervention (multimethodology); the development of the critical systems approach; autopoiesis and its applications; and the nature of information and meaning. He has published over 50 papers in these areas in journals such as the *Journal of the Operational Research Society*, *Systems Practice*, *Omega*, and the *Journal of Applied Systems Analysis*. He has published the first comprehensive study of autopoiesis – *Self-Producing Systems: Implications and Applications of Autopoiesis*, and has also edited *Multimethodology: the Theory and Practice of Combining Management Science Methodologies* (with Tony Gill) and *Information Systems: an Emerging Discipline?* (with Prof. Frank Stowell).

Richard Ormerod
Professor at University of Warwick
Richard Ormerod, having qualified as a civil engineer, pursued a careeer in engineering consultancy, factory management, operational research, corporate strategy and management consultancy. He is currently Professor of Management and Associate Dean Executive Programme at Warwick Business School. Previously he was Business Manager at PA Consulting Group in charge of the Information Technology Strategy Unit.

Jonathan Rosenhead
Professor at London School of Economics
Jonathan Rosenhead has been on the staff of the London School of Economics for over 30 years, and Professor of Operational Research since 1987. Prior to becoming an

academic he worked in the steel industry and as a management consultant. He is the author of over 70 professional publications. His fields of research interest, in addition to problem structuring methods, include health services planning, community operational research, OR in less developed countries, policy analysis, the social responsibility of OR, and the history of operational research. He has been President of the Operational Research Society, and holds its President's, Goodeve and Beale Medals.

Preface

Why this book has been written

The purpose of this book is to provide an introduction to a range of methods for structuring issues, problems and decision situations, rather than 'solving' them. Until the first edition of this book (Rosenhead, 1989) was published, accounts of some of these methods were available only in scattered articles in technical journals. Others had been expounded in books, each offering a substantial presentation of one particular methodology (Checkland, 1981; Eden, Jones and Sims, 1983; Friend and Hickling, 1987). There was therefore no easily accessible introduction to the full range of available methods. Indeed it was substantially the publication of the first edition of *Rational Analysis for a Problematic World* which led to their recognition as members of a single coherent field, that of problem structuring methods (PSMs), rather than being seen as a collection of unrelated methods.

In the intervening period, problem structuring methods have become widely accepted as a significant new direction for operational research and the systems movement. One quantitative index of this advance is given by a recent comparative analysis of citations of papers published in the *Journal of the Operational Research Society* between 1981 and 1999 (Ranyard, 2001). Of the 13 authors whose work had been cited more than 100 times, 5 are contributors to this volume. Consistently with this finding, the Journal's editor expressed the view that the first edition of this book was 'probably the most referenced book by JORS authors over the last 10 years' (Ranyard, 2000).

Since that first edition, a number of further books on PSMs have been published. These include Checkland and Scholes (1990), and Eden and Ackermann (1998) on particular PSMs; Eden and Radford (1990) on cross-cutting client interface issues in the use of PSMs; Flood and Jackson (1991) on a range of system-based methods which overlap to some extent with those in this volume; and Mingers and Gill (1997) on the combined use of more than one method. None of these invalidate the need for the current volume. For example, in order to understand the significance of, say, the interaction between consultant style and the effectiveness of decision support, or to see the relevance of combining methods, it is first necessary to have at least a basic grasp of the methods involved. Again, it is a considerable commitment to embark on, say, a 300-page book focused on just one method. How can I know that *this* is the particular approach that has something to offer in my particular circumstances? How can I know that *any* of these methods could help me to sort out my predicaments?

The present volume has been designed to make access to problem structuring methods less of a problem. Each of five methods is presented in a linked pair of chapters covering, broadly, theory and practice perspectives. For each approach, the first chapter lays out the justification for the method (what sort of situation it addresses, and why these are significant), develops the conceptual apparatus which is employed, and describes the sequence of activities by which the method is applied. The second chapter of each pair illustrates the application of the method by means of a practical case study. The linked chapter format is also used to describe and illustrate the use of PSMs (and other methods) in combination; and there is a further chapter providing condensed summaries of a number of other methods which have similarities of character or scope with, or which have been used in conjunction with, PSMs.

The paired chapter format should make it possible for the reader to establish an informed view of what each method claims to be able to do, and how. It will not, of course, convert the reader into a skilled exponent of the method. However it should enable her or him to decide which of the approaches merits follow-up, whether through further reading, attendance at training sessions, or consultation with an experienced practitioner.

Scope

The five principal methods described in this book are, in sequence,

Strategic Options Development and Analysis (SODA), together with its Journey Making
    variant and its technical component of cognitive mapping

Soft Systems Methodology (SSM)

Strategic Choice Approach (SCA)

Robustness Analysis

Drama Theory

In each case the authors include the principal architect(s) of the method.

A further chapter covers a small number of related decision support methods, namely the Viable System Method (VSM); System Dynamics (SD); and decision analysis and decision conferencing. Finally there are two chapters describing the theory and practice of 'multimethodology' – the creative combination of methods in order to suit the particular circumstances in which analytic assistance is being offered. And there are introductory and concluding chapters that place PSMs as a whole in a wider context.

The sequence in which the five principal methods are placed in the book does *not* correspond to any sequence of stages in problem solving or decision making. None of them has a field of application limited to, say, 'appreciating the problem' or 'making choices'. The issue of what method to use when has more than a single dimension to it, as will be discussed in the more general chapters.

The simple logic behind the sequencing which has been adopted for these five topics is that the earlier methods, SODA and SSM, are the most general, in the sense that they make fewest structural assumptions about the nature of the situation which is being investigated. They can therefore be used quite broadly to identify a possible framework of factors and issues that can constitute the agenda for further discussion and analysis – though each also offers procedures for advancing that discussion towards a conclusion. The other three methods each concentrates on a particular key dimension of decision-making situations. Strategic Choice and Robustness share a focus on uncertainty and ways of managing it, while it is the need to manage the tension between conflict and cooperation which is at the core of Drama Theory. They should be used when, and only when, these features are perceived to be central to the issues that need resolving.

What is the rationale for selecting the particular methods that are included in this book? Certainly the PSMs described here share a range of common characteristics, as will be explored in the following chapter. Among these are that they aim to provide elements of appropriate structure to help decision-making groups cope with strategic problem situations. They are not, however, the only methods that offer a contribution in this area. Approaches which have *not* been included in the book, but which might be thought to have a claim, include the Analytic Hierarchy Process (Saaty, 1980), Idealized Planning (Ackoff, 1974, 1979), and Strategic Assumption Surfacing and Testing (Mason and Mitroff, 1981).

Rather than give reasons for these exclusions (which could be done) I prefer to concentrate on the positive reasons for including the five principal methods that do feature in the book. These approaches score individually on grounds of transparency, activation of judgement, a focus on commitment, and practical applicability. However, there is a further collective reason for their inclusion: that they also constitute a coherent and distinctive contribution to the art and craft of structuring problems. All had their origins in the British operational research and systems movement; their originators and many active practitioners know each other well and over the years have shared insights or even worked together on joint projects. There is an evident advantage in grouping together a set of approaches that have sprung from broadly the same cultural matrix. A disjointed eclecticism can be avoided, enabling the coherence of the subject matter to emerge more sharply.

There are a number of audiences for this book. For graduate and even undergraduate students in a range of disciplines, this book can serve as a text for the courses in problem structuring methods and in strategic modelling now being taught. For the practitioner whose student days pre-date the emergence of such courses, it offers at least the first stage of updating in a significant growth area. And for the manager with a sophisticated interest in the potential of analysis, it offers an accessible state-of-the-art summary. There is no requirement for any particular level of mathematical preparation. This is not to say that the material in the book is easy – but just that the difficulties are not mathematical.

Changes from the first edition

There have been many advances in the field of problem structuring methods in the dozen years since the publication of the first edition of this book, and these are reflected in the current volume. Indeed it might almost equally well be described as a new book.

Topics introduced for the first time in this edition are the two chapters on multimethodology, and that providing condensed accounts of some methods closely related to PSMs. Another structural change is the removal of the original two pairs of chapters on Metagame and Hypergame Analysis, and the substitution of two chapters on Drama Theory – which has, in the interim, been formed by the merger of these two approaches.

Of the other four methods that were covered in the first edition, two (SODA and SSM) have entirely new case studies, and amendments or updates have been made to the others. All the 'theory' chapters have been substantially re-written. And of course the introduction and conclusions are new, to reflect the large strides which have been made in the development, application and understanding of problem structuring methods.

Jonathan Rosenhead

References

Ackoff, R.L. (1974). *Redesigning the Future*, John Wiley & Sons, Inc, New York.

Ackoff, R.L. (1979). 'Resurrecting the future of operational research', *J. Opl Res. Soc.*, **30**, 189–99.

Checkland, P.B. (1981). *Systems Thinking, Systems Practice*, John Wiley & Sons, Ltd, Chichester.

Checkland, P.B. and Scholes, J. (1991). *Soft Systems Methodology in Action*, John Wiley & Sons, Ltd, Chichester.

Eden, C. and Ackermann, F. (1998). *Making Strategy: the journey of strategic management*, Sage, London.

Eden, C., Jones, S., and Sims, D. (1983). *Messing About in Problems*, Pergamon, Oxford.

Flood, R. and Jackson, M.C. (1991). *Creative Problem Solving: total system intervention*, John Wiley & Sons, Ltd, Chichester.

Friend, J.K. and Hickling, A. (1987). *Planning Under Pressure*, Pergamon, Oxford.

Mason, R.O. and Mitroff, I.I. (1981). *Challenging Strategic Planning Assumptions*, John Wiley & Sons, Inc, New York.

Mingers, J. and Gill, A. (Eds.) (1987). *Multimethodology: the theory and practice of combining management science methodologies*, John Wiley & Sons, Ltd, Chichester.

Ranyard, J. (2000). 'Commentary on Checkland (1995): Achieving "desirable and feasible" change: an application of Soft Systems Methodology', *J. Opl Res. Soc.*, **51**, 1347–8.

Ranyard, J. (2001). 'Editorial', *J. Opl Res. Soc.*, **52**, 1–3.

Rosenhead, J. (Ed.) (1989). *Rational Analysis for a Problematic World: problem structuring methods for complexity, uncertainty and conflict*, Wiley, Chichester.

Saaty, T.L. (1980). *The Analytic Hierarchy Process*, McGraw-Hill, New York.

Acknowledgements

The editors are grateful for guidance and advice and the provision of material to, among others, Carlos Bana e Costa, Val Belton, Mike Cushman, Julian Pratt, Larry Phillips and Geoff Thomas; and to Lisa Dewar for organizing the final manuscript. Also to our contributors for their positive spirit of cooperation.

1 A New Paradigm of Analysis

Jonathan Rosenhead and John Mingers

This book describes a generation of methods that can help with the more intractable organizational problems of today and tomorrow, by using appropriate forms of analysis.

Making and taking decisions, solving problems, designing and re-designing systems nowadays all have to take place in conditions of unprecedented complexity and uncertainty. Complexity – because organizations (and individuals too) operate in an environment of densely interconnected networks, in which the wider ramifications of decisions cannot be ignored. Uncertainty – for more than one reason. Firstly, we don't know what those *other* decision-makers, whose choices will affect whether *our* choices pay off or not, are going to do. Secondly, the dynamics of this networked world are both poorly understood (it's not been like this for long enough for reliable patterns to have emerged) and turbulent (the day after tomorrow's world is likely to be very different). Thirdly, organizations are fluid in their missions and individuals increasingly unrooted; so we cannot be sure that what we want to do, even to be, today will have a very long half-life.

A generation or two ago, a form of analysis was developed to help decision-makers to deal with the level of complexity and uncertainty that was then prevalent. It is still in use, but mostly in situations shielded from the full rigours of our connected and turbulent world. Which is to say, not on the significant decisions that shape our organizational or individual potentialities. Its emphasis was, and is, on representing (modelling) the factors and relationships in a decision situation mathematically, and then using computer power to review the predicted consequences of alternative choices. Mostly the tools and techniques within this approach aim to find the 'best' solution.

The methods described in this book, problem structuring methods, are not like that. They accept as a fact that the most demanding and troubling task in formative decision situations is to decide what the problem *is*. There are too many factors; many of the relationships between them are unclear or in dispute; the most important do not reduce naturally to quantified form; different stakeholders have different priorities. Problem structuring methods use models (often in the plural, and with little or no quantification) to help (mostly) group decision-making – since it is rare for such issues to be resolved by single decision makers. The model representations are used to provide enough structure that those who must take responsibility for the consequences of the choices which are made, do so on a coherent basis and with sufficient confidence to make the necessary commitments.

So the aim of problem structuring methods is both more modest and more ambitious than that of the previous generation of optimizing methods. More modest, because they do not set out to capture a single truth about the situation from which the one best answer can be derived. More ambitious, because their aim is rather to provide useful assistance to those processes of dialogue and debate which prepare the way for decisions that significantly affect future prospects.

The Crisis

The function of this chapter is to set the scene for the descriptions of the particular problem structuring methods in later chapters. In it we will first outline the crisis that overtook conventional modelling methods when they attempted to impose structure on recalcitrant material, and the rethinking which this failure provoked. This critique was far from destructive, since it gave rise directly to propositions for an alternative way of providing model-based decision support. Indeed, as we will see, the problem structuring methods covered in this book demonstrate that this alternative approach was not just an abstract idea, but is both practical and widely applicable. We will leave it to the concluding chapter to assess the achievements of problem structuring methods (PSMs) to date, and their future prospects.

Foremost among the general-purpose decision-aiding practices which have sprung up over the past half-century is operational research (OR), also known as management science. It is in the context of OR that the crisis in decision-support will be discussed here – and the methods in this volume are an OR response to this crisis. (Similar issues and arguments have arisen in the systems movement more generally, and in urban planning – see Checkland (1983) and Fischer and Forester (1993).)

It is possible to see the traditional and alternative modelling approaches as competing 'paradigms', following Kuhn (1970). Very broadly, a scientific paradigm consists of a set of implicit rules for identifying a valid scientific problem, and for recognising what would constitute a solution to it. A paradigm crisis occurs when an established orthodoxy is challenged by an alternative view of boundaries, methods etc. Suggestions of a paradigm crisis in OR were advanced as early as 1973 (Thunhurst, 1973). By 1981 the concept formed the organizing principle of Dando and Bennett's (1981) influential paper 'A Kuhnian crisis in management science?'.

Indeed the signs of paradigm crisis accumulated rapidly over this period, most actively from the early 1970's to the mid 1980's. Prior to this time, there had been an almost total lack of critical discussion about OR's nature, methods, *raison d'être*. But major turmoil now erupted in the world's two largest OR societies. In Britain it was over plans to 'professionalize' the British OR community (1972–73), which some felt would fossilize the methods that could count as operational research. In the USA it was the Operational Research Society of America's attempt to establish a code of conduct and to discipline offenders (1971–2) which caused the trouble. The ORSA code in particular unleashed a torrent of critical comment (ORSA, 1971: Botts *et al.*, 1972; Churchman *et al.*, 1972), but this was not the only evidence of disarray.

Ackoff, a leading US academic, engaged in an extended exchange with radical critics from Britain (Ackoff, 1974, 1975; Chesterton *et al.*, 1975; Rosenhead, 1976). Ackoff himself launched a scathing attack on mainstream OR practice (Ackoff, 1979a) which evoked supportive responses for his diagnosis but not his proposed remedy (Ackoff, 1979b). The work of Ackoff himself, together with that of Churchman and Checkland, came under renewed critical scrutiny from Jackson, once more provoking a substantial debate (Jackson, 1982, 1983, Mingers, 1984).

These mostly ill-tempered exchanges certainly generated heat. To add some illumination it is helpful to use Dando and Bennett's (1981) identification of three principal positions in the debate. The 'official' paradigm held that skilful modelling based on accurate data could provide helpful advice, and very probably optimal solutions, for management. 'Reformists', notably Ackoff and Checkland, criticised the 'official' paradigm for its limiting, technical emphasis, and in this they were joined by the 'revolutionaries'. However the latter did not seek just a change in the subject's methods, but also in its clientele and establishment stance.

More considered dissections of the 'official' paradigm soon built on the initial polemics, and these will be examined next. We will use 'orthodox' and 'traditional' as more descriptive substitutes for the 'official' label.

The Critique

In the decade and a half following the outbreak of hostilities a considerable literature developed which attempted to understand what it was that the traditional modelling approach could, and especially could *not*, do. Significant contributions to this literature include Ackoff (1987), Eden (1982), Flood and Jackson (1991), Jackson (1987, 1991), Jackson and Keys (1984), Keys (1984), Mingers (1980, 1992), Rittel and Webber (1973), Rosenhead (1986, 1991), and Rosenhead and Thunhurst (1982) – and the account which follows draws selectively from these works. The resulting perspective, which is no longer controversial, is important to the understanding of PSMs. Evidently it is in the gaps – in the areas that conventional methods do not handle adequately – that the opportunities for an alternative approach must lie.

Operational research was not alone in losing its way and its self-confidence in the early 1970's – architecture, urban planning and policy sciences all suffered crises with onsets in or around 1973. They can all be seen as examples of a loss of faith in 'modernism'. Modernism holds the view that, since scientific knowledge can provide a better understanding of the way in which actions lead to consequences, it can help us to improve or even perfect social systems and arrangements. Indeed it is implicit that these improvements are ones that everyone would agree upon. It is the *model* of the problem situation, in conventional operational research, that encapsulates this understanding; and it is the model that enables 'optimal' decisions to be derived. In urban planning it was in particular model-based planning which proved particularly vulnerable to the attack, when it came; methods which had worked well on more limited problems were found to fall apart when applied to more ambitious projects (Lee, 1973). In policy analysis the 'moon-ghetto metaphor' was coined in the United States to describe the (false) assumption that the same methods which had got a human to the moon could be used to solve the problems of inner-city ghettos (Nelson, 1974).

Particularly revealing is the RAND Corporation's work in New York City, described by Greenberger, Crenson and Crissey (1976). There RAND attempted to apply its cause-effect modelling and optimizing approach, honed on aerospace and defence problems, to the dilemmas of big city government. The moon-ghetto metaphor in action! The results were very mixed. Success and implementation depended very much on the context. Traditional methods worked well to the extent that the relevant city agency was structured as a quasi-military hierarchy; few of its staff were analytically sophisticated; the agency performed a well-defined task whose repetition generated reliable data suitable for quantitative manipulation; and priorities between alternative objectives commanded almost universal consensus. All these features were in place for RAND's extensive work with the fire service. Diametrically opposite conditions held for the city's public health administration, and there RAND encountered comprehensive failure.

A Dichotomy of Problems

The RAND experience suggests a dichotomy of problem situations, with one of the two categories unsuited to the application of traditional modelling methods. This idea has been generated independently by many observers and commentators. We will review a range of these formulations here. It is not only that a closer specification of the reach of conventional methods will reveal the possible scope for an alternative approach. In addition, the explanations offered as to *why* conventional approaches are limited in particular ways can signal in what ways an alternative approach would have to be different if it is to overcome these limitations. Each author is listed with their disciplinary affiliation.

Ackoff *(OR/systems) – messes versus problems*

According to Ackoff (1979a) 'Managers are not confronted with problems that are independent of each other, but with dynamic situations that consist of complex systems of changing problems that interact with each other. I call such situations messes. Problems are abstractions extracted from messes by analysis; they are to messes as atoms are to tables and chairs.' Individual problems may be 'solved'. But if they are components of a mess, the solutions to individual problems cannot be added, since those solutions will interact. Problems may be solved; messes need to be managed. If we insist on the solution mode, analysts will be relegated to those relatively minor problems which are nearly independent, while messes go inadequately managed (Ackoff, 1981).

Rittel *(design) – wicked versus tame problems*

For Rittel, a 'tame' problem is one which can be specified, in a form agreed by the relevant parties, ahead of the analysis, and which does not change during the analysis. For a 'wicked' problem by contrast, there are many alternative types and levels of explanation of the phenomena of concern, and the type of explanation selected determines the nature of the solution. Alternative solutions are therefore not true or false, but good or bad. These judgements of worth must be made not by the analyst (who has no relevant expertise or standing in the matter) but by the interested parties themselves. According to Rittel 'the methods of Operations Research ... become operational ... only *after* the most important decisions have already been made, i.e. after the [wicked] problem has already been tamed' (Rittel and Webber, 1973).

Schon *(systems/management) – swamp versus high ground*

Schon (1987) captures the dilemma of how good analysis can be carried out in messy, wicked situations via a vivid metaphor:

> In the swampy lowland, messy, confusing problems defy technical solution. The irony of this situation is that the problems of the high ground tend to be relatively unimportant to individuals or society at large, however great their technical interest may be, while in the swamp lie the problems of greatest human concern. The practitioner must choose. Shall he remain on the high ground where he can solve relatively unimportant problems according to prevailing standards of rigour, or shall he descend to the swamp of important problems and non-rigorous inquiry?

Ravetz *(history and philosophy of science) – practical versus technical problems*

Technical problems are those for which at the inception of the study there exists a clearly specified function to be performed, for which a best means can be sought by experts. For a practical problem, by contrast, there will exist (at most) some general statement of a purpose to be achieved. The output of any study here should be, not a specification of optimal means, but an argument in favour of accepting a particular definition of the problem, together with its implication for the corresponding means of solution to be adopted.

Practical problems, therefore, cannot be solved by technical or analytic expertise alone. This expertise must interact with judgement as to the cogency of arguments among diverse stakeholders (Ravetz, 1971).

Checkland *(systems) – soft versus hard systems thinking*

Checkland distinguishes between what he calls hard and soft systems thinking. Hard systems thinking can be typified by the RAND approach already mentioned above. It assumes that the world consists of systems that can be objectively modelled; that there are well-specified and agreed objectives or goals; and that its main task is to determine the most effective or efficient means to realize those goals (Checkland, 1978). By contrast, soft systems thinking (Checkland, 1985) accepts that the rich complexity of the world cannot be assumed to consist of systems which can be modelled, let alone optimized. Rather, systems concepts can be helpful in structuring our thinking and learning about problematic situations and we should aim for debate and accommodation about the nature of the problem, rather than its solution.

These diverse analyses all point in the same direction. Problems for which there are uncontested formulations that can be specified in advance are susceptible to technical solution. But different methods, incorporating the engagement of human judgement and social interaction, are needed to make progress with problems for which these simplifying assumptions are invalid. Another way of putting this is that methods for the former type of problems adopt an *objectivist* stance that sees problems essentially as independent of individual participants' views and beliefs. By contrast, the latter type of problem requires a *subjectivist* stance that recognizes the importance of participants' perceptions in defining or even constituting a 'problem' in the first place. Schon, in the quotation above, makes the assumption that any investigation in this 'swampy' terrain must be non-rigorous. However it may be argued that in the more demanding, and more important, conditions of the swamp some kind of appropriate yet systematic approach is still more crucial. What is needed is a re-specification of rigour.

The Scope of Traditional Modelling Methods

No group of methods, indeed no paradigm, is applicable to an unlimited range of subject matter. Before the development of PSMs, what did operational researchers regard, explicitly or implicitly, as falling within their remit? According to Checkland (1981), it was problems that fitted the following abstract description: 'there is a desired state, S_1, and a present state, S_0, and alternative ways of getting from S_0 to S_1. "Problem solving", according to this view, consists of defining S_1 and S_0 and selecting the best means of reducing the difference between them.' Another way of putting this is that 'hard systems thinking', of which OR is an example, consists of 'systematically-ordered thinking concerned with means-definition in well-structured problems in which desirable ends can be stated'. There is seen to be only one problem 'out there'. The task of the analyst is to recognize it, and then turn the handle on the analytic sausage-machine. Of course some do this with greater skill or energy than others. But the method is, in principle, practitioner-free (Checkland, 1983).

Much, then, is taken as 'given' in the traditional OR study. There is no room for, and certainly no methods to deal with, arguments about objectives. Different departments, factions or organizations must not have different conceptions about what S_1 should be. The *context* of the problem is also taken as given – a continuation of present conditions or a projection out of current trend lines. And it is taken as given that within the (given) problem focus, means-ends relationships are all that need to be taken into account. Not, for example, the relationships between the people who are currently managing S_0, and their differential willingness and ability to adjust to the changed circumstances of S_1. Not the limitations on their knowledge of the future, let alone the present. Not the possibility that any study that is carried out may result, not in a solution of the given problem, but in a new formulation of the problem. The given problem may nevertheless be of daunting complexity, calling forth dazzling (though often misguided) feats of technical virtuosity – giving rise to Ackoff's (1979a) characterization of OR as 'mathematically sophisticated but contextually naïve'.

The clear and unambiguous specification of 'the problem' which traditional methods of OR are designed to tackle means that it will in general have one 'best' solution. The task of the traditional OR technique, like that of a well-trained gun dog, is to go out and retrieve it.

This is a slight exaggeration. For example there may be more than one equally good solution. And in cases where a plausible optimizable formulation cannot be reached, computer simulation may be used to find, not the true optimum, but which of a number of selected alternatives is best. What is not an exaggeration is that *academic* operational research has been dominated by the search for computable methods that can 'solve' bigger problems, or solve problems faster; or for novel formulations that can cast re-calcitrant problems in a shape that allows optimization to be performed. Practitioners have of course been more pragmatic. But the developed repertoire of techniques has not offered systematic support for a more sophisticated practice. Rather it has been a strait-jacket tending to limit organizational calls for OR assistance.

The result of all this has been a rather persistent malaise, a sense of disappointed ambitions. Ackoff (1979a) was early to observe the tendency in the United States for OR to be demoted from the corporate level to the study of secondary problems. Corbett and Van Wassenhove (1993) identified what they called the 'natural drift' of OR away from tackling unstructured problems, and towards applying standard techniques to standard problems. Operational research, in the dominant tendency that looked for technical solutions to well-structured problems, was largely excluded from those places and occasions where the 'givens' of those problems were decided. Or perhaps it had excluded itself.

We have suggested earlier that problem situations may be divided into those suitable and unsuitable for the use of traditional OR techniques. However the idea that there is a dividing line is of limited value unless we also have some way of recognizing, based on the characteristics of a particular situation, on which side of the line it falls. Establishing such a rule proves to take us into an interesting but productive tangle.

Hopwood (1980), based on a parallel experience with budgetary processes, identified *uncertainties* as the key factor determining the type of method that could be used for organizational decision making. In fact two types of uncertainty – over the consequences of action, and over the objectives of action. If both are low, he proposes, the appropriate mode is 'computation', corresponding to the traditional OR approach. If the former is high, the appropriate mode is 'judgement'; and if the latter is high, then it is 'bargaining'. If both types of uncertainty are high, then we only have 'inspiration' to fall back on. In terms of this categorization, traditional OR, with its computational tools, is necessarily confined to problem situations where uncertainties (and hence the stakes) are low.

Another categorization, that of Jackson and Keys (1984), has been widely taken up. As is summarized by Mingers (2000), their 'system of systems methodologies' (or SOSM for short) is based on two dimensions of problem situations. One dimension deals with how complex the problem context is (from 'simple' to 'complex'); the second concerns the relations between stakeholders, with the alternative possibilities of 'unitary' (i.e., general agreement); 'pluralist' (differing but reconcilable views); and 'coercive' (differing and irreconcilable views). The combination of these two attributes for a particular situation, it was proposed, could be used to specify the type of analytical approach that should be used. Only the simple-unitary type of situation was identified as suitable for the application of 'hard' methods such as traditional OR techniques.

Flood and Jackson (1991) subsequently built an elaborate method to operationalize the use of this scheme. This strand of work, it should be said, has come under criticism for its assumption that any problem context can be fitted unambiguously, at the outset of a study, into one of the six resulting categories (Mingers, 1992). Maybe the nature of the situation is one of the objects of study! Or perhaps different stakeholders would disagree about whether it was, say, pluralist or coercive. Nevertheless the argument about SOSM was broadly constructive, and contributed, for example, to the prevailing view on the importance of combining together different methods in the same intervention (see Chapter 12). This pluralist approach has been developed in different ways by Midgley (1997), Jackson (1999), and Mingers (2000).

Schemes such as SOSM suggest what observation confirmed. This was that the traditional OR approach of building a single model of cause and effect relationships, based so far as possible on objective data, and claiming to represent the truth about a problem situation, was necessarily confined to one corner of the field of organizational decision making.

Evidently the problem types which traditional modelling methods are well placed to solve are important. The fact that there exist powerful analytic methods available to provide solutions to these problems is of great value to many organizations – including financial institutions, extractive and manufacturing industry, airlines and rail companies – and to society as a whole. They can help to ensure that tasks of very considerable complexity are carried out efficiently and effectively; in some cases the avoidance of waste may make the difference between feasibility and infeasibility.

But the situations and issues that these methods cannot tackle include, as stated in the quotation from Donald Schon in an earlier section, 'the problems of greatest human concern'. Among the problems that do not sit within the frontiers of the low uncertainty, high consensus domain are those of a strategic kind in large organizations, where decisions will set the context for lower level tasks. Also excluded are most of those one-of-a-kind dilemmas which individuals or groups at any level will confront, whose resolution may determine what future development paths are left open to them, but whose troubling nature cannot be reduced to numbers.

What sort methods can provide help, not in the solution of well-defined problems, but in the structuring of unique and as yet ill-defined ones?

The Structure and Process of Problem Structuring Methods

This book is predicated on the view that problem structuring methods provide a repertoire of methods for making progress with ill-structured problem situations. This section will explore the justifications for this view, in two stages: first by clarifying the common characteristics of PSMs, especially in contrast to those of traditional problem *solving* methods, and second, by examining how PSMs engage with organizational decision processes.

Before starting on either of these essentially theoretical exercises, it may be helpful to provide some grounded evidence. Table 1.1 lists a few practical PSM applications that can illustrate the breadth of situations within which these methods have been used successfully.

It is unlikely that any of these situations could have benefited from a traditional modelling approach. Elements of the situations which stakeholders saw as essential to an adequate representation could not be captured in numbers without distortion. There were participants for whom backroom analytic modelling would have been mystifying and excluding. Judgemental inputs as well as judgement about model outputs were required. Participating individuals and organizations did not necessarily subscribe to the same objectives or world-view. In these cases PSMs have proved able in practice to reach both down to the grassroots and up into senior management domains, extending the range of contexts in which model-based decision support has something to offer.

Table 1.1 – Some practical applications of problem structuring methods

Application and source	Description	Methods
Bombardier (Ackermann, Eden and Williams, 1997)	Support for legal action over disruption to design and manufacture of 'shuttle-wagons' for the Channel Tunnel	SODA with system dynamics
Tower Hamlets (Friend, 1994)	Community groups opposing local hospital closure	Strategic Choice
Shell (Checkland and Scholes, 1991)	Organizational restructuring of a division of an international company	Soft Systems Methodology
Thurnscoe (Thunhurst *et al.*, 1992)	Community operational research for residents of an ex-miners housing estate	A range of hard and soft methods
Netherlands Government (Chapter 7)	Establishing national policy on transport of hazardous material	Strategic Choice
Sainsbury's (Ormerod, 1996)	IT strategy development for a major supermarket chain	Combination of 3 PSMs on 1 project

Putting a Problem Well

One of the earliest classics of the OR literature (Churchman, Ackoff and Arnoff, 1957) contained the following aphorism:

> There is an old saying that a problem well put is half solved. This much is obvious. What is not so obvious is how to put a problem well.

For thirty or so years this advice, or warning, was largely ignored. Too many modellers thought that it *was* obvious. The way to put a problem well was to quantify in preparation for computation.

In this section we will draw out the general characteristics which methods should have if they are to be useful in structuring problems. That is, we move on from critique towards prescription. However to highlight the distinctiveness of these characteristics, we will at a number of points contrast them with those of traditional, problem solving approaches.

One description of how the traditional paradigm of operational research works in practice (Rosenhead, 1981) is shown in Table 1.2.

Not all of these features have been touched on directly in our earlier summarized critique of the traditional modelling approach. However it should be evident that they form a coherent whole: a technical-fix approach to problems of attaining pre-set goals in an efficient way, on the assumptions that the context remains constant or is knowable, that the goals are not contested, and that there is complete control over implementation. In almost no situations will these assumptions hold precisely. But they may be approximated, more or less closely, in 'tame' (Rittel) or technical (Ravetz) problems. That is, the approach outlined in Table 1.2 is broadly representative of the methodology appropriate for use in problems on one side of the dichotomies identified earlier.

Table 1.2 – Characteristics of the traditional paradigm of operational research

1. Problem formulation in terms of a single objective and optimization. Multiple objectives, if recognized, are subjected to trade-off onto a common scale.
2. Overwhelming data demands, with consequent problems of distortion, data availability and data credibility.
3. Scientization and depoliticization, assumed consensus.
4. People are treated as passive objects.
5. Assumption of a single decision maker with abstract objectives from which concrete actions can be deduced for implementation through a hierarchical chain of command.
6. Attempts to abolish future uncertainty, and pre-take future decisions.

Table 1.3 – Characteristics of an alternative paradigm

1. Non-optimizing; seeks alternative solutions which are acceptable on separate dimensions, without trade-offs.
2. Reduced data demands, achieved by greater integration of hard and soft data with social judgements.
3. Simplicity and transparency, aimed at clarifying the terms of conflict.
4. Conceptualizes people as active subjects.
5. Facilitates planning from the bottom-up.
6. Accepts uncertainty, and aims to keep options open.

The purpose of the current section is to identify and justify an outline of a methodology appropriate for problems on the other side of these dichotomies – for 'wicked' and 'practical' problems. One simple, even simplistic, way of envisioning what such an approach might look like is to turn the traditional paradigm on its head. Perhaps if the natures of the two types of problem situations are so radically opposed, then the converse of the orthodox approach might have much to offer for wicked and practical problems. This might lead us to consider a methodology with the characteristics listed in Table 1.3.

When these characteristics of an alternative methodology were first proposed in the late 1970s they seemed quite theoretical: at best a blue-print for a form of analytic assistance that might one day come into being. It was encouraging, though, that this conceptual paradigm, like its dialectical opposite, is internally coherent. It would constitute appropriate analytic assistance for a process of accommodation between independent agents whose agreement is not subject to compulsion from some higher level. These agents have relevant experience-based judgement to contribute to the process which cannot be adequately be captured in numbers, may have different perspectives and interests, and are not blessed with second sight about what the future has in store. Could this, then be a characterization of desirable aspects of any method aiming to be of use for the less 'well-behaved' side of the dichotomy of problem situations?

Gradually over the last thirty years it has become evident that methods with this orientation are not just theoretical possibilities. They exist, and some of them are described in this volume. Indeed most of them existed, though in a relatively undeveloped form, before the existence of an alternative paradigm was postulated. Robustness

Analysis, Strategic Choice and Metagame Analysis (one of the parents of Drama Theory) were all conceived in the 1960s. Soft Systems Methodology can be traced to the early 1970s, and Hypergame Analysis (the other parent of Drama Theory) and Strategic Options Development and Analysis emerged in the later part of that decade. However their relative prominence is quite new. The methods themselves have grown in sophistication – in part due to cross-pollination. Also both analysts and decision makers have become more aware of the limitations of the orthodox inheritance. Since the early 1990's the joint identity of these problem structuring methods as an alternative paradigm of decision aiding has been increasingly accepted.

This is not to say that each of the methods described in this book exhibits all of the six characteristics of Table 1.3. (But then, neither do all approaches within the traditional paradigm correspond in every respect with Table 1.2.) The paradigm represents, as it were, an ideal type from which any particular example will deviate to some extent. How and why they deviate (for example, some methods emphasize uncertainty, others conflict, others multiple perspectives) will emerge from the descriptions of particular methods in the chapters which follow. The remainder of this introduction will concentrate, rather, on some common features of PSMs, in particular on their joint assumptions about the nature of the decision process that they are intended to aid, and the nature of the tools this allows them to deploy.

Working with Decision Processes

We can start from de Neufville and Keeney's (1972) position that

> typically large decisions are not made by a single group of like minded people . . . they are, rather, the result of extended negotiations, either implicit or explicit, between representatives of different points of view.

The same, it might be said, is often also true of relatively small decisions whose consequences are important to those who must take them. To project the output of some backroom analysis into such situations without a knowledgeable, even sophisticated awareness of the dynamics of the negotiations is unlikely to help them along.

The word 'negotiation' has been used here in a broad sense. In situations of overt conflict, formal sessions may be convened at which positions are outlined, threats conveyed and concessions horse-traded. Where overt conflict is absent it is more probable that the give-and-take of organizational and inter-organizational life will be at least superficially more amicable. Here the mutual modification of positions will occur in ways that if possible preserves positive future working relationships; the trade-off implicit in the accommodations may not even be explicitly acknowledged. When situations are not too complex, too urgent, too fraught with uncertainties or too important, these informal methods can work well. However in cases where these calm conditions do not apply, even skilful and experienced managers can be stretched. (And not all managers are equally skilful.) It is here that the significant opportunities for problem structuring methods lie.

If we take this view, in effect that 'wicked' problems do not have a client but rather a 'client system'(Tomlinson, 1984), this has implications for how analysis can be helpful. If a model-based support process is to be of value to members of the client system, then it will need to encompass their varying perspectives. It cannot select one of these world-views as superior or correct, nor impose the modeller's perspective.

The stakeholders in the client system will wish to do their negotiating on their own behalf – they certainly will not entrust that to some supposedly neutral analyst, perhaps with more computer know-how than sense. Model-based assistance will be of most value if it can be referred to as a common base of understanding during their direct contacts. These contacts may consist of different pairings or larger groupings distributed over time and space.

Alternatively, and often to the advantage of all concerned, meetings of relevant stake-holders may be called to resolve as many as possible of the outstanding issues. It is for these circumstances that PSMs have mostly been designed. Although they may also be used by individuals, PSMs realize their potential most fully in use with groups in work-shop format – that is, meeting without formal agenda or chairing but with a shared commitment to making progress with the issue at hand. Indeed PSMs have been called 'wide-band group decision support systems', where 'wide-band' indicates their ability to handle problems that have not been pre-formulated and may have quite diverse structures (Eden, 1995).

These circumstances for which PSMs are designed, so different from those assumed by earlier model-based approaches, have strong consequences for the role of the modeller. In the traditional paradigm she is appropriately called an 'analyst', whose model is developed and polished in the back-room, even if there is interface work to be done in collecting data, and in explaining, even 'selling' the results to the client. In the alternative paradigm it is the work with the group that is the distinctive activity, even if in some PSMs there are other activities preceding or interleaving workshop sessions. It is in the workshop that the model or models representing cause and effect are built up, integrated, amended, transformed through the collaboration of the modeller and the group. The modeller therefore has dual responsibilities, both for the development of a 'requisite' model (Phillips, 1984), and for the constructive management of the dynamics within the workshop group. Rather than an analyst, she is a 'facilitator' of the group's work.

Facilitated groups are now a common feature of organizational life. They are used to organize constructive conversations about situations that cannot be adequately captured in a pre-circulated agenda. *Model-based* facilitated groups offer additional advantages for problem situations with the full 'swamp' characteristics. However the model will only be of use if it becomes a common currency for group members. It is unlikely that an initial model constructed by the facilitator will be seen as valid – and if it were it would not become the property of the group. In most PSMs the model is in any case jointly constructed by the group members and the consultant. This model development is necessarily iterative, with trial versions of the model being successively improved by the group until such time as it is seen as adequate.

Group members may be present simply because they have different experiential knowledge bases, which can avoid gaps in the model and so increase the confidence with which the group can exercise its judgement. Frequently, however, there will be other factors at work in drawing up the invitation list. If a key stakeholder were to be un-represented at the workshop it could render the attempt to make progress with a thorny issue quite sterile. The presence of many (if not all) group members will also serve as a covenant that the outcome is not unacceptable to the constituency which they represent – though this assurance may be conditional on members checking back with their bases after the meeting.

From a subjectivist stance (adopted by several authors in this book) it may be the different *perceptions* of the problem situation by participants rather than their differing interests that is at the heart of their distinctive 'takes' on that situation. However, either type of explanation leads to the same consequence – that comprehensive solutions to some notional 'whole problem' are likely to be extremely rare. Different group members will be more or less willing to engage with and commit to action on particular aspects of the problem situation, depending on their particular interests or worldview. Negotiation and eventual agreement is likely to focus on the overlap area of these separate problem foci, together with some closely related elements.

It follows that no member's 'whole problem' will be dealt with – the remainders will need to be the business of other interactions of interested parties on other occasions in different fora. So each stakeholder can realistically hope to make progress only in-crementally with his or her key concerns. A good outcome will be partial commitments for which each can see the rationale – together with the improvements in mutual under-standing and working relations that flow from that, and the learning that has been achieved about the problem situation

Context, Process, Tools

Up to this point we have been arguing, broadly, that

1) there is a type of problem context for which 'hard' methods are unhelpful; and
2) appropriate methods for problem situations of this kind need to mesh with their interactive decision processes.

The third step is to examine how these two factors, of context and process, constrain and shape the type of analytic tools that can be deployed as part of these methods.

The three components of this ensemble are shown in Table 1.4. What we have for

Table 1.4 – Swamp conditions – process and technical requirements

'Swamp' conditions	Process requirements for appropriate methods	Technical requirements for appropriate methods
multiple actors	permitting alternative perspectives	diagrammatic
multiple perspectives	participative/interactive	exploration of solution space
incommensurable/conflicting interests	iterative	discrete options
	supporting partial commitment	possibilities
prominent intangibles		scenarios

brevity labelled 'swamp conditions' (after Schon) have already been discussed extensively in this chapter. It is these contextual attributes, which tend to make traditional modelling methods ineffective, that are picked out in the first column. Those in the second column are the process characteristics that are necessary if model-based methods are to be adequate to these conditions. It is the third column, on the nature of tools and techniques that can mesh with these processes, that will be discussed in what follows.

First, the means of representing the problem structure needs to be easily understandable by the client group. Yet it is precisely the complexity (taking this word in a broad sense) of the problem situation that makes structuring methods worth using. So the quandary is, how to represent complexity in a way that does not exclude lay involvement. Certainly, overt mathematics will render the analysis incomprehensible to most participants; even covert mathematics (say, embedded in computer software) is quite likely to promote unease – a sense that manipulations of the knowledge elicited from them are being carried out that they are asked to take on trust.

Both common sense and experience suggest that graphical methods have much to offer. Diagrams can display in spatial terms quite intricate networks of influence, causality, similarity or compatibility. Representations of considerable complexity can be apprehended visually with surprising ease. Even those without previous exposure to the particular graphical notation are often able to adopt the language readily, to the extent that they can in short order use it to suggest modifications to the diagrammatic model.

Such models cannot be annotated with mathematical symbols if they are to remain accessible. Indeed only if they are entirely non-quantitative can engagement of the whole group with the representation be expected. This obviously limits the range of manipulations that can be performed on the models. But this loss is scarcely relevant; the purpose of these representations is not to enable the consultant to find a solution, it is to enable the group to engage their experience and judgement more effectively. Indeed, more generally we could say that appropriate methods need to employ *language* rather than mathematics as their primary means of representation, whether it be (as we will see) in root definitions, cognitive maps or drama theory's 'card tables'. For it is only language itself that has the degree of richness and transparency suitable for participative modelling of complex reality.

This perception leads on to a further advantageous property for such methods. If the purpose of building a model is not to identify a single solution, this implies that the entire 'solution space' is in principle of interest. The difficulty here is that the set of all possible future systems, designs, plans or whatever can be unmanageably large. Even a few options in each of quite a few choice areas can show alarming combinatorial escalation of possibilities – while a decision making group can give serious consideration to just a handful. Methods are needed, therefore, which can select out just a few significant specimen 'solutions' for examination. For example, tools may screen out internal incompatibilities, or eliminate them through dominance (the existence of another option whose performance is at least as good in every circumstance). Thresholds of acceptable performance on a number of criteria may be adjusted to ensure that the number of options remaining is tractable. Where the range of possible commitments remains too great, they may be bundled into coherent packages; or alternatives may be selected to represent contrasting priorities.

To render this 'option scanning' both manageable in scale and also comprehensible to group members, another act of analytic self-denial is called for. Continuous variables can apparently represent an infinity of possibilities in a single symbol. They also offer the seductive appeal (to the mathematically able) of calculus, which can be used to derive optimal results. All this must be sacrificed. Instead, a small number of representative discrete options will need to stand in for the theoretically infinite spectrum of alternatives. The relative advantage of these options can then be analysed and displayed in ways that focus the act or process of choice.

So far this discussion has focused on accessible tools for representing and handling complexity. Uncertainty is another prime confuser of the intuition. In the orthodox paradigm, the answer to uncertainty is *probability*. Where there is lack of certainty about, for example, future values of some factor of interest, then the indicated action is to derive a probability distribution across its possible values. This enables averages and other handy measures to be calculated – not just of this factor, but also of other variables related to it.

Where data are available from previous experience in comparable circumstances, this process may well be legitimate. In the absence of such data, subjective probabilities – of how likely the events of interest are *felt* to be – may be elicited. This latter approach is common in decision analysis. However neither objective nor subjective probabilities can be central to the resolution of problems of the swamp. Indeed, if either version is applied to swampy problems, the resulting clarity is likely to be achieved at unreasonable cost.

Where objective probabilities can be calculated, it implies that the phenomena to which they apply have occurred repetitively in the past. If the probabilities are accepted as valid by all parties, it implies that the existence, relevance and interpretation of the phenomena are not at issue. In other words, they refer to aspects of the problematic situation that are relatively 'tame'. If leaving them unresolved causes group members confusion, then it may be helpful to simplify the problem by, as it were, some side calculations. But where the uncertainties (about what is currently happening, about future events, about what priorities to apply) are an integral part of the 'wickedness' of the situation, attempts to reduce them to numbers can only result in the analysis being unhelpful.

In this respect subjective probabilities are perhaps more dangerous because they can appear to offer quantified knowledge of the future in areas where repetitive observations (perhaps any observations at all) are lacking. This quantified version is a simplification of what to the participants is multifaceted and intangible; this is then subjected to mathematical manipulations in order to derive conclusions from the numbers. Participants' knowledge is thereby translated into the pre-set mathematical language of the analyst, and subjected to opaque transformations. In effect, it is now the analyst's, not the group's, problem.

As a general guide one could say that probabilities are likely to be a primary aid to choice only when what is at issue is of less than compelling importance. When an eventuality whose occurrence is uncertain is important enough to be considered in deliberations, it is that *possibility* that is relevant, more than any numerical expression of its *probability*. It follows that methods for wicked problems cannot employ probabilities (and none of those in this volume does so). Methods, rather, should confront the group in a structured way with the implications of those possibilities that cannot be dismissed from consideration.

What is important is that methods for wicked problems do not force the problem into a restrictive strait jacket, and particularly not into a mystifying quantitative one. It must be possible for participants to identify events, issues or outcomes that need to be taken into account, without being obliged to place (quite possibly meaningless) numbers on their significance. One aspect of this more appropriate approach is the use of scenarios as a way of embracing different possible futures within a study. A number of contrasting pictures of the future are developed. Each tells a coherent story, in words and diagrams as well as numbers, of how the relevant organizational environment might evolve.

Placing pressing decisions in the context of alternative future scenarios is a way of opening up discussion about threats and opportunities. The equivalent process within the orthodox modelling tradition is to generate numerical forecasts of key variables. A single forecast is a way of closing discussion down. Multiple forecasts, though usually preferable, are in effect a way of hedging ones' quantitative bets rather than a productive contribution to debate among diverse stakeholders.

Methods for Wicked Problems

Model-based methods for contributing constructively and appropriately to the resolution of wicked problems have only recently become widely known and practiced. They add an extra dimension to what analysis can offer to quite diverse groups – corporate executives, grass-roots community groups, health service managers, voluntary sector organizations, governmental task forces. PSMs extend both the clientele of operational research, and the range of types of situation to which model-based analysis can be applied. Given the dichotomy of problem types identified earlier, traditional modelling and PSMs are complementary rather than in conflict.

References

Ackoff, R.L. (1974). 'The social responsibility of operational research', *Opl Res. Q.*, **25**, 361–71.

Ackoff, R.L. (1975). 'A reply to the comments of Keith Chesterton, Robert Goodsman, Jonathan Rosenhead, and Colin Thunhurst', *Opl Res. Q.*, **26**, 96–9.

Ackoff, R.L. (1979a). 'The future of operational research is past', *J. Opl Res. Soc.*, **30**, 93–104.

Ackoff, R.L. (1979b). 'Resurrecting the future of operational research', *J. Opl Res. Soc.*, **30**, 189–99.

Ackoff, R.L. (1981). 'The art and science of mess management', *Interfaces*, **11**, 20–26.

Ackoff, R.L. (1987). 'OR, a post mortem', *Opns Res.*, **35**, 471–4.

Ackermann, F., Eden, C., and Williams, T. (1997). 'Modelling for litigation: mixing qualitative and quantitative approaches', *Interfaces*, **27**, 48–65.

Botts, T. *et al.* (1972). Letters to the Editor, *Opns Res.*, **20**, 205–46.

Checkland, P.B. (1978). 'The origins and nature of "hard" systems thinking', *J. Apl. Sys. Anal.*, **5**, 99–110.

Checkland, P.B. (1981). *Systems Thinking, Systems Practice*, John Wiley & Sons, Ltd, Chichester.

Checkland, P.B. (1983). 'OR and the systems movement: mappings and conflicts', *J. Opl Res. Soc.*, **34**, 661–75.

Checkland, P.B. (1985). 'From optimizing to learning: a development of systems thinking for the 1990s', *J. Opl. Res. Soc.*, **36**, 757–67.

Checkland, P. and Scholes, J. (1991). *Soft Systems Methodology in Action*, John Wiley & Sons, Ltd, Chichester.

Chesterton, K., Goodsman, R., Rosenhead, J., and Thunhurst, C. (1975). 'A comment on Ackoff's "The Social Responsibility of Operational Research"', *Opl Res. Q.*, **26**, 91–5.

Churchman, C.W., Ackoff, R.L., and Arnoff, E.L. (1957). *Introduction to Operations Research*, John Wiley & Sons, Inc, New York.

Churchman, C.W. *et al.* (1972). 'Discussion of the ORSA Guidelines', *Mgmt Sci.*, **18**, 608–29.

Corbett, C. and Van Wassenhove, L. (1993). 'The natural drift: what happened to operations research', *Opns Res.*, **41**, 625–40.

Dando, M.R. and Bennett, P.G. (1981). 'A Kuhnian crisis in management science?', *J. Opl Res. Soc.*, **32**, 91–103.

Eden, C. (1982). 'Problem construction and the influence of OR', *Interfaces*, **12**, 50–60.

Eden, C. (1995). 'On evaluating the performance of "wide-band" GDSS's', *Eur. J. Opl Res.*, **81**, 302–11.

Fischer, F. and Forester, J. (Ed.) (1993). *The Argumentative Turn in Policy Analysis and Planning*, UCL Press, London.

Flood, R.L. and Jackson, M.C. (1991). *Creative Problem Solving: Total Systems Intervention*, John Wiley & Sons, Ltd, Chichester.

Friend, J.K. (1994). 'Community involvement in health strategy in Tower Hamlets', in *Community Works: 26 Case Studies Showing Community Operational Research in Action* (Eds. C. Ritchie, A. Taket, and J. Bryant), PAVIC Publications, Sheffield.

Hopwood, A.G. (1980). 'The organizational and behavioural aspects of budgeting and control', in *Topics in Management Accounting* (Eds. J. Arnold, B. Carsberg, and R. Scapens), pp. 221–40, Philip Allen, Deddington.

Jackson, M.C. (1982). 'The nature of "soft" systems thinking: the work of Churchman, Ackoff and Checkland', *J. Apl. Sys. Anal.*, **9**, 17–29. See also replies in the same issue.

Jackson, M.C. (1983). 'The nature of "soft" systems thinking: comment on the three replies', *J. Apl. Sys. Anal.*, **10**, 109–13.

Jackson, M.C. (1987). 'Present positions and future prospects in management science', *Omega*, **15**, 455–66.

Jackson, M.C. (1991). *Systems Methodology for the Management Sciences*, Plenum, New York.

Jackson, M. (1999). 'Towards coherent pluralism in management science', *J. Opl Res. Soc.*, **50**, 12–22.

Jackson, M.C. and Keys, P. (1984). 'Towards a system of systems methodologies', *J. Opl Res. Soc.*, **35**, 473–86.

Keys, P. (1984). 'Traditional management science and the emerging critique', in *New Directions in Management Science* (Eds. M.C. Jackson and P. Keys), pp. 1–25, Gower, Aldershot.

Kuhn, T. (1970). *The Structure of Scientific Revolutions*, University of Chicago Press, Chicago.

Lee, D.B. (1973). 'Requiem for large-scale models', *J. Am. Inst. Planners*, **39**, 163–78.

Midgley, G. (1997). 'Mixing methods: developing systemic intervention', in *Multimethodology: The Theory and Practice of Combining Management Science Methodologies* (Eds. J. Mingers and A. Gill), pp. 250–90, John Wiley & Sons, Ltd, Chichester.

Mingers, J. (1980). 'Towards an appropriate social theory for applied systems thinking: critical theory and Soft Systems Methodology', *J. Apl. Sys. Anal.*, **7**, 41–50.

Mingers, J. (1984). 'Subjectivism and Soft Systems Methodology – a critique', *J. Apl. Sys. Anal.*, **11**, 85–104.

Mingers, J. (1992). 'Recent developments in critical management science', *Journal of the Operational Research Society*, **43**, 1–10.

Mingers, J. (2000). 'Variety is the spice of life: combining soft and hard OR/MS methods', *International Transactions in Operational Research*, **7**, 673–91.

Nelson, R.R. (1974). 'Intellectualizing about the moon-ghetto metaphor: a study of the current malaise of rational analysis of social problems', *Policy Sci.*, **5**, 375–414.

De Neufville, R. and Keeney, R.L. (1972). 'Systems evaluation through decision analysis: Mexico City Airport', *J. Sys. Eng.*, **3**, 34–50.

Ormerod, R.J. (1996). 'Information systems strategy development at Sainsbury's supermarkets using "soft" OR', *Interfaces*, **26**, 102–30.

ORSA *Ad Hoc* Committee on Professional Standards (1971) 'Guidelines for the professional practice of operations research', *Opns Res.*, **19**, 1123–258.

Phillips, L.D. (1984). 'A theory of requisite decision modelling', *Acta Psychologica*, **56**, 29–48.

Ravetz, J.R. (1971). *Scientific Knowledge and its Social Problems*, Oxford University Press, Oxford.

Rittel, H.W.J. and Webber, M.M. (1973). 'Dilemmas in a general theory of planning', *Policy Sci.*, **4**, 155–69.

Rosenhead, J. (1981). 'Operational research in urban planning', *Omega*, **9**, 345–64.

Rosenhead, J. (1986). 'Custom and practice', *J. Opl Res. Soc.*, **37**, 335–43.

Rosenhead, J. (1991) 'The dog that didn't bark: the unrealized social agenda of operational research', in *Operational Research '90* (Ed. H.E. Bradley), pp. 11–21, Pergamon, Oxford.

Rosenhead, J. and Thunhurst, C. (1982). 'A materialist analysis of operational research', *J. Opl Res. Soc.*, **33**, 111–22.

Schon, D.A. (1987). *Educating the Reflective Practitioner: Toward a New Design for Teaching and Learning in the Professions*, Jossey–Bass, San Francisco.

Thunhurst, C. (1973). 'Who does operational research operate for?' Paper presented at Operational Research Society Conference, Torquay (mimeo).

Thunhurst, C., Ritchie, C., Friend, J., and Booker, P. (1992). 'Housing in the Dearne Valley: doing community OR with the Thurnscoe Tenants' Housing Cooperative. Part 1 – the involvement of the community OR Unit', *J. Opl Res. Soc.*, **43**, 81–94.

Tomlinson, R. (1984). 'Rethinking the process of Systems Analysis and Operational Research: from practice to precept – and back again', in *Rethinking the Process of Operational Research and Systems Analysis* (Eds. R. Tomlinson and I. Kiss), pp. 205–21, Pergamon, Oxford.

2 SODA – The Principles

Colin Eden and Fran Ackermann

Introduction

The SODA method is an *approach* which is designed to provide consultants with a set of skills, a framework for designing problem solving interventions and a set of techniques and tools to help their clients work with messy problems. These problems are likely to be those that demand an ability to use model building to help work with both quantitative and qualitative aspects of the problem. It is an approach that aims to encourage the consultant to bring together two skills. Firstly, the skills of a facilitator of the *processes* involved in helping a problem solving team to work together efficiently and effectively in reaching workable – politically feasible – agreements. Secondly, the skill to construct a model of, and appropriately analyse, the *content* – interconnected issues, problems, strategies and options – which members of the team wish to address. The process management issues are not taken as independent of the content management issues. Rather, each aspect informs the way in which the other skill is best utilized (Eden, 1990).

In this chapter we acknowledge that the original SODA methodology (reported in the previous version of this book) has been developed. The developments have allowed the methodology to go beyond complex problem solving to encompass work by senior management teams on strategy making. The developed methodology – known as JOURNEY Making – encompasses the method known as Strategic Options Development and Analysis (SODA). As with SODA, JOURNEY Making focuses on the importance of process and negotiation in strategy making and strategy delivery – it suggests that the journey is as important as the outcome in ensuring the development of good strategy and the implementation of agreements. JOURNEY represents an acronym for Jointly Understanding, Reflecting, and Negotiating StrategY. Journey Making is presented in full in Eden and Ackermann (1998a).

With SODA and JOURNEY Making the traditional model building and analysis skills of the operational researcher are used to handle the complexity that faces a consultant working on messy issues. However, the nature of both the model and the analysis are powerful *facilitative devices intended to help manage political feasibility*. They facilitate the better management of the process by which the team will arrive at something approaching consensus and both emotional and cognitive commitment to action. Indeed the aim of seeking consensus (rather than compromise) and commitment produces a distinctive and multifaceted measure of success for the use of the SODA approach.

Underlying this notion of success is a view of problem solving that focuses on the point at which people feel confident to take action that they believe to be appropriate. This is in contrast to the idea of striving for the 'right answer'. (One way of conceptualizing this difference is as an orientation to 'problem finishing/alleviation' rather than 'problem solving' – see Eden, 1987.) Thus SODA's success cannot be measured by the rationality or optimality of the action portfolio in terms of content alone, but rather relates to energy and commitment generated for delivering the agreements.

For SODA, one can only evaluate success by consideration of the impact of personalities, roles, politics, and power dimensions of the *specific* group of individuals that make up the decision-making team. (The same may also be said of Soft Systems Methodology and Strategic Choice or indeed any of the so-called 'wide-band group decision support systems' (Eden, 1995 and 2000, Finlay 1998).) Some practitioners (for example Machol, 1980) have alleged that the recourse to social considerations is an attempt to shelter behind the obfuscation provided by 'sociological jargon' and so excuse improper OR practice. We would argue the contrary, that the exclusion of such considerations has often been a factor limiting OR's acceptability.

An OR consultant will be interested in employing a SODA approach to problems only when some or all of the following conditions prevail. Firstly, the consultant is personally interested in working face-to-face with problem-solving groups, that is in being explicit and reflective about managing a social process – being a facilitator as well as modeller. The consultant will often be happier operating 'on the hoof' than 'in the backroom'. The consultant will be more interested in designing and managing problem-solving workshops rather than in research and analysis of the problem characteristics. The personality of the consultant will be such that action satisfies more than discovery.

Secondly, the consultant will relate personally to a small number (say, three to ten persons) of 'significant' people as client. This is in contrast to some consultants who see themselves acting with respect to 'the organisation' as client. Thirdly, the consultant will tend towards a contingent and cyclic approach to working on problems. The approach will be 'to proceed flexibly and experimentally from broad concepts to specific commitments, making the latter concrete as late as possible' (Quinn, 1980). This tendency is to be distinguished from that of working steadily through a linear and deterministic process towards a clear goal. The consultant will be as pleased to work in a 'quick and dirty' manner as in a 'thorough and complete' manner.

These characteristics are not better than other laudable profiles for the 'good' consultant. They are intended to help the reader gain a rough impression of the sort of person most likely to enjoy working with SODA, and therefore more likely to be successful. Similarly, they importantly encapsulate the sort of client who will feel comfortable working with SODA. The client will need to be sympathetic to the above characteristics. In particular, the client group will be looking for *help* in thinking through analytically the issue they face, without expecting the consultant to act as an expert with respect to content. The expectation (Eden and Sims, 1979) to be established by both parties is that the consultant will contribute professional expertise in bringing together different perspectives, analysing the implication of those perspectives, and facilitating negotiation for agreed action.

A Framework and Context for 'SODA'

The framework of concepts shown in Figure 2.1 shows the four important and inter-acting theoretical perspectives that imply the need for an approach such as SODA. The figure shows four perspectives about the *individual*, about the *nature of organizations*, *about consulting practice*, and about the role of *technology and technique*. Each of these perspectives leads to the core notion that drives SODA: the application of a *facilitative device*. The following narrative discusses each of these perspectives in more detail.

The SODA approach has its foundation in 'subjectivism'. Each member of a client group is held to have his or her own personal subjective view of the 'real' problem. The wisdom and experience of members of the team is a key element in developing decisions with which participants feel confident. It is because of the complexity and richness that arises from attention to subjectivity, that a focus for SODA work is on the managing of *process* as well as content. This view of behaviour, judgement, and decision making in organizations sees experience-gathering as an act of 'scientific' endeavour, where man-agers experiment with their organizational world, learn about it, develop theories about how it works, and seek to intervene in it.

This *'focus on the individual'*, or on the *psychology and social psychology* of problem solving, is guided by the 'Theory of Personal Constructs' (Kelly, 1955). This particular body of psychological theory is a *cognitive* theory. It argues that human beings are continually striving to 'make sense' of their world in order to 'manage and control' that world. In

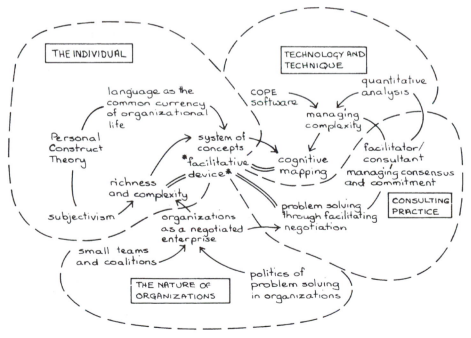

Figure 2.1 Theory and concepts guiding SODA

this way it implicitly sees the individual as a problem finder/problem solver, using concepts rather than emotion to guide action. Therefore, it suits the particular purpose of working with individuals who are constrained by a need to *explain* their actions within their organizational world. (Other psychological theories are appropriate for other purposes.) Within SODA, construct theory has practical significance because cognitive mapping, the 'technology and technique' (in Figure 2.1), works with 'language as the common currency of organizational life'. A 'cognitive map' is a model of the 'system of concepts' used by the client to communicate the nature of a problem. The model represents the *meaning* of a concept by its relationship to other concepts through an action orientation. Any statement about an aspect of the problem is given meaning through the role the statement plays in expressing a means to an end – the consequences and purposes of the statement as if it were an action. We ask why is this 'fact, assertion, proposal' important to managing and controlling the situation. In addition, we seek to understand the explanations for the circumstance that the statement describes. We ask how this 'circumstance, proposal' might have come about. In other words, statements are made as a way of representing a person's 'making sense' of the situation/problem they believe is faced by the group. The meaning of a statement is derived from it's implications and explanations – theories of means/ends.

Thus, the manager is taken to be involved in the psychological *construction of* the world rather than the *perception* of an objective world – 'if men define situations as real, they are real in their consequences' (Thomas and Thomas, 1928). So it is the interpretation of an event that is reality, rather than the perception of it. Action arises out of the meaning of situations, and the meaning will vary from one individual to another even if the characteristics of the event are agreed by both individuals to be similar. Thus individuality is legitimate and allowed to blossom within a SODA project. Protecting individuality is designed to ensure that the outcome of the project is both creative and also consensual.

This orientation is reflected in the distinction Silverman makes between the Systems Framework and the Action Framework (a distinction explored more fully in Eden and Graham, 1983). Thus,

> while behaviour may be viewed as a reflection of the organizational structure and its problems ... it is equally as valid to suggest that an organization itself is the outcome of the interaction of motivated people attempting to resolve their own problems. ... The environment in which an organization is located might usefully be regarded as a source of meanings through which members defined their actions and made sense of the actions of others. (Silverman, 1970)

In organizations, teams are deliberately created in order that each member of the team may bring a different perspective to an issue. A different construction of problems comes from having a different role and from a different set of experiences and wisdom. In the SODA approach we simply aim to exploit this fully as a benefit. However, exploiting individuality implies deliberately encouraging more richness in problem construction by accentuating complexity within problems.

The individual, within an organizational setting, will use all methods of communication in order to negotiate with and persuade others. However, SODA focuses on that form of communication that is most legitimate in organizations, i.e. language. This means ignoring, to a very considerable extent, the role of non-verbal communication in its own right. It assumes that the consultant will use language as an adequate (to the client) modelling medium to capture the meaning that derives from emotion expressed also through intonation, body movement, and personality.

The above discussion has focused on the segment labelled 'the individual' in Figure 2.1. Following the figure in an anticlockwise direction leads to a consideration of *'the nature of organizations'*.

A facilitator considering the use of the SODA approach needs to be clear about, and in sympathy with, a particular view of decision making in organizations. This is one that emphasizes the role of the individual, in contrast to an inclination to 'reify' the organization or parts of it as if it were an individual. Many practitioners prefer to work with 'the organization' or 'the department' as the focus of attention. We do not wish to argue here that this is wrong, but rather to be clear that it does not inform the SODA approach. The purpose of the organization is defined in practice by its participants rather than by written documents – theories in use rather than espoused theories (Argyris and Schon 1974). Thus purpose is neither presumed by the consultant or determined by reference to anything other than the problem solving group, even though what is written elsewhere in the organization may be introduced and used by the consultant as a reference point during the modelling and facilitation processes of negotiations within the group

A view of organizations which focuses on the individual will inevitably also focus on the organization as a changing set of coalitions in which politics and power are significant explanations of decision making. That is to say, 'organizations are a negotiated enterprise' (Strauss and Schatzman, 1963), whose participants are continuously negotiating and renegotiating their roles within it.

These two perspectives, on organizations and individuals, come together to form a *'consulting practice'* (the third segment of Figure 2.1) which centres on the role of negotiation in effective problem solving. The consultant is the instrument for facilitating this negotiation, and for managing consensus and commitment. The consultant is taken to have a central professional role in both designing *and* managing this negotiation.

These three perspectives on the individual, the nature of organizations, and the characteristics of consulting practice each derive from seeing *an organization as a negotiated enterprise*. Through appropriate *'technology and technique'* (the final segment of Figure 2.1) these building blocks come together through the concept at the core of Figure 2.1 – 'a facilitative device'. Our approach is aimed at providing a device that can be used to facilitate managing the messiness of deciding on action. In this way we are attempting to create an analytically sound method of dealing with both content *and* process. The effective management and analysis of process is informed by the effective management and analysis of content, which in turn is informed by the issues of managing process.

In the case of SODA the technique is 'cognitive mapping', and the technology to help manage complexity is computer software called Decision Explorer and Group Explorer.

Cognitive Mapping as a Formal Modelling Technique

The technique or methodology of 'cognitive mapping', within the context of JOURNEY Making and SODA, does not exist independently of the framework described above. It exists, rather, as one of the key techniques which are employed in the prosecution of SODA and JOURNEY Making. SODA is the *approach* to working with clients, out of which has grown the particular *technique* of cognitive mapping.

'Cognitive mapping' is the label for the general task of mapping a person's thinking within the field of psychological research on perception. It is important to note that cognitive mapping is *not* simply a 'word and arrow' diagram, or an influence diagram (used by System Dynamicists (see, for example, Wolstenholme, 1990)), or a 'mind-map'/'brain-map' (Buzan and Buzan, 1993). It is a formal modelling technique with rules for its development; without such rules it would not be amenable to the type of analysis expected of a formal model. Often cognitive maps are reasonably large – over 100 nodes on the map. Group maps that are developed from merging several cognitive maps derived from each member of the problem-solving group are inevitably much larger – over 800 nodes. Thus, the ability to conduct formal analyses, that are meaningful to the client group, is of paramount importance. Without good analysis the richness cannot be addressed by enabling a group to focus on what is at the 'nub of the issue' they face. Some consultants use some of the principles of cognitive mapping and SODA through the use of 'word-and-arrow' diagrams where the formality of how nodes are phrased and the rules for determining the direction of arrows is not regarded as important. Nevertheless, SODA mapping processes often lead, in our own practice, to the later development of influence diagrams as a lead in to System Dynamics simulation modelling (for example, Ackermann, Eden, and Williams, 1997; Eden, 1994).

The term cognitive map was first used by Tolman in 1948, and has been used widely since then by researchers in a wide variety of disciplines. In this chapter we are introducing a version of cognitive mapping which has been specifically developed to help internal and external consultants/facilitators deal with some important aspects of their job. It is also distinctive because it is a modelling approach which is directly derived from a substantive theory within cognitive psychology (Kelly, 1955).

The SODA-based version of 'cognitive mapping', as a modelling system, is founded on the belief expressed in Figure 2.1 that language is a basic currency of organizational problem solving. Whorf (1956) has vividly expressed the underlying view that 'the world is presented in a kaleidoscope flux of impressions which has to be organized by our minds – and this means largely by the linguistic systems in our minds … we cut nature up, organize it into concepts, and ascribe significances as weights largely because we are parties to an agreement to organize it in this way'.

As we have said, a cognitive map is a formal model – a model amenable to formal analysis. It is a model designed to represent the way in which a person defines an issue. It is not a general model of someone's thinking, neither is it intended to be a simulation model of decision making. It is a network of ideas linked by arrows; the network is coded from what a person says. The arrows indicate the way in which one idea may lead to, or have implications for, another. Thus a map is a network of nodes and links (a 'directed graph'). Some years ago it seemed helpful to devise computer software that would help with storing the maps and with their analysis. In consequence, software called 'COPE' (Eden, Smithin and Wiltshire, 1980), and now called 'Decision Explorer' (Banxia, 2000), was developed to act as an aid in developing the methodology for working with teams. It became an integral, but not essential, part of the process of working on problems. We shall comment later upon the role that computer software and associated computer technology may play both in the management of process and in the management of content complexity.

When managers talk about an issue, and what should be done, they use language which is designed to argue why the world is 'like it is and how it might be changed'. Take a simple example of one person expressing a view about profit sharing. (This view was expressed well before the Labour Party in the UK reached the position of government during the 1990's. It is no longer of relevance to Labour Party industrial policy, though it does have historical interest . . . .)

'The latter-day Labour Party, aiming to appeal upmarket, is in a more ambivalent position. At a time when they are looking for a concordat with the unions, union opposition to profit sharing – because of the fear of collective bargaining – is hard to avoid. American experience with Employee Share Ownership Plans since the early 1980s has led to a drop in union membership in firms with these profit sharing schemes.'

[Extract from the *Guardian* newspaper 'Who gains from profit sharing?' by Jane McLoughlin, 14 May 1986 (slightly modified).]

Figure 2.2 shows how this piece of written, rather than spoken, argument may be converted into a cognitive map. Important phrases are selected to capture the essential aspects of the arguments. An attempt to capture the meaning of each phrase is made by trying to identify the contrasting idea. Thus 'Labour support for profit sharing' is contrasted with 'ambivalence towards profit sharing', and 'upmarket appeal' is contrasted with 'working class appeal'. This latter contrast is a possibly incorrect attempt by the coder to understand the meaning of 'upmarket' by making a guess. The *meaning* of a phrase together with its contrast (a 'concept') is further elaborated by considering the argumentation that links the concept with others. In a cognitive map this is shown by linking arrows.

Thus 'concept A leading to B and explained by C and D' has a different meaning from 'concept A leading to E and explained by C and F'. The meaning of a concept is given by the contrasting pole as well as the explanatory and consequential concepts; not by any dictionary definition.

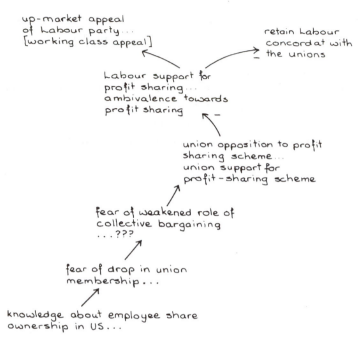

Figure 2.2 An example of a small cognitive map (is read as 'rather than' and separates the first pole of the concept from the contrasting pole)

The phrases and linking arrows are not precisely a replication of the language used by the person speaking: they have been modified to reflect the need for an *action, or problem solving, orientation*. Each of the concepts in Figure 2.2 is written as a 'call to action' and is intended to suggest an option for changing the nature of the situation in a positive way. Similarly, the argumentation (direction of the arrows) is such that an option always leads to a desired outcome, with the most important outcome hierarchically superior to others. The means to an end is always the subordinate concept, and placed at the tail of the arrow linking two concepts. In Figure 2.2 the highest order goal is taken to be the 'Labour Party seeking an upmarket appeal', alongside the other presumed goal of 'retaining Labour's concordat with the Unions'. All the options are taken to have implications for these goals.

In addition, the map indicates the nature of the argumentation by adding a negative sign to the end of an arrow if the first phrase of one concept relates to the second phrase of the other concept. Thus 'union opposition' leads to 'ambivalence *rather than* support'. The reasons for coding so that a negative sign is needed are several, it is not designed deliberately to complicate the map! The most obvious reason is that chains of argument often join up, so that one or other chain will need a negative sign in order for them to come together. An example of a more subtle reason is that it is sometimes helpful for the map to be constructed so that the first poles of concepts are those at the forefront of the client's thinking. In this way a map depicts the overall definition of the situation. Sometimes a glance at all the first poles (the definition of the situation which is predominant for that person) reveals that a situation is problematic because, in effect, the 'world is tumbling around about me, and I don't like it'. In other cases it will reveal that the client sees the situation as problematic because 'my world could be a better place, and I'm not there'. In the first case the client sees disaster and wants to remove himself or herself from it, in the second the client sees a better future and is striving to get there. This difference in construing the situation will have some bearing on how the consultant sets about managing the problem solving process. Early in a project it is important to build a map that reflects the client's, and no one else's, orientation to the problem (and particularly not that of the consultant).

Changing the language used by the client, so that it becomes oriented to action rather than problem description, without the client losing 'ownership' of the model, is not a trivial exercise. Equally, deciding which concept is the goal/outcome/end and which is the action/option/means of a linked pair of concepts is an important part of the model building. For example, looking for a concordat with the Unions' sounds like a goal (particularly given the use of the phrase 'looking for'), and so has been coded as a goal in Figure 2.2. However, if we were able to converse with Jane McLoughlin (as would be the case if she were a client), then we would be keen to establish whether 'a concordat' is regarded as a goal (a good outcome in its own right), or as an option which contributes to 'ambivalence towards profit sharing'. The overall sense of the text on its own makes us feel uncertain about our coding. Nevertheless, in some circumstances the hierarchical order of concepts can be decided more easily. When a concept is a generic label for a variety of possible options, then it will be hierarchical to each of the possible options that are encompassed by the generic label. Thus if we say 'helping the reader understand the point we are making leads us to include a diagram' then it would not be coded as spoken (arrow from 'helping' to 'diagram'). Instead, 'helping' would be the generic concept of which 'diagram' would be one option leading to the outcome of 'help'.

Working with Cognitive Maps

The map in Figure 2.2 is exceedingly small. Typically, a map created when working with one member of a problem solving team might contain 40 to 120 concepts; that for the issue as represented by the aggregation of maps for several team members could consist of several hundred. 'Strategic management' maps, which are to be used over long periods of time as a part of a managerial decision support system, can contain several thousand concepts. Nevertheless, the above example serves to demonstrate the principles of analysing the structure of maps.

There are two principal ways of working on a map with the client. The first is to explore the goal system further, and then gradually work down the map towards increasingly detailed options for achieving goals. Alternatively, one can start from the detailed options and gradually work up the map towards goals by exploring each concept in turn as a potential option. Which of these two approaches is chosen depends upon the professional judgement of the consultant about process issues concerning client attitudes. Some clients will become more excited by expending energy on elaborating and questioning the goals implied by their view of the problem. Others, in contrast, may regard the goals as self-evident and be more motivated by working on possibilities for action. This issue is discussed in more detail in the case study presented in the next chapter.

Each of these ways of working with a single client presumes that the consultant is satisfied that the model is a fair representation of the situation as it is seen by the client, and so is likely to be 'owned' by the client. The model above was constructed from written text; this origin apparently simplifies but actually complicates the process of understanding a client.

Working from text denudes the meaning that derives from intonation, from body movement, and more significantly from the results of consultant-client *interaction*. One of the powerful attributes of mapping as a model building method comes from the ability to create the model as the client is talking. This makes it possible to explore the implications of the model, with the client, during the interview.

When interviewing each member of a problem solving team, each interview is normally planned to last for an hour, although it is best to run them on a 2 hourly basis to provide a) enough time to continue the interview if the interviewee is inclined and b) enough time to tidy up and 'finish' the map. Four interviews in a day is normally considered the maximum possible. During the interview the model is explored interactively so that it is more likely that ownership will be assured as the consultant checks possible misunderstandings as the interview unfolds. This way of working also ensures that the consultant develops the questions asked during the interview from the interview data itself, rather than from a tight agenda of prepared questions. This allows for a warmer, more trusting consultant-client relationship to grow, and more importantly gives the control of the interview over to the client.

This style of operating allows the consultant to move in a gentle fashion from an 'empathetic' to a 'negotiative' paradigm of consultant-client relationship (Eden and Sims, 1979). Early in the project the consultant must attend to understanding the world of the client from the client's perspective; later, and after trust has grown, the consultant can suggest alternative views. These alternative views may be based upon those of the consultant's substantive and content-related expertise from working on other similar projects, or can be based on injecting views from others in the problem solving group (but without identifying sources). The process of working with the client for checking and further elaboration slides into working on options which are defined in enough detail that they can be acted upon. In the interview this comes from 'laddering' down the map by continually seeking further explanation (see Eden and Ackermann 1998a, chap 5). Each explanation is, in principle, an option – every time we explain why something has happened or might happen we are identifying a possible intervention for changing the world.

As checking for an adequate model becomes less important, the consultant will move to one of the two more proactive, or negotiative, modes of working – working with the client on an analysis of the goal system and then down the model towards options, or working from options towards goals – 'laddering up' or 'laddering down'.

Working in the first mode, with the goal system, implies concentrating on the concepts at the 'top', or hierarchically super-ordinate, part of the map. Consultant and client together will consider the overall network of goals, and their relationship one to another. In our example this means concentrating on questions such as 'why is up-market appeal important to the Labour Party?' The client is invited to expand the chain of goals by moving to successively higher levels in the hierarchy. In this case we may suppose that something like 'wider electoral appeal ... appeal to electorate in the North' might be a further elaboration. Both client and consultant may find it illuminating to go on extending such questions until it becomes 'obvious' to both that the concept at the top of the model, with no further consequences, is 'self-evidently' a 'good thing'. Once this stage has been reached the client may be invited to work back gradually down the hierarchy by answering the question 'what options come to mind for changing this situation, other than those already mentioned?' For example, 'what other ways come to mind for shifting "ambivalence towards profit sharing" to "support", other than "reducing the fear of a weakened role in collective bargaining"?'.

The second mode of working with the client focuses on action by identifying each 'tail' (the concept at the bottom of a chain of argumentation, that is with no further explanations) and testing it as a possible intervention point. Therefore, 'knowledge about share ownership in the United States' is tested as a possible option – is there any way in which this 'first pole' of the concept creatively suggests a 'contrasting pole'? It may seem more natural to regard this particular concept in the example as simply a part of the context within the original statement, rather than as a means to the end of 'reducing fear of a drop in union membership'. However, consideration of such concepts as potential options often leads to creative suggestions for action – in this case 'rubbishing the knowledge from the United States' might be such an option. The next part of the problem solving process is to consider other means by which it might be possible to reduce the 'fear of a drop in union membership'. So, we proceed to elaborate the map by inserting new options/tails as subordinate concepts to that being considered.

Further exploration of options moves up the concept hierarchy, by considering ways of making 'weakened role' an option. This is done in the same way as in the above example: in this case we had supposed that there was an action which might be taken to 'reduce the fear of a weakened role for collective bargaining', and had inserted '???' in Figure 2.2. This was to serve as a prompt for guiding the client to consider possible contrasting poles. In addition we would invite the client to consider other ways of, 'reducing fear', by asking 'are there any other reasons why unions have a fear of weakened role of collective bargaining?'. For example, the client might respond by suggesting that the contrasting pole is weakened role seen as strength, not reduced role as we had thought. If the client suggested this contrasting pole, we would seek to discover from the client how such a view might come about. For example delegating negotiating power down to local shop stewards may be preferred as a possible explanation. This additional concept now becomes a new 'tail', as an explanation for weakened role seen as strength (an arrow into the 'role' concept from 'delegating', with a negative sign on it). After working with the client on other ways of countering weakened role by developing other new 'tails' we would then move to the next concept up the hierarchy and consider other ways of countering union opposition. And so on, elaborating the map by seeking to discover further explanations for why the situation is as it is.

Looking for options in this way reveals the importance of trying to identify contrasting poles of concepts – for the contrast is the essence of action. For example, in considering how to counter weakened role it is important to identify the nature of the contrast. This might have been strengthened role or less weakened role, or the contrast suggested above of weakened role seen as strength. Each contrast has significantly different implications for identifying possible interventions and further explanations. Each explanation, in its own way, becomes a new option to be considered. In the original map, the 'tail' 'knowledge about employee share ownership in the United States' could have been regarded as an option, in the sense of negating it by ensuring knowledge is not transmitted.

A 'SODA' (or JOURNEY Making) Project

Figure 2.2 is a 'cognitive' map because it is supposed to be a model of the *thinking* of one person. In a SODA project the cognitive map of each member of the client team will be merged to form an aggregated map called a 'strategic map'. This process of merging maps is a crucial aspect of how the consultant takes account of process as well as content issues. The aim is to produce a 'facilitative device' to promote psychological negotiation amongst team members so that, in the first instance, a definition of the problem can be established. During the initial model building with individual clients, the aim was to help them 'change their minds' about the nature of the problem through a combination of self-reflection with respect to the map, and gentle negotiation with the consultant. The map is used as the device to facilitate the negotiation.

Similarly, the initial purpose of the merged map is to change the minds of each member of the client group, without their feeling compromised. The aim is to secure enough agreement about the nature of the problem that each team member is committed to expending energy on finding a *portfolio* of actions, where that portfolio is the strategy for dealing with the issue. The group negotiation approach is informed by some approaches to international conciliation, where the intention is to gain agreement to *enough* group ownership of the problem definition (the group map) and then move towards using the map as a way of encouraging the development of new options (or portfolios/systems of options) on which politically feasible agreement can be reached, rather than fighting over 'old options' (Fisher and Ury 1982, Fisher and Brown, 1988).

Because the aim is to facilitate negotiation, the individual maps are merged with a significant regard for the anticipated dynamics of negotiation. This means that when a concept on one map is overlaid on a similar concept on another map, it is a matter of concern as to which person's wording is retained on the strategic map. Similarly, as the strategic map is analysed prior to creating an agenda for a SODA workshop, to be attended by all or most team members, then the extracts from the strategic map that are to be used in the workshop are carefully monitored to ensure balanced representation from key team members.

Consider the (unlikely) possibility that Jane McLoughlin is a member of a problem solving team and that one of her colleagues had said:

'It is possible that the Labour Party might support profit sharing schemes if opinion polls demonstrated support from Union members ... however the tabloid newspapers would need to give some education on profit sharing instead of continuing to ignore the idea ... with support from these newspapers it is likely that some popular support might result – at the moment there is support only from the middle classes ... it is also important that the "man-in-the-street" is made aware of the benefits US workers have seen from profit sharing schemes in the US ... the trouble for the Labour Party is that if there were popular support then other opposition parties might also support profit sharing ... nevertheless I believe the crucial question for the Labour Party is whether their support could decrease antagonism from key members of the CBI ... I suspect that if there were mechanisms for applying profit sharing to public sector workers then this would be a powerful argument for the party supporting something which at present only seems to apply to the private sector. '

These views might have resulted in the map shown in Figure 2.3, which would need to be merged with that of Figure 2.2.

The cognitive maps built with each of these team members might be merged along the lines shown in Figure 2.4. We might overlay the two concepts that relate to profit sharing (concepts 1 and 5 in Figure 2.4), and then link concepts elsewhere within the two maps (4 leads to 2, 6 leads to 9, and 14 leads to 12 and 13). Unless there is a process reason for doing otherwise (for example, if the concept that is to be overlaid belongs to the boss then it *might be* worth considering deliberately retaining it regardless of other considerations), then the concept that is lost is that which is less rich. Thus in this example concept 5 will be lost in favour of concept 1 which has a contrasting pole. As other concepts are linked, the consultant uses judgement to maintain the hierarchical relationships within the final merged map. This judgement is not to be treated lightly, for the consultant will be beginning a process of negotiating his own view of the problem on to the model by inserting new links between 'owned' maps. For example, in the merged model, we have decided to *suggest* that a decrease in antagonism from key members of the CBI will have the likely consequence of creating upmarket appeal. By so doing we are implicitly (and later during a workshop explicitly) inviting consideration of options for decreasing antagonism other than that of providing support for profit sharing.

Figure 2.4 shows instances of two paths of argumentation from one concept to

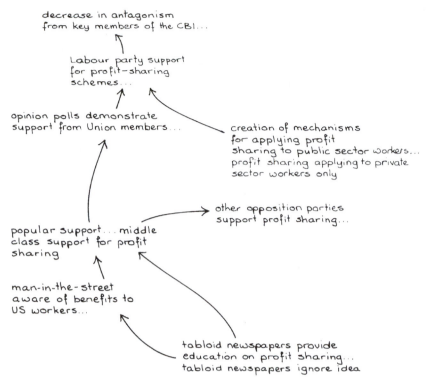

decrease in antagonism
from key members of the CBI...

Labour party support
for profit-sharing
schemes...

opinion polls demonstrate
support from Union members...

creation of mechanisms
for applying profit
sharing to public sector workers...
profit sharing applying to private
sector workers only

other opposition parties
support profit sharing...

popular support... middle
class support for profit
sharing

man-in-the-street
aware of benefits to
US workers...

tabloid newspapers provide
education on profit sharing...
tabloid newspapers ignore idea

Figure 2.3 Possible cognitive map for a second team member

another. For example, in the merged map concept 1 leads directly to concept 2, and indirectly through concept 4. In these circumstances it is helpful to ask whether there are genuinely two paths – it is often possible that the direct route is the same as the indirect route, the indirect route being a useful elaboration of the direct route. If the two paths indicate different argumentation – as appears to be the case in the above map – then it will be useful to add in at least one further concept to explain the different means to the same end. In the example we might ask the clients to elaborate, and this might result in a further concept such as 'Labour seen to be supporting trendy new ideas'. We may also note that there are now ten (!) paths of argumentation from concept 14 to concept 2 (a path is any unique sequence of concepts, for example the path 14,13,12, 8,6,1,2 is different from 14,12,8,6,1,2). The option represented by concept 14 of rubbishing knowledge is a *dilemma* in that it leads to a desirable outcome following some paths and an undesirable outcome following others. It is also tempting for the consultant to insert a tentative negative link from the current undesirable negative-outcome of 'other opposition parties support profit sharing' to the goal of 'upmarket appeal'.

The SODA process is built around working with a team, on their aggregated data, having paid the fullest possible attention to the individuality of problem construction. The process is designed to facilitate negotiation and the broadening of problem definition,

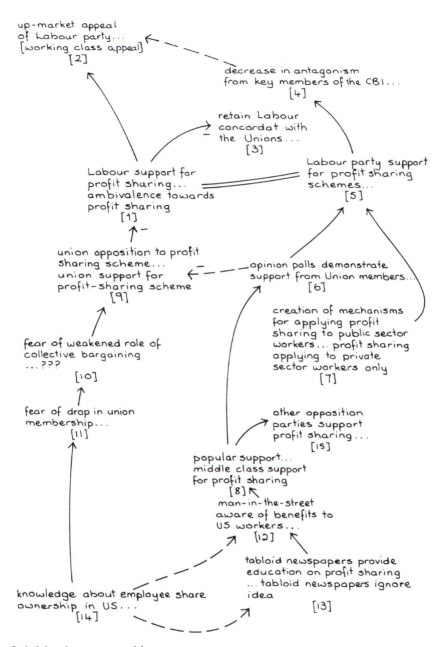

Figure 2.4 Merging two cognitive maps

that is, a deliberate attempt to increase complexity rather than reduce it. And it must be noted that increasing complexity can be disabling to a client (Eden, Jones, Sims and Smithin, 1981), unless the consultant has a method for managing this complexity *without* losing richness and subtlety. The process is also structured to decrease the possibility of 'group think', and increase the possibility of identifying creatively pleasing strategies. The most important element of the methodology is a SODA *workshop*. The workshop is carefully designed to address the aggregated data in a manner that does not lose any of the richness and detail of the owned cognitive maps.

After maps have been merged, the consultant must analyse the content and structure of the model in order to generate an agenda for the workshop – an agenda which has sensibly managed complexity without losing richness. While this can be done manually, it is obviously easier using a computer and associated software – the strategic map is likely to be of several hundred concepts. The overall richness of the structure of the data will be difficult to appreciate fully without the help of sophisticated clustering and mapping algorithms. The initial task is to analyse the data to identify 'emerging themes' (bundles or clusters of material that are tightly linked nodes), and 'core concepts' (those nodes, that if deleted, would fundamentally change the structure of the model). See Eden, 1988; Eden, Ackermann and Cropper, 1992; Eden and Ackermann 1998b for more detailed discussion of analysis possibilities.

The computer software (Decision Explorer) that performs these tasks has been designed at the Universities of Bath and Strathclyde. It is passive software that is non-prescriptive in use or outcome. It is deliberately designed to help the skilled professional consultant manage the complexity and richness that arises when working large amounts of interrelated qualitative data. It contains several algorithms for automatically drawing maps, for identifying clusters of nodes, for comparing subsets of data, for 'collapsing' maps, for creating expert system specifications, and for allowing clients to interact directly with a large strategic database. It provides the user with the opportunity to custom-design analysis routines through the use of its own high level language.

The software is most often used in real time in conjunction with data projection facilities as the core technology in a SODA workshop (Eden and Ackermann, 1992). In addition many workshops are designed to use Group Explorer (a further extension of Decision Explorer, where a local area network of laptop computers enables participants to interact directly with the public screen through 'chauffeur' software to manage the collection of data and Decision Explorer as the driver (Phrontis 2000)). However, the use of Decision Explorer is not essential to the approach, and in many projects is deliberately excluded because it would not fit with the style and culture of the client group, or alternatively because time constraints do not make it efficient. Nevertheless the use of Group Explorer can increase significantly the effectiveness and productivity of the group (Ackermann and Eden, 2001).

The design of the SODA workshop is initially influenced by an identification of the *system of interacting problems that make up the issue* being addressed. (The principle purpose of this analysis is not dissimilar to the exploration and analysis of interconnected decision

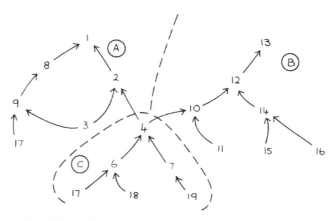

Figure 2.5 An example of clustering

areas undertaken in Strategic Choice – see the chapters by Friend and Hickling in this volume). A variety of methods for analysis of the data is available to the user of the software. These help the consultant to use professional judgement to identify clusters within the map. In this way clusters of about 15–30 concepts are identified. Each cluster represents a problem arena within which there will be problem-related goals at the 'head' of the cluster, strategic options within the cluster – that is, options that are of strategic significance, requiring considerable effort to implement, usually demanding a range of actions within several different clusters, and options at the 'tail' of the cluster. Each cluster, therefore, will probably be linked to other clusters. The goals of one problem lead to the options of another, and the options within one problem are consequences of the goals of a subordinate problem.

Figure 2.5 shows the principle of clustering maps. In this example complexity has been managed by visually (rather than mathematically) breaking the map into three clusters that are relatively independent of one another. (Deleting the relationships from concept 4 to concepts 2 and 10 would make each cluster completely independent.) The clustering in this example has been undertaken with apparently no regard for the content and complete regard for structure, however the map structure is determined by content and so the analysis is not only paying attention to structure but also to content. A structural analysis is always a good starting point but rarely a good finishing point for the analysis of maps. It must then be followed by attention to content of clusters and to process considerations, and the clusters modified accordingly. Similarly, each cluster is tested by making a judgement about the validity of the analysis in suggesting a sensible problem with goals and options.

It is only by using judgement that the essentially reductionist cluster analysis can guide the consultant towards capturing the holistic properties of the aggregated data. Each cluster may be given a label to describe the 'nub of the problem' it represents. An overview map may then be constructed which identifies the problems/clusters and their hierarchical relationship one to another.

The Workshop

Armed with these clusters, each produced either by hand or by the computer as large (newsprint size) maps, and taking full account of the process issues, the consultant must establish a rough agenda for the workshop. Typically, a workshop will be arranged to take anything from 2 hours to 2 days, depending on the availability of team members and the perceived importance of the issue. The scheme for the workshop is, in principle, similar to that for the interaction between consultant and single client. The consultant may choose to start from a goal orientation or an action orientation. An important consideration is to design an agenda which will allow a *cyclic process* to unfold. (See Friend and Hickling, 1987 for further discussion of the nature of cyclic processes in problem solving workshops.) The objective of working with a cyclic process is to ensure that participants in a workshop are helped with the process of gradually absorbing the overall emerging issues, yet get to grips with the detail, and then move to action.

This can be achieved most effectively by taking participants quickly through an overview of the *system of goals, interrelated problems (clusters), strategic options, and assumptions.* This first pass through the data is undertaken by the consultant without extensive discussion – it is 'billed' as an introductory pass. The aim of the first pass is to begin the process of participants 'taking on board' alternative views – the gradual psychological negotiation of a new construction of the problem, and ownership by enough of the group view for negotiation to occur. The first pass contributes to gaining this ownership by a controlled 'walk' through the model to demonstrate that concepts belonging to each participant have been included in the model. The potential for each of the participants 'changing his or her mind' is largely dependent upon the help the model provides in extending ownership beyond those concepts that belong to a single participant. Extending ownership occurs by a participant seeing his or her own concepts now set within the context of concepts that are known to belong to other participants. Cycling through the data on several occasions gives the time for each participant to absorb the change in *meaning* implied by a new context for concepts. This is the model acting as *facilitative device*, whereby a person can concentrate on the concepts themselves rather than who is presenting them, or on the social needs of debate.

The first pass creates a 'backdrop' against which the second pass, focusing on individual issues/clusters, can unfold. The preparatory work on the agenda for the workshop will have located the key issues, their interdependence, and the order in which they will be addressed. The consultant must decide whether to work on a cluster top-down (goal system mode) or bottom-up (option mode). In this second pass the 'rules' change and discussion is encouraged. As discussion continues the consultant will be publicly elaborating and extending the maps. (See Eden and Ackermann, 1998a for discussion of this process as a computer assisted group decision support system.)

For the operational researcher, the clusters within the strategic map will have alerted him or her to opportunities for more extensive project work. It is usual for a SODA workshop to identify opportunities for further analysis, such as financial model building, simulation modelling, market research, and statistical analysis. The software has provision for 'collapsing' an ideas-oriented map down to a smaller map focusing on those concepts that may form the basis of an 'influence diagram' for use in system dynamics model building. In addition the software will identify all feedback loops and calculate the nodes that are most central. Alternatively, the same sort of collapsed model can provide a direct input to 'spreadsheet' software. However, the attraction of undertaking this further work, for both consultant and client, lies in the clear understanding that it will be carried out within the context of broader qualitative issues. This means that work within one problem cluster will have known ramifications for work on other interacting problems. For example, it is not unusual to discover key relationships (arrows), within a cluster/problem, about which there is a high level of uncertainty. Often these relationships express a crucial belief about how the market place works. When such circumstances occur the client may call for market research to validate particular concepts and their links.

Review and Summary

The aim of this chapter has been: (i) to set out the key assumptions which underlie the SODA/JOURNEY Making approach to working with groups on messy problems; and (ii) to exemplify this approach through the use of 'cognitive mapping' as the core technique within SODA. As we hope we have shown in this chapter and in the following case study, the SODA approach and cognitive mapping as a *consultancy* tool has been developed independently of other work with cognitive mapping, because it has a different purpose and a different body of theory and concepts underlying it.

As readers evaluate its appropriateness or otherwise for their own practice, we suggest that the following questions be considered. Firstly, does the body of theory and the concepts that have been outlined here make sense? If you draw upon your own experience of organizations and consulting, does the view of organizational life and the nature of problems presented here fit with that experience? Does the emphasis on the design and analysis of process fit your own personal style and capabilities? Secondly, do you believe that the SODA approach, and cognitive mapping, adequately relate to the theory, concepts, and declared aims? And thirdly, does the application of the analytical techniques designed into the software seem to be a useful and powerful addition to the package of tools available to you? These questions are intended to be hierarchical – it is possible to answer 'yes' to the first questions and 'no' to the others, 'yes' to the first two sets of questions and 'no' to the last, or 'yes' to all three – in any of these events the reader might expect some part of this chapter to inform their professional practice. However, the reader should not adopt the method without being in sympathy with the underlying theory and aims.

Finally, as with all of the methods reported in this book, using the SODA approach with cognitive mapping can look deceptively easy. The experience of a wide range of practising consultants is that it is not easy. Its power derives from the ability of the consultant to employ contingently a coherent body of theory and concepts within the practical world of small group problem solving. Nevertheless, as with any other powerful approach of substance, some training and practice coupled with commitment is a basis for many consultants becoming skilled and valued facilitators of this approach. Ashby's Law of Requisite Variety applies as much to our work as problem solving consultants/ facilitators as in any other field – complexity of problems and the people who have to act in relation to them needs to be matched with complexity in method.

Our experiences, of training practitioners and other consultants, suggest that it is an approach that others can learn without too much effort. Nevertheless, a difficulty with SODA, and other approaches in this book, is that there is likely to be disappointment with first use. This is particularly likely if the user believes that a cursory absorption of the principles will suffice.

In the next chapter we consider the processes of using the principles of cognitive mapping for problem structuring, but in a group setting. The process uses an approach called the 'Oval Mapping Technique' (OMT) (described in Bryson, Ackermann, Eden and Finn, 1995; and more fully in Eden and Ackermann, 1998a). Here the statements that make up the map derive from individual members of the group, but the map itself is not the thinking of any person, and so it is usually called a Cause Map, Group Map or Strategy Map. All of the principles of mapping presented in this chapter apply equally to the building of OMT maps.

References

Ackermann, F. and Eden, C. (2001). Contrasting single user and networked group decision support systems for strategy making, *Group Decision and Negotiation*, **10**(1), 47–66.

Ackermann, F., Eden, C., and Williams, T. (1997). 'Modeling for Litigation: Mixing Qualitative and Quantitative Approaches', *Interfaces*, **27**(2), 48–65.

Argyris, C. and Schon, D.A. (1974). *Theories in Practice*, Jossey Bass, San Francisco.

Banxia. (2000). Decision Explorer. See www.banxia.com

Bryson, J.M., Ackermann, F., Eden, C., and Finn, C. (1995). 'Using the "Oval Mapping Process" to identify strategic issues and formulate effective strategies', in *Strategic Planning for Public and Nonprofit Organizations* (Ed. J. Bryson), 2nd ed., pp. 257–75, Jossey Bass, San Francisco.

Buzan, T. with Buzan, B. (1993). *The mind map book*, BBC Books, London.

Eden, C. (1987) 'Problem Solving or Problem Finishing?', in *New Directions in Management Science* (Eds. M.C. Jackson and P. Keys), pp. 97–107, Gower, Hants.

Eden, C. (1988). 'Cognitive Mapping: a review', *European Journal of Operational Research*, **36**, 1–13.

Eden, C. (1990). 'The Unfolding Nature of Group Decision Support', in *Tackling Strategic Problems: the role of group decision support* (Eds. C. Eden and J. Radford), Sage, London.

Eden, C. (1994). 'Cognitive mapping and problem structuring for system dynamics model building', *System Dynamics Review*, **10**, 257–76.

Eden, C. (1995). 'On the Evaluation of "Wide-Band" GDSS's', *European Journal of Operational Research*, **81**, 302–11.

Eden, C. (2000). 'On evaluating the performance of GSS: furthering the debate', *European Journal of Operational Research*, **120**, 218–22.

Eden, C. and Ackermann, F. (1992). 'Strategy Development and Implementation – the role of a Group Decision Support System', in *Computer Augmented Teamwork: A Guided Tour* (Eds. S. Kinney, R. Bostrom, and R. Watson), pp. 325–42, Van Nostrand and Reinhold, New York.

Eden, C. and Ackermann, F. (1998a). *Strategy Making: the Journey of Strategic Management.* Sage, London.

Eden, C. and Ackermann, F. (1998b). 'Analysing and Comparing Idiographic Causal Maps', in *Managerial and Organizational Cognition* (Eds. C. Eden and J.C. Spender), pp. 192–209, Sage, London.

Eden, C. and Graham, R. (1983). 'Halfway to infinity', *Journal of the Operational Research Society*, **34**, 723–28.

Eden, C. and Sims, D. (1979). 'On the nature of problems in consulting practice', *Omega*, **7**, 119–27.

Eden, C.; Ackermann, F., and Cropper, S. (1992). 'The Analysis of Cause Maps', *Journal of Management Studies*, **29**, 309–24.

Eden, C., Jones, S., Sims, D., and Smithin, T. (1981). 'The intersubjectivity of issues and issues of intersubjectivity', *Journal of Management Studies*, **18**, 37–47.

Eden, C. Smithin, T., and Wiltshire, J. (1980). 'Cognition Simulation and Learning', *Journal of Experiential Learning*, **2**, 1–13.

Finlay, P.N. (1998). 'On evaluating the performance of GSS: furthering the debate', *European Journal of Operational Research*, **107**, 193–201.

Fisher, R. and Brown, S. (1988). *Getting Together: Building a Relationship that Gets to Yes*, Houghton-Mifflin, Boston, Mass.

Fisher, R. and Ury, W. (1982). *Getting to Yes,* Hutchinson, London.

Friend, J. and Hickling, A. (1987). *Planning Under Pressure: The Strategic Choice Approach.* Pergamon, Oxford.

Kelly, G.A. (1955). *The Psychology of Personal Constructs*, Norton, New York.

Machol, R. (1980). 'Comment on "Publish or Perish", *Journal of the Operational Research Society*, **31**,1109–13.

Phrontis. (2000). Group Explorer. www.phrontis.com

Quinn, J.B. (1980). *Strategies for Change: Logical Incrementalism*, Irwin, Homewood, Illinois.

Silverman, D. (1970). *The Theory of Organizations*, Heinemann, London.

Thomas, W.I. and Thomas, D.S. (1928). *The Child in America: Behavior Problems and Programs.* Knopf, New York.

Strauss, A. and Schatzman, L. (1963). 'The Hospital and its Negotiated Order', in *The Hospital in Modern Society* (Ed. E. Friedson), pp. 147–69, Macmillan, New York.

Whorf, B. (1956). *Language, Thought and Reality.* MIT Press, Cambridge, Mass.

Wolstenholme, E. (1990). *System Enquiry: A System Dynamics Approach*, John Wiley & Sons, Ltd, Chichester.

3 SODA – Journey Making and Mapping in Practice

Fran Ackermann and Colin Eden

Getting Started – Developing the Consultant–Client Relationship

This chapter focuses upon a recent (and potentially ongoing) project that will illustrate how the 'precepts' of SODA and mapping are used in practice. However, whilst the general design of this project is one that has been found to be effective on a number of occasions, this project nevertheless is unique and has therefore demanded various adaptations. This is true of all projects and therefore professional judgement in designing the intervention is always necessary. To attempt to apply the contents of this chapter as a 'precise formula' in other circumstances would be to court disaster. The idiosyncrasies of the client, the organization and the issue must be taken into account. In order to appreciate this point more fully, contrast this case study with previously published case studies for example those noted in Eden and Ackermann (1998a), Ackermann and Eden (1997), Ackermann and Eden (2001).

The project this case study is designed around focused on providing the National Audit Office (NAO) with help when designing an audit. This was a new area for mapping and soft Operational Research methods in general, and therefore working in this area would allow both the NAO team to learn more about soft OR methods, and the two consultants to try out the techniques in a new environment with a different remit. In addition, as part of the agreement, the organization agreed that they were happy for the engagement to form part of a published case study (provided issues of confidentiality were respected).

The initial interest for the work came about when one of a series of presentations to promote the potential for using Management Science/Operational Research methods in the NAO coincided with the 'client' considering the best way to proceed with a particular piece of work. This almost serendipitous beginning is not untypical, in the authors' experience, of the process of getting started. Managers are often unaware of, or unfamiliar with, a large number of OR techniques, particularly those concentrating on the qualitative side of modelling, and yet these same managers have problems/issues that would benefit from their application. Thus, the combination of presentation and issue provided a valuable impetus. The client subsequently contacted the consultant and discussed the possibility of using mapping as a means of working on the issue.

The client's organization, the NAO, is the external auditor of governmental departments and many other public sector organizations. They examine the accounts of most of these bodies and carry out value for money examinations into the economy, efficiency and effectiveness with which the bodies have used their resources. The results of these 'value for money' examinations are published primarily for the benefit of Parliament.

The client and his team were currently undertaking a value for money study into how HM Customs and Excise counter VAT avoidance. Customs have been concerned at the number of traders seeking 'to avoid' paying tax by artificial means that have little or no business purpose and it was on this remit that the value for money exercise was focused. VAT avoidance however, is a complex and sensitive area, partly because of the nature of the subject but also because of Customs arrangements for dealing with it. For example, there are concerns that publishing guidelines clarifying what is and isn't avoidance may open the door to those looking for loopholes. Therefore the client was keen to ensure that this sensitivity would be taken into account, as the outcomes from this study would influence future work of his team and the NAO in general (audits usually receiving significant amounts of scrutiny from the public and political arena). As with most OR interventions, recognizing the culture of the organization, the different pressures and constraints, the future life of the group/team, and stakeholders is important. All these factors influence the design of the intervention and the success of the outcomes.

In the initial scoping conversation, the client, Daniel[1], started by stating that he was interested in getting the consultants to help the audit team to identify the issues that needed to be examined and to design a methodology for their study. However, although he was interested in using the mapping approach he wasn't sure exactly what this would involve. After providing the consultants with some background both to the organization and to Customs and Excise/VAT avoidance he was interested in how they might approach the topic. This initial dialogue between client and consultants is often a critical moment in building the relationship, as it is the point at which it is possible to begin to surface alternative courses of action, explore these in the light of the environmental conditions and begin to design the way forward.

Due to time pressures – the value for money (VFM) study had already begun – and the available resources (the VFM study itself had to be cost effective), it became evident that the Oval Mapping Technique (Eden and Ackermann, 1998, Bryson et al, 1995) would be the better option for surfacing and structuring the thinking. This was in contrast to individual interviews using cognitive maps (see previous chapter). This move to a group process was a break from 'traditional' methods: Daniel and his team had previously used interviews to elicit data, that they subsequently analysed back in the office and then confirmed with the client. However, in these traditional interviews the NAO team had not used the cognitive mapping approach to capturing data and therefore was not familiar with its power and benefits. Moving to OMT would involve both a new technique and a different way of working.

---

[1] The names have been deliberately changed, but the characters are real

Using the Oval Mapping Technique would allow the work to be 'collapsed' into a single session and, whilst not eliciting the depth and richness normally associated with individual interviews using mapping, the technique has other benefits. One of these benefits is the ability to involve more people. As the oval mapping technique is designed to be used with groups (it is a manual *group support system* – rather than one employing facilitator-driven or direct entry computer support (see Ackermann and Eden, 2001) it is possible to involve between 6–12 participants. This enables more participants to be involved than might be the case if interviews were to be used. In addition, as the technique results in a map being built in front of the group, thus participants are able to see the different contributions and explore how they fit together. As a result, they are able to rapidly build up a shared view/common understanding of what the key issues are (thus increasing the knowledge of all). Having the entire map in front of them (rather than a single section – as dictated by the necessities of working with computer screens – see Ackermann and Eden, 1994) allows members to rapidly gain not only an overview of the issue being discussed but also the details. Finally, in a manner similar to the interview-based process noted in the previous chapter, as part of being involved in the process, developing a shared understanding and working as a team, the participants gain ownership and commitment to the outcome. This increases the likelihood of any actions that are forthcoming being implemented.

Although this initial conversation regarding the possible alternatives was held over the phone, rather than in the client's office (which is the more usual process), the discussion allowed both parties to begin to build the consultant–client relationship. The process of explaining the options and their various merits and disadvantages meant that Daniel was able to shape the intervention, taking into account the culture of the organization and the particularity of the issue. As he explained why particular issues were or were not important, this in turn gave the consultants valuable insights into the organization, helping them refine the process further. This process of joint design is critical as it enables the process to be fine-tuned so that it best addresses the situation.

As the discussion continued a further option emerged (based on the growing knowledge base). This was that as a result of using OMT to elicit views, time would be saved and therefore it was possible to try the technique out first with the NAO team before using it with Customs and Excise. This would allow Daniel to see how the process 'looked' and therefore give him more confidence in the process and its outcomes. As a result, it would enable him to better explain what was involved to Customs and Excise. It would also provide a means of ascertaining in advance what the NAO team thought were the main issues (i.e. those that were key to the discussion), for comparison with what would emerge from the Customs and Excise group.

In addition, it was agreed that one of the consultants would take an active role in facilitating the process (process facilitator), while the second (content facilitator) would capture the material in the mapping software – Decision Explorer (DE). The first advantage of capturing the material on line was that it would reassure the participants that they were being taken seriously – since efforts were being made to ensure their views were held onto. A second benefit was that the resultant electronic model then could be used with the group, allowing them to see that it matched their wall picture, and enabling them to extend and refine the computerized model. Finally, through having a computerized model, the material could be subsequently a) analysed to determine the emergent properties (see Eden and Ackermann, 1998a) and b) organized in a format that would aid feedback to the client (and his team). The feedback would normally be done within a week (so as to ensure that the emotional and cognitive commitment is capitalized upon) and would involve the provision of a combination of maps and associated text allowing easy identification of what was agreed and why it was agreed.

Use of OMT to Surface the Issues

The first issues to consider for the NAO workshop were those of timing, and of who would participate. If they were to both surface and structure the material, and then work on the results using the electronic model (the DE model), it would probably require a full day. In this manner they could spend the morning concentrating on the OMT, which works best when around 3–3.5 hours are allocated. The lunch break could then be used as a useful time for catching up with any material the facilitators had missed or not quite captured fully, carrying out some quick analysis and pulling the material into a form for presentation back to the group. The consultants and Daniel could also discuss how they felt the session was going and if necessary make adjustments. The afternoon would then be spent examining the issues that had surfaced, exploring how they might impact one another, and detecting any missing areas.

Choosing who should participate in the NAO workshop meant considering who would be involved subsequently in the Value for Money audit (as they would need to buy into the outcomes). To promote the wider use of the process within the NAO, Daniel was also interested to involve a few people from outside his own team. Thus, a member from the training team was invited to attend. During this initial conversation the consultants recommended that the size of the group stay around 8 participants – in this way the workshop would provide participants with plenty of airtime and ensure that the different perspectives could be fully expressed. They were both keen to make this first workshop a success.

The next step was to agree the wording of the issue question that would provide the focus for the OMT session. When asking participants for their contributions, some indication of the area to focus upon is important. Therefore one of the first steps is to generate a question reflecting the boundary/area for consideration. The question works best if it is

• Not one that is prescriptive – implicitly suggesting a particular direction,
• Not ambiguous – this is difficult as it is important to be clear about the focus while not making the focal area too narrow, and
• Not one that demands a yes/no answer.

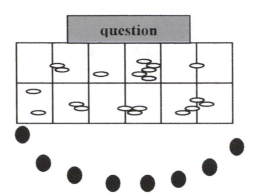

Figure 3.1 An example or room layout

Daniel and the consultants worked hard at getting the question 'right'.

Another issue to be discussed was the room design and other such 'trivialities'. These aspects of workshops can have a major impact on the success of the intervention (Huxham, 1990, Hickling, 1990). As the OMT is a manual technique that allows the participants to see the 'big picture' i.e. all of the contributions at once – ample wall space is necessary. Through experience the consultants knew that at least 12 sheets of flipchart paper attached to the wall (portrait) would be necessary, although they preferred 16 or 18 (see Figure 3.1). This amount of space provides enough working room to a) prevent participants from subconsciously ceasing to contribute, as the wall appears full and b) facilitate moving material around to form clusters. The facilitators agreed to bring ovals, flip chart pens, participant pens[2] and blu-tack with them.

Finally Daniel and the consultants considered carefully what Daniel would say to the participants when inviting them to attend. They wanted to ensure that the participants were clear about the purpose and logistics whilst at the same time not raising too many expectations or causing concern.

Starting the First Workshop

The first workshop started with Daniel thanking the participants for coming, providing some context for the workshop and then introducing the two consultants and handing over to them. The consultants began by providing an overview for the day explaining what the different tasks were and how the day would unfold. They had already written

---

[2] Ensuring that all of the participants have the same pens allows for additional 'anonymity' (most people do not recognize one another's handwriting and therefore if the writing is in the same colour it is harder to identify proponent). In addition, through dictating the shape/size of the nib, it is possible to ensure that the writing is sufficiently large to ensure all can read the material. Alongside this, the facilitator ensures that they have a black pen for drawing in the links, a purple one for marking the key issues and a red one for numbering the ovals. Water based pens are best as they tend not to leak through the flipchart paper and therefore leave a mess!

this agenda up on a flip chart for easy reference – to be used both at the beginning of the day and later to show progress. It is important to give the group a clear sense of progress; ticking off the various items on the agenda can provide clear milestones for the group. Providing a clear introduction and setting the scene is critical for the success of the workshop (Ackermann, 1996, Phillips and Phillips, 1993).

The next step was to introduce the technique itself. Participants were informed that all the material would be generated by them, and that neither of the consultants would be adding to the content. (Indeed it was pointed out that neither of them was familiar with the area and might therefore have to ask questions about the contributions). It was therefore an opportunity for them to surface all of their knowledge including what were the issues, concerns, hopes, assertions etc relating to the audit. Participants were told that any material not written on the ovals would probably not get captured and taken into consideration – so they were encouraged to write down their thoughts. This didn't mean that participants couldn't discuss the issues between themselves, merely that they should then capture the results of their discussion on the ovals. Finally, participants were reassured that consensus was not necessary at this stage.

Although the oval mapping technique is fairly straightforward a small number of guidelines were reviewed. The first was a request to stick to one statement per oval, and with around 8–10 words per statement. This is partly to help with the readability of the oval's content – more than around 10 words results in smaller handwriting making it difficult for other participants to read and therefore 'piggy back' off the contributions. A second reason is that when the process moves on to structuring the contributions, it is easier if each oval contains only a single statement and limiting the statements to 10 words helps. For example, when using the cause mapping technique (see previous chapter) in structuring material around the statement 'increase and improve research output' options such as 'write high quality (Category A journals) articles' might support the second element of the statement (improve) but actively prevent the first element (increase). Finally the consultants suggested that participants use more than one or two words for each contribution as this helps with clarifying the meaning of the statement, as does using an action orientation when wording the contributions.

A second guideline was the request for participants not to remove another partici-pant's oval even if they disagreed with it! Rather, where agreement or disagreement occurred, they were encouraged to consider the reason for this response and to write that on an oval and place it alongside the original contribution. This guideline, as usual, caused participants to laugh as they recognised the value of the point (and their own in-clinations) and were reassured by its explicit mention. The third guideline was not to stockpile contributions; participants were asked to stick their ovals up on the wall (using blu tack*) as soon as they had written two or three. By doing this, other participants are able to read the material and have the chance of responding to them, so enhancing the creativity of the group.

---

* Oval-shaped stickers of a convenient size are now available from *www.ovalmap.com*

Figure 3.2 Getting started – initial contribution being placed on the wall

Finally the roles of the two consultants were explained – one of them helping with the process of capturing and structuring the material (the process facilitator) and the other capturing this in the computer (content facilitator). The consultants then handed out ovals, blue tack and pens to the participants. Giving participants pens rather than letting them use their own makes a non-trivial contribution to the technique. The main reason is that if all the participants use a standard pen then a degree of anonymity is achieved. Most participants don't recognise one another's handwriting with any certainty. However if someone is writing with a distinctive pen – for example green – then this is more easily recognisable. The second reason for providing pens is to ensure that the thickness of the nib is sufficient to force larger writing – and thus an increase in legibility.

The issue question was posted at the top of the flip charts and participants were encouraged to start capturing and putting up their contributions. Figure 3.2 shows a similar group getting started.

Structuring the Contributions

At first participants were a little hesitant, but once a few ovals had appeared on the walls confidence grew and before long there were over a hundred. While the participants were writing and posting their contributions, the process facilitator focused on trying to arrange them into clusters, and on numbering each contribution to aid the data entry process (as well as linking later on). Identifying the clusters took a little time as usual (the clusters don't always appear immediately), but from previous experience the consultants had found that one way of helping this process is to start by reading each oval and moving them around – this helps to see emergent patterns through 'playing' with the material and structuring it in different ways.

Facilitators should be prepared to change the clusters as more contributions are posted and new insights gained. This might mean breaking down a big cluster into two or three sub-clusters – particularly if there appears to be sub-themes (for example internal communication and external communication). Another useful tip is to ask participants to put their ideas directly into the clusters. However, this doesn't always work – it is easier for them to simply put them on the wall map! Nevertheless continual reminders do help. Finally, those that didn't seem to fit anywhere were moved into a 'dump' cluster – but this was not a concern as they generally sort themselves out during later stages of the process. Having ample wall space does help with this whole process as it enabled ovals to be moved around more easily.

After about 30 minutes some of the participants were beginning to dry up, and so to keep the energy going (and to allow those still writing down contributions to finish their work) the process facilitator prompted participants to focus on existing material. She encouraged participants to consider what were the constraints, options, and objectives of the audit and asked them to consider how or why the issues being surfaced might be addressed. Finally, before taking a coffee break (as a reward to the participants for their hard work), the process facilitator reviewed the emergent clusters. This provides a good milestone and is an effective way of giving participants a sense of what has surfaced.

The break also gave Daniel and the consultants' time to catch up, review progress and do some tidying of the clusters. The aim was to have the oval that appeared to be the most super-ordinate at the top of each cluster and the ovals that support – lead into – it further down. Thus the shape of the structure would be similar to a teardrop with the most detailed contributions at the bottom (see Figure 3.3). Headings were identified for each cluster.

After about 15–20 minutes the group reconvened and the process of structuring the material began. This is probably the most valuable (and difficult) part of the Oval Mapping Technique. The links are causal links – that is 'means-ends' or 'options-outcomes' links (see previous chapter). Through linking the material both within and across clusters, the participants began to gain a sense of shared understanding – and the process also surfaces new contributions as the process of linking highlights differences in interpretation. The group's first step was to revisit the clusters – in order to refresh their memories – and then select one for working on first. The material in this selected cluster was then reviewed and the process of linking explained.

The process facilitator asked participants how the different statements in each cluster related to one another (starting with one cluster and moving on to others once that had been completed). This can prompt a range of different interpretations. For example one participant might argue that statement A leads to Statement B. To do this he would provide a chain of argument to defend his case. The process facilitator would then en-

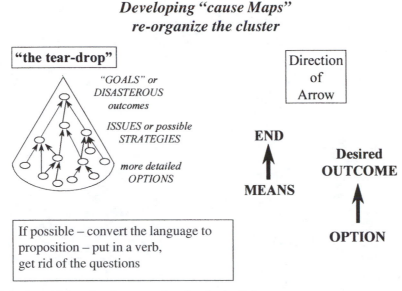

Figure 3.3 Organizing the clusters – drawing in the links

courage this to be written down on ovals and put up on the wall with its links. However, in response to this clarification another participant might argue that 'no, statement A leads to Statement D in another cluster' – and present his rationale. The process facilitator would again ask for this new material to be captured and linked into the existing material.

The numbering of ovals meant that rather than draw a long link between a contribution in the bottom left corner to something in the top right, it was possible simply to draw a small arrow from the oval to a hand written number. As is always the case, whilst work done in the coffee break had helped in doing some of the structuring, and the process facilitator was careful not to draw in the arrows until the chain of argument had been agreed, there were times the arrow had to be crossed out and an alternative link drawn in. Sometimes this is due to an enhanced appreciation of the material by the participants or a lack of understanding by the facilitator. This process of structuring and teasing out the different nuances begin to develop a sense of shared understanding amongst the participants.

Despite requests participants had nevertheless posted some single worded ovals on the flip chart sheets. During the structuring process these contributions were elaborated. This was achieved by the process facilitator asking the proponent of the oval for further clarification – particularly aiming to get an action orientation to the contribution[3].

---

[3] This process has to be carefully managed to preserve anonymity. Presenting the contribution positively (and thus reassuring the participant that his/her statement is of value) helps. Where information is not forthcoming, asking participants, if they could at a later stage (over lunch/break) help clarify the meaning, also may assist in weaving the contribution into the overall picture

Figure 3.4 Working through the clusters – making the links between the various contributions

Again, as further clarification was provided alternative perspectives emerged and so further new material was added to the oval map. Whilst on the whole participants were good about writing down the new material on the ovals, the process facilitator found herself at times working hard to capture contributions as participants moved on to another angle of the topic. Figure 3.4 illustrates this process showing the process facilitator, with a similar group, working with the ovals in a cluster.

At regular intervals, and once each cluster appeared to be structured, the process facilitator reviewed the links with the group to check their validity. At first participants had to work hard to understand the process of linking and structuring. However, once the first two or three clusters had been completed they became more fluent and were able to work on the remaining clusters much more quickly. The 'dump' cluster also began to disappear as participants, through the process of structuring the contributions, began to understand more about the different clusters' contents and therefore could see where these homeless contributions fitted. It wasn't long before all were incorporated into the overall picture (for an example see Figure 3.5).

The morning finished with an overall review of the wall picture and a commendation to the group for working so hard. Through the numbering system it was possible to inform the group just how many contributions they had surfaced. A final review of each of the clusters – now representing the issues – was also undertaken.

Over lunch both consultants worked hard at getting the remaining material into the

Figure 3.5 A final wall map showing the clusters, issue question (top centre) and links

Decision Explorer mapping software. To help with this process they used the software's analytical capabilities. For example, they used the 'orphan' analysis to identify contributions that hadn't been linked up. In the morning session, as part of the review of each cluster, the process facilitator had, with the group's aid, identified which of the ovals best represented each theme/cluster. These contributions were usually positioned at the top of the teardrop, and in some cases were existing ovals, in other cases new ones generated that described the cluster. Each had been asterisked for easy identification and assigned the category of 'key issue'. Key issues are usually broad based, costly in terms of resources, possibly irreversible and may take some time to implement. They may be either extensively elaborated or supported by only one or two statements. During their tidying up process, facilitators asked the software to list those contributions that they had categorized as potential key issues to check that all had been captured and categorized accordingly.

They also used this period of time to ask Daniel how he had found the process so far. Regularly checking in with the client helps him/her feel more in control of the process. This in its own right helps build a good relationship as well as potentially giving insights into content or process issues that might otherwise have been overlooked. Daniel commented that he had found the process fascinating and very beneficial. He was interested in the clusters that had emerged – and that particular emphases had been taken. He was keen to see what would happen next.

Working with the Decision Explorer Model

Once the consultants were confident they had a reasonably accurate copy of the OMT map in the software they began to use the inbuilt analysis features to help them prepare for the afternoon session. The first task was to create a number of views that allowed the group to just focus on clusters or sections of the model (rather than the whole 200 concept model). A view was created that displayed, in map format, those contributions that had been marked as key issues. This view allowed the consultants to see which key issues were linked to one another directly and which were currently unlinked. To explore the links further the collapse[4] analytical routine (Eden et al, 1992, Eden and Ackermann, 1998b) was used. From this it was possible to see whether some of the key issues were linked to one another through contributions not on the current map view[5]. This view (a form of overview) would make a good starting point for the afternoon session. Other views were also created so that each of the OMT clusters could be displayed if needed. A further analysis that was undertaken was listing the 'heads'. These were contributions that currently had no further consequences. Where these were substantive (i.e. good in their own right) this was noted for the afternoon session, however where they dealt with supporting argumentation, then the consultants returned to the wall map to see if they had missed a link.

The afternoon session began with the consultants explaining what they had been doing during the lunch break and outlining the process for the afternoon. To ensure that working with the electronic model went smoothly the consultants had paid careful attention to the number of contributions they displayed on each view and that they had a good, high resolution, projector. Keeping the number of contributions (concepts) down to around 20 means that it is easier for participants to absorb the material – the consultants had found on previous occasions that displaying more than that resulted in participants becoming overwhelmed with the mass of information. However, once the group had absorbed the material on the screen it was possible to bring more contributions on and gradually enlarge the picture. Having a good projection facility was also important. Ensuring that the projector produces a clear bright image (an XGA 1200 lumens specification is best) helps reduce eyestrain (and therefore mental fatigue) as well as reducing or removing the need to darken the room. As the session followed lunch this was important! In addition, having a good projector did mean that as the afternoon unfolded and new material was added to the model, the expanding views could be displayed without loss of clarity.

The process then moved on to exploring the previously created key issue/overview map. The consultants explained how the map had been produced (including the 'collapse'

---

[4] The collapse analysis focuses upon a selected group of concepts (in this case the key issues) and checks whether there are any direct or indirect links between them. For example key issue A might be linked to key issue B via some additional argumentation not on the map. The software allows a 'direct' route to be viewed

[5] The model acts as a relational database with the 'views' acting as windows onto a selected set. Therefore the user has complete control over how much, and what type of statements, they bring on to the view

process) and asked the participants to examine it for completeness. In particular they asked whether there were any key issues relating to the audit that hadn't yet surfaced and/or whether there were any missing links. Because the software mirrored the mapping technique used in the morning (i.e. through being able to capture, link, move and edit contributions) participants quickly made the transition between the oval maps and the electronic form. After an initial period of familiarizing themselves with the map's contents, participants began discussing how the different key issues related to one another. Participants began by focusing upon those that had been found to have no links to other key issues (noted from the earlier analysis). Once these had been discussed and where necessary changes made to the structure (e.g. additional links made), other relatively sparsely linked contributions were scrutinized and their relationship to the key issues determined. It was during this part of the process that a further potential key issue was identified and added to the map[6]. After about 30 minutes the participants felt that they had a good overview of the issues around the audit and were ready to move to the next stage.

Given that there was less than 2 hours remaining there was not sufficient time to examine all of the key issues in depth and arrive at possible actions. Consequently the consultants asked the participants to carry out a preferencing exercise. A flip chart list of the key issues that had been detected during the OMT session had been prepared, and the new key issue that had been recently surfaced had been added to it. They gave the participants a number of self-adhesive spots or 'resources'[7] and asked them to place these against the key issues that they felt were the most important ones for the group to tackle that afternoon. Participants, if they wished, could put all of their spots/resources against one key issue if they felt that it was of paramount importance, or alternatively scatter them among various issues.

The results were quite revealing. There was one key issue that nearly everyone wanted to work on and in addition to this three other areas that scored highly. It was agreed that each of these key issues would be given around 20 minutes, leaving approximately 10 minutes for a quick review of the day. The view of the particular key issue cluster being examined (each of which had been produced over lunch for this purpose) was then displayed, and discussion about what was important, what needed to be done and what might be some of the constraints ensued. The computer-based model thus took the place of a dialectic allowing members to see how their contributions fitted in with the other material and to use this understanding to consider what steps might be taken. A new style (i.e. category[8]) was created for those items that appeared as potential actions – and contributions that were considered as actions were categorized accordingly. It had already been agreed with Daniel that no firm agreement to the actions

---

[6] Even though in its current state it had no supporting statements

[7] The usual method for doing this is to make the number of resources issued to each participant about ⅔ of the number of key issues. In this manner normally the key issues selected will include at least one of the key issues chosen by each participant

[8] The software allows for different styles (representing categories) to be set up and used. These are usually a combination of colours, fonts, sizes etc

would be made in the workshop as they would wait and see what the Customs and Excise workshop surfaced. Whilst 20 minutes didn't really give enough time to do each issue justice, it did allow some further material to be captured and some agreement about possible ways forward to emerge.

Finally, just before it was time to finish, the consultants made a quick review of the progress achieved by the group. Starting with the agenda they were able to 'tick' all of the tasks completed. Moving to the electronic DE model, they noted a) how many contributions had been captured, b) the value of structuring the material (especially the overview map detailing the key issues) and c) that the group had generated a number of possible ways forward. Following this, Daniel once again thanked participants, hoped it had been a useful and enjoyable day for them, and brought the workshop to a close. Both consultants were pleased when a number of the participants commented spontaneously that they had indeed found the day productive and informative – it is always nice to have feedback.

Although both the consultants had planes to catch, they made sure that they had some time with Daniel to review how he felt the day had gone and to reflect on the outcomes. Through such discussions the consultant–client relationship is further developed. Daniel was keen to hear what the consultants had made of the day – had it gone as they had anticipated? The consultants wanted to know what Daniel thought – was he pleased? During this discussion Daniel asked about the process of getting feedback from the day and in what format this would appear. The consultants promised to get it back to him within a couple of days and informed him that the format would comprise the maps (i.e. the overview (key issue) map, along with each of the clusters), and some analysis of the model as it currently stood. (It was, however, acknowledged that some issues had not been examined, which would therefore affect the results.) Finally just before leaving Daniel also confirmed his desire to hold a similar workshop for Customs and Excise – and would therefore be in touch regarding dates and participants.

The Second Workshop

To keep the momentum going, and due to the time constraints of the VFM study, the date for the second OMT workshop was agreed to be two weeks later. The workshop would take place in Customs and Excise's building, and whilst Daniel now appreciated why careful attention to room design was so important (having experienced the process) he was not sure that he had managed to convey this to Customs and Excise. He hoped that the room made available would be suitable. This is often problematic, as until the process has been experienced it is hard to convince clients of the importance of good design.

A three-way conversation was held regarding participants, as the consultants relied on Daniel to ensure that the right mix of people from Customs and Excise would attend. In addition, Daniel was keen that he and one of his team attend the second workshop.

This was partly because he wanted to be able to participate in the discussion of the issues (and gain first hand experience of how others viewed the situation) and partly, as he had asked Customs and Excise for their time, he wanted to be able to welcome and thank the group. A group of 7 was finally agreed upon including the head of the Customs and Excise Department and a number of her staff.

Some modifications to the design of the workshop had to be made. Firstly there were issues around whether Daniel and his colleague should contribute to the oval map. Daniel was keen to do this, as it would enable him to surface issues he would like to see Customs and Excise consider: however the consultants were a little concerned that if he participated too much he might inhibit the Customs and Excise staff. Daniel agreed to keep his contributions to a minimum. He also agreed as before to do a 'welcome and thank you' introduction to the workshop. The second change was to the issue question, whose language was modified slightly. This was partly due to the consultants and Daniel reflecting on how participants at the previous workshop had interpreted the question, and partly to reflect the different nature of the group.

The workshop unfolded in a very similar manner to the previous one. Not withstanding Daniel's efforts the room was not ideal – one wall was just glass allowing those walking by to see straight into the room, which was potentially disrupting to the process. To manage this difficulty the glass wall was identified as the surface for the oval map, and visibility was reduced through covering the wall in flip chart sheets! In addition there was a large, heavy and almost unmovable table in the center of the room, but with the help of the participants this was shifted towards the opposite wall giving a clear working space for the morning's session.

As with the previous workshop, the participants generated a large number of ovals – with Daniel and his colleague contributing to the overall picture but not in any great number. The participants subsequently worked through the ovals, structuring and refining the clusters and becoming quite engaged in the process. Whilst a number of the clusters were similar to those previously identified some new ones appeared – food for thought for the audit team. In addition, by being able to put up some ovals himself, Daniel was able to get some clarification on those issues that had emerged at the previous workshop as items where further detail and Custom and Excise's perspective was important.

Another difference between the two sessions came after lunch when the group was reviewing the overview map. In addition to working on linking the existing key issues together, the Customs and Excise group laddered up the hierarchy further and began to consider the purpose or goals of their department. This proved insightful both to the Customs and Excise team but also to Daniel, as it revealed the priorities and emphasis of the department.

This overview, and the material captured by the wall map, not only provided the audit team with some extremely useful information but also, judging from the informal comments made by the participants, was of value to the Customs and Excise team. They too wanted copies of the feedback material and said that they had found the day an enjoyable one. Once they had left, Daniel and the consultants reviewed the day and discussed next steps. All of them felt that it had been a positive experience, that it had built good relations with the Customs and Excise team (important as no one likes being audited) and that it had revealed some useful information. The next question was how was this going to be used alongside the material from the audit team workshop.

One option was for Daniel and two key members of his team to get together with the consultants and work through the two models, identifying the key areas and determining which of the many options could be done within the remit of the audit. Another option was for the consultants to 'merge' the two models, and then analyse the implications of the combined model. If this second option were to be undertaken, it would be necessary to weave the material from the two models together[9]. This would require some judgement on behalf of the consultants and therefore a further workshop might be necessary to validate the final model. Since both Daniel and one of his colleagues (Mark) were keen to learn more about the techniques, they found the possibility of working on it together attractive. A date was set when Daniel and Mark would work with the consultants.

The Final Session

Although it was only two weeks after the Customs and Excise workshop, it seemed worthwhile starting the day by spending some time looking through the material and getting reacquainted with the various issues and options. This review of the material also provided a useful time for Daniel and Mark to provide the consultants with some further feedback on the second workshop, in particular Customs and Excise's response which was very positive.

The group then moved on to examining the two overviews (the maps containing the key issues of the two workshops). It became clear that there was a considerable similarity between the two maps, and potential merges and cross-links were suggested. The consultants had created (using the software) a new model containing the material from both workshops. Contributions from Customs and Excise were readily identifiable from those of the NAO from their numbering sequences. The changes suggested by Daniel and Mark were made to this new model and the results examined further.

Once Daniel and Mark felt comfortable with the overview structure they began to explore the material that supported each of the key issues. Using the hierarchical set analysis facility of the software (see Eden and Ackermann, 1998a for more detail) it was possible to identify all of the material that supported each key issue and to produce corresponding maps. These maps were similar to the clusters produced during the OMT sessions – they were teardrop in shape with the key issue appearing at the apex supported by the explanatory material. As in the previous workshops, Daniel and Mark (constituting the group) made changes, added new material and began to agree on the

---

[9] (See Eden and Ackermann, 1998a pages 400–14)

best way forward. Those contributions that they agreed should be actions were categor-ized accordingly, clearly marking them out from the remaining material.

Finally, having covered all of the issues, the consultants recommended that Daniel and Mark do a quick review of all of the proposed actions. This would ensure that there was sufficient resource to put them all into action (Eden and Ackermann, 1998a). The results from this final session provided a clear direction for the audit – entailing the overview (what were the objectives), along with the detailed actions as the means of achieving it. Daniel and Mark left feeling that they had made good progress and had something concrete to work with.

Final Comments

Daniel has continued to support the techniques (both OMT and the use of interactive modelling). When asked to comment on the process he remarked that 'the NAO team's view was that the oval mapping process was a means of getting a great deal of information from each participant on their understanding of the key issues and how the arrangements worked with Customs. It was also very difficult for anyone to opt out or for any individual to control or dominate the information that was being put forward. There is a risk in some situations such as with focus groups that the most senior person takes charge and only their point of view is put forward. In addition, the NAO team consider that the session has increased their reputation with the Customs staff as they have shown that they can quickly come to grips with a difficult subject and focus on the key issues'.

Furthermore, since the workshop, the consultants have carried out another OMT workshop with NAO (but for a different department) and are currently exploring how the process can become more established in-house. It is hoped that the Oval Mapping Technique and the use of Decision Explorer with groups can become an established way of working, and that it can be applied to a number of different areas within the organization. In addition, the work has led to a continuing involvement with Customs and Excise using multi-criteria modelling methods and, separately, visual interactive simulation.

Acknowledgement

The authors would like to thank Professor Val Belton for initiating the workshop, which was a consequence of a longer term collaboration with NAO to explore the potential for OR/MS approaches in their work.

References

Ackermann, F. (1996). 'Participants Perceptions on the Role of Facilitators using Group Decision Support Systems', *Group Decision and Negotiation*, **5**, 93–112.

Ackermann, F. and Eden, C. (1994). 'Issues in Computer and Non-Computer Supported GDSSs', *International Journal of Decision Support Systems*, **12**, 381–90.

Ackermann, F. and Eden, C. (1997). 'Contrasting GDSSs and GSSs in the Context of Strategic Change: Implications for Facilitation', *Journal of Decision Systems*, **6**, 221–50.

Ackermann, F. and Eden, C. (2001). 'Contrasting Single User and Networked Group Decision Support Systems', *Group Decision and Negotiation*, **10**, (forthcoming).

Bryson, J.M., Ackermann, F., Eden, C., and Finn, C. (1995). 'Using the "Oval Mapping Process" to identify strategic issues and formulate effective strategies', in *Strategic Planning for Public and Nonprofit Organisations* (Ed. J. Bryson), 2nd ed., pp. 257–75, Jossey Bass, San Francisco.

Eden, C., Ackermann, F., and Cropper, S. (1992).'The Analysis of Cause Maps', *Journal of Management Studies*, **29**, 309–24.

Eden, C. and Ackermann, F. (1998a). *Making Strategy: The Journey of Strategic Management*, Sage, Chichester.

Eden, C. and Ackermann, F. (1998b). 'Analyzing and Comparing Idiographic Causal Maps', in *Managerial and Organizational Cognition: Theory, Methods and Research* (Eds. C. Eden and J.C. Spenders), pp. 192–209, Sage, London

Hickling, A. (1990). '"Decision Spaces": A Scenario about Designing Appropriate Rooms for Group Decision Management', in *Tackling Strategic Problems: The Role of Group Decision Support* (Eds. C. Eden and J. Radford), pp.169–77, Sage, London.

Huxham, C. (1990). 'On Trivialities in Process', in *Tackling Strategic Problems: The Role of Group Decision Support* (Eds. C. Eden and J. Radford), pp.162–8, Sage, London.

Phillips, L. and Phillips, M.C. (1993). 'Facilitated Work Groups: Theory and Practice', *Journal of the Operational Research Society*, **44**, 533–49.

4 *Soft Systems Methodology*

Peter Checkland

Introduction

The only man-made object on our planet which is visible to astronauts in space is the Great Wall of China. Its creators over several thousand years, or, to take a more recent and less awe-inspiring example, the creators of the American telephone network in the early years of this century, must have been engineers and managers of considerable skill. In both cases they successfully accomplished what in today's language would be called major 'projects', though that word has become popular only in recent times. The notion of a project implies bringing together the materials and skills necessary to create both some complex object and the way it will be used. A project implies the exercise of a combination of engineering and management skills. In the case of the latter, not only does the project itself have to be managed, but also the project content must include creating a way of using (managing) the physical object or objects. In the case of the Anglo-French Concorde project, for example, the overall task was to create both the world's first supersonic passenger aircraft and ways in which it could be manned, flown, serviced, and fitted into airline operations.

Given the number of impressive projects throughout human history, it is perhaps surprising that it is as recently as the 1950s and 1960s that ways of defining and carrying out projects were set down formally in a methodology to be followed by aspiring project managers. What is less surprising is that engineers played a big part in that development. The thinking of engineers extended from designing and making single objects to creating systems, the latter thought of as both a connected set of objects and the way of using them. In the 1950s, phrases such as 'the systems engineer' and, 'systems engineering' became current, and methodological accounts of how to do systems engineering – something intuitively grasped by the builders of the Great Wall and the engineers of the American telephone network – began to appear. Hall's classic account of 1962, *A Methodology for Systems Engineering*, was generalized from the experiences of Bell Telephone Laboratories in carrying out research and development projects, and the approach is now well established.

This kind of systems engineering is both the intellectual and the practical parent of the Soft Systems Methodology (SSM) to be described in this chapter. SSM is best understood in relation to its origins. It is the problem solving approach developed from systems engineering when that approach failed. And systems engineering – impressive enough as a way of carrying out technological projects – failed when attempts were made to apply it, not to projects in the sense described above, but to the messy, changing, ill-defined problem situations with which managers have to cope in their day-to-day professional lives.

In this chapter the nature of systems engineering will be described briefly, in order to explain the conditions under which it will inevitably break down. An account will then be given of the emergence of SSM as a response to that breakdown, and an account of it as a problem solving methodology suitable for messy problem situations will be given. Finally, it will be useful to reflect on just how far the systems thinking in SSM has moved beyond that in systems engineering.

In the following chapter a detailed account of SSM in action will be given.

Systems Engineering

Professional engineers make sense of their world by thinking about it in the following way. A specification is produced which gives a careful description of something which is required, whether a physical object (for example, a particular kind of valve for an oil rig) or a complete system (for example, a petrochemical complex). The professional skill of the engineer is then used to meet the specification in the most efficient, economic, and elegant way. Finally, the finished object or system has to be described – often in 'manuals' – in ways which enable others to use it. The acclaimed engineer is the person who invents new ways of meeting a specification (for example, a jet engine instead of a piston engine) or who finds solutions which use less materials, perform better or are more elegant (for example, basing a bridge on the idea of the keystone).

How, then, does the engineer go about his or her task of *meeting the specification?* Engineering thinking is teleological; it asks: what is the *purpose served* by the object or system? The engineer works back from the purpose, or objective, and creates an object or system which will achieve that objective. The whole design realization process is driven by the discipline of having to meet a declared objective (Machol, 1965; Chestnut, 1967; Wymore, 1976).

Out of this kind of thinking, which, in the case of Bell Telephone Laboratories, was 'generalized from case histories' (Hall, 1962), comes a methodology for systems engineering as a series of steps in a process. These steps start by defining the need to be met and the objectives of the system which will meet them. Alternative systems are appraised in the light of the objectives, and the most promising alternative is selected for development. The criteria for 'promising' include such considerations as fitness for purpose, and economic aspects. Finally, the selected system is realized, operated, and maintained. Many techniques exist to help with each stage of this process.

In a sentence, the essence of the approach is *the selection of an appropriate means to achieve an end which is defined at the start and thereafter taken as given.* The American moon landing provides a sharp example of this. The President himself defined the objective as 'before this decade is out ... landing a man on the Moon and returning him safely to Earth' and declared an open-ended commitment to providing whatever resources were required (Kennedy, 1961). Once the NASA project was underway, questioning the objective was inconceivable.

This is the core of the systems engineering approach whose failures in normal management situations led to the emergence of SSM. In fact the thinking which has been described here as characteristic of the engineering tradition parallels in time, and matches in content, the thinking underlying the establishment in the 1950s and 1960s of the whole group of methodologies for rationally intervening in real situations in order to bring about improvements. These go under different names and were developed in somewhat different contexts.

'Systems analysis', for example, as originated by RAND Corporation and subsequently developed by many different groups (Smith, 1966; Optner, 1965; Quade, 1975; Miser and Quade, 1985,1988) brings together ideas from engineering and ideas from economics and seeks to help a real-world decision maker faced with carrying out a major project. As described by one of its pioneers, the systems analysis approach assumes an objective we desire to achieve; alternative systems for achieving it; costs or resources required by each system; models showing the interdependences of objectives, systems, resources, and environment; and a criterion for choosing the preferred alternative (Hitch, 1955).

'Operational research', as we now know it, grew out of the application of the scientific method not to unchanging Nature but to wartime military operations. OR discovered that the scientific method could be used to understand, if not the unique idiosyncrasies which characterize human situations, at least *the logic of situations* (Blackett, 1962; Waddington, 1973). Operational researchers went on to work out the applied mathematics of the logic of some common situations which recur, such as managing queues, locating depots, deciding when to replace capital equipment, or assembling an investment portfolio (see any university textbook on classical OR, such as Wagner, 1975). Traditionally, the approach seeks to apply the empirical method of natural science to real-world operations. It does this by defining the objective to be achieved in a real-world activity, and then exploring how that objective might be achieved by manipulating a model. The well-known algorithms of OR are simply ready-made manipulations for some well-structured problems which recur.

It is obvious that the fundamental thinking underlying systems engineering, systems analysis, and operational research is very similar. Though they have different names as a result of their different histories, these three approaches to rational intervention in human affairs can readily be shown to represent *one* approach (Checkland, 1981, 1983). They all assume that an important class of real-world problems can be formulated as a search for an efficient means of achieving objectives known to be desirable. The search can be conducted systematically by defining the objective to be achieved and manipulating models of the situation or of alternative forms it might take. This approach has been named as 'hard' systems thinking, to distinguish it from the 'soft' systems thinking which grew out of it (Checkland, 1985).

The Emergence of SSM

With hindsight the emergence of SSM from failed attempts to use the methodology of systems engineering seems inevitable. At the time, of course, the usual confusion which characterizes any research programme in a changing subject, seemed to reign supreme! The research intention, in a university postgraduate Department of Systems, was to find out what happened to systems engineering methodology when the word 'engineering' was read in its broad sense (you can 'engineer' an agreement, as well as a nitric acid plant) with the approach applied to typical managerial problems in organizations, rather than to the better-structured projects of systems engineering embodying 'hard' systems thinking.

'Hard' systems thinking entails starting from a carefully defined objective which is taken as given. This is the starting point in systems engineering, systems analysis, and classical (textbook) OR. But in many, perhaps most, managerial problems at any level the questions – What are the objectives? What are we trying to achieve? – are themselves part of the problem. In our research we found ourselves seeking an approach to problem solving which would cope with messy situations in which objectives were themselves problematical.

In one formative experience the work was being carried out in a textile company with 1000 employees which was in grave difficulties. The company had spent its spare cash on a new technology (extrusion of polypropylene tape) which it had failed to master. And it had failed to pay a dividend for the first time in its history. It had recruited from outside (also for the first time in its history) two senior managers, a Marketing Director and a Finance Director, who felt very uncomfortable in the parochial culture of the firm. Every aspect of the company activity – production planning, controlling quality, distribution, etc – exhibited many obvious deficiencies.

We were asked to do whatever seemed helpful to ensure company survival. The Managing Director declared that the objective was 'to survive', but this was hardly an *operational* definition. What exactly should survive: the traditional business, a rationalized version of it, or one based on the new polypropylene technology? Senior managers had very different ideas on what should be done. The Production Director, for example, attributed the company's problems to the Marketing Department's failure to lay down achievable technical standards for each of the company products. More important, the managers lacked any mechanisms for exploring different views and achieving agreement on action.

The methodological model provided by systems engineering seemed quite irrelevant to this mess. What was 'the need'? What 'system' would meet that need? What were 'the objectives' of that system? These seemed very naive and simplistic questions in the face of the failings, fears and farce of the actual situation. Systems engineering – like the other 'hard' approaches – assumes a relatively well-structured problem situation in which there is virtual agreement on *what* constitutes the problem: it remains to organize *how* to deal with it. However, for most managers most of the time both what to do and how to do it are problematical, and questions such as: What is the system? What are its object-ives? ignore the fact that there will be a multiplicity of views on both, with alternative interpretations fighting it out on the basis not only of logic but also of power, politics, and personality. An approach which assumes these questions have been settled, and concentrates only on getting together a response, will pass by the problems of real life, applicable though it may be once a particular project has been decided upon.

Another formative experience was a study of the Anglo-French Concorde project, based in what was then the British Aircraft Corporation. Again we had the situation, welcome for research purposes, that 'the problem' was not tightly defined. We were to make a study and see where systems thinking could contribute to the success of the project. This was a very much more sophisticated environment than that in the textile firm which could not cope with polypropylene extrusion! But this perhaps made it more difficult for us to see how our methodology was failing us. The context of the work was that serious consideration was being given at that time as to how computerized infor-mation systems could and should be introduced into BAC, and our study could be seen as part of that effort. We had recently, in a quite different study, developed a way of modelling information flows by deriving them from models of operational decisions which recur, these being forerunners of the activity models which are now a central feature of SSM (Checkland and Griffin, 1970).

With some vague idea of using this method to define the basic information flows necessary in the Concorde project, and examining existing flows, we did not pause over questions of objectives at the start of the systems engineering methodology. We took it without question that the need was obviously to develop the innovative aircraft and get it into service. 'The system' was the Concorde project; and 'the objectives of the system' were to develop, jointly with the French, an aircraft to meet a particular specification within a certain time at minimum cost. All this was taken to be completely obvious, and it was anticipated that work would eventually concentrate on alternative ways of meet-ing the information-flow requirements of such models.

It was subsequently extremely difficult for us to appreciate that the models we pro-duced, which represented projects to develop Concorde, were simply *not meaningful* to the managers with whom we tried to discuss them and their implications! Since 'the Con-corde project' was the phrase everyone used, it was not easy for us to step back and perceive that project thinking was not in fact the way BAC managers made sense of their world, even though the need for a supersonic passenger aircraft was taken as given. BAC was not then managed, as are many aircraft manufacturers, on the basis of project man-agement. BAC was organized at that time in functional groups, with *ad hoc* task forces formed to tackle particular crises, and what was referred to as 'the project' at BAC at Filton had only a reporting, not a managing, role, the reporting being to the government in Whitehall.

Here again, our systems-engineering-based methodology was not capturing the rich-ness of the situation. We did not stop to consider whether to take the Concorde project to be essentially political (collaborating with the French; beating the Americans to at least one advanced technology), economic (providing much employment in the British engineering industry), legal (the question of possible cancellation as costs soared) or technological. The most obvious technological objective was taken as given. And we failed to perceive that the project-management language of our models did not get heard in the particular culture we were in. Here was a case in which, even though what was called 'the Concorde project' had been established, the methodological concepts of systems engineering, with their focus on the logic of achieving an objective, missed much of the human richness of the specific problem situation in BAC. And there are few human situations in which getting the logic right is enough to bring about action.

These experiences in management situations in the textile and aircraft industries, like many similar experiences in the early years of the research programme, emphasized that the use of systems engineering methodology in 'soft' (multi-perspective) problem situations had severe limitations. Any situation in which human beings try to act together will be complex simply because individuals are autonomous. Shared perceptions – essential for corporate action – will have to be established, negotiated, argued, tested, in a complex social process. Any human situation, in fact, will be characterized by more than facts and logic. It is true that a distribution means will *have* to be appropriate to the product distributed, that continuity of product supply will be contingent upon a continuity in supply of raw materials, etc. But the facts and logic will never supply a complete description of a human situation. Equally important will be the myths and meanings by means of which human beings make sense of their worlds. Systems engineering, by taking objectives as given, assumes that the myths and meanings are in place, and static, and that effort can focus on the facts and logic. This is explicitly recognized. In a significant passage near the end of their book on *Systems Analysis for Engineers and Managers* de Neufville and Stafford (1971, p. 251) remind analysts of their limited role:

> It is important that engineers, planners, and economists recognize not only their incapacity to determine a social welfare function, but also the legitimacy of the political process to decide social priorities.

This is clear advice to engineers, planners, and economists to stick to their fields of facts and logic, leaving aside broader social issues.

In many public projects, for example in health care or public water systems, the political process will be embodied in *representative* institutions which will generate the objective to be taken as given. In a company or other organization there is unlikely to be a political system based on representation, but politics in whatever form will still have an important bearing on the priorities which determine whether a project goes forward or not. De Neufville and Stafford, in the quotation above, are reminding users of the 'hard' approach they describe that politics, much concerned with myths and meanings, is *outside its scope,* that their approach assumes 'whats' have been decided and gets down to providing an efficient 'how'.

A systems-based methodology for general management problem solving would evidently have to change significantly the process of systems engineering. That is what happened. A rudimentary form of SSM as an alternative emerged in a dozen projects of the kind discussed briefly above (Checkland, 1972). What is now to be described is a mature version of SSM several hundred projects later, to which very many users in industry, the public sector, and universities have contributed.

Soft Systems Methodology

A full account of the emergence of SSM and some rethinking of systems ideas which that entailed has been given elsewhere (Checkland, 1981, 1984, 1988; Wilson, 1984, Checkland, 1999). Here will be summarized the main features of the approach as they appear to be after much experience in organizations large and small, public and private, together with some experience in studies not based within organizations.

Whereas systems engineering methodology is a system concerned with achieving objectives, SSM is a learning system. The learning is about a complex problematical human situation, and leads to finding accommodations and taking purposeful action in the situation aimed at improvement, action which seems sensible to those concerned. SSM articulates a process of enquiry which leads to the action, but that is not an end point unless you choose to make it one. Taking that action changes the problem situation. Hence enquiry can continue; there are new things to find out, and the learning is in principle never ending. This learning process or cycle can be *thought of* as a sequence of stages, and will be described later in this chapter in this way, even though the experienced user does not use it as a sequence from Stage 1 to Stage 7. But first it is useful to describe some general features of this approach, some assumptions which it takes as given, which make it the process it is.

Firstly, SSM is a process for managing, and must therefore take a particular view of what 'managing' is and what a manager does. Managing is interpreted very broadly as a process of achieving organized action; it is not restricted to the activities of the particular professional class which emerged as a result of the Industrial Revolution. In the broad sense relevant to SSM, the activities of a peasant craftsman, of an industrial company, of a cooperative, of a trade union, of the NHS, of a terrorist cell or anarchist political group all have to be *managed*, in that they all entail deliberate, thought-out action, not simply random thrashing about. And the view of this deliberating which SSM takes, is that anyone who is a manager in any field of activity is reacting and trying to cope with an ever-changing flux of interacting events and ideas. The world immerses all of us in such a flux. 'Managing' means reacting to that flux: perceiving and evaluating (parts of) it, deciding upon action, and taking action which itself becomes part of the on-going events/ideas flux, leading to new perceptions and evaluations and further actions. Although management 'problems' may occasionally be temporarily 'solved' out of existence, this is only a special case of the continuing process. Choose the right time frame and all is seen to be flux. The process is shown in Figure 4.1 [based on Checkland and

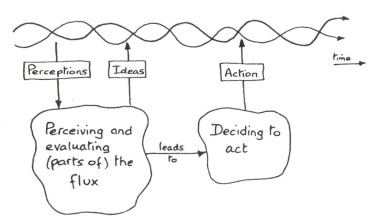

Figure 4.1 A broad concept of managing (after Checkland and Casar, 1986)

Casar, 1986. See also the Appendix to Checkland (1999): Systems Theory and Management Thinking.]

Given this broad view of managing, SSM then assumes that different individuals and
groups, being ultimately autonomous, will make different evaluations leading to different actions. This creates 'issues' with which the manager must cope. Gregarious life
would not be possible if perceptions and evaluations did not to some extent overlap.
Such an overlap is virtually a condition for the existence of what we call 'an organization' (Checkland and Holwell, 1998, Chapter 3). But the overlap will never be complete, and the issues which arise from the mismatch provide much of the substance of
managerial work. The issues themselves will derive both from interpreting the facts and
logic of a situation and from engaging with the myths and meanings through which
other managers and participants make sense of it.

The third major assumption of SSM is that in consciously articulating the process of
Figure 4.1, systems ideas will be helpful. 'System' is a concept of a whole which has
properties as a single entity, so-called 'emergent properties' (Checkland, 1981, Ch. 3).
(For example, the ability to confer degrees is an emergent property of a university as an
entity: the property has meaning only in relation to the institution as a single whole.)
Since the world outside ourselves appears to be densely interconnected – more like a
hedge than a handful of marbles – it seems worth exploring the extent to which systems
ideas can be mobilized to help explain the tangled reality we perceive.

The fourth general assumption behind SSM stems from the experience of developing
it. When this was done in the 1970s, systems thinkers had already developed the concepts of 'natural systems' (a possible name for wholes created by Nature) and 'designed
systems' (a name for wholes created by human beings). Such ideas had been helpful in
understanding such things as frogs and foxgloves, tramcars and telescopes. They did

not, however, seem rich enough concepts to cope with the complexity of human situations. These, in every study we undertook, wherever situated, involved human beings
trying to take purposeful action. The idea was developed that a set of activities linked
together in a logical structure to constitute a purposeful whole (the ability to pursue the
purpose being an emergent property of that whole) could be taken to be a new concept
of system to set alongside 'natural system' and 'designed system'. The name adopted for
the new concept was 'human activity system' (the phrase being borrowed from Blair and
Whitston's book on industrial engineering, 1971).

In order to make use of this idea, however, by forming concepts of human activity
systems and trying to map them onto real-world action, it was necessary to achieve some
important learning about the way in which people talk and think about purposeful action.

Where it will be possible fairly easily to get an agreed and testable account of a frog
regarded as a natural system, or a bicycle treated as a designed system, accounts of
purposeful activity are usually given in terms of an *interpretation* applied by the speaker.
Ask someone how he or she would regard a prison as a purposeful human activity
system and he or she will usually describe it as 'a rehabilitation system' or 'a punishment
system' or 'a system to protect society' or, more cynically, 'a system to train criminals'.
These answers, all *relevant* to debating, or understanding, the notion of 'a prison', are all
heavy with interpretation. It is rare to get an answer as relatively neutral as 'a system to
accept and store labelled people for a defined length of time'.

This readiness to talk of purposeful activity only in terms of a particular interpretation, bias, prejudice or value system means that we have to accept a) that there will be
multiple possible descriptions of any named real-world purposeful action, and b) that
any description of purposeful activity which is to be used analytically will have to be
explicit concerning assumptions about the world which that description takes as given.
German has the strongest word for this. We need in naming a system of purposeful
activity to declare the *Weltanschauung* which makes that description meaningful. The
usual translation is 'worldview', but that has a rather bland air, as does 'point of view'.
Our *Weltanschauungen* are the stocks of images in our heads, put there by our origins,
upbringing and experience of the world, which we use to make sense of the world and
which *normally go unquestioned*. It is a difference of *Weltanschauung* which causes the
Government of Nicaragua in the 1980s to describe the guerrillas known as the Contras
as 'terrorists' while the President of the United States refers to them as 'freedom
fighters'. Systems engineering ignores *Weltanschauungen*. SSM cannot afford to.

In order to engage with the concept of using systems language to give accounts of
purposeful activity, SSM was *forced* to take account of the need to describe any human
purposeful activity in relation to a particular declared image of the world. And similarly
it had to accept that any *real-world* purposeful action could be related to several
human-activity-system descriptions, based on different assumptions about the world.
(The alert reader will have noted that I use 'activity' to describe what goes on in models
on paper, 'action' to describe what goes on in real life. Users of SSM never take the
models to be *descriptions* of the real world, only as devices to explore it.)

These considerations lead to the fifth basic characteristic of SSM as an enquiring process. SSM learns by *comparing* pure models of purposeful activity (in the form of models of human activity systems) with perceptions of what action is going on in a real-world problem situation. Thus we could learn about real prisons by comparing what goes on in them with the activities in a set of models which might include, among other possibilities, a rehabilitation system, a punishment system, a system to protect society, a system to train criminals and a storage system. Intuitively this seems to be what we do anyway in the process of consciously thinking about something. We try out various mental constructions; indeed, our ability to do this consciously seems to be one of the significant things which distinguishes us from cats, crabs, and cuckoos. SSM simply provides a highly explicit kind of comparison based on system models used in an organized process which is itself a learning system.

The purpose of this comparison, carried out in the later stages of the SSM approach, is to achieve a readiness to take action purposefully in the problem situation in question, action which is defined in the debate initiated by the comparison stage (model versus perceptions of the real world).

Thus, finally, SSM is an articulation of a complex social process in which assumptions about the world – the relevant myths and meanings as well as the logics for achieving purposes which are expressed in the systems models – are teased out, challenged, tested. It is thus intrinsically a *participative* process because it can only proceed via debate. SSM does not in principle call for a professional expert who makes a study and draws conclusions, although the legacy of attitudes in the management science world in which it was developed means that it has on many occasions been used in that mode. Of course, someone familiar with the approach, who is skilled at naming human activity systems and building models of them, can greatly facilitate a study. But the most important aim of such a person is to give away the approach, to hand it over to people in the problem situation, to leave behind not only some specific action taken but also the process by which the decision on that action was reached.

The 'Stages' of Soft Systems Methodology

Having described five important general features of SSM, we are now in a position to give a more detailed account of it. For the sake of clarity of exposition this will be done by describing SSM as a series of 'steps' or 'stages'. This was indeed how it was thought about in the early years of its development, and a user could always, as a deliberate choice in a particular situation, elect to use it in this way; but as users gain experience of SSM, as they internalize it, they cease to think of it in this algorithmic fashion. Instead of thinking of it as the process in Figure 4.2, which was how it was thought about in the 1980s, they retain, rather, the image of Figure 4.3 and use that not as a prescription but as an *aide memoire* of its principles as they fashion a form of it suitable for a particular situation.

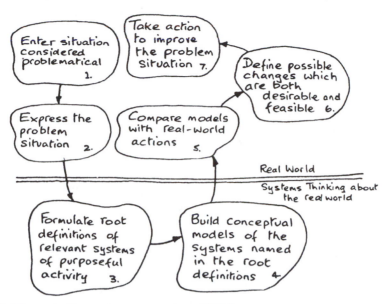

Figure 4.2 The early '7-stage' representation of SSM

Speaking logically, then, SSM articulates a process of organized finding out about a problem situation, the finding out then leading to taking deliberate action to bring about improvement in the situation. In the everyday world a common route from finding out to taking action is to rely upon experience. Experience is certainly not to be despised, but SSM supplements it by an explicit use of systems thinking, in the process shown in Figures 4.2 and 4.3. The systems thinking starts by naming (in so-called 'root definitions') some systems of purposeful activity (human activity systems) which are hopefully *relevant* to exploration of the problem situation. This oblique approach is necessary because, as has been argued above, it is never possible simply to describe real-world purposeful action once and for all. We can only describe a range of interpretations which are relevant to *debating* the real-world processes and structures. There will always be many possible, more or less plausible, accounts of a prison, a production process, a distribution function or a health care system. We have to learn our way collaboratively to the most relevant perceptions in a particular situation in order to take action to improve the situation.

Activity models are built of a number of named relevant systems. These models are brought into the everyday world of the problem situation, and compared with real-world action going on there. The models, being only logical machines for pursuing a purpose, built on the basis of declared pure *Weltanschauungen*, will not in general precisely map the observed real world action. If they do, then more radical root definitions are needed!

The purpose of the comparison is to provide the structure of a debate about possible changes, that debate focusing on differences between models and real-world action. The object of setting up the debate is to *learn your way to possible implementable changes*, changes

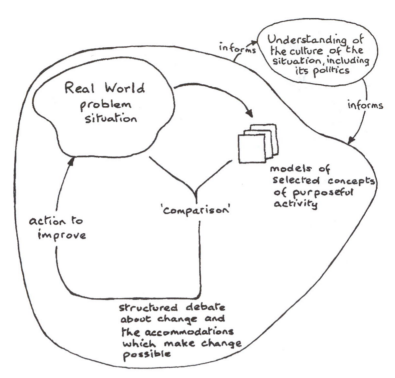

Figure 4.3 The representation of mature SSM

which are expected to constitute improvements in the problem situation. In general, the implementable changes will represent an *accommodation* between the different conflicting views developed and presented in the debate. An accommodation, entailing a version of the situation which people holding different views can nevertheless live with, does not eliminate conflict – which is endemic in human situations – but may make corporate purposeful action possible. The purpose of the debate is to find the way to that action.

Since human situations embody myths and meanings as well as facts and logic, the search is for changes which meet two criteria simultaneously. The changes must be both *systemically* desirable (on the basis of the logic of the models), and *culturally*, feasible for the people in the problem situation, given the unique history of the specific situation in a particular culture. The debate both defines changes which would bring about improvement, and seeks to motivate people to take action to implement the defined changes.

The problem situation – a portion of the flux of events and ideas in Figure 4.1 – may well have been changed by the systems thinking about it; it certainly will be changed by the action taken to improve it. A cycle of learning and action is thus complete, the flux moves on, the cycle of learning and action can begin again . . . .

The cycle of SSM will now be described in more detail, following the logic of Figures 4.2 and 4.3.

Finding Out

It will not be possible for any would-be problem solver, whether an outsider or part of the problem situation, to simply 'find out' about the situation in a neutral manner. The personality traits, experience, knowledge, and interests of our investigator will all affect what is noticed and what is taken to be significant. The finding out has to be done, seriously but lightly, with this in mind.

Three phases in developing ways of finding out, and expressing, the problem situation can be discerned in the evolution of SSM. Initially, pictures of the situation in question were assembled by recording elements of slow-to-change structure, recording the dynamic elements of continuously changing process, and forming a view of how the two relate to each other in creating the climate of the situation. Examples of this are described in Checkland (1981). The approach was found to be helpful, especially the representation of important relationships in the situation literally in 'rich pictures', but many people found these guidelines too abstract when faced with the specific, often alarming, energy and emotion in a human situation regarded as problematical.

An alternative approach was developed of using the cycle of SSM itself to the initial finding out. This was done by quickly moving to modelling, building models of systems to carry out some declared, official, primary task relevant to the situation (e.g. the storage and loan of a body of written and recorded material, in the case of a library) and using the comparison between these models and real-world action to direct and constitute the finding out. This approach has been successful in many cases but suffers from the disadvantage that it can tend to channel subsequent thinking in only one (somewhat boring) direction, namely improving the efficiency of existing operations.

Lately, experiments with a third approach proved useful, and became a normal part of SSM. This involves three related analyses. Analysis One takes the intervention in the situation as its subject matter and identifies the occupiers of the roles 'client(s)' [who cause(s) the intervention to take place] and 'would-be problem solver(s)' [who conduct(s) the study] (see Checkland, 1981, pp. 237–40). Then, whoever is in the latter role names a list of possible people who could be taken to be 'problem owners'. This list will normally include whoever is 'client', but also many different people with an interest in the situation or likely to be affected by changes in it. This list is a very good source of potentially relevant systems for later modelling.

Analysis Two looks at the problem situation as a 'social system' – using that phrase in its everyday-language sense. Analysis Two establishes what social *roles* are significant in the situation, what *norms* of behaviour are expected from role holders, and by what *values* performance in role is deemed to be good or bad. This analysis ensures that basic attention is paid to the problem situation as a *culture*.

Finally, Analysis Three examines the situation *politically* by asking questions about the disposition of power. This is done by asking through what 'commodities' power is manifest in the situation, and finding out how these commodities are obtained, used, preserved, passed on [Stowell (1989)]. (Typical commodities included role-based, sapiential or charismatic authority; privileged access to certain people or information; command of resources, etc.) The three analyses are described more fully in Checkland (1986). They yield a rich account from which some systems of purposeful activity relevant to exploration of the problem situation can be selected.

While carrying out the analyses just described, which constitute finding out about a complex, problematical human situation, the fluent SM user will constantly be representing aspects of the situation – or the situation as a whole – literally in pictures. SSM's 'rich pictures' follow from the realization that where human affairs are concerned, their complexity always stems to a large degree from the existence of multiple interacting *relationships*. And since linear prose is a rather poor medium for representing relationships, SSM users develop their skills in drawing pictures which enable the complexity being tackled to be viewed more holistically than is possible via strings of words. Checkland and Scholes (1990) and Checkland (1999) give a number of examples of rich pictures used in actual studies, and one is included later in this chapter, drawn in this case in the slightly different context of appreciating the full implications of a statement of purposeful activity before building a model from it.

Formulating Root Definitions

The formal expression of systems thinking in SSM begins by writing down the names of some systems for carrying out purposeful activity, systems thought to be *relevant* to that deeper exploration of the problem situation which will lead to action to improve it. In the early years of SSM much effort was spent in trying to select the most relevant of all possible relevant systems. This is now seen as wasted effort. As the user becomes familiar with the approach, he or she finds that insight is most effectively generated by entertaining many possibilities. Thus we *learn* our way to those which turn out to be most relevant by passing quickly round the SSM cycle a number of times.

Early in the research 'root definitions' (RDs), as the names of relevant systems are called, were written rather casually, covering essentially only the purpose which the system in question pursued. Later, when RDs from many studies were examined against a completely general model covering any purposeful activity (Smyth and Checkland, 1976) a rule was derived for ensuring that RDs are well formulated. RDs should be constructed by consciously considering the elements of the mnemonic CATWOE, which is explained and illustrated in Figure 4.4.

The core of an RD is T, the transformation process which changes some defined input into some defined output. This simple concept is frequently misunderstood, and the systems literature is full of inadequate representations of system inputs and outputs. Figure 4.5 illustrates the idea and some pitfalls. The usual error is to confuse the system input (that entity which gets changed into the output) with the resources needed to bring about the transformation, quite a different concept. Everyone who has ever used systems thinking will have made the mistake more than once! However, it is very important to

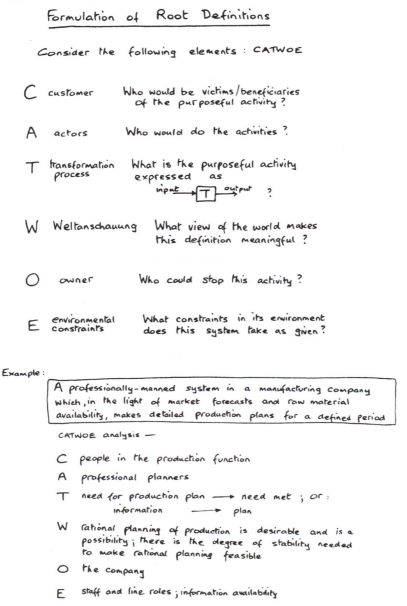

Formulation of Root Definitions

Consider the following elements : CATWOE

C customer — Who would be victims/beneficiaries of the purposeful activity ?

A actors — Who would do the activities ?.

T transformation process — What is the purposeful activity expressed as input →[T]→ output ?

W Weltanschauung — What view of the world makes this definition meaningful ?

O owner — Who could stop this activity ?

E environmental constraints — What constraints in its environment does this system take as given ?

Example:

> A professionally-manned system in a manufacturing company which, in the light of market forecasts and raw material availability, makes detailed production plans for a defined period

CATWOE analysis —

C people in the production function

A professional planners

T need for production plan → need met ; or : information → plan

W rational planning of production is desirable and is a possibility ; there is the degree of stability needed to make rational planning feasible

O the company

E staff and line roles ; information availability

Figure 4.4 Formulation of root definitions

get a correct representation of T, since once that exists, model building is straight-forward. What is looked for is the coherent formulation of some RDs which can be related to the CATWOE questions and from which models can be built.

When the work which yielded the CATWOE mnemonic was carried out, it was noticed that historically we had been very prone to write RDs which excluded both A

Purposeful systems as transformation processes

T changes, transforms I into O. I must be
present in O but in a changed state.
An abstract I must yield an abstract O.
A concrete I must yield a concrete O.

Example: Possible T's relevant to a football match:

Players ——→ Tired players
Pitch ——→ Churned-up pitch
Rules ——→ Rules having been applied

Football skills ——→ Football skills developed
Team spirit ——→ Team spirit increased/diminished
Need for entertainment ——→ Need met by mounting a
football match

Two wrong answers :

Players ——→ Football skills displayed

Players
Referee
Rules   }   ——→ Entertainment
Pitch
Ball

Figure 4.5 The concept 'transformation process'

(the actors who would do the activities of the system) and O (the system owner who could
demolish it). The reason for this, it was eventually realized, lay in the legacy of systems
engineering ideas which were only gradually being stripped off as SSM evolved. We had
tended to miss A and O in CATWOE because we had been far too ready to think
only of notional systems whose boundaries corresponded with real-world organization

groupings such as sections, departments, divisions – in which case A and O were too obvious to be noticed. This readiness to think of real-world departments, etc., as *being* systems, a common thought in hard systems thinking, gave far too much importance to organization boundaries, which are in the end arbitrary, created by human beings, hence changeable.

Nowadays we would always try to include amongst the relevant systems not only some 'primary task' definitions expressing official, declared, tasks but also 'issue-based' definitions which lead to systems not likely to be institutionalized in the real world (Checkland and Wilson, 1980). For example, in an organization which carries out a number of disparate tasks, a useful issue-based RD might express the idea of 'a system to resolve conflicts on resource use'. You would not expect to find a department of conflict resolution in the organization: nevertheless such systems, which cut across organizational boundaries, are very useful in freeing up thinking, and in generating new ideas at the comparison stage. Selected relevant systems should always include some with issue-based root definitions.

In summary, well-ordered formulation of RDs yields a handful of definitions, both 'primary task' and 'issue-based', which can then be modelled for use in a debate about change.

Building Conceptual Models

In SSM the core of the language for modelling activity systems is both very simple and very sophisticated: simple because the user knows it already – it is 'all the verbs in English'; and sophisticated because there are a great many verbs in English, allowing fine nuances of meaning to be expressed!

The model-building process consists of assembling the verbs describing the activities which would have to be there in the system named in the RD and structuring them according to logical dependencies. An arrow from activity x (say, 'obtain raw material') to activity y ('convert raw material to product') shows that y is *contingent upon x*. These considerations govern the assembly of the operational part of the system which would achieve the transformation process(es) named in the RD. It is a useful aim, for most models, to describe the operational activities in 'the magical number 7 ± 2' activities. The quoted phrase is from Miller's famous paper in cognitive psychology (Miller, 1956) in which he suggests that the human brain may have limited channel capacity for processing information: 7 ± 2 concepts we can perhaps cope with simultaneously.

The final model is that of *a system*, that is to say a notional entity which could adapt and survive, via processes of communication and control, in a changing environment. Because of this it is necessary to add to the operational sub-system a monitoring and control sub-system, which examines the operations and takes control action to change and/or improve them. Any system model is thus a combination of an operational system and a monitoring and control system, in the structure shown in Figure 4.6.

We may unpack the concept 'monitoring and control' by asking: how could the system fail? In general there are three kinds of answer to that (Forbes and Checkland, 1987). Firstly, failure could stem from doing the wrong thing and hence failing to contribute to high-level, longer-term aims. For a purposeful 'system to do x', the question as to whether x is the right thing to do, given higher-level aims, tests the *effectiveness* of the system in its wider context. Secondly, the system must show a means of carrying out the transformation expressed in the RD which in principle could actually work. Asking whether the selected means does work tests the *efficacy* of the system. Finally, an effective system with an efficacious means could still 'fail' because the operations of the system do not achieve the desired end with economy of resource use. The degree to which achieving the transformation uses up resources measures the *efficiency* of the system. Any monitoring and control system must pay attention to all three of these 'Es'. For example, consider setting up a notional 'system to wash cars' in which a small boy works with a bucket of water and a cloth, the intention being to earn a living from this operation. Monitoring effectiveness means asking the question: do we accept that we are getting an adequate income from this, or should we think of doing something else? Monitoring efficacy asks whether or not the small boy with his limited resources could in fact do the job: do customers regard the output as 'clean cars'? Finally, we need to ask if the small boy is making. a minimum use of resources (here, time and materials) while producing properly cleaned cars: we need to measure the system's efficiency in that sense.

These considerations show that it is useful to express purposeful activity in the form of

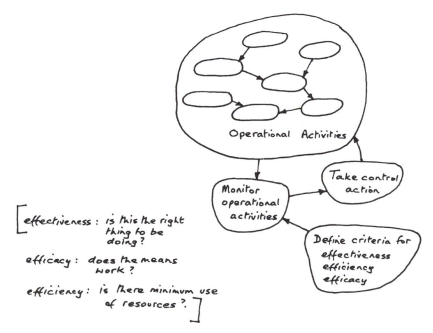

Figure 4.6 The general structure of a model of a purposeful activity system

an imperative statement: do P by Q in order to help achieve R, where P and Q relate to an input-output transformation. This addresses questions of 'what'(P) 'how'(Q) and 'why'(R). We need then to ask what would serve as measures of effectiveness, efficacy, and efficiency. With these defined, control action could in principle be taken if the system were not performing well according to these measures.

More detailed consideration of the concept of monitoring and control shows that in circumstances in which questions of effectiveness are especially important, it may be useful to express the structure of the systems modelled in the form shown in Figure 4.7.

This is a more sophisticated version of Figure 4.6, and draws attention to the fact that questions concerning the effectiveness of a system can be answered only by taking account of the wider system(s) of which the system in question will be a part. The owner of a system described in an RD (CATWOE's 'O') will reside in a wider system and could in principle decide to demolish the operations of the system and do something else instead. One of the reasons for including 'system owner' in CATWOE, in fact, is to ensure that thinking is not restricted to one level (that of the system as a logical machine pursuing its purpose). Thinking about 'O' forces us to take into account the meta-level

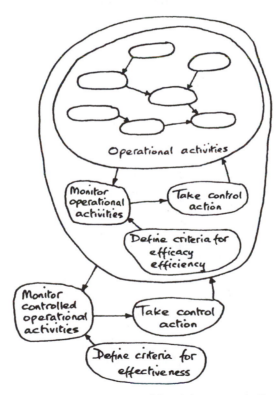

Figure 4.7 The structure of a model of a purposeful activity system indicating that effectiveness is decided in the wider system which owns the system

which can discourse *about* the system in question, while the activities within the model comprise the names of its sub-systems.

This last consideration is an example of the importance of the system concept of 'hierarchy' – or, if you want to avoid the unhelpful coercive connotations of that word, 'stratified order'. According to this idea, no system can ever be conceptualized in isolation, only as existing at one level in a stratified order of sub-systems, system and wider systems, etc.

A second way in which the concept is important in model building is that it allows detailed models of notional systems to be built without breaking the useful rule of '7±2 activities'. Having built a complete model with a handful of activities in the operational sub-system, we may now take any or all of those activities, as sub-systems, to be sources of root definitions which can themselves be modelled in more detail: 'obtain raw material' can be expanded into the structured set of activities which make up 'the system to obtain raw materials'. Similarly, the system originally modelled may itself be regarded as *one* purposeful activity in a wider system, one whose root definition will be suggested by examining the effectiveness criteria. For example, conceptualizing a system to provide health care for the elderly might lead to modelling a wider system which provides resources for all health care services, and has to weigh the priority given to each.

We have worked in some studies with detailed models containing more than 200 activities, but we would not have known how to build them except in a stratified order of wider systems, systems, sub-systems and sub-subsystems!

Perhaps the greatest difficulty in conceptual model building lies in disciplining yourself to work only from the words in the root definition. Since RDs are *relevant to* real-world activity, it is easy to slip into feeding into the model elements from real-world versions of the purposeful activity being treated as a system, elements not justified by the words of the RD.

Model building should focus only on the RD; every phrase in it will lead to particular activities in the model; every element in the model should relate to a particular part of the RD. The aim is *a justifiable combination* of RD and conceptual model. It is not expected that different modellers will derive exactly the same model from an RD, simply because words carry different connotations for different people. What is sought is a model which is coherent and defensible rather than 'correct' or 'valid'.

Figure 4.8 gives an example of an RD and a model which derives from it. The model in Figure 4.8 cannot possibly include unjustified real-world knowledge since it is, deliberately, an RD without meaning! It is included to show how a defensible *logical* structure for a model can be created from an RD, even though the RD does not refer to the everyday world.

Consider the task of producing the conceptual model consisting of the necessary linked activities called for by the RD of Figure 4.8, namely:

> A dag-owned gor tonking system which, within legal
> constraints, tonks those gors which meet criteria gog.

Model Building :

> A defensible logical structure for a model may
> be derived from a root definition even though
> knowledge of any real-world version of the
> purposeful activity is lacking!

Root Definition

> A dag-owned gor tonking system which,
> within legal constraints, tonks those gors
> which meet criteria gog.

C   gors
A   not stated (skilled tonkers implied)
T   gors ⟶ tonked gors
W   gor tonking is a good thing to do
O   dag
E   legal constraints

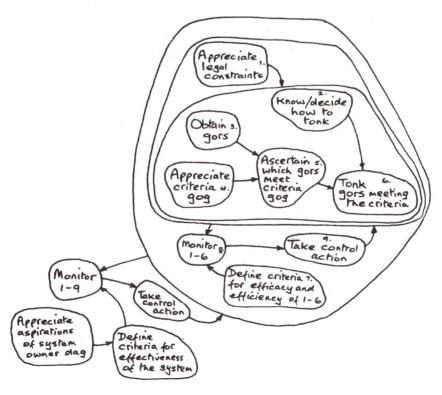

Figure 4.8 Model building from a root definition and CATWOE

Even though we know nothing of gor tonking, we can model the logical machine necessary to carry it out according to this definition. In doing this kind of model building it is always useful first to get into your head an holistic concept of the purposeful system to be modelled. A useful starting point is the construction of a 'rich picture'. Earlier in this chapter, the concept of rich picture was introduced in the context in which it was developed, namely in getting a grip on the relationships constituting the problem situation being studied. But any RD necessarily describes a hypothetical 'situation': one in which an instrumental transformation process, converting some defined input into an output, is being carried out under various constraints. So the relationships inherent in this can be expressed in a rich picture. In order to do that in this case we need to represent three kinds of gor (those meeting criteria gog; those not meeting that criteria; those which have been tonked). We need a representation of the legal constraints under which the system operates, a representation of the owner dag who could act to abolish the system, and a means of dealing with the ambiguity in CATWOE: the absence of A. There, we may make the reasonable assumption that we would have to have knowledge of the tonking process (and hence skilled tonkers who could carry it out). Given invented icons for these elements, we can express the situation described in the RD in a rich picture, as in Figure 4.9. Producing such a picture makes clear the transformation process, and helps the model builder to assemble and structure the minimum necessary activities to meet the requirements of the root definition, as is done in Figure 4.8. Armed with that model we could formulate some cogent questions to ask about the gor tonking process. Checkland and Scholes (1990) give several examples of rich pictures drawn to help complex model building (see Chapter 9) as well as examples of rich pictures drawn

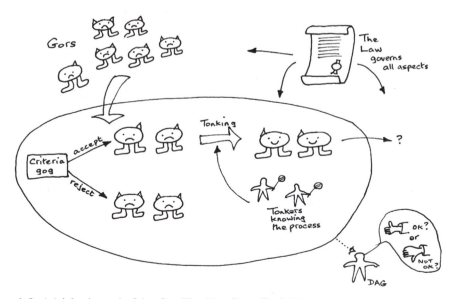

Figure 4.9 A 'rich picture' of the Gor Tonking Root Definition

to illustrate the perceived nature of problem situations (pp. 46, 47, 98) – which was their original role.

Although fanciful, the gor tonking example illustrates starkly that modelling in SSM is not a process of *describing* (parts of) the real world. It is a process of creating systemic instrumental devices with which to explore the real situation. (For those disconcerted by the magic realism of a gor tonking system, Figure 4.10 provides a feet-on-the-ground RD, with its CATWOE and a model defensible against the definition.)

In summary, model building in SSM yields a number of models of activity systems, each built according to a particular pure view of the world which is declared in the W of CATWOE.

The models may then be used to structure exploration of the problem situation in order to help find feasible and desirable ways of bringing about improvement, and to find or create the motivation to take action.

Using Models, Defining Changes

The models provide a means for perceiving reality afresh and initiating a discussion from which changes to improve the problem situation can be sought. This is achieved by focusing upon differences between the models and perceived reality. Since the models are all based upon pure, carefully expressed worldviews, the discussion directs attention to taken-as-given assumptions about the world, highlights alternatives and, in general, provides an opportunity for rethinking many aspects of real-world activity. This is always an exciting, sometimes a painful experience! And it is very often the point from which one recycles to earlier stages in the methodology, as learning is achieved through the comparisons between models and real world.

Four ways of conducting the model/real-world comparison have emerged. Whichever approach is adopted, the initial comparison is usefully done at the level of the RD itself. How does it reflect current perceptions? Could it? Should it? For example, in a study aimed at improving the operations of a local public library, an RD might be based on viewing the library, not as a well-understood mechanism for book and record loan, but as a part of the local education system. It would be useful, even before considering the model, to compare and contrast this concept with those of the professional librarians, potential actual users of the library and local educationists.

When it comes to comparing activity models with what is currently going on in the situation, we are at the point at which the often unquestioned, informal and intuitive perceptions of reality are brought up against the systems constructs. The constructs (both issue-based and primary task) are those considered *relevant* to reconsidering present perceptions and activities, with a view to improving them. Since human situations are diverse, it is not surprising that different ways of carrying out the comparison stage have seemed sensible in different studies (Checkland, 1981; 1999 pp. A28–A31).

The first of four ways of conducting this stage is the least formal: simply record

Root Definition

> A hospital-owned system which provides records of spending on drugs so that control action by administrators and doctors to meet defined budgets can be taken jointly.

C   Administrators, doctors

A   Not stated

T   Need to know   →   Need met by
      spending on drugs   recording information

W   Monitoring spending on drugs is possible and is an adequate basis for joint control action

O   Hospital

E   Hospital mechanisms; roles administrators and doctors; defined budgets

Figure 4.10 Another example of model building

differences which stand out between the handful of models and current perceptions and happenings. List the differences and discuss whether or not they matter. This approach is often relevant where roles and/or strategies are an issue. If the concern is more detailed – improving operations and necessary information flows, for example – then a more formal listing of differences yields the second approach. Here, each model is used to define a series of specific questions concerning activities, and links between activities, for which answers are then sought in the situation itself; this often involves further finding out beyond that carried out initially. Thus we can ask of every activity and every link in the model: Does this happen in the real situation? How? By what criteria is it judged? Is it a subject of concern in the situation? Tables of answers to such questions are assembled. This ordered questioning is the most common way of carrying out this stage.

A third approach is to 'operate' the activity system, on paper, and so write a scenario describing how things might happen given the RD in question. Such scenarios can often be compared with historical happenings known to people in the problem situation.

The fourth method of comparison consists of trying to build a model of a part of reality similar to a model thought to be *relevant* to it, following as closely as possible the structure of the latter model itself. If this can be done then overlay of the two models reveals the differences starkly. (In the unlikely event that the two models were identical – unlikely because reality is more rich and complex than logical models – this would mean that more radical RDs were needed.) This is the most formal method of doing the comparison, and naturally it can only be used if there is in the real world some fairly direct manifestation of the purposeful activity of the model. This is not as common an occurrence as might be thought, given that the models are intellectual constructions intended to structure debate, not would-be descriptions of reality. So this fourth method of doing the comparison can be used only rarely.

In summary, this 'comparison' provides the structure and substance of an organized debate about improving a situation thought of as problematical.

In practice it merges into the phase in which changes to be implemented are defined.

The purpose of the comparison stage is to use the differences between models and reality to discuss possible changes which could bring about improvement in the problem situation. The models are not necessarily thought of as designs, as happens in 'hard' systems engineering. Here the thought may be to make reality either more *or less* like the models: the purpose is to make the debate a coherent one.

What is looked for in the debate is possible changes which appear to those taking part to constitute potential improvements worth trying. Such changes, which may include any or all of changes to: structures, processes, attitudes (Checkland, 1999 pp. A28–A31), have to meet two rather different criteria simultaneously. Firstly, the comparison of a fecund reality with a number of models (which are simply logical machines) will generate ideas for changes which are *systemically desirable,* such as instituting mechanisms for assessing effectiveness, making sure resources are appropriate, ensuring that logical dependencies are reflected in real-world sequential actions, etc. But this logic is not enough. People will not always be motivated to implement change which is justified merely by logic! The debate must find its way to *accommodations* between people holding conflicting views if changes which are *culturally feasible* in the particular human situation in question are to be found. (The *history* of the situation, its myths and meanings, for instance, will always affect this issue.) This is one reason why it is so important to think carefully about the *Weltanschauung* of each RD and model: CATWOE's W is a way of ensuring the cultural aspects cannot be completely ignored.

This need for cultural feasibility as well as systemic desirability is something which scientists and engineers sometimes find difficult; they tend to overemphasize the importance of logic, and fail to notice cultural aspects which in fact determine whether or not change will occur. In one study the logic of information flows required by an activity model to monitor expenditure on drugs in a large general hospital had little impact in the face of the heavily-defended clinical autonomy of the hospital consultants. And the example has already been given of the project models which were simply not meaningful within the engineering culture of the British Aircraft Corporation at the time of our study.

If both logical and cultural criteria are not kept in mind, then the chance of achieving change will be much reduced; though equally it must be said that what is culturally feasible in a given situation will itself be changed in and by the debate structured by the models used. Cultures are never static, and SSM can be seen as a way of exploring them and enabling them to change.

Taking Action

When some changes accepted as 'desirable and feasible 'have been identified, and accommodations between conflicting views have been found or created, then the cycle of SSM is completed by implementing these changes. The readiness to make the changes, of course, changes perceptions of the initial problematical situation – which in any case will have been moved on by the very processes of SSM. There is now a somewhat more structured problem situation, and addressing it (that is, implementing the changes) can itself be tackled by using SSM in further cycles. 'Relevant systems' will now include 'a system to implement the defined changes', and modelling it via RDs and CATWOE can help make implementation a coherent process.

The cycle of SSM, together with the recycles which normally occur within any application of it, thus provides a way of articulating the cycle of Figure 4.1, an approach to 'managing' in a broad sense of the word. It is an approach 'validated' by having been found useful in several hundred studies as well as transferable to users other than those who developed it. It makes use of systems ideas together with a concept of purposeful activity, in a combination which tries to address not only the facts and logic of a problem situation, but also the myths and meanings through which the people in the situation perceive it and relate to it.

The Nature of SSM

Anyone wishing to make effective use of SSM needs to be aware of its status as *methodology*. This is a much misunderstood word, especially by desk-bound academics, who are prone to use it when what they really mean is *method*. Practitioners, honed and chastened by experience of the complexity of the everyday world, are, in my experience, much more likely to understand SSM as methodology and to bring to it the necessary flexibility, the light-footedness, which effective use calls for. The point is that a methodology is, as the structure of the word indicates, a *logos* of method, a set of *principles* which have to be adapted in use to a particular situation which will be the product of a particular history, that history both creating and being created by a particular culture. Thus, a sophisticated user of SSM will remain situation-oriented, not methodology-oriented, and will create an approach appropriate to the particular situation studied which draws on and embodies the methodological principles which are SSM. What happens when SSM is properly used can be generalized in the LUMAS model shown in Figure 4.11: Learning for a User by a Methodology-informed Approach to a Situation. The study described in the next chapter illustrates this process in a large acute hospital.

Conclusion

How different is SSM from the systems engineering (SE) which spawned it 30 years ago? In particular, how different is the systems thinking in 'soft' systems methodology from that in 'hard' systems engineering?

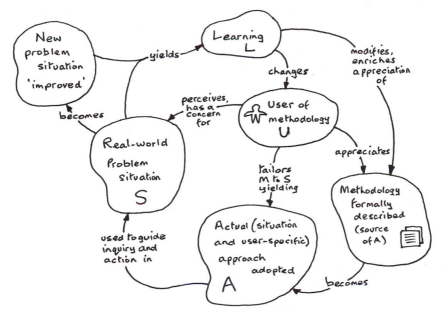

Figure 4.11 Methodology in use: the LUMAS model

SE works with a defined need or objective, and systematically finds its way to a system to meet the need, achieve the objective. In the experiences which produced SSM, it was found necessary to regard as problematical precisely what is taken as given in SE, namely the need or objective. SSM treats *what to do* as well as *how to do it* as part of the problem. It does so via the device of modelling systems which pursue a pure purpose from a declared point of view. It accepts that real-world action will be much messier than these pure models, and uses the models to structure a debate in which different conflicting objectives, needs, purposes, interests, values can be teased out and discussed. In this way it tries to encompass cultural myths and meanings as well as publicly testable facts and logic. It thus seeks to articulate a process in which an accommodation between conflicting interests and views can be sought, an accommodation which will enable action aimed at feasible improvement to be undertaken. This means that SSM is a learning, not an optimizing system; learning has to be participative, so that SSM is not – or should not be – the skill of an external expert.

Finally, it will be clear that ending a systems study which uses SSM is an arbitrary act: the flux of events and ideas moves on, there are no permanent solutions, and systems thinking has to be envisaged as a process which is in principle never ending.

All these differences between SSM and SE make SSM the general case of which SE is a special case. The special case becomes relevant when ends are agreed (or can be imposed), and the question is not what to do but only how to do it.

SE takes 'system' to be the name of something in the world which could be 'engineered'. SSM takes 'system' to be the name of an epistemological device which can be used to investigate some of the problems in the world. Thus the crucial distinction between the hard and soft systems approaches is that the former takes the world to consist of systems, whereas the latter shifts systemicity from the world to the process of enquiry into the world: in SSM 'the system' is not something out there in the situation but is the process of enquiry, a process which happens to make use of pure systems models (Checkland, 1983; 1985; 1999).

In the next chapter an application of SSM as the basis of a process of enquiry leading to real-world action will be described.

References

Blackett, P.M.S. (1962). *Studies of War*, Oliver and Boyd, Edinburgh.

Blair, R.N. and Whitston, C.W. (1971). *Elements of Industrial Systems Engineering*, Prentice Hall, Englewood Cliffs, NJ.

Checkland, P. (1972). 'Towards a systems-based methodology for real-world problem solving', *J. Sys. Eng.* **3**, 87–116.

Checkland, P. (1981 and 1999). *Systems Thinking, Systems Practice*, John Wiley & Sons, Ltd, Chichester.

Checkland, P. (1983). '*OR* and the systems movement: mappings and conflicts', *J Opl. Res. Soc.*, **34**(8), 661–75.

Checkland, P. (1984). 'Systems thinking in management: the development of soft systems methodology and its implications for social science', in *Self-organisation and Management of Social Systems* (Eds. H. Ulrich and G.J.B. Probst), pp. 94–104, Springer-Verlag, Berlin.

Checkland, P. (1985). 'From optimizing to learning: a development of systems thinking for the 1990's', *J. Opl. Res. Soc.*, **36**, 757–67.

Checkland, P. (1986). 'The Politics of Practice', IIASA Roundtable, 'The Art and Science of Systems Practice', Laxenburg, Austria, November 1986.

Checkland, P. (1988). 'Soft systems methodology: an overview', *J. Appl. Sys. Anal.*, **15**, 27–30.

Checkland, P. (1999). *Soft Systems Methodology: A 30-year Retrospective*, John Wiley & Sons, Ltd, Chichester.

Checkland, P. and Casar, A. (1986). 'Vickers' concept of an appreciative system: a systemic account', *J. Appl. Sys. Anal.*, **13**, 3–17.

Checkland, P. and Griffin, R. (1970). 'Management information systems: a systems view', *J. Sys. Eng.*, **1**, 29–42.

Checkland, P. and Holwell, S. (1998). *Systems, Information and Information Systems*, John Wiley & Sons, Ltd, Chichester.

Checkland, P. and Scholes, J. (1990 and 1999). *Soft Systems Methodology in Action*, John Wiley & Sons, Ltd, Chichester.

Checkland, P. and Wilson, B. (1980). 'Primary task and issue-based root definitions in systems studies', *J. Appl. Sys. Anal.*, **7**, 51–4.

Chestnut, H. (1967). *Systems Engineering Methods*, John Wiley & Sons, Inc, New York.

de Neufville, R. and Stafford, J.H. (1971). *Systems Analysis for Engineers and Managers*, McGraw-Hill, New York.

Forbes, P. and Checkland, P.B. (1987). 'Monitoring and control in systems models', Internal Discussion Paper 3/87, Department of Systems, University of Lancaster.

Hall, A.D. (1962). *A Methodology for Systems Engineering*, Van Nostrand, Princeton, NJ.

Hitch, C.J. (1955). 'An appreciation of systems analysis', in *Systems Analysis* (Ed. S.L. Optner, 1965), pp. 19–36, Penguin, Harmondsworth.

Kennedy, J.F. (1961). Message to Congress on urgent national needs.

Machol, R.E. (1965). *Systems Engineering Handbook*, McGraw-Hill, New York.

Miller, G. (1956). 'The magical number 7 ± 2', *Psych. Rev.*, **63**, 81–96.

Miser, H., and Quade, E.S. (Eds.) (1985). *Handbook of Systems Analysis: Overview of Uses, Procedures, Applications, and Practice*, North-Holland, New York.

Miser, H. and Quade, E.S. (Eds.) (1988). *Handbook of Systems Analysis: Craft Issues and Procedural Choices*, North-Holland, New York.

Optner, S.L. (Ed.) (1965). *Systems Analysis*, Penguin, Harmondsworth.

Quade, E.S. (1975). *Analysis for Public Decision*, Elsevier, New York.

Smith, B.L.R. (1966). *The Rand Corporation*, Harvard University Press, Cambridge, Mass.

Smyth, D.S. and Checkland, P. (1976). 'Using a systems approach: the structure of root definitions', *J. Appl. Sys. Anal.*, **5**, 75–83.

Stowell, F. (1989). Change, organization, power and the metaphor 'commodity', PhD Dissertation, Lancaster University.

Waddington, C.H. (1973). *OR in World War 2*, Elek Science, London.

Wagner, H.M. (1975). *Principles of Operations Research*, Prentice-Hall, London.

Wilson, B. (1984). *Systems: Concepts, Methodologies and Applications*, John Wiley & Sons, Ltd, Chichester.

Wymore, A.W. (1976). *Systems Engineering Methodology for Interdisciplinary Teams*, John Wiley & Sons, Inc, New York.

5 Soft Systems Methodology in Action: Participative Creation of an Information Strategy for an Acute Hospital

Peter Checkland

Introduction

The previous chapter has described how SSM emerged from the interaction of ideas and experience in a programme of action research. It emerged as a replacement for the systems engineering approach, which was found to be too one-dimensional to cope with the complexity of problem situations of the kind managers have to face in day-to-day life in organizations. SSM took the form of an organized process of inquiry and learning which used systems models of purposeful activity as devices to provide structure to a discussion/conversation/debate aimed at finding (or creating) accommodations between conflicting perspectives which enabled 'action to improve' to be taken. Most important, SSM emerged as methodology in the true sense of that word: as a set of principles (the *logos* of method) which a user can draw upon to create a specific approach relevant to *this* particular situation involving *these* particular people with their particular history, culture and worldviews. The generic LUMAS model (Figure 4.11 in the previous chapter) expresses this process, providing a language in terms of which the history of the several hundred experiences in the action research programme over 30 years can be captured.

What follows is an account of a particular use of SSM by a large group of people who took part in a study which aimed to create a new information strategy in a large acute hospital in the National Health Service. The study took place in the mid-1990s, and represents a now-common situation: one in which experienced facilitators familiar with SSM use it to orchestrate a study by people in the problem situation who are not themselves required to know about SSM. In this particular case about 40 of the NHS professionals who worked in the hospital carried out the work; but they had no previous interest in or, indeed, knowledge of SSM. Facilitation was by a senior manager in the hospital and two outsiders: a professional management consultant and the present author. That work of this kind is possible is for me evidence that SSM is essentially a 'natural' process, and one which is equally relevant to a specific highlighted project with a de-clared objective and duration or to the general process of managing in organizations, which is on-going. If that were not so SSM would soon sink to the 'back-room' status of most management science.

It is obvious that a number of problems face anyone trying to describe a real experience. For one thing, it will be impossible for any written account to approach the rich complexity of the lived experience itself. This would be true even if we were to abandon the would-be scientific approach and write a novel out of the experience. For the novel would be from the author's point of view: is that the 'true' account? Is there in fact any 'true' account of the study, given that the happenings were experienced by a group of people each having his or her own (changing) *Weltanschauung?* And even if all participants agreed an account of the study, and agreed on the study's value – an unlikely event in itself – then that account, if regarded as advocating the approach adopted, would be defenceless against a number of criticisms. There is no answer to anyone who asserts that the study should have been done more quickly or more competently, or that some other approach would have been more effective. Since the same human problem situation cannot ever be tackled twice, such criticisms are not ultimately very interesting, being incapable of refutation; but they do indicate that case histories are tender flowers, easily trampled under the boots of unreason.

Given these problems, the author can only declare the stance from which the study is described, and hope that he gets readers ready to see if the story provides some learning for them! What is described here, then, is an account from the author's point of view of a systems study using SSM in which he participated. In the true spirit of SSM the study was carried out by people in the problem situation in question, with three other people acting as facilitators. Their role was to help the study along, providing occasional *enabling* help.

This account of the study enriches the brief account in Checkland and Holwell (1998) and a conference paper (Checkland, Clarke and Poulter (1996)).

The Study Situation

The NHS

Most Western economies provide their citizens with health care through insurance: either via subsidies to private insurance or through compulsory national insurance schemes. In the UK, however, the National Health Service is funded from general taxation, so that its services are free at the point of delivery regardless of the individual patient's ability to pay. This principle of nationally-provided health care for the whole population 'from cradle to grave' has made the NHS not only the largest organization in the UK but also one of the most popular. In the words of Webster's excellent short historical review of the NHS, written to mark its fiftieth anniversary in 1998:

> The new health service dramatically eliminated all the humiliating disqualifications of the old system. In the popular imagination the new service seemed realistically equipped to confront the awesome task of providing the entire community with a first-class and com-

prehensive level of care from 'the cradle to the grave'. On the basis of the rapid strides made to fulfil this expectation, the NHS quickly established for itself a unique status of esteem among the public services that has proved capable of withstanding all the trials of economic turbulence and political transformation experienced over the last fifty years.

(Webster, 1998 p. 2)

The fifty-year history of the NHS has been characterized by this 'turbulence and transformation', and the general shape of the story is well-captured in the sub-headings of Rivett's fine comprehensive history (1998), also written for the anniversary of the Service: Establishing the NHS ('48–'57); The renaissance of general practice and hospitals ('58–'67); Re-thinking the NHS ('68–'77); Clinical advances and financial crisis ('78–'87); New influences and new pathways ('88–'97). Webster's 'economic turbulence and political transformation' started in a major way in Rivett's period from 1968–1977: 'Re-thinking the NHS'. Following Green and White Papers from Government in the early 70s, and discussion of the need for better linking of GP, hospital and community-based services, the NHS underwent a major reorganization in 1974. 14 Regional Health Authorities were formed together with 90 subordinate Area Authorities, whose boundaries mapped those of local authorities, and 192 District Health Authorities (DHAs). The aim was to integrate health services for districts with a population of about 250 000–300 000 people, involving clinicians in management, and managing through 'consensus decision-making'. By the end of the decade Rivett reports

NHS reorganization was not a success. The oil crisis led to recession and the building programme was cut to save jobs. Devolution downwards was long in coming. Far more rapid was the increasing centralisation of powers and the issue of immense amounts of detailed guidance epitomized by a turkey circular that advised hospitals to cook the Christmas fowl fully. (p. 279)

Webster has more recently written of the period leading to the 1974 reorganization in the following terms:

From the mid-60s on, a decade of deliberation over reorganization represented a staggering record of ineptitude on the part of both Labour and Conservative governments. The result was a worst-of-worlds blueprint in the form of the 1974 reorganization ... (which) was a gigantic mistake.

(Webster, 2000)

Industrial action had also become a new feature in the life of the NHS, making the life of politicians more difficult as they sought to balance increasing demands from patients and limitation of resources – the permanent 'crisis' of the Service.

Following a report from a Royal Commission on the NHS in 1979, which called for simplification of structure and strengthened local management, Area Health Authorities were abolished in 1982, making the DHAs the crucial tier at which services were delivered. In 1983 the then Secretary of State for Health invited a senior manager from the food marketing industry – Roy Griffiths, deputy chairman and managing director of J. Sainsbury – to advise him on the management of the NHS. Not surprisingly the Griffiths Report identified a lack of management in the NHS compared with private industry, remarking, in a famous sentence, that

> If Florence Nightingale was carrying her lamp through the corridors of the NHS today, she would almost certainly be searching for the people in charge.

He proposed a Chief Executive for the Service as a whole, with similar posts at Regional and District levels. Within a DHA its units (for example: an acute hospital, a chronic unit and a unit providing community-based services) would be headed by Unit Managers. This introduction of 'general management', as it was called in the NHS, neglected the fact that, for example, no hospital consultant could be required by an executive manager to act in a way which he or she considered harmful to patients. This rather undermines the concept of appointing budget-holding accountable managers; providing health care is not equivalent to selling groceries, and not surprisingly a number of managers who joined the NHS from industry at this time soon left. The Service struggled on, kept going as always by the dedication of its employees, and coping *ad hoc* with the ambiguity which this latest reform had introduced.

By the late 1980s expenditure on the Health Service in England and Wales was around £25 000 million (and this would rise to over £40 000 million a decade later). There was a general feeling that although expenditure on the Service continued slowly to increase in real terms, it could never cope with the combination of a growing public demand, an increasing number of old people in the population and the steady availability of new and costly medical techniques. The scene was set for what Rivett calls 'the next managerial drama' (1998 p. 361). This was the drama that was unfolding when the study described in this chapter was carried out: the attempt to improve efficiency and effectiveness of the NHS by the introduction of an 'internal market'. The then Government hoped that the disciplines of a market situation might drive the Service towards efficiency and effectiveness in a way that the introduction of 'general management' had not.

The changes were announced in the White Paper 'Working for Patients' (Cm. 555) in January 1989 and implemented in April 1991. The central concept was to separate the running of hospitals from their financing, or, more generally, to separate the provision of all health services from the commissioning (purchasing) of them. Also, GPs could choose to become fundholders, thus becoming informal purchasers for their patients; and hospital and community units would become autonomous Trusts as 'providers' of services, while the old DHAs would fill a new role in which they would become 'purchasers' of health care services for their local population – though with the activities of fundholding GPs cutting across their activity. The link between DHA's as purchasers and Trusts as providers would be through a series of negotiated annual 'contracts' to provide a particular service over the coming year for an agreed sum of money. In spite of the use of the word 'contract', the NHS and Community Care Act 1990 explicitly rejected the legal connotation: they were agreements which

> Shall not be regarded for any purpose as giving rise to contractual rights or liabilities
> (NHSCCA, 1990, quoted in Flynn & Williams (Eds.), 1997 p. 86)

In spite of this disclaimer, the political rhetoric at the time was strong, with a document from the NHS Executive in 1993 declaring the need for 'creative tension and robust negotiations between purchasers and providers'.

An action research team from Lancaster University, researching numerous examples of the evolving relationship between 'purchasers' and 'providers' of health care, found a very complex situation, one which could not be described adequately as 'a market driven by contract negotiation', nor as 'a managed market characterized primarily by contract negotiation'; on the other hand the NHS was far from being a command structure managed from the centre, even though pressure from the centre was a daily reality for Trust and Health Authority chief executives (Checkland, 1997a). Looking back from the year 2000 it seems to this observer that here was a situation in which the NHS professionals worked to meet their statutory obligations (sometimes with a 'contract' as no more than one side of A4 signed at the eleventh hour!) without being convinced that an internal market was a satisfactory mechanism for provision of a public service. Individual pairs of purchasers and providers learned their way to a version of their local situation which they could both live with; then there were, in some cases, interventions from Regional Authorities where agreement was not possible.

This was the situation in the NHS when the work to be described here was carried out. One useful consequence of the purchaser–provider split in its original form, with its requirement for annual 'contracts' for service provision, was that both the purchasing Health Authorities and the providing Trusts had to think more seriously than they had in the past about their information systems. The very concept of two separate organizations coming to time-bound agreements about service delivery, even if those agreements were not legally binding, implies the availability of significant good-quality information about a service, its costs and the month-to-month story of its delivery over the period of the 'contract'. So it was not surprising during the 1990s to find a situation like that described here: large acute hospital (a Trust) wishing to re-think its information strategy.

Like many (perhaps most) organizations, the Trust in question had bought computer systems quicker than it had developed ways of thinking out clearly, in advance, exactly what information was needed to support those who carried out the hospital's on-going activity at both tactical and strategic levels. The hospital's Information Manager felt that it was necessary to re-define their information strategy, this time starting not from an examination of available IT, but from a careful look at the purposeful activity the hospital exists to carry out. He initiated the participative systems study using SSM which is described below.

As indicated above, this study was done when the purchaser–provider 'contracting' arrangements were in place, and the rhetoric was strong. But in highly political situations change can be very rapid, and the need for 'creative tension' and 'robust negotiations' (quoted above from an NHS Executive document of 1993) had become, in the 1996/97 *Priorities and Planning Guidance* 'the need to reinforce and realise the commitment in the NHS to partnership, collaboration and teamwork'. Then in 1997 the latest White Paper 'The new NHS: modern, dependable' declared that it

> sets out how *the internal market will be replaced* by a system we have called 'integrated care', based on partnership and driven by performance. It forms the basis of a ten year programme to renew and improve the NHS ... (Cm. 3807 para 1.3 p. 54; present author's italics)

Given this change it might be thought that a study carried out in an acute hospital under the 'contracting' arrangements is now of only historical interest. But this is not so. The 1997 White Paper has retained the crucial split between purchasing organizations which decide the pattern of services required for a particular population, and organizations (Trusts) which provide those services. The 'service agreements' (no longer 'contracts') now run for several years and are linked to a 'Health Improvement Plan' for the population in question. But the requirement for purchasers and providers to think carefully about the information needed to define, deliver and monitor delivery of services is as great as ever. The need for a hospital to develop a well-thought-out information strategy is undiminished.

The Hospital Situation

The Royal Victoria Infirmary (RVI) in Newcastle is a large teaching hospital linked to the Newcastle University Medical School. At the time of the study it was merging organizationally with Hexham General Hospital, a much smaller hospital twenty-five miles away, so it was now becoming a very big hospital indeed, on two sites. Hexham's Steve Clarke became the Information Officer of the new hospital, and he saw the need for a new information strategy for the combined hospital. He wanted this to be developed not by the IS and IT professionals – in which case it would be too much to hope for user-ownership of the strategy – but by people working at the two hospital sites. He saw SSM as a suitable approach for achieving this, and asked me to give methodological help. I was very happy to do this but was somewhat disconcerted to find that the project, initiated in March, was required to formulate the new information strategy by September! This seemed a very tall order, given that the work would be done by busy doctors and nurses who would somehow have to find the time to work on the project without being relieved of their normal responsibilities. However, Steve Clarke and I were not the only people responsible for organizing and orchestrating the work. We were joined by John Poulter, then a senior management consultant from the SEMA Group, who had won the contract for the work following a tendering process. So there were three of us as project facilitators; and I can report that the delivery of the new strategy within seven months was due entirely to the exercise of fine professional management skills by Steve and John. I was very impressed to observe this. Having worked in a university for more than twenty years after leaving industry, I had become unused to seeing management skill routinely exercised, universities being administered rather than managed (Checkland, 1997b.)

It was also important for the project that both Steve Clarke and John Poulter are natural holistic thinkers, excellent examples of what Donald Schon describes as 'reflective practitioners' (1983). In my experience it is such practitioners, rather than academics, who are the best source of insights into the use of an action-oriented approach such as SSM.

The funding for the RVI project came from the HISS initiative in the NHS. This was a remarkable centrally-funded project to take sixteen NHS acute hospitals from being organizations with fragmented and disparate systems (one for patient administration, one for the pathology laboratory etc) to being hospitals supported by a single integrated computer-based information system, and to do this in a single technological leap. It was 'remarkable' in that most professionals in the IS and IT fields regarded such an aspiration as absurdly over-optimistic, especially in an organization like the NHS with a then rather unsophisticated knowledge of IS and IT. And so it turned out. The HISS project was harshly treated when evaluated by the National Audit Office (1996), and savagely attacked in the trade press, being described as 'impossibly ambitious' and as having 'underestimated the risks of failure and ignored early signs of disaster' (Collins 1996). However, modest HISS funding was also available for smaller more realistic projects, and Steve Clarke achieved the RVI's new information strategy for less than half of one percent of the total of £8.3m spent at Greenwich, one of the sixteen HISS main sites.

The Methodology – SSM and IS

Steve Clarke understood that experience suggests that the most fruitful way to use SSM is participatively, with people in the problem situation carrying out the study helped by experienced facilitation. In such circumstances it is usually best to conduct the study in the everyday language of participants with only the minimum necessary recourse to the language of SSM. This was readily accepted by the three facilitators, as was the constraint of a necessarily tight timetable for the work. This entailed producing activity models for the major activities of the hospital (such as 'providing general surgery' or 'providing a nursing service') and using them as a basis for discussion of the information support needed by those carrying out the activities. This support could then be compared with that currently available from existing systems, with capabilities, gaps and opportunities identified. These would then provide the basis for a re-formulated information strategy. Given the September end point the timetable envisaged producing activity models by April and information requirements by June; identification of capabilities, gaps and opportunities by July would then enable the strategy, the information plan, to be produced on schedule in September.

Methodologically this was reasonably straightforward. Given that an organization's information strategy is necessarily at a high level, being a generic account of the information systems necessary to enable an organization to fulfil its explicit, 'official' function, we needed only to build 'primary task' models, that is ones having boundaries which map onto existing hospital structures. (It is in any case never easy to change hospital structures, given that they derive from the boundaries which define professions: doctors, nurses, radiologists, physiotherapists, accountants etc. Current efforts to render such boundaries more flexible within the NHS are making very slow progress.)

As far as the focus on information systems is concerned, the methodology adopted is a straightforward reflection of the approach to IS work which the use of SSM calls for. This is described in detail and copiously illustrated in *Information, Systems and Information Systems* (Checkland and Holwell, 1998) and will be baldly summarized here:

1. Information systems (IS) are not created for their own sake. Once they exist they may of course be used for various purposes, and usually play a large role in the drama of organizational politics, but in a formal sense they are created because people acting purposefully need to know various things: they need information support; information systems meet that need. They can therefore be conceptualized as systems which serve, help or support people undertaking tasks.
2. Whenever one system serves or supports another, the system which serves can be coherently thought about, designed and implemented only if there is a prior clear concept or account of the system served. This must be so because how the system served is conceptualized will define what counts as 'help' or 'support' (Checkland, 1981; Winter, Brown and Checkland, 1995; Checkland and Holwell, 1998).
3. Therefore, in order to create an IS it is first necessary to agree a conceptualization of the system served – in this case a system of purposeful activity as modelled in SSM from a declared perspective or worldview.
4. Once the system served (the purposeful activity) is carefully described then, if this is done by an SSM-style activity model, we may ask of each activity in the model: What information would have to be known by someone doing this activity? And: What information would be generated by doing the activity? Extending from these basic questions we can specify the IS and coherently think about how it might be realized, nowadays usually by use of IT.
[5. Of course it is also the case that as 1–4 above are followed, we need also to keep in mind that modern IT can enable us to do new purposeful activity, activity which would not be possible without the IT. So the thinking process is not simply a linear one from 1 to 4 but an iteration which also involves possible re-definition of activity.]

This argument rests upon a particular analysis of what it means to attribute meaning to our observed and experienced world, an analysis of such concepts as 'data', 'information', 'knowledge'. Checkland and Holwell (1998) conduct an analysis of how these categories are created. The literature shows a rough consensus that 'information' is 'data' to which human beings have attributed meaning in a particular context. Over time larger bodies of structured information will be assembled; we may use the word 'knowledge' to describe such structures, which we expect to have some reasonable lifetime, to change relatively slowly.

One other concept was found useful to complete this analysis. There are masses and masses of data, only a tiny fraction of which we pay attention to, think about or take seriously at a given time. As I sit writing these words one morning in North Lancashire, I am at the back of my mind aware of the following as a plausible possible data set: the present weather pattern (temperature, pressure, precipitation, wind speed and direction etc) in Tokyo and Osaka. I pay this possible data set no attention, it does not interest me. If, however, I were travelling to Japan to visit those cities next week I might well wish to find out the current content of that data set in order to know what to expect and to plan my stay there. That data would have become something different: it would now be *selected* data to which I pay attention, which I seek out, take seriously. This is always the first step in the thinking which leads to information and knowledge (though in everyday discourse the steps may be virtually simultaneous).

We use the word 'capta' to indicate this tiny fraction of all possible data which we have a concern for. ['Capta' comes from the Latin verb *capere*, to take, where 'data' comes from *dare*, to give (Checkland, 1982; Checkland and Holwell, 1998 pp. 86–98)].

So, in the RVI project our task as facilitators was to organize a process in which a large group of NHS professionals could think in a coherently structured way about core hospital activity, express that in models of purposeful activity and then, based on their professional knowledge and experience, work out what capta, and hence what information and knowledge was needed by people working in the hospital. Through comparison with existing provision, this would enable the following question to be answered: What IT-based information systems should the hospital put in place in order to support the achievement of its core purpose as an acute hospital within the NHS?

The Work Done

Getting Started

The team facilitating the project felt that if the study was to achieve the delivery of a new information strategy to the Board within six months, it should not be slipped quietly into the day-to-day activity of the Newcastle and Hexham hospitals but should be given a more prominent profile. Steve Clarke, given responsibility for delivering the strategy, therefore arranged for the project to be launched by the Chief Executive of the RVI. This was done at a meeting of about 100 people in one of the hospital's tiered lecture theatres. The CEO, speaking first, explained the importance of the project in the context of the NHS reforms and then Steve himself, John Poulter and myself all made contributions, explaining how the work would be tackled. The CEO's involvement gave the project a certain cachet; it ensured that those taking part understood that this study was considered significant by the Trust, also that people not present at the meeting would hear about it, and it emphasized that the strategy would emerge not from 'management' but from a group of people drawn from all areas of the hospital's activity. My methodological input restricted itself on this occasion simply to indicating that information systems exist to provide necessary support to those carrying out important tasks, and that this support can be sensibly defined only if there is a careful prior definition of the purposeful tasks. We would ask them to use their knowledge and experience to define the hospital's core tasks in a particular way, and use those definitions to work out what information was needed to support the people undertaking the tasks.

With Steve Clarke's help, since he knew all the people involved, each hospital was asked to nominate fifteen to twenty doctors, nurses and managers who would meet in groups of three or four to carry out the work. Each group would be asked to examine the core purpose, activities and information needs of several functions performed at the two hospital sites. These included such functions as surgery, medicine, nursing, pathology, anaesthetics, theatres, estates, business management, accounting and human resources. The teams were deliberately mixed, bringing together people from different functions but always including someone who worked in a function being examined. The group work was helped by facilitation by Steve Clarke, John Poulter or members of the IM and T (Information Management and Technology) departments at the two sites. Each month a joint workshop was held at which representatives of the groups described their progress and problems, with the three project facilitators using these meetings to monitor the extent to which the work as a whole was keeping its intended shape, and to assess whether additional help was needed. I found that my role at each of these meetings was always the same: to articulate afresh the whole process being followed, reminding the participants of what had been done so far, where we now were and where we were going next, and why. It may seem surprising that this emerged as necessary each month, but remember that the members of the groups were having to fit the group meetings into their very busy professional lives. No group member was relieved of any of his or her normal duties and responsibilities. In fact the whole participative study confirmed the familiar adage: if you want to get something done, ask a busy person! This may be a sad reflection on human nature, but this work certainly confirmed the insight on which the aphorism is based.

In addition to the group meetings and the monthly plenary workshops, the progress of the whole exercise was reviewed by a steering group consisting of directors and senior managers from the Hexham and Newcastle sites. Always the eye was on the clock, given the tight schedule ending in the September Board meeting at which the new strategy was to be presented.

When it came to expressing the functional activity of the hospital in SSM-style activity models, a mode of expressions which then makes relatively straightforward an analysis of what people carrying out the activities would need in the way of information support, we faced a dilemma. No one in the groups of hospital professionals was familiar with SSM and its activity modelling, and there was no time for, or value in expositions of SSM in any depth. On the other hand, working out coherent descriptions of purposeful activity is not easy without the intellectual discipline which building models from root definitions brings. In the circumstances of this study, however, the dilemma was relatively easily solved.

Had we been making a systems study of the RVI as a whole, its role in its changing context and the issues it faced, there is no doubt that it would have been necessary to explore many 'issue-based' models as well as ones mapping current structures (i.e., ones based on 'primary task' definitions). More time would have been needed for this (including time for in-depth cultural analysis via SSM's Analyses Two and Three) as well as the active involvement of many more people, including the RVI's senior medics and managers. However, in the context of the creation of 'an information strategy' we were trying to answer the questions: What IS does the RVI need in fulfilling its role as a large acute hospital, and how might IT enable those systems to be realized? This meant that in *this* particular study we could take existing organizational structure as given, and focus on primary task definitions of the core functions which an acute hospital has to fulfil in order to *be* such an organization. The solution to the dilemma, therefore, lay in my preparation, at several levels, of *generic* models relevant to being an acute hospital. These models, described below, were given to the groups with the advice that they use them as a starting point in any way they felt was useful to their deliberations: adopting them, adapting them, or using them as a base for models of their own. The exposition of SSM, apart from the fundamental position it takes with regard to information systems and their role, already discussed, needed then to consist only of an account of CATWOE as a means of enriching accounts of purposeful activity, together with a basic account of models as notional wholes in which purposeful activity, the result of a structure of linked activities, is monitored, and adapted if necessary, by using carefully thought out measures of performance: those measures covering at least the key instrumental criteria for efficacy, efficiency and effectiveness which are relevant to any expression of purposeful activity as a transformation process.

The fact that the models used in this study were all PT models stems from the explicitness of the question addressed: what information systems does the RVI need to fulfil its role as an acute hospital? In general a user of SSM would anticipate using both PT and issue-based (IB) models. In many cases an initial use of PT models quickly leads to IB models. This is because in many studies where issues await resolution IB models may seem most cogent. In this particular study PT models were sufficient. But in a study concerned, for example, with *implementing* an already-formulated information strategy, something which cuts across internal organization boundaries, IB models would almost certainly emerge as relevant right from the start.

Modelling

Since the object of the study was to develop an information strategy for the RVI as a single entity, an organizational whole, the first model built was a high-level account of the fundamental activity implied by the phrase 'an acute hospital'. In the NHS context a number of functions are obviously relevant to the expectations which people have of a hospital of this kind. Any such organization will be expected to deliver a range of services to patients referred to it by GPs or entering it as a result of accident or emergency. It will have to match its offered services to its capabilities, and to develop its services over time as a result of both the monitoring of its own performance and external changes – including developments in medical science and practice and policies imposed by the NHS Executive. At the time of the study an acute hospital was required to negotiate 'contracts' with purchasing health authorities, which brought with it many requirements for recording the delivery of health care, since hospitals themselves were a main source of the information needed by a *purchaser* in order to define its requirements for a particular population. Considerations of this kind suggest that a relevant 'primary task' root definition would be:

> A system, operating under a range of external influences, which in the light of a strategy based on its capabilities and costs, delivers services defined in 'contracts' with purchasers within the context of NHS norms and policies, that service delivery itself contributing to the on-going development of its strategy for service provision.

The CATWOE elements for such a definition can be defined as follows:

C those receiving hospital services; purchasers
A hospital professionals
T need for acute services   →   need for acute services met
W acute services may best be provided by an organization dedicated to developing and delivering such services
O hospital management board; NHS executive
E NHS structures and norms; the purchaser–provider split

The core criteria for monitoring and controlling such a system could be defined as:

- efficacy   demonstrable delivery of a portfolio of services of suitable quality
- efficiency   minimum use of resources (expressible in money and time)
- effectiveness   satisfaction of patients treated, purchasers and NHS Executive; contributions to hospital reputation (i.e., contributions to long-term viability)

As is frequently the case with the efficiency criterion, this would be judged not in absolute terms for a single period, but in terms of a trend over time: could the system demonstrate that it was now delivering more for a given resource use than it had been

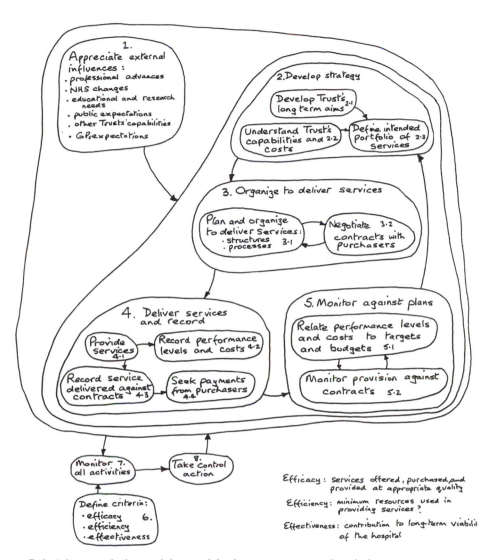

Figure 5.1 A low-resolution activity model relevant to an acute hospital

doing over the past few years? Note also that although this is, like all such definitions, a root definition of a *system* to do something . . . , since this is a primary task definition, with the system boundary coincidental with the organizational boundary of (in this study) the hospital located in Newcastle and Hexham, the language used for CATWOE and the three Es refers to the *hospital* as a systemic entity. This reflects that in choosing a primary task system as relevant in a particular study we are *consciously choosing to view* some organized chunk of the everyday world *as* a system.

A model meeting the requirements of the root definition and CATWOE is shown in

Figure 5.1. This is a low-resolution activity model relevant to any acute hospital in a purchaser-provider relationship. It consists of five main activities (the 'magical number' 7 minus 2 in this case!) in an operational sub-system, together with a monitoring and control sub-system in the now classic representation in a model of purposeful activity. Activities 2–5 are themselves expanded at a higher level (though still one far from being detailed) and are all carried out under the flock of external influences in activity 1. Activity 2 develops strategy. For example, in real life a big teaching hospital like the RVI with an international reputation in several research areas would have to decide whether its portfolios of surgical services, which would undoubtedly include doing hip replacements, should be expanded to include, say, heart transplants. Activity 3 covers the necessary organizing (covering both structures and processes) to provide services under negotiated 'contracts', while activity 4 covers what most people would regard as the core activity of an acute hospital: providing services to patients. Doing activities 2, 3 and 4, and monitoring that activity, would itself yield knowledge about the hospital's capabilities and costs; this, together with appreciation of the external influences of activity 1

Figure 5.2 An activity from Figure 5.1 expanded

would provide a rational contribution to the development of hospital strategy in activity 2: hence the internal feedback from activity 5 to activity 2.

The model in Figure 5.1 provides an overall, helicopter view of acute hospital activity and could define the main categories of IS needed by the RVI, but it is at too low a resolution level to engage with the considerations which will concern the hospital's professional staff and engage their energies and emotions as they go about their day-to-day work. For example, activity 4.1: Provide services, covers an enormous range of the happenings and activities which will, in the real situation, constitute the drama, turmoil and politics which make up the context of their work for those in the front line of hospital activity: the treatment of patients. Here, in a Primary Task root definition, we are concerned only with the core activities which *constitute* 'provide a service to patients' rather than with day-to-day *issues* which will arise concerning that provision. Nevertheless, the activity 'provide services' can usefully be expanded to provide a more detailed functional account of what 'provide services' entails. Given this, several activities in the model were expanded at a higher resolution level. Figure 5.2 expands activity 4.1 in the initial model for a particular clinical service. Given the position of the 4.1 (Provide services) activity in the hospital-level model, carrying out that activity would require a prior appreciation of the hospital's clinical capability and the requirements contained in the negotiated contracts for each particular service. This would make possible the activities which most would think of as core hospital activity: receive a request for the service, accept a patient, diagnose the patient's clinical problem, provide appropriate treatment and discharge the patient (activities 4.14 – 4.18 in Figure 5.2). All this would have to be recorded, and the treatment could call on a range of supporting services such as pathology laboratory tests, taking X-rays etc. The CATWOE analysis for the model in Figure 5.2 would be:

C patients, ancillary support services
A providers of a clinical service
T need for service S   →   need for service S met
W the capability and organization for professional provision of this service is available and appropriate
O senior hospital managers, including doctors
E NHS norms; hospital organization structure; contract requirements.

As a subsidiary model of a primary task (PT) parent, this model is by definition itself also a PT model: its boundary would map onto the boundary of a unit providing a particular clinical service, such as general surgery or an orthodontics service. Note, however, that if the present study were not restricted to PT models, as discussed above, a model like that in Figure 5.2 might itself provoke ideas about relevant *issue-based* models. For example, activities 4.13 and 4.19, concerned with establishing and using a range of ancillary support services, suggest that the hospital will repeatedly face the issue of deciding resource allocation between the numerous support services needed to underpin the treating of patients. Had we been doing a general systems study of the RVI, rather than a more focused study concerned only with an information strategy, an issue-based root definition of 'a system to allocate resources between ancillary support services' might well have been modelled as a highly 'relevant' system, one which would have explored the pattern of resource allocation and the criteria which might perhaps lead to increased investment in one service at the expense of another.

A certain amount of further generic modelling was carried out, expanding some of the activities of Figure 5.2 in yet more detail, but no complete models at this fourth resolution level were felt to be necessary. In general there is nothing to stop more and more detailed activity modelling, the limits being set by judgements about where lie the most problematical features of the situation under investigation. In principle it would be possible to model right down to the level of activities such as 'press computer key' or 'dip paint brush in tin of paint'. Experience over 30 years, however, has produced no examples of a need to model at more than two or three levels, the top level being typified by that of an organization taken as a whole.

The generic models were presented to the groups carrying out the present study as a starting point for their work. They served to emphasize the role of models in SSM as devices for structuring discussion, rather than would-be descriptions of anything in the real situation, and groups made use of them in any way they were comfortable with: using them, changing them or treating them as exemplars.

Defining Information Needs

Once the groups had models they were happy with, the next phase of the work could start, namely, using the models as statements of purposeful activity about which the hospital was serious, enabling attention to turn to the exploration of the information support needed by those undertaking the activity. This was done by the classic variant of SSM's 'comparison stage', used when the focus is on information rather than activity. Normally models are used to initiate and structure debate by asking activity-related questions such as: does this activity occur?; who does it?; how is it done?; when?; how is it judged? (i.e., how do people tell whether or not they are satisfied with it?) etc. When the focus is on information this questioning is extended to include questions of the kind: what information should be available to someone doing this activity?; what information is currently made available?; and: what information would be generated by doing this activity? To whom should it go? etc.

The period May/June was spent carrying out the information analysis, the group members bringing to that exercise both the prompting from the models and their own experience of information issues in their own work in the RVI.

Table 5.1 shows an illustrative comparison chart of the kind produced during the study, though for reasons of confidentiality its content does not derive directly from the

Table 5.1 – An illustrative comparison chart

Activities from the Model	How the activity is done	Measures of performance	Information needed	Information Support provided by	Information gaps and opportunities
4.1.4 and 4.1.5 Receive request for Service, and accept patient	Letter, phone call	Speed with which the Request is handled	Patient's details, clinical condition, and history Contract situation	PAS (Patient administration system)	Automatic generation of Letters to patient and Referrer Up-to-date contract Situation
4.1.6 Diagnose problem	Consider history Examine patient Conduct investigation	Medical audit	Case notes Results from investigations		Case notes often missing Much duplication of recording of patient's details Delays in receiving test results
4.1.7 Treat patient	Conduct procedures/ Operations Prescribe drugs	Medical audit	Availability of facilities (theatres, anaesthetists, etc) Drug effects and interactions	Theatre booking system	Systems not available at ward level
4.1.8 Discharge patient	Discharge summary, discharge letter	Speed with which produced	Post-treatment test results Availability of discharge facilities coding	PAS	Links to ongoing providers of care Automatic generation of discharge summaries and letters Support for Read coding

RVI. In conducting such a comparison the cogency attained stems from the column recording differences between current information provision and that required to support the activities in relevant models. These differences define gaps and opportunities and, in a study of this kind, provide the basis for the information strategy. Note that the gaps and opportunities emerge from *the discussion and debate* which the models stimulate and structure, not necessarily exclusively from the models as such. There is no point in being prissily purist about this, but if the discussion massively expanded the analysis based on models this might lead to querying the relevance of the models being used and a search for more relevant ones. This reinforces the point, which cannot be over-emphasized in soft systems thinking, that the models are only useful devices, and are not intended to be descriptions of reality.

The identification of information gaps and opportunities was being worked on by July, and in spite of the arrival of the main holiday period and the consequent 'dead' month of August, the new information strategy was delivered on schedule in September. In the lead up to this the 'information gaps and opportunities' columns of the comparison charts provided the basis for the evaluation of IT options, and also solutions which included both process definitions and technology. These were presented to a final workshop of the teams and then to the steering group prior to the presentation of the information strategy to the Trust's Board.

Given what had gone before, the actual development of the strategy was relatively straightforward. It entailed setting out how, given the existing technology, the gaps could be filled and the opportunities revealed exploited.

Learning from the Experience

This was one of the smoothest systems studies I have been associated with, by which I mean that it was one of the best-managed. Its intention was clear, its level – strategic – meant that it was never blown off course by any of the day-to-day issues arising in the life of the hospital, and its management by Steve Clarke and John Poulter ensured that momentum and enthusiasm were maintained throughout. For Steve and John this was a first experience with SSM; but they are both natural holistic thinkers and they immediately grasped its principles, finding that it provided a sense-making frame which added understanding to what they would do 'naturally'. (I always find that grasping SSM is much easier in a live situation than in a classroom, where the lack of any imperative to action encourages the convolution of rhetoric.)

Looking back at the experience retrospectively yields a number of lessons which can in principle help to reinforce or modify earlier learning, and may influence future studies. These lessons emerge in several different areas. Although the work in the RVI/Hexham hospital was problem-oriented rather than methodology-driven, it adopted a particular approach, that of SSM, and hence yields lessons concerning methodology. Its specific content concerned information systems and information technology, and hence there are also potential lessons in that field. These two areas are discussed in turn.

Methodology

Intellectually this study was relatively straightforward, with 'primary task' root definitions being used because the focus throughout was on the easily-defended logical view that a large acute hospital absolutely requires a coherent information strategy which will enable it rationally to develop the IT-based information systems which will enable it to fulfil its core role. I feel sure that the use of an explicit methodology to develop the strategy played a part in allowing a very tight schedule to be met, for such a use of methodology reduces the amount of irrelevant or aimless discussion. It also helps to generate enthusiasm among those doing the work. This stems from the participants feeling that here, for once, there is a well-defined task to be done and an organized way of going about it. The members of large complex organizations usually feel as if they are trying to sail a small boat through turbulent seas, with no definite course to follow and no knowledge of the direction from which the next onslaught will come. A methodology which feels natural rather than esoteric can help to counter this feeling.

For me the RVI experience did support the argument mounted in *Soft Systems Methodology in Action* (Checkland and Scholes, 1990 pp. 300–302, especially Figure 10.10) that the SSM process is one which feels familiar even when it is being used for the first time. This is because the SSM process resembles the shape of human discourse prior to taking action. There, we select a subject and make up sentences having different predicates; these may then be compared with each other and with perceived external reality, enabling judgements to be formed about what action to take. SSM offers a sharpened-up version of this, based on the use of systems ideas: 'predicates' become conceptual models, and comparison of them with each other and with perceived reality leads to action being taken.

Certainly in the RVI the participants' lack of knowledge of SSM never held up the work, and a number of them became interested in the methodology being followed. I believe that the participants' acceptance of the process being followed stemmed from the fact that it felt natural. Also the regular plenary meetings reinforced the feeling that a definite process was available, was being followed, and was leading to steady progress.

A specific example of how an explicit methodology which feels natural can help to stimulate and structure thinking occurred with a group who were considering the question of what is entailed in providing a nursing service in an acute hospital. CATWOE having been introduced at one of the early joint workshops, a group working towards a model of a system to provide a nursing service in the hospital decided that before modifying one of my generic models they would define the CATWOE elements. Starting with C (for 'Customer') and its question: who would be victims or beneficiaries of this system's activity? They immediately wrote down: patients. This reflected the motivation of those who choose to become nurses, and seemed the obvious answer. But as the group moved on to the other CATWOE elements a senior nurse in the group pulled them back; she had just realized that in the purchaser-provider contract situation then in place it could be argued that the answer was no longer simply 'patients'; it could also be defined as 'the hospital contracts manager'. Given the so-called 'internal market' in the NHS it could now be argued that the role of nurses was to provide precisely that amount and quality of nursing care which, being specified in the contract, would be paid for by the purchaser. Nor surprisingly, this led to a long and animated discussion within the group! For the senior nurse who brought this story to a joint (plenary) workshop, this incident explained why she was against the introduction of an internal market in health-care. She had had for some time a feeling of antipathy towards that aspect of the Government's NHS reforms, feeling that her professional autonomy as an experienced trained nurse was being chipped away. Now she understood and could clearly articulate the reason for her unease, thanks to the use of CATWOE.

This is an example of insight coming from a detail of methodology use. As far as the broader issue of tackling a problem situation using declared methodology is concerned, a number of participants found the exercise liberating in the sense that it gave them a broader-than-usual view of their role in the hospital. This was most cogently expressed by a medical consultant who told me that although he had worked in the RVI for many years, this study had given him, for the first time, a sense of the hospital activity as a whole, and his part in it. It is not at all unusual to find the use of SSM helping to free people from the tunnel vision which is hard to avoid if you are doing a specific job within one function of a large and complex organization.

Finally, at a methodological level, this experience provided another example of the lesson which is captured and expressed in the LUMAS model (Figure 4.11 of the previous chapter). In that model a methodology, as a set of principles (M), is embodied in a specific approach (A) which is taken to be appropriate for a particular set of users (U) in this particular situation (S). Use of A then generates learning (L), SSM being funda-mentally a learning system. Here the strategic nature of the problem addressed (create an information strategy), together with Steve Clarke's perception that SSM is at its most powerful when used participatively, led to an adaption of M to A which consisted of the mode of small-group working already described and the view that generic primary task models at three levels would here provide an adequate intellectual structure for the work. Had this intellectual structure proved inadequate, the joint workshops provided a mechanism by means of which this would have been recognized, enabling A to be suitably modified. In the event this was not necessary, and the initial embodiment of the principles of the methodology in A proved to be appropriate in this particular situation.

Note, finally, that the approach adopted, A, is defined in terms of both 'what' is to be done methodologically and 'how' the study will be conducted. The 'what' included the use of 'primary task' models followed by information analysis; the 'how' was the choice of small group working with monthly joint plenary workshops. This is another illustration of the already-learnt lesson that SSM can make use of the concept of working with models of purposeful activity in two different ways. The ubiquity of would-be purposeful action in human situations means that the 'problem content' can be usefully addressed by using such models to ask cogent questions of the perceived problem situation. But since *tackling* a problematical situation is itself a would-be purposeful action, it too can be examined using human-activity-system models. As indicated in Checkland (1981, pp. 238–241), Checkland and Scholes (1990, pp. 45–48) and Rodriguez-Ulloa (1988), the first model built in a study is often a model of 'a system to carry out the study'. (This usefully directs attention to the worldviews which will inform tackling the study.) In the case described here this thinking took place, but informally in the heads of the three facilitators; I used, but did not bother to put down on paper, a mental model of 'a system to do the study', such a model being especially useful to ensure that the 'monitoring and control' activities will – in the real situation – enable the study to flexibly respond, if necessary, to changing circumstances.

Information Systems and IT

In every case in which SSM is used it is likely that the specific focus and content of a study will yield lessons relevant to that content as well as methodological lessons. In this case the experience in Newcastle and Hexham was one of the studies which helped in building up a core concept of what we really mean when we use the ambiguous phrase 'an information system'. Such a concept is developed and illustrated by Checkland and Holwell (1998). The phrase is a poor one, since the broad consensus in the IS and IT field is that 'information' comes into existence when human beings attribute meaning to data (or, better, to *selected* data – or 'capta' – in which we have an interest). Since the creation of information is a human act, what we casually call 'information systems' are, more accurately, 'capta processing systems'. The crucial act is then the *selection* by people in an organization of the capta they have a concern for (out of the limitless masses of available data) in order to transform it into information in their context for their purposes (Checkland and Holwell, 1998, Chapters 3 and 4). Thus in this particular study the forty hospital professionals who did the work were – to express it precisely – engaged in defining relevant capta and their transformation into the information fundamentally necessary to function as a large acute hospital in the NHS under the purchaser-provider contract arrangements.

At a broader level the project provided a real-world example of the core nature of the process of information system development, a process which, according to the analysis by Checkland and Holwell (1998, Chapter 4 and Figure 4.9) must, in logic, start by exploring and defining the nature of the purposeful action which the IS will support, rather than from evaluation of IT possibilities. It was gratifying to find that all the participants with whom I discussed the matter thought this to be completely obvious. I am sure that it *is* obvious, but the astonishing fact is that the hegemony of IT is such that many organizations still make the fundamental mistake of initiating work on information systems by talking to IT vendors and buying computers and their ancillary technology. How much better armed they would be when entering dialogue with vendors if they took with them a well-thought-out account of the purposeful action which the IT-based IS will support!

Conclusion

The intention in this chapter has been to illustrate SSM by giving an account of its use. The account tries to describe the experience, but, of course, the experience itself was much richer than any account of it could be. This account has concentrated selectively on making the use of the methodology clear.

The study was successful in that the new information strategy was delivered on time and helped to bring about change in this particular situation. But the account of this 'successful' study is completely defenceless against assertions that it should have been done better, or quicker, or that some other approach would have been even more successful. Since the same human situation, located in time, cannot be investigated twice, methodology is *undecidable*: 'successes' might have been greater with some other approach, and 'failures' might be due to incompetence in using the methodology rather than to the methodology itself (Checkland, 1972; 1999). An individual can only test a methodology by seeing if he or she finds it useful. Ultimately, the only powerful argument in favour of SSM is that it has been found to be transferable to people beyond those who developed it, and has been used in several hundred projects around the world.

Acknowledgements

The author wishes to thank Mr. M. Robson, Executive Director of Finance and Information, Royal Victoria Infirmary and Associated Hospitals NHS Trust, Newcastle upon Tyne, for permission to use the descriptions of the work done at Newcastle as an example in this chapter. The authors also wish to record their appreciation of the contributions made by all of the many people who have been involved with this kind of work in many NHS Trusts. The interest and encouragement provided by Neil Devlin of the NHS IMG HISS Central Team is also much appreciated.

The author is grateful to the Leverhulme Trust for the award of an Emeritus Fellowship, during the period of which this and the previous chapter were prepared.

References

Checkland, P. (1982). An organized(?) research programme in information systems? Internal Discussion Paper 1/82, Department of Systems, Lancaster University.

Checkland, P. (1997a). 'Rhetoric and reality in contracting: research in and on the National Health Service', in *Contracting for Health: Quasi-markets and the NHS* (Eds. R. Flynn and G. Williams, (Oxford University Press, Oxford.

Checkland, P. (1997b). (New Maps of Knowledge), Valedictory Lecture, Lancaster University, 19 Nov. 1997 and *Systems Research*, **17**(S1), S59–S75.

Checkland, P. (1999). *Soft Systems Methodology: A 30-year Retrospective*, John Wiley & Sons, Ltd, Chichester.

Checkland, P., Clarke, S. and Poulter, J. (1996). 'The use of soft systems methodology for developing HISS and IM & T strategies in the NHS Trusts', *Healthcare Computing*, BJHC, Weybridge.

Checkland, P. and Holwell, S. (1998). *Information, Systems and Information Systems*, John Wiley & Sons, Ltd, Chichester.

Checkland, P. and Scholes, J. (1990 and 1999). *Soft Systems Methodology in Action*, John Wiley & Sons, Ltd, Chichester.

Flynn, R. and Williams, G. (Eds.) (1997). *Contracting for Health: Quasi-markets and the NHS*, Oxford University Press, Oxford.

Rivett, G. (1998). *From Cradle to Grave: Fifty Years of the NHS*, King's Fund Publishing, London.

Rodriguez-Ulloa, R.A. (1988). 'The problem-solving system: another problem content system', *Systems Practice*, **1**(3), 243–57.

Schon, D.A. (1983). *The Reflective Practitioner: How Professionals Think in Action*, Temple Smith, London.

Winter, M.C., Brown, D.H., and Checkland, P. (1995). 'A role for soft systems methodology in information systems development', *European Journal of Information Systems*, **4**, 130–42.

Webster, C. (1998). *The National Health Services: A Political History*, Oxford University Press, Oxford.

Webster, C. (2000). 'Cure or curse?' *The Guardian* 26.7.00.

6 *The Strategic Choice Approach*

John Friend

Introduction

This chapter introduces a distinctive approach to coping with complexity – the *strategic choice approach* – which deals with the interconnectedness of decision problems in an explicit yet selective way. The most distinctive feature of this approach is that it helps people working together to make more confident progress towards decisions by focusing their attention on possible ways of managing *uncertainty* as to what they should do next. Because it combines a concern for complexity with an emphasis on real time decision making, the strategic choice approach has been described as an approach to *planning under pressure* (Friend and Hickling, 1997).

Origins and applications

The origins of the strategic choice approach (sometimes abbreviated to SCA) are to be found in the experience of two pioneering research projects of the 1960's. In these, researchers with very different backgrounds worked together in observing strategic decision-makers in action and discussing with them the day to day dilemmas that they faced. One of these projects was concerned with communications in the building industry (Crichton, 1966), and the other with policy making in city government (Friend and Jessop, 1977). Both projects were conducted by mixed teams of operational research scientists and social scientists from the Tavistock Institute of Human Relations.

The insights obtained in the course of these two seminal projects were to provide foundations for the development of a set of relatively open, participatory methods for representing the structure of interrelated decision problems and the various sources of uncertainty – technical, political, structural – that made them difficult to address. Subsequently, these methods were put to the test in a programme of collaborative 'action research' projects, in which operational research scientists acted as advisers to teams of decision makers faced with particular planning tasks. Gradually, the use of these methods has spread, to the extent that they are now being used in addressing complex decision problems in many parts of the world, at a variety of scales and in a variety of organizational and inter-organizational settings (Friend, 1997).

The case study to be presented in Chapter 7 offers one example of a high level application to national policy making in the Netherlands. Yet the approach is a versatile one, which can also be applied quickly and informally at more modest levels of decision making. For the term strategic choice, in the sense to be used in this chapter, is intended to signify not so much a high level of decision making within some particular organizational framework, as a readiness to address interconnected decision problems and to manage uncertainty *in a strategic way*.

It is no accident that the principles of the strategic choice approach first emerged from research experience in two realms of decision making – the construction industry and city government – in which powers of decision are widely diffused, so that progress may depend on negotiations cutting across many areas of responsibility. Of course, complexity in the relationships among decision-makers is by no means absent within the conventional hierarchical control structure of the classical commercial firm. Yet the prevailing assumption has long been that it is the firm that should offer the model for the design of effective decision processes in any planning context. One important point that is demonstrated by the history of the strategic choice approach is that there is substantial scope for the transfer of innovation from other more diffuse organizational settings into the world of the commercial corporation; a scope which has for long been undervalued or ignored.

Philosophy: Managing Uncertainty in a Strategic Way

The origins of the approach to be presented in this chapter are more empirical than theoretical. They reflect not so much any idealized principles of decision making, as an explicit recognition of some of the ways in which people who face complex decision problems in practice learn to cope with the dilemmas of their work, even if only at an intuitive level.

In such situations, decision makers must learn to make judgements as to how broadly or closely to focus their attention; how to strike a balance between current commitment and future flexibility; and which other people should be brought into the decision process, at what stage and through what channels. When working under real-time pressures for commitment, the judgements and negotiations through which such choices are handled can have deep influences on the decisions made. Furthermore, they can shape the charting of a course through a labyrinth of possible organizational channels.

The strategic choice approach views the steering of any non-routine decision process as governed by perceptions of the relative importance to be attached to three broad types of *uncertainty*, each calling for a different type of response. These three categories of uncertainty can be introduced as follows:

Uncertainties About Our Working Environment: UE for short

This is the kind of uncertainty that can be managed through responses of a relatively *technical* nature: by surveys, research investigations, forecasts, requests for detailed estimation of costs. The form of the response can range from an informal telephone conversation with an expert at one extreme, to the initiation of an elaborate exercise in mathematical modelling at the other.

Uncertainties About Our Guiding Values: UV for short

This is the kind of uncertainty that calls for a more *political* response. This response might take the form of a request for policy guidance from a higher authority; a structured exercise to clarify declared objectives; or a programme of consultations among affected interests. Again, the level of response may vary from the most informal of soundings to the most elaborate of procedures to agree strategic goals.

Uncertainties About Choices on Related Agendas: UR for short

This is the kind of uncertainty that calls for a response in the form of further exploration of the *structural* links between the decision currently in view and others with which it appears to be linked. The call here may be to move to a broader planning perspective, or to negotiate or collaborate with other decision-makers. The wider the links, the more likely it becomes that some at least of the related choices will be 'owned' by other people, who may be working to different time horizons for decision.

This view of three primary types of uncertainty, calling for different kinds of response, is summarized in Figure 6.1. This picture can be seen as representing a snapshot view of

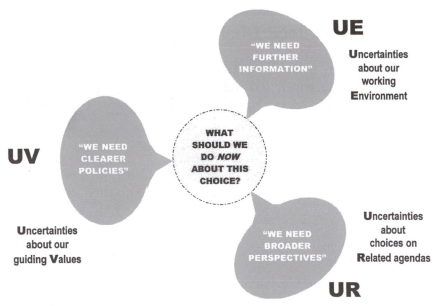

Figure 6.1 Three kinds of uncertainty in decision making

any moment at which one or more decision-makers are experiencing some degree of difficulty in deciding what they should do next. So the picture may appear to be a static one; yet it is one that has profound implications for the wider *dynamics* of any complex decision process.

It is tempting for any set of decision makers, faced with a complex and seemingly intractable decision problem, to agree that all three kinds of uncertainty are significant, and so that all should be vigorously addressed. However, this is a counsel of perfection, ignoring the costs and delays incurred by initiating different kinds of response – which may also yield different levels of *benefit* in terms of the confidence with which important decisions can be made. Research can be expensive and time consuming; so can consultation with affected interests; so too can large-scale planning exercises. Indeed it is not hard to find examples of situations in which major investments of effort in any of these directions have yielded disappointingly meagre results.

So decision-makers continually face important practical choices about how far to invest in different kinds of response to uncertainty. The return on any such investment can be conceived in terms of more confident decision making. The outlay can be viewed not only in terms of scarce resources such as money and demands on the attention of busy people, but also in terms of delays in the taking of decisions to which particular urgencies apply. The choice of how best to *manage uncertainty through time* is one that implicitly faces all decision-makers faced with complex problems. It is such choices that the strategic choice approach aims to articulate in a more explicit – and indeed strategic – way.

The Dynamics of Strategic Choice

Figure 6.2 presents a more dynamic view of any process of strategic choice, which will provide a framework within which to introduce a set of simple yet appropriate concepts and techniques. This framework distinguishes four complementary modes of decision-making, defined as follows:

- *The shaping mode:* When functioning in this mode, decision-makers are addressing concerns about the structure of the set of decision problems that they now face. They may be debating in what ways choices should be formulated, and how far one decision should be seen as linked to another. They may be considering whether their current focus should be enlarged or, conversely, whether a complex web of related problems should be split into more manageable parts.
- *The designing mode:* When functioning in this mode, the decision-makers are addressing concerns about what courses of action are feasible in relation to their current view of problem shape. They may be debating whether they have enough options in view, or whether there are design constraints of either a technical or a policy nature that might

restrict the scope for combining options from linked areas of choice in particular ways.

• *The comparing mode:* When functioning in this mode, the decision-makers are addressing concerns about the ways in which the implications of different courses of action should be compared. They may be considering a variety of different criteria, and debating in what ways assessments of consequences should be made. It is in this mode that uncertainties of the three types shown in Figure 6.1 come into sharpest focus, even though some of them may have emerged earlier.

• *The choosing mode:* When functioning in this mode, the focus for the decision-makers is on how to agree commitment to actions over time. This may mean considering not only whether there are some commitments to substantive action that could be undertaken straight away, but also in what ways the future process might be managed. It is in this mode that the dimension of time becomes critical, and strategies for managing uncertainty through time must be explored.

Figure 6.2 depicts a process in which opportunities exist to switch freely from work in any one of the four modes to work for a while in any of the others. Similarities can be seen between this general model of a decision process and other more familiar models in which a sequence of logical steps or stages is defined, often with feedback loops to allow for possible recursion to earlier stages. Yet observations of decision-making groups suggest that people working under pressure tend to switch their attention flexibly between

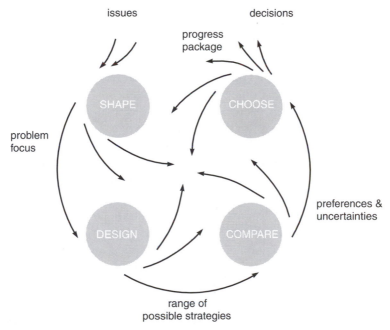

Figure 6.2 Four modes in any process of strategic choice

one mode and another in the more fluid and adaptive way suggested in Figure 6.2. This is clearly illustrated in the case presented by Allen Hickling in Chapter 7.

Sometimes, this switching process may seem to become entirely random, generating no more than a sense of going round in circles without any progress having been made. Yet at other times it may lead to a sharing of insights and perceptions that can make a valuable contribution in sustaining the sense of momentum within a decision-making group.

In terms of the framework of Figure 6.2, there is evidence that the majority of the more conventional management science techniques are addressed primarily to the activities of the designing and comparing modes. Some may be concerned with a search for an optimum within a closely defined problem structure, while others may be concerned with exploring the consequences of adopting alternative courses of action through the use of formal predictive models. In so far as uncertainties are explicitly considered, these are generally perceived as of the UE type, enabling them where possible to be expressed in terms of probability distributions. Yet it is now recognized that the probabilistic approach has severe limitations in coping with many of the forms of complexity and uncertainty encountered in practice. It is such limitations that the strategic choice approach is designed to overcome.

Introducing a Toolbox for Strategic Choice

The purpose of the next four sections is to introduce a set of basic concepts and methods that have come to form the basic 'toolbox' of the strategic choice approach, taking each of the four modes in turn. Because these tools are intended to support communication among decision-makers rather than back room analysis, many of them are graphical rather than quantitative in form. Together, they can be seen as offering an *appropriate* – as opposed to an advanced – technology of strategic choice.

Yet the strategic choice approach, as it has evolved through practice, has come to offer more than merely a *technology* to support strategic decision-making. As discussed in more depth in the core text on the approach (Friend and Hickling, 1997), it can be compared with other approaches not only in terms of its technology but also in terms of the three complementary facets of *organization*, *process* and *products*. It will therefore be briefly reviewed in these terms towards the end of this chapter.

There are many variations in the way that the strategic choice approach can be introduced in practice, and these too will be reviewed later in this chapter. In the case study of Chapter 7, Allen Hickling tells the story of an actual series of inter-ministerial workshop sessions held in the Netherlands to explore policy alternatives for the transport, storage and distribution of Liquid Petroleum Gas. This story is illustrated by photographs – accompanied by English translations – of the actual freehand graphs and other representations of problem structure drawn by the workshop facilitators on flipcharts at the time.

In this present chapter, a different example – commercial rather than governmental – will be used to introduce the key concepts and methods of the Strategic Choice Approach in a logical sequence. This case is also based on a real situation, which has been simplified for didactic purposes. The situation is one of a medium-sized company assembling instruments for small boats, here given the name MARINTEC[1]. This company currently faces a set of linked locational and marketing choices, some of them quite specific and urgent while others are broader and longer-term in their implications.

The case study approach is adopted in this chapter because it has been found unhelpful to introduce the core ideas – such as those of the decision area, the uncertainty area and the comparison areas – in a purely abstract form, devoid of any context. It has been found essential to convey something of the context of a realistic decision situation if the reader is to appreciate the variety, complexity, difficulty and potential ambiguity of the choices being addressed in a typical process of strategic choice.

Methods for Shaping

In a typical strategic choice workshop, the facilitator begins by helping the group to build up a shared picture of the main areas of choice that they see ahead of them. This process can generate considerable debate, which usually enables the participants to learn much about the views of others. The facilitator has a crucial role to play in listening to what is said, in asking questions for clarification, and in seeking agreement to a form of words to be written on the wall. This initial list contributes to a shared record of progress that will grow over the course of the workshop.

In the strategic choice approach, the starting point for the work of the shaping mode is the basic concept of the *decision area*; a concept that is simple in essence yet has demonstrated that it has wide application. For a decision area is no more than a description of any area of *choice* within which people involved in decision-making can conceive of more than one possible course of action that might be adopted, now or at some future time. It is of the essence of the decision area concept that it can be used to describe decision problems of many different kinds – and of different levels of importance and urgency – as a starting point from which to discuss the structural relationships among the choices to be made. This variety can be seen in the list of nine decision areas for Marintec[2] presented in Figure 6.3.

To give a little further background at this point, the core business of the company is supposed to be that of assembling instruments for use in small boats. Also, through a second factory on an adjacent site, it manufactures packaging materials both for its own use and for sale to other industrial customers. It will be noticed that some of the decision areas in the list of Figure 6.3 relate to specific current opportunities, while others

---

[1] I am grateful to Allen Hickling for the material on which this case is based

[2] In this and later Figures relating to the Marintec case, a flowing italic font is used to simulate the kind of easily legible handwriting in which this kind of information would normally be recorded by a facilitator on a flipchart

Decision Area	Label
Which operations to move from present site?	OPSMOVE?
When to invest in new packaging technology?	NEWTECH?
Whether to retain reserved site?	RESVD SITE?
Enter new instrument markets?	INST MKTS?
Expand market for packaging?	PACKMARKET?
Whether to lease a plot in new industrial park?	IND PARK?
Acquire local transport firm?	TRANSPORT?
Raise new capital?	NEWCAPITAL?
Change company name?	COMPY NAME?
....	

Figure 6.3 An initial set of decision areas for Marintec

describe broader policy issues some of which may have been under discussion for some time, yet may perhaps have acquired added urgency through recent events.

The process used to arrive at such a list can be varied according to the circumstances. In a typical workshop, a group of between six and twelve participants sits in a semicircle, facing the facilitator who has arranged a number of blank flipcharts side by side on a wall behind. The facilitator asks for suggestions of 'issues' that any of the participants see as relevant to the present situation – with the particular intention of identifying issues that can be seen as areas of choice for the participants. Most of these suggestions will then be added to the first list of *decision areas*, after discussion about how they might be most clearly worded, and any potential overlaps.

Some of the issues suggested may however be best recorded on a separate list of *uncertainty areas* – where they represent matters over which the participants seem to have little influence – or in another parallel list of criteria or *comparison areas*. This last category can be especially useful in recording issues relating to broad aspirations or goals; from experience, these may be more usefully introduced later as a means of making comparisons among options within more specific areas of choice.

In the list of Figure 6.3, each decision area is recorded first in terms of an agreed description, of sufficient length to describe clearly the nature of the choice. Then later a brief working label is added against each, usually on a Post-it type semi-adhesive sticker that can then be removed and transferred to another blank flip chart, as a starting point for the next stage of the shaping process.

This next stage involves the construction of what is called a *decision graph*, in which connecting lines are drawn between some pairs of decision areas but not others. Such a line is usually referred to simply as a *decision link* – or often simply as a *link* once the participants have a clear enough sense of what the concept means. Such a link merely indicates a working assumption that this particular pair of decisions is directly interrelated, in the sense that there is judged to be some possibility of a difference in preference if the two choices were considered together rather than one at a time. It is worth noting that

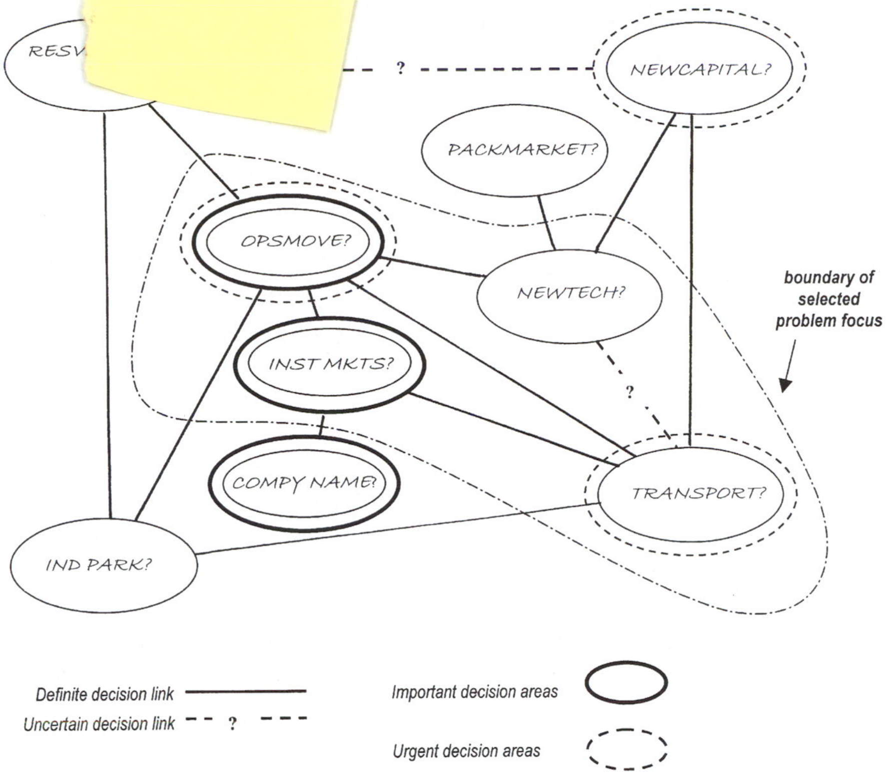

Figure 6.4 A decision graph for Marintec: typical flipchart format

the strategic choice approach differs from some other methods for mapping complexity in that such links are not normally represented as directional; that is, no use is made of arrowheads to indicate supposed causal or sequential links between one decision area and another.

Figure 6.4 shows an example of the type of decision graph that might be agreed after a period of group discussion among the participants in the Marintec workshop. This graph is normally drawn freehand by the facilitator – sometimes more than once – as shown by the photographs used to illustrate the actual case study of government policy-making in Chapter 7. The use of semi-adhesive stickers offers a useful aid to flexibility, especially in the early stages[3]. In Figure 6.4, as elsewhere in this chapter, the presentation has been tidied up, merely to make the content and structure of the graph more clear.

Among the conventions illustrated by the example of Figure 6.4 are the following:

- Different line styles (broken lines, or sometimes differences in colour) are used to record links about which there are elements of doubt or disagreement;

---

[3] Oval-shaped stickers of a convenient size are now available from *www.ovalmap.com*

- decision areas of especially high importance or urgency are identified – in this case by the use of double and/or broken boundaries, or perhaps by the use of different colours.
- an agreed choice of *problem focus*, selected by the group after discussion as a starting point for deeper investigation in the designing and comparing modes, is recorded by means of a boundary enveloping some subset of decision areas.

It is important that the facilitator should provide generous opportunities for group discussion between the stage of agreeing on an initial list of decision areas, as in Figure 6.3, and the stage of arriving at an agreed decision graph and a problem focus within that. The process of discussion can be varied according to circumstances, but a typical sequence is as follows:

- after working labels for all decision areas have been recorded on Post-it-type semi-adhesive stickers, these are transferred to a blank flipchart and rearranged so that any that are judged to be closely related are positioned close to each other;
- once the participants are broadly satisfied with an arrangement, pairs of decision areas that are judged to be directly linked are recorded by drawing connecting lines – using broken lines to indicate any doubts or disagreements over such decision links;
- additional boundaries or symbols, preferably in colour, are added to identify those decision areas that are agreed to be most important or most urgent (or both);
- the facilitator leads a discussion of which decision areas should be included within the agreed problem focus for the next stage of the work, taking into account considerations of importance; urgency; and intensity of links to other decision areas. These decision areas are then enclosed within a boundary.

There may be many different lines of reasoning behind the inclusion or exclusion of decision links. For example, the link in Figure 6.4 between the choice on retention of the reserved site and the choice of which operations to move might arise from an assumption that this reserved site would be suitable for relocation of the packaging factory, but not the instrument side of the business. Meanwhile, the link between the choice as to which operations to move, and the choice of when to invest in new packaging technology, might reflect an assumption that it would be uneconomic to install this technology at this time if the packaging operation were later to be relocated.

In general, the greater the number of decision areas, the more important it is to be sparing in the introduction of decision links. A graph in which every decision area appears to be connected to almost every other will not only be impenetrable to the eye; it will also contain less structural information of value to decision making than one in which links have been inserted in a more selective way.

In practice it is rarely advisable to select a focus of more than three or four decision areas as a basis from which to proceed to closer exploration in the designing and comparing modes; sometimes, indeed, there will be a case for choosing a focus of only one or two. In some contexts a useful means of proceeding is to select two or more different problem foci, with or without some overlap between them. These can then be assigned to different subgroups of participants for closer examination of alternatives and their implications. For the choice of focus can always be altered at a later stage, in keeping with the adaptive style of switching between modes indicated in Figure 6.2.

All the basic tools of the shaping mode – the decision area, the decision link, the decision graph, the problem focus – are simple enough in essence. Yet there can be considerable challenges in applying them effectively to real-life problems that are likely to be perceived differently by different participants in a decision-making group. A skilled facilitator will respond to these challenges by listening to doubts and disagreements, and by being ready to alter the developing picture of problem structure at any stage. For example, the labels of decision areas may then be struck through and replaced by improved wording – preferably leaving the original wording visible as a record of the learning that has taken place. Decision links and indicators of importance or urgency can also be changed at any time.

When working on flipcharts, the cumulative outcome of such changes can sometimes make the graph so untidy that it becomes worth redrawing it to make its structure more transparent, while retaining the earlier one beside it as part of the cumulative record of work done. The positions of some of the decision areas can then be altered, to make the pattern of connections clearer – in particular, by eliminating any crossovers between decision links that have no structural significance.

In Figure 6.5 below, the same decision graph is presented in the form of a computer display, using the conventions of the STRAD2 software[4], which has been developed as an additional resource for users of the strategic choice approach. This software has proved especially useful when working informally with small groups of decision-makers, or in a consultant/client interaction, without setting up a full-scale facilitated workshop. It also has a variety of other uses that will be briefly discussed at the end of this chapter. A note on Figure 6.5 outlines some of the additional facilities that the software offers.

When working on a computer with STRAD2, the procedures of the *focus window*, illustrated in Figure 6.5, enable decision areas to be repositioned by hand, with any that it is wished to exclude from current consideration dragged to an *ex graph* column to the left. In Figure 6.5, the strip below the graph records a sequence of previous versions of the decision graph, which may differ in terms of both size and layout. Where a graph contains too many decision areas and links for its structure to be visually clear, a set of focusing aids, accessible on a toolbar, can be used to recommend a possible choice of problem focus within it. However, as a matter of principle; the final choice of focus is left to the users, rather than treated as a matter for the computer alone. For it is vital that this choice should be viewed not as a matter of technicalities, but as necessarily involving elements of value judgement for the participants.

---

[4] For the latest information on this software, see the website www.btinternet.com/~stradspan/

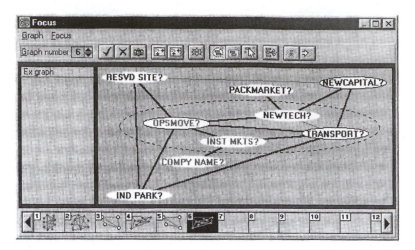

Note: less thick lines in a distinctive colour are used in STRAD2 to identify uncertain decision links.
Coloured labels are used to identify important decision areas, and boundaries to identify urgent
ones. The strip below the graph enables earlier versions of the graph to be displayed and edited.

Figure 6.5 A decision graph for Marintec: the focus window format in STRAD2

Methods for Designing

Once an agreed problem focus has been chosen, enclosing a manageable number of
decision areas, a next step is to agree a representative set of options within each decision
area. Then options from different decision areas within the focus can be examined in
pairs, so as to judge how far it is feasible to combine them with each other. This provides
a basis from which to generate a range of possible ways forward to carry forward for
comparison, using a logical approach to combinatorial design that has become known
as the *Analysis of Interconnected Decision Areas*, or *AIDA* for short[5].

Figure 6.6 illustrates the concept of a set of *options* within a decision area, with reference to the example of the focus of four linked decision areas for Marintec that was
selected in Figure 6.4.

In practice, it often happens that the choice of options within at least some of the
decision areas comes up for discussion – and may indeed be put on record – at the time
the decision areas themselves are first identified. For example, the opportunity to
acquire a particular local transport firm may appear to present two clear options of 'yes'
or 'no' – even though later discussion might throw up more subtle options, relating for
example to different bidding strategies.

Before finalizing a list of options within any decision area, it is important to consider
whether the options as so far specified are fully *representative* of the range of choice within

---

[5] See Luckman, J., 1967

Decision Area	Label	Options
Which operations to move from present site?	*OPSMOVE?*	☐ *Instruments* ☐ *Packaging* ☐ *Both*
Enter new instrument markets?	*INST MKTS?*	☐ *Agricultural* ☐ *Aircraft* ☐ *None*
When to invest in new packaging technology?	*NEWTECH?*	☐ *Now* ☐ *Later*
Acquire local transport firm?	*TRANSPORT?*	☐ *Yes* ☐ *No*

Figure 6.6 Generating options for the decision areas within the Marintec problem focus

that area, and also as far as possible *mutually exclusive*. For example, in the first decision area OPSMOVE?, Figure 6.6 assumes that there is an option of moving both operations as well as options of moving either on its own; while the 'null option' of moving neither is excluded because, in this case, the extent of congestion on the existing site makes some relocation essential. In contrast, in the decision area INST MKTS?, the option of entering *no* new instrument markets is included as realistic, but the option of entering more than one new market is excluded as too ambitious.

Where the definition of options is subtle, it is often worth recording both a careful description and a briefer label for working purposes – as in the case of decision areas. In practice, it is rarely found necessary to list more than four or five representative options within any decision area. Even when the range of options available may seem to be more open-ended, as where it is possible to choose any point along a continuous scale – the range can be expressed in terms of a few judiciously spaced points within the feasible range. Such a simplified representation might be considered unacceptable when applying more sophisticated techniques to a more precisely structured management control problem. Yet it can be quite adequate for a broad exploration of the more open-ended and evolving type of problem situation for which the strategic choice approach comes into its own.

Once a set of two or more options has been agreed in each decision area, the next step is to explore the *compatibility* of options between different decision areas within the problem focus, as shown in Figure 6.7. The format of the *option graph* illustrated here can be seen as an expanded version of that of the decision graph. In this case the option graph is restricted to the four decision areas in the problem focus of Figure 6.4 – the labels of the decision areas being now written rather than inside the boundaries so as to make room to enter the names of the options within them.

The expansion of any part of a decision graph into an option graph enables the pattern of decision links to be replaced by a pattern of what are called *option bars*,

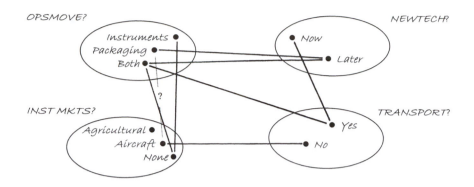

Links between options represent incompatible combinations or *option bars*

Figure 6.7 Expanding the problem focus within the Marintec decision graph into an option graph

INST MKTS?	*OPSMOVE?* Instrum'ts	Packag'g	Both
Agricultural	•	•	•
Aircraft	•	?	•
None	✗	•	✗

NEWTECH?	Instrum'ts	Packag'g	Both	INST MKTS? Agricult'l	Aircraft	None
Now	•	•	•	•	•	•
Later	•	✗	✗	•	•	•

TRANSPORT ?	Instrum'ts	Packag'g	Both	Agricult'l	Aircraft	None	NEWTECH? Now	Later
Yes	•	•	✗	•	•	•	✗	•
No	•	•	•	•	✗	•	•	•

✗ incompatible combination (option bar)
? compatibility doubtful
• compatible combination

Figure 6.8 A compatibility grid for the four decision areas within the Marintec problem focus

connecting combinations of options from different decision areas that are assumed to be *incompatible*[6] with each other. Sometimes, an option bar may represent a logical incompatibility; in other cases, it may be more judgemental, as when some combination is deemed to be too costly or to have other unacceptable consequences. As in the case of

---

[6] It might seem strange that the connecting lines on the option graph are used to indicate incompatible rather than compatible pairs of options. However, experience has confirmed that it is in practice usually only a minority of combinations that are ruled out by option bars; so a graph which shows incompatible rather than compatible combinations is in practice almost always simpler to draw and to interpret

links between decision areas, option bars that are doubtful or in dispute can be recorded as broken lines.

Figure 6.8 presents the same information on incompatibilities between options in an alternative tabular arrangement known as the *compatibility grid* or matrix. In this format, a definite option bar appears as a cross, while a doubtful one is represented by a question mark. All cells representing compatible pairings are here marked with a spot; alternatively, they may be left blank.

The two definite option bars linking options in OPSMOVE? and INST MKTS? have the effect of reducing the number of available combinations within these two decision areas from 9 to 7, of which one is doubtful. When the two options for NEWTECH? are added, in the second row of the grid, the overall number of possible combinations to be examined rises from 9 to 18. The further addition of the two options for TRANS-PORT? increases this total again to 36.

The more decision areas are added, the more complicated it becomes to find out how many combinations of options are feasible once the various option bars are taken into account. Although a formula[7] was devised by Luckman for arriving at a quick estimate, the only way to arrive at an exact enumeration is to take the decision areas in an agreed sequence and then follow methodically through all possible combinations, checking for feasibility at each stage. The logic of this procedure is shown in Figure 6.9.

The upper display of Figure 6.9 shows the outcome of the logical procedure of working systematically through the options in each decision area in the problem focus. First, the four decision areas are listed from left to right in any chosen sequence; in this case the sequence of Figure 6.6 is used. Then the options are considered in turn, checking at each point whether the latest option added is or is not compatible with any of the options in the decision areas appearing earlier in the sequence. The outcome of this procedure is that the 36 possible combinations are reduced to 11 – of which one is un-certain, because of the uncertainty recorded against the combination of the Packaging option in the OPSMOVE? decision area with the Aircraft option in INST MKTS?

The lower display of Figure 6.9 shows the logic of this procedure in more detail. It examines in turn all possible branches of what is sometimes called the *option tree*, terminating a branch with a cross as soon as an option bar is encountered. Any combination that encounters no option bars is then recorded as a feasible *decision scheme*[8].

The more compact format of Figure 6.9(a), in which with all the closed or 'dead' branches are omitted, provides a practical point of departure in proceeding towards comparisons, even though it does not reveal the full logic by which the range of feasible schemes was developed.

Figure 6.10 shows the same information as presented in Figure 6.9(a) in the format of STRAD2 software, using what is known as the *schemes window*. One of the benefits of introducing a computer program such as STRAD is that the range of paths available

---

[7] see Friend and Hickling (1997) pp. 154–5

[8] or a feasible strategy or plan. The term *decision scheme* – or *scheme* for short – is used here as it helps to indicate that the term is being used in a special sense, relating to a feasible combination of options in different decision areas

(a) Option tree showing all feasible decision schemes after taking into account option bars

OPSMOVE?	INST MKTS?	NEWTECH?	TRANSPORT?		count of decision schemes
Instruments	Agricultural	Now	No	✔	1
		Later	Yes	✔	2
			No	✔	3
	Aircraft	Now	No	✔	4
		Later	Yes	✔	5
			No	✔	6
Packaging	Agricultural	Now	No	✔	7
	?----Aircraft ----?------	Now ------- ?-----	No	?	8?
	None	Now	No	✔	9
Both	Agricultural	Now	No	✔	10
	Aircraft	Now	No	✔	11

(b) Full option tree showing excluded (dead) branches - *added to demonstrate logic of exclusion*

OPSMOVE?	INST MKTS?	NEWTECH?	TRANSPORT?		count of decision schemes
Instruments	Agricultural	Now	Yes	X	*(Yes with Now barred)*
			No	✔	1
		Later	Yes	✔	2
			No	✔	3
	Aircraft	Now	Yes	X	*(Yes with Now barred)*
			No	✔	4
		Later	Yes	✔	5
			No	✔	6
	None X				*(None with instruments barred)*
Packaging	Agricultural	Now	Yes	X	*(Yes with Now barred)*
			No	✔	7
		Later X			*(Later with Packaging barred)*
? ------	Aircraft ----- ?------	Now---- ?.----	Yes	X	*(Yes with Now barred)*
		?.----	No	?	8? *(Packaging with Aircraft?)*
		?---- Later X			*(Later with Packaging barred)*
	None	Now	Yes	X	*(Yes with Now barred)*
			No	✔	9
		Later X			*(Later with Packaging barred)*
Both	Agricultural	Now	Yes	X	*(Yes with Now barred)*
			No	✔	10
		Later X			*(Later with Both barred)*
	Aircraft	Now-	Yes	X	*(Yes with Now and Both barred)*
			No	✔	11
		Later X			*(Later with Both barred)*
	None X				*(None with Both barred)*

Figure 6.9 An option tree displaying all the feasible decision schemes for the Marintec problem focus

can be developed and displayed almost instantaneously. Also, the structure of the tree can quickly be displayed with the decision areas appearing in different sequences; and it is easy to test the sensitivity of the resulting range of choice to changes of assumptions about the availability or the mutual compatibility of specific options.

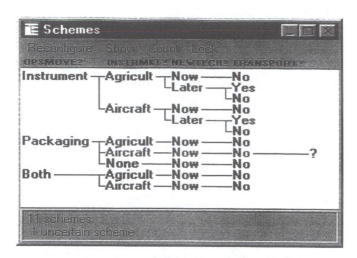

Note: menu options in STRAD2 enable the sequence of decision areas to be altered or shortened; uncertain or excluded schemes to be shown or hidden; the frequency of appearance of each option in a decision area to be counted; and a preferred option in the first few decision areas in the sequence to be chosen and "locked"

Figure 6.10 An option tree for Marintec developed using the STRAD2 software.

Experience in workshops over many years has shown how laborious it can be to follow through such logical operations without computer support – with risks of human error always to the fore. In such workshops, the advice is therefore to restrict a problem focus to no more than three decision areas at a time. Indeed, it has become quite usual to reduce the focus to no more than one or two decision areas.

The availability of computer support has brought a renewal of interest in the use of the AIDA design method as a means of generating quickly a relatively wide variety of ways forward within a focus containing several linked decision areas. This has the effect of opening up a wide 'decision space' within which multiple criteria can be brought to bear in comparing different ways forward. In turn, this creates a more open setting for decision-making than the familiar one where discussion focuses on one or two alternative proposals, each perhaps advocated by an interested party – leading to a confrontation rather than creative discussion in exploring mutually acceptable pathways.

When the number of decision schemes appears to become too large to handle, then the assumptions as to what combinations are admissible can be tightened up, or more doubtful options can be removed. Yet this process of cutting down the range of choice by introducing new constraints is one that it is unwise to pursue too far. For the purpose of work in the designing mode is not to come up with a single 'optimum' solution, but rather to generate a rich yet manageable set of possibilities amongst which explicit comparisons can be made, taking any significant sources of uncertainty into account.

Methods for Comparing

So the set of strategies to be compared at any point may range from a restricted set of options in a single decision area to a wider set of feasible schemes within a focus containing several linked decision areas. However wide or narrow the range of choice may be, the question arises as to how to move towards *comparisons* among them, as a starting point in building a basis for decisions. At the most basic level, where only two alternatives are to be compared, is one alternative clearly preferable to the other? Or is there so much uncertainty about this as to suggest that further explorations should be made before either of them is discarded?

The strategic choice approach recognises that choices of any significance almost invariably mean striking a balance between multiple criteria – especially where different participants in a workshop represent a range of divergent interests or 'stakeholders'. The general concept of a *comparison area* has been introduced into the strategic choice vocabulary, alongside those of the *decision area* and the *uncertainty area*. In the cut and thrust of a workshop, however, the shorter and more familiar term *criterion* is often used instead. The value in principle of the special term *comparison area* is that it need imply no more than a space within which comparisons may be made, whether intuitively or more systematically. The word *criterion*, on the other hand, suggests to some people a requirement to introduce some kind of linear scale with which to measure differences in performance.

An example of an initial set of five comparison areas that might be agreed in the case of the Marintec problem is presented in Figure 6.11. Such a list will normally be developed through debate among the participants. Among the questions raised may be whether further comparison areas should be added, or whether any of those already listed should be subdivided or amalgamated. In Marintec, for example, it might be agreed to add further areas relating to differences in profitability, or environmental impact, or flexibility in the face of foreseeable contingencies or risks. Then some participant might raise the question of whether acceptability to employees might be subdivided into two or more separate comparison areas to reflect differential impacts by length of service or by category of employee.

Where many decision schemes have been generated in the designing mode, it can become hard to compare them all simultaneously in terms of the full set of agreed criteria

Comparison Area	Label
Capital outlay:	CAPITAL:
Expansion potential:	EXPANSION:
Acceptability to employees:	EMPLOYEES:
Impact on internal communications:	COMMUNICN:
Impact on company image:	IMAGE:

Figure 6.11 A set of comparison areas for Marintec

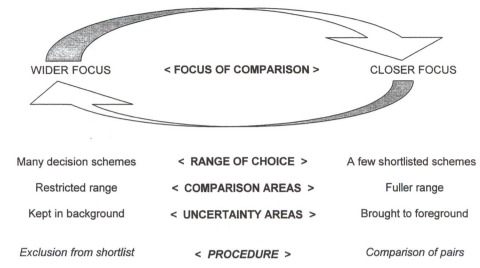

Figure 6.12 A Cyclic Approach to Comparison

– especially if it is intended to draw out significant information on areas of uncertainty in the process. Even the set of eleven decision schemes for Marintec displayed in Figure 6.9(a) can be seen as quite a large number to examine simultaneously using the full set of five comparison areas.

In strategic choice workshops, a *cyclic approach* to comparison is often adopted as a practical means of dealing with this problem of variety in comparing decision schemes. The principle of this is shown in Figure 6.12.

Figure 6.12 presents a general principle for dealing with a situation in which it is wished to compare many possible strategies or decision schemes. First, some quick and relatively informal procedure is introduced for narrowing the focus of comparison to a working shortlist containing a few of the more promising schemes. Then closer comparisons are made among successive *pairs* of alternatives within this shortlist, bringing key sources of uncertainty to the foreground. Sometimes, one scheme emerges as a clear preference; more often in practice, however, the preference across all the chosen criteria is less clear. Often, the discussion of difficulties yields fresh insights that suggest that the initial basis for shortlisting might be re-examined. So it may be agreed to go through a further cycle of shortlisting followed by pair comparison, taking these new insights into account. Where the decisions to be made have major resource or social implications, it may be worth repeating this kind of cycle many times.

When working with flipcharts in a workshop, it has become customary to resort to very crude yet transparent methods of shortlisting; methods that can be much refined where computer support is available. One such crude approach involves first assessing all the schemes quickly by asking for group judgements of their scores in a few at least of the more critical comparison areas. Where some monetary or other numerical scale of measurement already exists for a comparison area, this can be used as a means of calibration. In other cases, special interval scales can be devised and calibrated for the purpose. It is usual to use a distinctive symbol in each such comparison area, so as to discourage attempts to treat all assessments as commensurable. A practical instance of this kind of broad approach to comparison will be found in Figure 7.5 of Chapter 7.

In the case of Marintec, it might be agreed to compare the CAPITAL: impacts of schemes in terms of whatever currency unit applies in the context; while EXPANSION: impacts might be compared in terms of an estimated percentage increase in relation to the present Marintec market. Where no agreed scale exists, a pair of schemes judged to occupy the extremes of the range might be used to define a scale of four or five points within which all other schemes can be placed. For example, the scheme judged to bring the least disruption in terms of internal communication might be awarded a minimum score of one (*), and that bringing the greatest disruption awarded a maximum score of five, marked (*****). All other schemes can then be awarded scores at appropriate points within this interval range.

One simple yet transparent means of shortlisting is then to rule out all schemes that cross some threshold of acceptability, taking one comparison area at a time. For example, all schemes for Marintec requiring capital investment above some limit reflecting the company's current circumstances might be excluded; so might those with scores higher than, say, *** for disruption to internal communications. A different approach is to search for and discard any scheme that scores less highly than some other scheme – or at least no more highly – in terms of *each* of the selected comparison areas. In the language of multi-criteria analysis, the less advantageous scheme is said to be *dominated* by the other.

The use of the STRAD software enables more powerful methods of shortlisting to be adopted. These methods will not be described here; in principle, they entail developing a shortlist using several comparison areas in combination, after introducing a set of working assumptions about their relative value weightings. Whether using flipcharts or software, the object of any shortlisting process is the same. It is to generate a limited range of what appear to be relatively *promising* schemes – typically between three and six – within which closer comparisons between selected pairs can be made.

To guide such a process of pair comparison, a simple form of grid has been developed for the visual assessment of *comparative advantage* between options or decision schemes. In this format, one alternative – which may either be an option in a single decision area or a scheme covering several decision areas – appears on the left side and the other on the right. Figure 6.13 presents an example in which such a grid is used to compare two of the 11 schemes for Marintec that were presented in Figure 6.9. It is here supposed that these two schemes, together perhaps with a few others, have been selected from the eleven through a shortlisting process as discussed above – in the course of which a new numbering sequence is supposed to have been introduced[9].

---

[9] The schemes numbered in Figure 6.13 as 2 and 3 in the shortlist will be found numbered as 10 and 5 in Figure 6.9

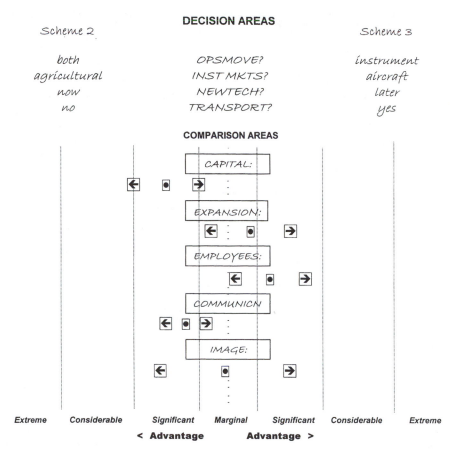

Figure 6.13 An advantage comparison grid for a selected pair of decision schemes for Marintec

The grid of Figure 6.13 is divided into vertical strips representing zones of *marginal, significant, considerable* and *extreme* advantage to either the alternative on the left or that on the right. In the centre is a feint vertical line representing *negligible* advantage to either alternative. Judgements can then be made of the expected level of advantage to either the left or the right, in a way that relates to similar judgements for other comparison areas entered elsewhere on the grid.

This overall advantage scale is deliberately not calibrated in terms of any numerical scale; rather, it is calibrated through a grading of zones based on adjectives in common use[10]. What is to be considered 'marginal', 'significant', 'considerable' or 'extreme' will of course vary with the context in which people are working. In a workshop, it may initially take some time to negotiate agreement on how to interpret these levels, until a shared sense of meaning develops.

[10] These adjectives have close counterparts in several European languages other than English

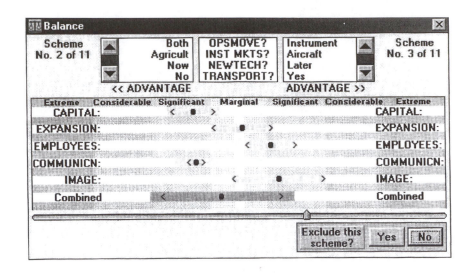

Note: In this window, further adjustments to positions and ranges can be made. The "combined" row presents the mean position of all the advantage assessments in the rows above; a formula is used to aggregate the ranges. A pointer can be placed at any advantage level at which it is wished to raise questions about exclusion of the alternative less likely to have a combined advantage over the other.

Figure 6.14 Comparing schemes for Marintec through the balance window of STRAD2

Indeed, an important part of the learning process in a workshop is to expose and record any differences of opinion on the relative importance of different comparison areas. These can then be recorded as uncertainty areas of type UV, in relation to the categories of Figure 6.1.

Figure 6.13 illustrates how, for each comparison area, it is possible to enter judgements of not only the *expected* level of advantage to one alternative or the other, but also of how wide a range of uncertainty is thought to exist on either side. When using flip-charts, small adhesive stickers are often used to place a single 'spot marker' and a pair of 'range markers' on the row corresponding to each comparison area. Their positions can then be changed easily in the course of discussion among the participants.

Figure 6.14 shows the STRAD2 equivalent of the advantage comparison grid of Figure 6.13 – known as the *balance window*[11]. It is possible on each side of this window to scroll down from one decision scheme to the next, so altering the scheme to be considered on either the left or the right. If the schemes have already been ranked in order of descending preference through some shortlisting process, then the most promising schemes – and so the most significant comparisons – will be displayed first.

---

[11] This is accessible at any time through a toolbar that allows rapid switches to be made across a set of eight *process windows*, two corresponding to each mode as shown in Figure 6.2. The *Overview* and *Focus windows* relate to the shaping mode; the *Compatibility* and *Schemes windows* to the designing mode; the *Assess* and *Balance windows* to the comparing mode; and the *Uncertainty* and *Progress windows* to the choosing mode

It will be noted that the balance window of STRAD includes a *combined advantage* row at the foot. Here the advantage assessments for the different comparison areas are brought together, using reasonable assumptions about additivity and statistical independence that are built into the program[12].

Sometimes, the end result of this process will be a conclusion that the overall balance of advantage lies clearly to one alternative or the other. More often, however, a substantial level of uncertainty will remain. The choice then arises of whether to carry out further pair comparisons; or to switch to further shaping or designing activities; or to proceed to the choosing mode, to discuss in what ways the key uncertainties might be managed as a means of making progress towards decisions.

Methods for Choosing

When switching from the comparing to the choosing mode, the question of how to manage uncertainty moves into the foreground. For any of the three types of uncertainty introduced in Figure 6.1 can get in the way of agreement on preferences as to choices within key decision areas. The most distinctive feature of the strategic choice approach is the framework that it provides within the choosing mode *for managing different types of uncertainty in a strategic way*.

Whether consciously or otherwise, people faced with complex and interconnected problems must find ways of managing uncertainty through time if they are to make sustained progress towards decisions. When the process is guided by the strategic choice approach, the critical areas of uncertainty tend to surface most clearly when the participants start focusing on comparisons of promising pairs of options or schemes. Yet, as indicated from the Marintec story so far, many areas of uncertainty may also have arisen during earlier work in the shaping and designing modes.

In a workshop, it is an important discipline to start recording all potentially significant areas of uncertainty on a separate flipchart as soon as they arise. This list will then gradually lengthen as work proceeds from mode to mode; and it may require rearrangement and consolidation from time to time. In the process, some issues earlier expressed as decision areas may be reformulated as uncertainty areas.

Among the stages at which new uncertainty areas may have been added to such a running record are:

- When encountering doubts over the capacity to choose within suggested decision areas *(shaping)*:
- When encountering doubts over the existence of links between pairs of decision areas *(shaping)*;

---

[12] The mid-point is the mean position of the mid-points of the range on each comparison area; the range is derived from the separate ranges using the statistical sum-of-squares principle

- When encountering doubts over the feasibility of options within decision areas *(designing)*;
- When encountering doubts over the compatibility of options between decision areas *(designing)*;
- When encountering doubts over judgements of advantage within a comparison area *(comparing)*;
- When encountering disagreements about the relative value weightings of comparison areas *(comparing)*.

Figure 6.15 lists a set of uncertainty areas that might have been built up, on one or more flipcharts, by an advanced stage of the Marintec workshop. Each is first described in full then, as in the case of a decision area, given a brief working label. So as to distinguish an uncertainty area from a decision area, a convention sometimes used is to place a question mark before rather than after the label.

Having agreed a working list of uncertainty areas, it is useful to try classifying them according to the three categories of Figure 6.1. The facilitator can now ask whether each seems to be of a kind which might be tackled by more technical forms of investigation (UE); or by explorations of a more political nature (UV); or by extending the problem focus to cover choices on other related agendas (UR). Sometimes, the classification of an uncertainty area may be unclear, because it embraces elements of more than one category. In that case, a mixed classification can be entered.

In Figure 6.15, a four-point scale has been introduced to grade the uncertainty areas for their relative importance, or *prominence*[13], in relation to the current focus of comparison. It is important to reassess this grading whenever the focus of comparison changes. For, especially when the focus has been narrowed down to a few selected pairs of promising schemes, a switch from one pair to another may alter significantly the relative prominence of the uncertainty areas.

The next question is what if anything might be done to reduce the level of uncertainty

Uncertainty Area	Label	Type	Prominence
? Growth potential of aircraft market	?AIRPOTL	UE	***
? Value of established maritime image	?VALIMAGE	UV	****
? Disposal of disused storage building	?STOREDISP	UR	***
? Gain from investment in new telecoms	?TELECOMS	UR/UE	**
? Extra cost to move instrument factory alone	?INSTMOVEX	UE	*
? What is policy value to company of growth	?VALGROWTH	UV	***
? Marketing strategy of chief competitor	?COMPETITOR	UR	**

Figure 6.15 A set of uncertainty areas for Marintec

[13] Earlier known as *salience* – see the discussion of Figure 7.8 of Chapter 7

Uncertainty Area	Exploratory Options		Cost	Delay	Gain
?VALIMAGE - value of established maritime image (UV) (****)	■	no action	...	...	...
	■	place on Board agenda	##	●●●	+
	✔	consult key directors	#	●●	++
?AIRPOTL - growth potential of aircraft market (UE) (***)	■	no action	...	...	...
	■	report from consultant	###	●●	++
	✔	phone an expert	#	●	++
?STOREDISP - disposal of disused storage building (UR) (***)	■	no action	...	...	...
	✔	open negotiation	##	●●	++
?VALGROWTH - policy value to company of growth (UV) (***)	✔	no action	...	...	...
	■	ask company owners	###	●●●	+

Figure 6.16 Comparing exploratory options in the more prominent uncertainty areas for Marintec

in the more prominent areas. Figure 6.16 illustrates one format that helps to stimulate discussion of this question[14].

On the left-hand side of Figure 6.16, the four most prominent of the seven uncertainty areas in Figure 6.15 are listed in descending order, with the type and the prominence score of each alongside. To the right of the display is recorded the outcome of discussions as to what *exploratory options* might be available. In a workshop, this information might be spread across two flipcharts mounted side by side.

As the example shows, there is always an option of taking no action to reduce the level of uncertainty in an uncertainty area. In Figure 6.16 this 'null option' is listed in each case, so as to demonstrate the principle as clearly as possible. However when working under pressure it may be omitted, so long as its existence as a reference point is borne in mind. The level of uncertainty in some areas may seem so irreducible that the null option offers the only realistic course; usually, however, one or more particular exploratory options can be conceived that might reduce the level of uncertainty to a significant degree.

Exploratory options might take the form of proposals for investigation (UE); for policy consultations (UV); or for some form of negotiation or joint planning with other parties (UR). Often, formal channels of response will spring to mind first: perhaps a debate in some official policy forum (UV) or the commissioning of some kind of systematic data analysis (UE). However, as suggested in the first two rows in Figure 6.16, in such cases options may also be available of adopting some more informal route. Often, such a route may yield good returns in terms of reducing uncertainty, while taking less time and perhaps incurring less cost. In many contexts, it may be important to view this concept

---

[14] An alternative format is that of the *uncertainty graph*, reflecting the format of Figure 1 – see Figure 7.8 of Chapter 7

of *cost* not only in terms of money, but also in other terms such as calls on the energies of busy people.

The columns at the right of Figure 6.16 show a set of three general criteria that are often used in strategic choice workshops to help in assessing the relative *resource-effectiveness* of different exploratory options. Here, different symbols are used to compare exploratory options to the 'no action' reference point for each of the following broad criteria:

- The COST of an option, whether gauged in monetary terms or in terms of opportunity cost;
- The DELAY that pursuit of the option would involve in the making of urgent decisions;
- The GAIN in confidence expected through a reduction in the prominence of this uncertainty area.

In the case of the ?VALIMAGE uncertainty area in Figure 6.16, a discussion around these three criteria could lead to agreement that an informal approach of consulting key directors might yield greater gain than the formal alternative of placing it on the board agenda – and do so more quickly and at less cost. This option might or might not also be agreed to be preferable to the option of taking no action at all.

As shown in Figure 6.16, the outcome of the discussion might be an agreement to adopt the less formal option within each of the first two uncertainty areas, and the option of negotiation within the third, while taking no action within the fourth. These agreements – recorded by check marks against these options in Figure 6.16 – then describe a deliberate strategy for managing uncertainty at this particular stage of the decision-making process.

Such an explicit discussion about ways of managing uncertainty can be especially worthwhile once work in the comparing mode has narrowed the range of choice down either to two or three promising schemes. Yet in practice a switch from comparing to choosing is sometimes agreed at an earlier stage when the choice remains more open, in order to view more clearly the challenges ahead.

Another important consideration in switching from comparing to choosing concerns the relative *urgency* of the decision areas within the selected problem focus. Such judgements may have already been made before selecting a problem focus, if the more urgent decision areas were then identified. Such earlier judgements may now need review in the light of changing circumstances. In choosing, they become significant in so far as they create opportunities to restrict the choice of early action to only the more urgent decision areas.

At this point, the opportunity arises to consider the relative merits of options in the more urgent decision areas in terms of the relative *flexibility of future choice* they allow in other decision areas. This can be done by rearranging the display of decision schemes so as to bring the more urgent decision areas to the front as illustrated in Figure 6.17. Here

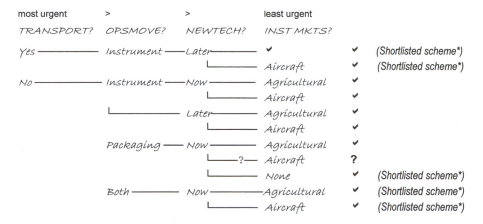

Structure of option tree as in Fig 6.9(a), but decision areas now ordered from left to right in sequence of decreasing urgency

* a shortlist of more promising decision schemes is here supposed to have been developed with reference to a restricted range of significant comparison areas, using the principles indicated in Figure 6.12

Figure 6.17 Comparing options in more urgent decision areas in Marintec for flexibility of future choice

the sequence of the option tree in Figure 6.9(a) is altered to bring to the front the two most urgent of the four decision areas within the selected problem focus, as was indicated in Figure 6.4. It is supposed here that the more urgent of these is TRANSPORT? as the choice here calls for a quick response to an opportunity that has suddenly arisen to acquire a particular local business.

If the number of decision areas is small, it is not too hard to alter the sequence of decision areas using a flipchart; with a larger number, this becomes harder without computer support. The outcome of such a rearrangement for Marintec is illustrated in Figure 6.17; this presents exactly the same information as Figure 6.9(a), but with the sequence changed to present the decision areas in descending order of urgency.

Figure 6.17 shows immediately the extent to which the 'Yes' option for transport restricts any future choice in both OPSMOVE? and NEWTECH? – at least on the assumptions currently made about option bars, which it might be wise to revisit at this stage. However the 'No' option for TRANSPORT? can be seen to leave open a much wider range of choice in these other decision areas.

If the more promising decision schemes have already been shortlisted using some or all of the comparison areas, then these can now be identified, as shown in Figure 6.17. So also can any schemes of doubtful feasibility. Figure 6.17 reveals that the first two schemes, both based on the 'Yes' option of acquiring the local transport firm, are judged to be promising, as are three of the nine based on the 'No' option.

What the participants choose to do next may depend on aspects of their situation not reflected in the analysis so far, such as any information on deadlines for acquiring the local transport business, or the likelihood of competing bids. For the present exposition, it will be supposed that they agree to forego the opportunity to bid for the transport business, and start discussing whether they should now select any option within the second decision area in the 'No' branch of the tree. In judging whether to select any of the three options available for OPSMOVE?, they can now take into account the number of shortlisted options remaining open for the third and fourth decision areas. This is a direct application of Rosenhead's robustness criterion, reflecting the capacity to choose in future among paths that currently come above some agreed threshold of acceptability.

The work of the choosing mode has now been brought to a point of climax, with attention focused simultaneously on the making of early decisions and on the management of uncertainty within a broad framework of discussion about how to make progress towards commitment through time. The process is an incremental one, in which critical points of commitment may arise in succession: for example, the agreed closing hour of a workshop, or an urgent requirement to present a set of recommendations to some group of responsible decision takers the following day.

At such a point, the current political context of the workshop becomes critical. It may now be important to draw together many aspects of the problem situation, including some choices that may have now become urgent in the light of recent developments, even though they may have been excluded from the particular problem focus selected for closer exploration within the workshop. The framework that is usually introduced to structure this task of synthesis is a form of grid that has become widely known as the *commitment package* grid. Recently, the phrase *Progress Package* has tended to supersede this, especially when such a grid is being developed on a trial basis. The term *commitment package*, with its more definitive ring, can then be reserved for such time as a preferred version is explicitly adopted as an agreed basis for commitment or recommendation to others.

An example of an agreed progress package for Marintec is presented in Figure 6.18 opposite.

Many variations of this kind of grid have been adopted in practical applications of the strategic choice approach[15]. Figure 6.18 shows a common variant in which the framework is divided vertically into two main parts, one relating to steps to be taken now and the other to steps to be deferred until some future time. Each section is subdivided into two columns relating to decision areas and uncertainty areas respectively. In a workshop, the NOW and FUTURE sections of the grid are usually drawn up on separate flipcharts mounted side by side, so as to give plenty of working space. The grid may also be subdivided horizontally into a sufficient number of rows to reflect areas of responsibility for different types of decisions. In the Marintec example, these are taken as departments; in many public policy contexts they may be separate organisations working within a joint planning framework.

---

[15] See Friend and Hickling, 1997, Chapter 8

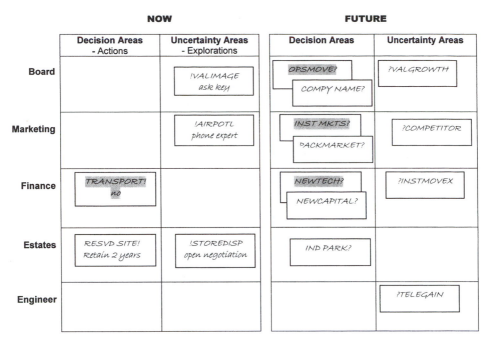

Labels of decision areas within current problem focus are shown **highlighted**

Figure 6.18 A progress package for Marintec

The use of Post-it-type stickers is recommended in placing the labels of decision areas and uncertainty areas within the grid, with any supporting information. The stickers can then be removed and repositioned flexibly as the discussion develops. In the Marintec case, the building of the package might start by positioning a sticker for TRANSPORT? in the relevant row of the first column, with the agreed 'No' option against it. Stickers for the other three decision areas in the current focus can then be positioned in the relevant rows of the third column. At this stage too, any of the other decision areas not included in the focus can also be positioned within the grid. Some of these – distinguished by normal rather than highlighted typeface in Figure 6.18 – may be brought forward to the first column, if they are sufficiently urgent and if, even without formal analysis, the choice of preferred option can be agreed.

Any of the uncertainty areas that have been generated can also now be positioned on stickers in either the second or the fourth column, according to areas of responsibility wherever these are agreed. Where an active exploratory option has been selected – as in the cases of ?VALIMAGE, ?AIRPOTL and ?STOREDISP in Figure 6.18 – then the uncertainty area can be positioned in the second rather than the fourth column, with the nature of the selected exploratory action indicated. There is an important logical link between the second column of the grid and the third. For the timing and other arrangements for addressing any decision areas currently deferred will normally be linked to the execution of any exploratory options addressed to uncertainty areas on which they critically depend.

In practice, it has become the usual practice to record in a structured form, either on the progress package grid or elsewhere, various types of additional information relating to the intended implementation of the more important of the agreed actions and explorations. In particular, answers can be recorded to the following types of implementation question:

WHO?   Questions of which person or group within an agency will be responsible.
WHEN?   Questions of scheduling or sequencing relating to a proposed action.
HOW?   Questions of procedure, budgetary provision or any formal approval to be sought.

Such information can also be recorded in relation to at least the more important of the decision areas to be addressed in future. In the case of some of the uncertainty areas for which no exploratory actions are agreed at this stage, arrangements for future monitoring or contingency planning may be specified.

Figure 6.19 shows how the concept of the progress package is reflected in the *progress window* of the STRAD2 software. Here, decision areas and uncertainty areas can be dragged from one part of the grid to another; and a *details window* for any area can be called up in which to record or view supporting information including implementation details. The software also enables users to generate and store alternative packages if they

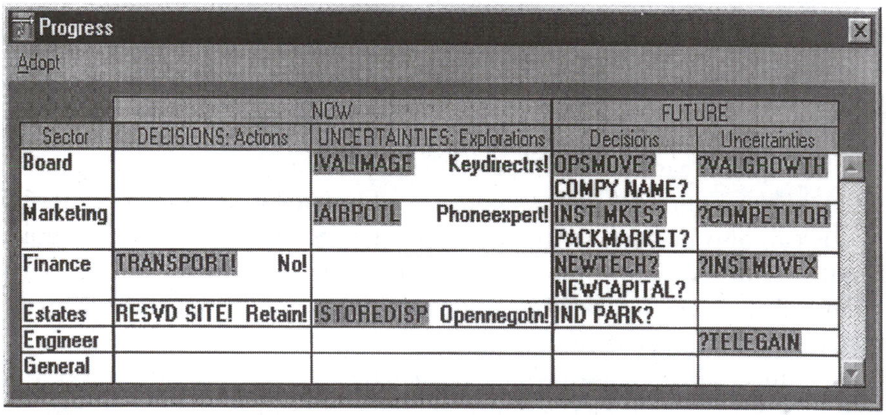

Progress				☒
Adopt				
		NOW	FUTURE	
Sector	DECISIONS: Actions	UNCERTAINTIES: Explorations	Decisions	Uncertainties
Board		!VALIMAGE Keydirectrs!	OPSMOVE? COMPY NAME?	?VALGROWTH
Marketing		!AIRPOTL Phoneexpert!	INST MKTS? PACKMARKET?	?COMPETITOR
Finance	TRANSPORT! No!		NEWTECH? NEWCAPITAL?	?INSTMOVEX
Estates	RESVD SITE! Retain!	!STOREDISP Opennegotn!	IND PARK?	
Engineer				?TELEGAIN
General				

Note: The position of any decision area or uncertainty area can be changed by dragging, so as to explore the effects of locking or unlocking actions or explorations. Double clicking on an area opens a details box in which any agreement on responsibility, timing and/or procedure for a proposed action or exploration can be recorded. An agreed progress package can then be adopted as a commitment, a recommendation or a strategic option.

Figure 6.19 Using the progress window of STRAD2 to develop a progress package for Marintec

wish, before formally adopting an agreed package as a basis for commitment or recommendation to others.

So the construction of a progress package does not necessarily mark a definitive end point in a process of strategic choice. For any deferred choices will still have to be addressed according to whatever deadlines, sequences and procedures have been agreed. Also, new decision areas may present themselves unexpectedly; new uncertainty areas may rise to the surface; and new participants may have a role to play in the continuing process of strategic choice, leading to further cycles of work in the shaping, designing, and comparing modes. For, the more complex the issues, the less realistic it becomes to suppose that the process of strategic choice will ever fully run its course.

Reviewing the Emphases of the Strategic Choice Approach

This concludes an introductory tour of the strategic choice approach, structured according to the four linked modes of shaping, designing, comparing and choosing as presented in Figure 6.2. A typical workshop begins with an identification of issues that are on the current agendas of the participants, and concludes with the development of an agreed progress package containing agreed actions and explorations to be taken back to those agendas. To this extent, the typical strategic choice workshop can be said to be *agenda linked*. This distinguishes it from other types of workshop that can be described as *agenda detached*, in that they aim to take people away from their day-to-day agendas so that they can start thinking at a broader, more systemic level.

The following five statements of emphases have been developed as a means of highlighting the main distinguishing features of the strategic choice approach:

more emphasis on **STRUCTURING COMMUNICATION** than on *REINFORCING EXPERTISE*
more emphasis on **FACILITATING DECISIONS**   than on *EXPLORING SYSTEMS*
more emphasis on **MANAGING UNCERTAINTY**   than on *ASSEMBLING INFORMATION*
more emphasis on **SUSTAINING PROGRESS**   than on *PRODUCING PLANS*
more emphasis on **FORMING CONNECTIONS**   than on *EXERCISING CONTROL*

Significantly, all these choices of emphasis draw on extensive experience in observing and subsequently supporting and facilitating decision-making groups, rather than on received theories of management or planning. This background is discussed more fully in the core text of the strategic choice approach (Friend and Hickling, 1997). Reference can also be made to two earlier books that report how the approach grew out of extensive field research in both corporate and inter-corporate contexts of group decision making (Friend and Jessop, 1977, Friend, Power and Yewlett 1974).

As will be apparent from the Marintec case, the practical application of the approach to complex and interrelated issues usually calls for extensive interaction among participants in workshop settings, with skilled guidance from a facilitator if progress towards agreed outputs is to be maintained. The nature of the judgements required is discussed more fully elsewhere (Friend and Hickling, 1997). In Chapters 4 and 9 of that book, the strategic choice approach is reviewed from the four complementary perspectives of *Technology, Organisation, Process* and *Products*. From each perspective it can be contrasted with other approaches to strategic decision making – especially with those more tightly structured approaches that tend to be designed for purposes of formal planning and control within large corporate organisations. The key differences can be summarized as follows:

In terms of *technology*, the strategic choice approach sets out to provide a set of tools not so much for backroom use by experts as to facilitate and structure *communication* among participants with varying perspectives and skills, and also often with varying account-abilities to outside interests. To this end, the emphasis is on methods that are transparent and make extensive use of graphical forms of representation – whether the medium be that of flipcharts or a computer display. Also important in a workshop is the arrange-ment of space and the availability of appropriate materials. An ideal room is large enough so that people can work informally, with tables pushed aside so that they can move freely. Usually, they sit in a semicircle, facing the facilitator. Behind the facilitator is a sufficient area of uncluttered wall space for progress to be continuously recorded, with flipcharts displayed side by side to form a developing picture of the problem struc-ture as it is being agreed through the discussion.

In terms of *organization*, the emphasis of the strategic choice approach is on temporary groupings that bring people together for a few hours at a time to interact intensively on issues of shared concern, cutting across more formal boundaries of departmental or corporate responsibility. Indeed, the lack of insistence on agreement on shared object-ives means that the approach has become recognized as particularly appropriate in contexts of inter-organizational planning of the kind that pervade the world of public policy, at levels ranging from the neighbourhood to the international stage.

In terms of *process*, the strategic choice approach emphasizes flexibility as opposed to a rigorous conformity to ordained procedures. This is illustrated by the many possible loops between modes shown in Figure 6.2. Often, this basic map of process is displayed on a flipchart as a point of reference during a workshop. The facilitator can then share with other participants an awareness of the need to balance progression towards early decision outputs against a readiness to loop back to earlier stages in the interests of group learning. In Chapter 9 of *Planning under Pressure*, a range of significant *process roles* is dis-cussed – including not only facilitation and recording roles within a workshop, but also roles relating to the work to be done between one workshop and the next.

In terms of *products*, it is important to recognize that a process of strategic choice can yield not only *visible products* in the shape of agreed actions and policy changes, but also more subtle *invisible products* in the perceptions of the individuals taking part. While visible progress is captured in the record of group progress on the growing array of flip-charts around the walls, the products of any workshop will also include more subtle

adaptations in the outlooks and appreciative judgements of some or all of the participants. Towards the end of a workshop session, it can be worth distributing simple evaluation sheets designed to bring these invisible products to the surface. After these are
collated, it can be important to allow plenty of time for group discussion of the lessons to
be learnt.

Continuous Development in the Strategic Choice Approach

Since the first experimental applications of the Strategic Choice Approach in the early
1970's, much further development has taken place not only in the methods themselves;
but also in the articulation of good practice guidelines and in the consolidation of the
underlying theory. Indeed in recent writings (Friend 1997) an argument has been developed for viewing the approach as helping to pave the way for an emergent science of
developmental decision making. This can be seen as drawing on a widespread existing *practice*
of developmental decision-making; to which the strategic choice approach aims to
provide operational support. The field of developmental decision science can be seen as
distinct from that of systems science, with its concern to take a more synoptic view; yet as
broader than that of classical decision science. For its concerns extend to address continually changing patterns of relationships both among areas for decision and among
decision-makers. It therefore offers a perspective within which the existing methods and
practices of the strategic choice approach can be critically reviewed, and the contributions of other complementary approaches can be evaluated.

    Many people have contributed to the evolution of the strategic choice approach over
more than three decades. Among them have been workshop participants engaged in
such varied fields as urban planning, business management, social policy, community
action and governmental and inter-governmental policy making, as well as the many
consultants and researchers who have at various times come to play facilitation or other
process management roles.

    What has now become the classical format of the strategic choice workshop, relying
on the use of flipcharts, pens and other such low-technology materials in a sparsely
furnished room, still remains the norm in most applications of the approach. Yet there
have been many significant adaptations to other contexts of decision making. At one
extreme, there have been applications by small informal groups working under pressure
in their own offices, where the setting up of any kind of special workshop environment
can scarcely be justified. At the other extreme, there have been adaptations to large and
diffuse aggregations of stakeholders in important areas of environmental and social
policy concern. Here, the variety of political and more technical roles is such that it cannot easily be accommodated in a single workshop or succession of workshops. Rather, it
calls for the design of more subtle developmental networks of interaction among stake-

holders, geared towards the delivery of a succession of products of different forms within agreed overall time schedules.

Some adaptations to the latter circumstances are presented in Chapter 11 of the second edition of *Planning under Pressure* (Friend and Hickling, 1997), drawing largely on the experience of Allen Hickling and his associates in large environmental policy projects in both western and eastern Europe. In the more microscopic context of the small 'intimate group', meeting casually in a conventional office environment, the use of the STRAD software, as illustrated in Figures 6.5, 6.10, 6.14 and 6.19, has been demonstrating its potential as an aid to on-line facilitation and recording.

It may seem surprising that the use of the computer to support the approach has so far been explored mainly in the informal setting of the small *ad hoc* group rather than in that of the more ambitious group workshop. Yet the special workshop environment calls for a greater level of advance organisation: dates must be reserved in many diaries, and a room with the right facilities must be made available.

Meanwhile, computer workstations have now become ubiquitous in most modern office environments. So, provided at least one member of an ad hoc group is familiar with the basic conventions of the software, files recording past progress on issues can quickly be retrieved so that the implications of more recent events and developments can be explored.

The software for strategic choice has recently been put to a growing range of additional uses. These range from the on-line recording of progress in a traditional strategic choice workshop, to the provision of interactive training courses in strategic choice methods, whether to experienced managers or consultants or to students of management, planning and public policy on the threshold of their careers. Meanwhile, there are other potential developments in the use of information technology in strategic choice which, at the time of writing, remain relatively unexplored.

The more immediate prospects include the development of procedures whereby individual members of a group can use linked workstations to enter independent inputs – for example, suggestions for new decision areas, or personal assessments of differences between options in agreed comparison areas. Computer-mediated methods would then have to be designed to merge these individual inputs and display the results. There already exist several computer-mediated group decision support systems that have made significant progress in this direction. More recently, there have also been experiments in strategic communication among participants in remote locations, with the World Wide Web demonstrating its increasing potential as a flexible vehicle for technological support.

A note of caution must be introduced before concluding that such developments will soon make the conventional 'low-tech' strategic choice workshop obsolete. The use of flipcharts in a workshop can always be replaced by wall projections from computer screens, as some modest experiments in the use of STRAD in this way have shown. Yet the risk is then that all eyes become drawn to the picture projected on the wall, reducing the incentive for participants to interact with each other in an informal way – and thereby placing in jeopardy some of the important invisible products of interactive working.

In conclusion, it is important to stress that the ideas presented in this chapter have already proved their value as a versatile form of support to strategic communication through numerous applications such as that reported in Chapter 7, without support from any kind of electronic resource. What is important about the strategic choice approach is that it is firmly rooted in an appreciation of the practical experiences of many decision-makers working across functional and organizational boundaries. In turn, the approach has shown how it can help such people respond to the ever-changing and imperfectly understood challenges that come their way during the course of their working lives.

References

Crichton, C. (ed.) (1966). *Interdependence and Uncertainty: a Study of the Building Industry*, Tavistock Publications, London.

Friend, J.K. (1997). 'Connective Planning: from Practice to Theory and Back', in *The Social Engagement of Social Science. Volume III: the Ecological Perspective* (Eds. E. Trist, F. Emery, and H. Murray), University of Pennsylvania Press, Philadelphia.

Friend, J.K. and Hickling, A. (1997). *Planning under Pressure: the Strategic Choice Approach*, 2nd ed., Butterworth-Heineman, Oxford. (1st ed., Pergamon, Oxford, 1987).

Friend, J.K. and Jessop, W.N. (1977). *Local Government and Strategic Choice*, 2nd ed. Pergamon, Oxford. (1st ed., Tavistock Publications, London, 1969).

Friend, J.K., Power, J.M., and Yewlett, C.J.L. (1974). *Public Planning: the Inter-Corporate Dimension*, Tavistock, London.

Luckman, J. (1967). 'An Approach to the Management of Design', *Operational Research Quarterly*, **18**, 345–58.

7 Gambling With Frozen Fire?

Allen Hickling

Disaster strikes

The 1978 disaster in the small Spanish town of San Carlos de la Rapita involved over 400 horrifying casualties. An LPG[1] lorry had crashed into the crowded Los Alfaques holiday campsite creating a ball of fire which consumed everything in its path. Nearly 200 died on the spot, and many of the injured were not to survive (*The Times*, 12 July 1978).

This was the first really serious accident with this highly dangerous, but otherwise very useful substance. It came at a time in The Netherlands when there was a trend towards increased use of LPG. The main causes were the rising price of naphtha (for which LPG is a substitute as a chemical feedstock), and expected surpluses of LPG on the world market. Dramatic increases were expected in the use of LPG as a chemical feedstock. It was also expected to take a larger share of the traditional market, serving as a substitute for petrol as a motor fuel. Plans had already been drawn up by private companies for the development of LPG terminals in several locations in The Netherlands. These were intended to receive shipments from the Middle East, which would then be used at facilities close to the terminal, or be transported to other users, including export to Germany.

But now, clearly, it was also a recognized hazard. The question had to be faced: 'Were we gambling with frozen fire?' (van de Graaf, 1985).

About the Presentation of this Case Study

This is a case study of the use of the strategic choice approach in practice. It is not an idealized fiction of what a project might have been like if the approach had been applied 'according to the book'. In this it is unlike the example used by John Friend in the previous chapter, which he cleaned up and adapted in order to present the strategic choice approach as clearly as possible. The experience is that tackling really difficult

---

[1] LPG stands for Liquefied Petroleum Gas. It consists mostly of propane or butane, and it can be a mixture of both. At room temperature under atmospheric pressure the substance is gaseous. It is transported and stored either under pressure (17 atm) or frozen (−50T)

problems is messy. However, to describe what really happened would be to condemn the reader to an almost impossible task akin to unravelling the proverbial Gordian knot. For, in working with the strategic choice approach in practice, the messiness is handled through its characteristic non-linear development of understanding, which takes various forms:

- the essential looping and switching between the modes of work;
- the incompleteness of analyses, which is an inevitable result of the fast learning process;
- the replication of effort caused by the need to work things through with different groups.

Actually, to talk about analysis at all may be misleading. The normal perception of analysis is that of working through a problem using predetermined methods, techniques, and procedures in a pre-established order, which produces the solution to that problem. But strategic choice is not like that – it is a dynamic learning process. Also there was a lot of work to be done. If one considers only the four-month period during which the strategic choice consultants were involved, there were probably 350 man-days put in by the team of eight alone. Of course not all of this could properly be described as strategic choice work – at least in the technical sense – and the consultants were only contracted for 30 man-days.

Thus only about fifteen days were spent in the typical interactive workshop sessions of strategic choice, which played a key role in directing the work undertaken in the intervening periods. Much of the team's time went into preparing working papers, consulting with colleagues and so on. Then there was the preparatory networking and 'back room' work which they had to do as an essential prerequisite to effective inter-active working.

In an attempt to portray the spirit of the strategic choice manner of working, photographs of the original documents have been used in conjunction with the translated figures. Two characteristics are noticeable:

- the hurried writing which is a direct result of trying to keep up with the interactive process (exacerbated for the reader of this case study by Dutch being the working language);
- the many erasures and the over-writing which came from the cyclic 'learning-by-doing' nature of the approach.

In this case, the difficulties of presenting a full story have been accommodated by excluding some of the cycles and describing separately parts which were actually overlapping in time. Those parts of the work selected for detailed description are followed through only as far as the evidence will allow. However, every attempt has been made to demonstrate the contribution each part made to the end result.

The Process of Updating the Interim Policy is Blocked

Four days after the disaster in Spain, there was an article about LPG in the *Sunday Times*. After another horrifying account of the accident itself, the situation was summed up as follows:

> And the rest of the industrial world, reminded of the growing stream of corrosive, poisonous, explosive and inflammatory substances constantly on the move past its front doors, is joltingly forced to ask: 'Could it happen here?'
>
> *(Sunday Times*, 16 July 1978)

The answer in The Netherlands was immediately positive. Public perception of the risks rose alarmingly. It soon became a hot political issue, and the Government reacted by setting up the necessary organization, and providing the necessary resources, to produce an immediate policy. In 1979 interim policy guidelines were laid down in a White Paper. This restricted further development by confining landing activities to the Rijnmond area, with distribution by pipeline. More importantly, in terms of this case study, the policy explicitly included time for further studies into the risks involved, and for further policy analysis to be carried out. The process was to be guided by an inter-ministerial Government Commission (RPC).

As early as the end of 1981 it was becoming clear that the interim policy would not stand up for long. Thus it was decided that the process of preparing a new policy should be started without delay. Consequently, a small project group was set up to service the Government Commission. This group was comprised of civil servants representing four very different sections of government. Each was a well-established centre of power representing interests which were difficult to satisfy in combination:

- the Ministry of Economic Affairs;
- the Ministry of Transport and Public Works;
- the Environmental Hygiene arm of the Ministry of Environmental Affairs;
- the Physical Planning arm of the Ministry of Environmental Affairs.

And work on the new policy began.

Extensive risk analyses had already been carried out for the Commission by recognized experts in the field, and towards the autumn of 1982 many of the results were already available. It had been expected that, at this point, the way forward would be reasonably clear-cut. In the event it was not. Although the results were not yet final, it was becoming clear that they would not be enough. In fact all three of the classic characteristics of a difficult decision problem were clearly evident – complexity, uncertainty, and conflict.

Thus, late in the autumn of 1982, the scene was set for a prime example of a blocked decision process – and further, one which had reached a state of urgency. Not only was there a lack of any real progress towards a proper policy, but the level of conflict in the project group was also causing no little concern. And time was running out. A situation which seems to be not uncommon in government policy making.

It was at this point that the Government Commission sought the advice of two decision process consultants – Arnold de Jong and Allen Hickling. These two, both experts in the use of the strategic choice approach, were consulted in the first instance about the management of uncertainty. However, other related difficulties, with respect to the complexity and conflict, soon became apparent.

A Decision Focus for the Shaping Mode

As might be expected after eighteen months of deliberation over a revised policy, much work had already been done. Among other things there was the on-going risk analysis. Although this was heavily focused on uncertainties about the environment (UE) as opposed to those about values (UV) or related areas of decision (UR), it was none the less identifying some of the more important uncertainties.

There was also the work of the project group itself. They had spent some considerable time defining the LPG 'system' in and through The Netherlands. In addition they had already submitted 96 alternative so-called scenarios (actually theoretically possible combinations of policies) to the Government Commission (RPC, 1982). This work had produced a useful level of understanding on which to base the shaping of the problem. Thus the first cycle through the shaping process was accomplished relatively quickly. However, much of the shaping work typical of strategic choice was never used in any formal way. In its place a sort of translation was carried out, from the hard systems-thinking framework, which had prevailed before, to one which was decision-centred. This is entirely consistent with the strategic choice philosophy – accepting that there are many sensible ways to approach a problem.

This background accounts for the way in which that earlier systems thinking is strongly reflected in the results at this stage (see the left-hand side of Figure 7.1), although in successive cycles this became less obvious (see the right-hand side of Figure 7.1). Had the starting point been different – as, more usually, when strategic choice is used from the beginning – then the decision graph would have been different also, probably with a wider variety of decision areas at various levels of concern.

Analysis of the decision graph was used to identify a problem focus for further work. The connectedness of the decision areas had already been used implicitly during the process of translation, and had produced five main possibilities. Urgency, importance, and controllability were used as criteria to provide the basis for further discrimination. The possible focus which had to do with market demand was easily identified as being uncontrollable, in the sense that it depended to a great extent on the future choices of others. In this way it was really a major uncertainty rather than a problem focus. As such

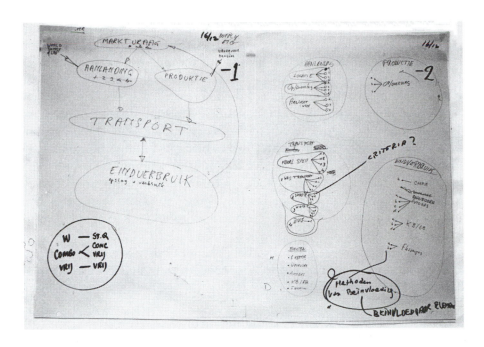

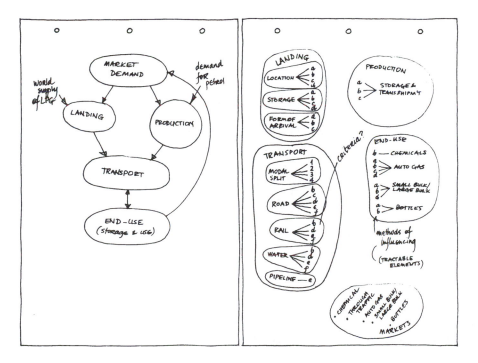

Figure 7.1 Shaping – the LPG system in decision graph form

it was felt to be a safe one to leave aside for the time being. There was, in any case, already an assumption that demand was going to increase, even though it would not reach the high levels earlier predicted. Indeed this was the reason for the project in the first place.

The other four possibilities represented the four main concerns of the project – the landing, storage, transportation, and use of LPG. Thus all of them would have to be addressed sooner or later. However, on the basis of the groups current understanding of the issues, it was relatively easy to identify two as being more important than the others. As it happened these two, the choice of location for landing areas and the choice of which transportation system to favour, were also urgent in a political sense, the Government Commission having said that they wanted to look at them next. This being the case, the other two (together with the one about the market) could clearly be left aside for the time being.

During this process a record was also being kept of other decision areas of a more operational nature, which were going to be of concern later, in effect leaving them aside as well. For example:

- the choice of how to handle safety in transhipment;
- the choice of type(s) of technical improvement to be fitted to ships using inland waterways;
- the choice of alignment for the proposed pipeline (through Noord Brabant or through Belgium);
- and so on.

Actually any listing provides in itself a sort of implicit problem focus. But any shaping at the operational level tended to be carried out more informally. When the lower levels of concern came into consideration, decision areas such as these were just brought into the work as they became relevant. As it happened, shaping at any level became the primary mode of work hardly at all in later cycles of the project. It was mostly carried out in the form of quick loops out of the other modes of the work, using the understanding achieved in earlier cycles as a basis for further development.

Each problem focus evolved over time, splitting and re-forming as the level of concern changed. For example, the transportation focus first evolved into one of 'modal split' (the balance between different forms of transport). Then in later cycles it split into two – one focused on 'mainstream' (bulk) transportation, and the other on 'diffused' (local) distribution. Soon after this, through traffic came back into consideration as a problem focus rather than an uncertainty, and was absorbed into the mainstream focus. And there were, of course, other activities in other modes of work taking place concurrently. It is impossible to work exclusively in one mode at a time. Quick loops into other modes were taking place frequently and, while the results were not immediately used in the shaping mode, the understanding gained did enable the work to be better directed. What is more, this work was not wasted. The results were recorded on the wall, along with the problem focus as it developed. In this way lists of aims, constraints, assumptions, and uncertainties were prepared for future use in other modes.

AIDA in the Designing and Comparing Modes

Throughout the shaping work, assumptions were being made as part of the formulation process. Many of these were, in effect, the result of quick loops into the design mode of working made to clarify the definition of decision areas. Examples of such assumptions were:

- that the existing terminal and landing point in the Westerschelde could not be closed, while that at Rijnmond could not be increased in area;
- that the choice of any particular landing location(s) would not exclude the landing at others where the LPG was to be used directly;
- that no form of transportation could be altogether excluded, thus any choice would be about which form(s) to encourage and which to discourage;
- and so on.

These, plus the more operational concerns which had been listed at the same time, were the starting point for the use of the Analysis of Interconnected Decision Areas (AIDA). This required more detailed development of the decision areas, the options within them, and the option bars between them.

Unfortunately it is impossible here to follow progress through more than one problem focus. For this, the one about transportation has been chosen. Taking the decision graph literally, it was thought that there would be five decision areas in the problem focus (see Figure 7.1): one each for choices about the pipeline; the railways; the waterways; and the road system – and one for the balance to be struck between them ('modal split'). In the event, each of these was quickly formulated as a cluster of four or five decision areas in its own right – a sort of lower level problem focus in fact.

The question of water transportation (canals) can be taken as an example. Early attempts to clarify the choices to be made led almost immediately to the identification of five separate decision areas (see Figure 7.2). In addition to the expected decision about the extent to which water transport should be used, there were choices to be faced about technical provisions on the vessels; physical improvements to the infrastructure; the introduction of selective routing; and the use of traffic control measures.

The group found it difficult to formulate the options within the decision areas at a consistently strategic level of abstraction. This is not uncommon. Options are not always discrete – nor mutually exclusive. However, it is necessary to start somewhere, even though it is inevitable that the results will have to be reworked almost immediately – and maybe several times. A form of representation was used here. For example, the two

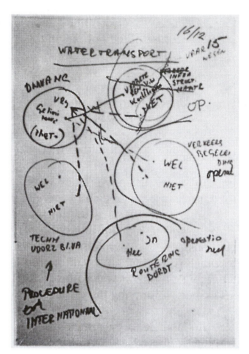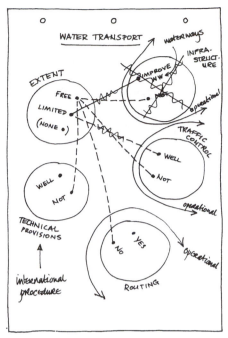

Figure 7.2 Designing – early option graph

options 'free' and 'limited' were used to represent the extent of use of water transport. Although the former may indeed have meant totally unconstrained – thus providing a discrete option – this was certainly not so of the latter. The limited option actually represented a number of different levels of constraint. (One could imagine, in another case, options such as 'very limited'; 'somewhat limited'; and 'slightly limited'.)

   In passing it should be mentioned that there was a third, discrete and mutually exclusive, option included in this decision area in the early stages. However, the extreme of prohibiting use of the canals for transportation of LPG ('none') was abandoned in the light of the assumption about impracticability which was listed earlier.

   The choice about improvements to the infrastructure was the next decision area to be considered. At the outset the options were expected to be composed of different sorts of improvement and areas of application. Thus one option was identified as improvements to the canals themselves. However, further analysis showed that other improvements could be better accommodated in the other decision areas, so that the only other option was to make no improvements ('none'). The structure of the options in the other three decision areas then followed this pattern, and they were all formulated in yes/no terms. As is quite usual, the placing of option bars proved particularly difficult initially. Often at a strategic level of policy choice there are no logical option bars at all. This was not the case here, but there was reasonable certainty about only one; it was agreed that expenditure on improvements to the waterways was definitely incompatible with limiting the use of water transport.

There was a feeling of uncertainty about all of the other five option bars, which were therefore shown with broken lines. But it was difficult to relate this to specific external uncertainties. It was more to do with the formulation as a whole. For example, while a specifically formulated 'no' traffic control option might have been considered incompatible with a higher level one of 'limited' water transport in some cases, it could not be totally excluded. It depended to a great extent on how it was to be combined with the other operational choices – about improving the infrastructure and selective routing.

It was concluded at this stage that two of the decision areas – those concerned with traffic control and routing – should be put aside for reintroduction later at an operational level. A third – the one about improving the infrastructure – was at first eliminated, but later reinstated (notice the crossing out, and then the crossing out of the crossing out, in Figure 7.2) also for use at the operational level. As time went on, this sort of analysis was carried out for all the clusters within the transportation problem focus. Some were more fully worked out than others – not always because they were inherently easier, but more due to the 'learning-by-doing' effect.

One of the more difficult ones was that about 'modal split'. This later turned out to be the only truly strategic level choice to do with transportation, and some of the difficulties of formulating options at this broad level began to emerge (see Figure 7.3). One common way of handling this sort of difficulty is through use of representation. Thus the 'free' and 'limited' options, referring to the extent of use of water transport, were used again. However, another way of handling the difficulty is to concentrate on what one can actually do. The two options 'consciously controlled' and 'not consciously controlled' with respect to the railways, are of this type.

There is a danger that concentrating on what can be done can easily lead to formulation at too specific a level. For example, the options for the pipeline were formulated in terms of which of several alignments it could take, rather than the more strategic choice of whether to go ahead with one or not. The purpose of showing this clearly incomplete part of the analysis is to demonstrate the value of 'learning by doing'. It is important to move ahead quickly simply because it speeds up the learning effect – especially in group situations. The work shown in Figure 7.3 also serves as a good example of how any analysis should be abandoned as soon as the learning effect drops off. No further work was necessary to draw two sorts of conclusion – one was visible and concerned with the content of the problem, and the other invisible and concerned with the process. The former was simply that it is not sensible to adopt the promotion of a pipeline without limiting transportation by rail and water, and vice versa. The latter was that any formulation of the modal split choice would probably require four decision areas. And, although the options within them would have to be at a relatively high level of abstraction, they might need to be based on more detailed analysis in the first instance.

This learning was a signal for the start of a second cycle through the design mode. But at this point once again, in the interests of simplicity and given the space available, the

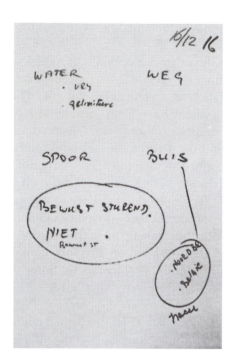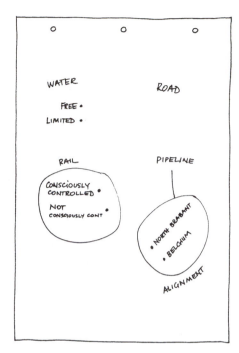

Figure 7.3 Designing – early option graph (modal split)

full analysis has to be represented by only a part. For these purposes it has been chosen to pick up again on the choices surrounding the use of water transport. In the following cycle, three decision areas were developed out of the original five (see Figure 7.4). The one about the extent to which water transport would be used came through unchanged. The other four, which had been posed at a more operational level, were reformulated as two at a broader level. One decision area was designed to embrace technical improvements of all sorts, including physical improvements to the canals as well as engineering changes on the vessels and other apparatus. The second dealt with the selection of routes, which included the possibility of traffic control systems.

The options changed little, although the possibility of 'no water transport' at all was finally omitted from the decision area about extent of use. The other two retained their basic 'yes'/'no' form, but took on a considerably different meaning with the redefinition of their decision areas. Two option bars were identified. What was not carried out was their annotation – keeping track of the logic on which they were based – probably in the interests of moving ahead fast at this stage. However, it is reasonably easy to reconstruct one argument: that the restriction of traffic to specified canals would hardly be consistent with free use of water transport. And the argument underlying the second option bar was similarly straightforward. The requirement of expensive technical upgrading of the vessels and other privately owned apparatus would be resisted strongly by their owners if, at the same time, their operations were to be limited. The resulting decision schemes were listed on the same sheet of paper – and as it was such a simple option graph, this was done directly as an option table. More usually, if this is done at all, it is via an option tree which is easier to construct.

At this point the group chose to compare these decision schemes. Early work on comparison areas had taken the form of lists of national policies relevant to the project. Some were very broad and represented the basic rationale for the project as such. For example:

- energy saving and conservation;
- the limitation of air pollution;
- the promotion of economic development;
- and so on.

These were so fundamental that they were more in the nature of implicit constraints operating throughout the whole project – especially in the formulation of decision areas, options, and option bars. Others, which proved to be more applicable to the LPG problem, were more relevant to the work in the comparing mode. For example:

- the promotion of public safety;
- the promotion of diversification in sources of energy and raw materials;
- maintenance of the Dutch international position in the area of transportation;
- and so on.

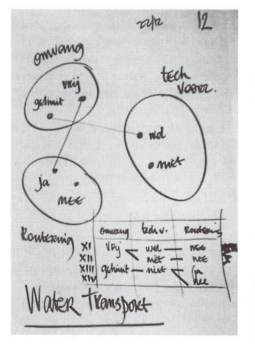 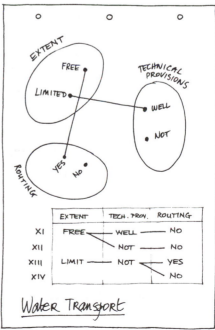

Figure 7.4 Designing – option graph and table (water transportation)

This earlier work was taken up again at this point, and formed the basis for a set of comparison areas for the emerging decision schemes concerning transportation. These areas were the reduction of risk; flexibility in loading; transportation costs; effects on the Dutch economic position; and the demand on space – the last two being typical of criteria used throughout the Dutch National Government.

The comparison table formed by these comparison areas and the decision schemes (see Figure 7.5) was filled in as a group process. The source of knowledge used was the current level of understanding and common sense held by the participants, enhanced by the synergy created through the interactive work style. This analysis took place in at least two cycles, one in which the main body of the table was completed, and another which can be seen in the workings on the extreme right. No numerical quantification was attempted; symbols representing relative effect were considered more appropriate to the rigour (or lack of it) of the exercise. The aim was not to select one best solution, but rather to find a number of good decision schemes for further analysis.

Looking now at only the transportation decision schemes, and taking the 'reduction of risk' comparison area as an example, the larger the black spot the greater was the estimated reduction in risk. Thus the decision scheme now identified as XII (see also Figure 7.4), allowing unlimited use of water transport with no special improvements of any sort, was given a very small spot indicating a very low rating with virtually no reduction whatsoever. On the other hand, the group rated the installation of technical improvements very highly, and decision scheme XI was given a correspondingly large spot.

A similar exercise was carried out for each comparison area in turn. Notice that the use of different symbols petered out after a while, and simple rankings took their place. These rankings, carried out for one comparison area at a time, are used extensively in strategic choice. The rank order is listed within the table – here numbered in reverse order simply because that is the way the group wanted to do it (the first is numbered '4', the second '3', and so on).

Understanding was recorded as it developed, even though it may not have been immediately relevant. Examples are the note attached to decision scheme XII, which was actually added later, and the question marks which can be seen in the comparison table. The latter indicated that the group was finding it very difficult to assess the transportation costs of decision schemes XI and XII, and attributed this to uncertainty. The exact nature of the uncertainty was not shown, because it was added separately to the growing list of those to be managed later.

There followed a simple evaluation to derive a working shortlist. Close inspection of these results enabled the group to identify decision scheme XII as being substantially inferior to decision scheme XI. Further, decision schemes XIII and XIV were seen to be dominated by decision scheme XI. This is not always a reliable criterion for reducing the number of alternatives under consideration, but it is a useful guide. In this case they were also thought to be so consistently low-scoring across all the comparison areas that they were crossed out. On second thoughts, however, this meant that limitation of water

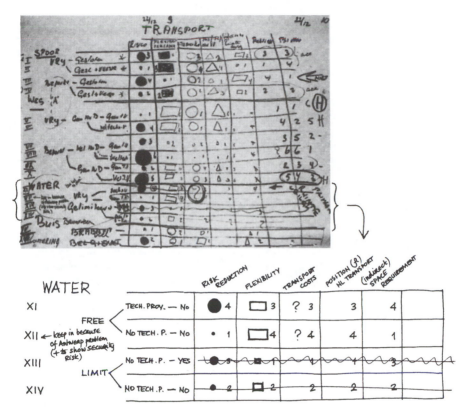

Figure 7.5 Comparing – preliminary work on decision schemes (with a focus on water transport)

transport was completely eliminated as an option, and the group was not ready for that yet. Consequently, alternative XIII, limitation of traffic by allowing the use of only selected routes, was brought back in again – hence the crossing out of the first crossing out. Thus decision schemes XI and XIII were carried forward for further analysis.

When this sort of analysis had been carried out for all four forms of transportation, the remaining decision schemes for each were used as options in a higher level option graph for the modal split question. In this way decision schemes XI and XIII were entered as options in the water transport decision area – with scheme XII being brought back in later (see Figure 7.6).

The work had now reached a stage where keeping track of the argumentation was beginning to be more important. The options were based on considerable analysis, and each simple Roman numeral represented a quite detailed definition. (For example, 'XI' meant promoting free use of the waterways system, with the safety of vessels controlled only via regulations concerning technical provision.)

The option bars now also needed to be clearly defined. The underlying logic of each was recorded and linked to the relevant bar(s) by a code letter. This simplified the

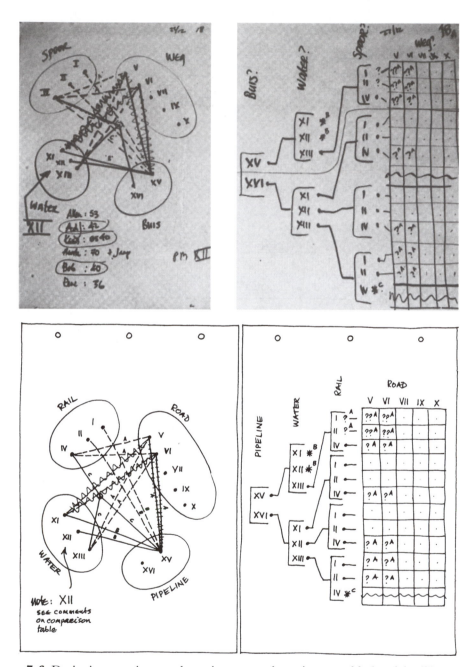

Figure 7.6 Designing – option graph, option tree and consistency table (model split)

recording process where a number of bars were supported by the same argument. For example:

A There was uncertainty about the viability of putting all transportation on to the road system.
B Promotion of two forms of mainstream transportation at the same time would have been counter-productive (e.g., pipeline versus water transport).

There was also a special form of option bar – a sort of three-way bar which connected options in three separate decision areas, meaning that all three used together would not work, although any one or two out of the three would be feasible. In this case the argument was as follows:

C The limitation of all three forms of bulk transportation together would provide too low a level of service.

The decision schemes for the three 'heavy' transportation decision areas – pipeline, water, and rail – were listed in the form of an option tree. In this case, in order to save space, the fourth decision area to do with roads was added using a consistency matrix – a variation on the compatibility matrix described in the previous chapter. While this use of the consistency matrix gave an indication of how many decision schemes to expect, and the pattern of compatibilities between the options, it did not make it easy to carry the analysis forward into comparison. But it did help in looping back into the shaping mode to reformulate the problem focus, so the chosen graphic structure served the team well.

They concluded from the analysis so far, and through discussion around it, that two main forms of distribution had to be provided for. One, described as 'mainstream', had to do with the major bulk transport flows to a few principal locations, while the other would serve a more diffuse network of destinations. Each of these now formed a separate problem focus. For common-sense reasons the pipeline was dropped from consideration for diffuse transportation, and to avoid traffic congestion road transport was dropped for mainstream transportation.

The next cycle of work using AIDA in the design and comparing modes was one of the last concerning policy about modal split, and the results were presented to the Government Commission in one of several working papers (RPC, 1983a). But, once again, it is impossible to follow the analysis completely through in all its aspects, and a part only must stand in as an example. For this purpose the analysis of the modal split for local transportation has been chosen.

Of the four decision areas in the analysis up to this point, two remained more-or-less unchanged – but now the group felt confident in going back to more broadly formulated (although paradoxically better defined) options. Thus the 'free' and 'limited' options reappear for the use of roads and rail (see Figure 7.7). The pipeline decision area had by this time fallen out of consideration. The fourth, about the inland waterways, was

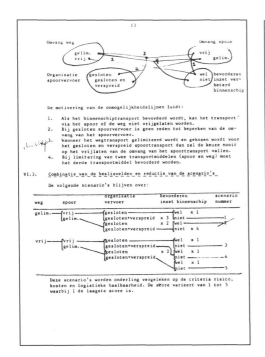
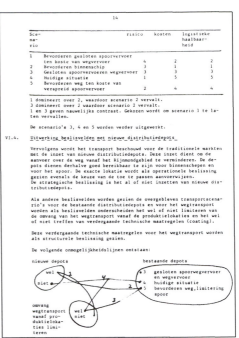
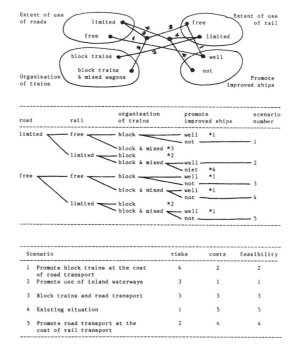

Figure 7.7 Interim presentation of local transport decision schemes (option graph, option tree and comparison table)

reformulated as a choice of whether to promote the technical improvements. An additional railway decision area concerning the organization of trains was introduced ('block trains' (all LPG) or 'block trains and mixed wagons').

The resulting decision schemes, of which there were five, were presented in an option tree and another cycle of comparison undertaken. For this the aims of the project, originally set up by the Government Commission and formulated while the shaping work was going on, were picked up again. Using these together with the experience gained in earlier comparisons, the group was able to identify three key comparison areas: risk, cost, and (logistical) feasibility. In this cycle the five decision schemes were assessed only by rank order, within each comparison area separately. No weighting of the comparison areas, beyond that implied in their selection, was thought to be necessary at this stage. However, a simple dominance analysis revealed that alternative 2 was inherently inferior to alternatives 1 and 3. Then further examination showed that alternatives 1 and 3 were so nearly the same that one could be selected to represent them both. Decision scheme 3 was so selected and the analysis continued with only three alternatives – numbers 3, 4, and 5.

At this point the use of a comparative advantage analysis would have been very helpful. Unfortunately this technique was not so well developed at that time, and the project group chose another direction. Instead they started integrating the work which had been carried out on different foci. The three short-listed alternatives were brought together with the results of similar work on the location of depots and other local distribution centres.

This work was presented to the Government Commission, and decisions were taken leading on to the writing of policy statements; and the analysis switched more into the comparing and choosing modes.

Management of Uncertainty in the Comparing and Choosing Modes

The management of uncertainty played an important role throughout the project. At the outset this took the form of listing for future reference any areas of uncertainty as they were identified. For example:

- What were the intentions of Belgian Government with respect to regulation of inland shipping which had to pass through Dutch waters en route to Antwerp?
- How well developed was the new Walradar chain (an augmented shore radar system)? How far had it already been installed, and when could it be expected to be fully operational?
- How was the trade-off to be made between the costs of the various possible measures and the level of risk?

Some of these could be reduced within the time-frame of the project through:

- seeking preliminary results from the ongoing risk analysis (thus reducing uncertainty of type UE);
- use of the inter-organizational structure of the group (thus reducing uncertainty of type UR);
- interactive working which included consultation with others (thus reducing uncertainty of type UV).

Some areas of uncertainty emerged too late in the process, or were not amenable to quick reduction in this way. Thus, as time went on, it became more necessary to adopt working assumptions in order to make progress. Choices were being made in all modes of work through repeated cycles of reformulation – some going deeper into more detail, others focusing more broadly and thus extending the scope of the analysis. In each case any significant assumptions were listed as they were made. From lists made in the shaping mode we have for example:

- the demand for LPG in The Netherlands would not grow as much or as fast as was predicted in 1979, but would be fairly substantial at least to the year 2000;
- in order for the pipeline to be feasible, all other forms of bulk transportation would have to be limited;
- and so on.

Constraints applied through the introduction of option bars, or in short-listing directly from the comparison table, were often based on assumptions about the availability of scarce resources, or about the behaviour of others. For example:

- the Government would continue to promote their policy on deregulation, with its concerted effort to reduce the exercise of control required of all levels of government;
- mutually satisfactory financing arrangements for the Walradar system could be negotiated with the Belgian Government;
- the spatial requirements for the safe shunting of mixed freight trains (including LPG wagons) would not be so great as to be impossible;
- and so on.

As the time for formal policy making approached, the explicit analysis of uncertainty became more pressing.

The lists of uncertainties – both those listed directly and those implied by the assumptions being made – had become quite considerable. And now they needed to be interpreted as uncertainty areas. Because it was not possible to analyse all of them, a selection had to be made. Indeed a sort of selection process had been going on all the time – not all the uncertainties and assumptions were being recorded. Only those

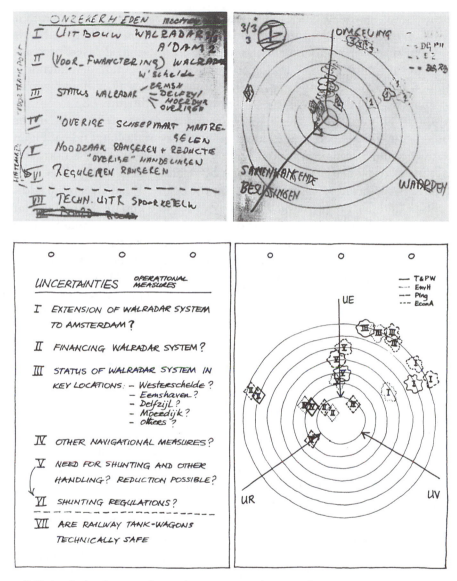

Figure 7.8 Analysis of uncertainty using an uncertainty graph

uncertainties which made the group feel less confident that they were doing the right thing, and those assumptions which threatened the validity of the results if they were proved incorrect, had made it into the lists.

One such cycle, in which a selected few of the outstanding uncertainty areas were analysed, is presented here as an example (Figure 7.8). The problem focus was the issue of 'mainstream' transportation which, at this stage, had been reduced to a combination of water and rail. For the identification of such uncertainty areas, the synergy of the group process was used – in quick loops between the choosing and comparing modes. Judgements were based on the nature of the emerging decisions – whether they were to be full-blown long-term commitments, or of a more interim, delayed or contingent nature – in terms of the possibilities for accommodation to, and/or reduction of, the uncertainties. Seven uncertainty areas were identified in this way, although two of them were combined during the analysis (see the left-hand side of Figure 7.8).

At this point an uncertainty graph was introduced, and analysis of the uncertainty areas could begin. In this case a radial form was used (see right-hand side of Figure 7.8), with the uncertainties of types UV and UR on opposite sides to those normally used. Uncertainties were plotted according to type by relating them to the three axes (UE, UV, and UR), with the more salient ones nearer the centre. What is more, in addition to the use of type and salience as characteristics by which to compare them, the group also used strength. Hard diamond shapes were used for those it was thought difficult to reduce, while soft jelly-like shapes were used for those more easily reduced.

One slight complication was that different opinions about the assessment of the uncertainty areas became apparent almost immediately. These differences were accommodated by allowing each of the four sectors of government represented in the group to plot the uncertainty areas separately, using a simple colour code to differentiate them.

As is commonly the case in using the strategic choice approach, the analysis was not carried out in full. Nevertheless, some useful conclusions could be drawn from it. There was, for example, strong consensus about uncertainty area III. And differences of opinion were only significant in the case of uncertainty area II – and then only in terms of its salience. That it was a mixture of uncertainties of type UR and UE, and that it was going to be very difficult to reduce, was agreed.

The identification of exploratory options was carried out quite informally in this case. These can be seen in the short-term work programme which was being compiled in parallel (see Figure 7.9). This interim product can be seen as a commitment package, though this framework was not used explicitly. However, the deadline was stated ('18 March'), and those responsible were noted ('T & PW', 'EnvH', and so on).

This programme was still quite tentative. Thus there was an emphasis on reducing uncertainty on all items. Nevertheless, preferred policy options could be implied from some of them. For example item 8 implied an already quite specific area for extension, and item 9 was taking the choice of pressure tanks in preference to refrigerated ones into its final stages (see right-hand side of Figure 7.9).

As it happened, the shift into more formal use of the commitment package framework occurred very shortly after this. The move took place quite quickly, and the work was completed in about half a day. The combination of being pressured to produce something and feeling ready to do so was enough to get the process going. The group sat in the project room with the photo-reports of much earlier sessions and the more formal working papers on the table. On the wall was hung a selection of flip charts – mostly the more recent ones, but also key ones from earlier cycles of the process. Also on the wall

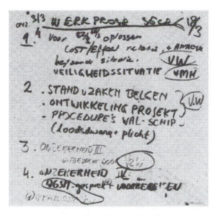
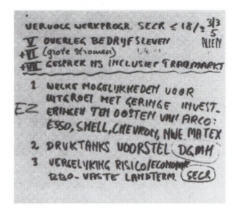

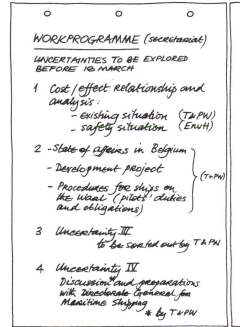
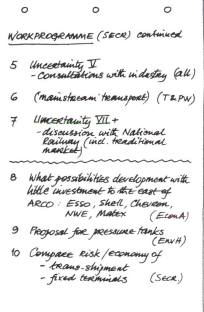

Figure 7.9 Choosing – an interim work programme

were a number of sheets with the empty commitment package already printed on them (see Figure 7.10 for the format). These provided the basic vertical structure of actions (*actie*), explorations (*onderzoek*), deferred choices (*uitgestelde maatregelen*) and contingency plans (*eventualiteitenplan*), and the horizontal structure of decision areas.

In addition, provision was made for the broader choices of who the commitment package was to be aimed at, in terms of who the decision taker (*besluitnemer*); the primary orientation (*strategie, scenario, alternatief enz*); and the time horizon (*tijdsperiode*). For

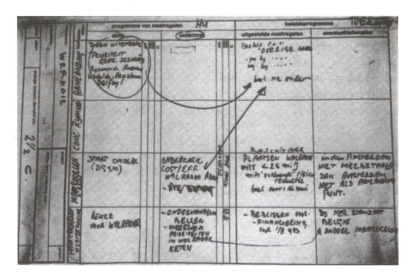

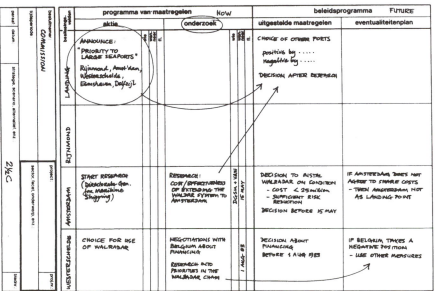

Figure 7.10 Choosing – use of a commitment package framework

each action columns were provided for the more operational issues of who was responsible *(wie);* the appropriate deadline *(wanneer);* and the available budget *(fl).*

These were filled in using the understanding gained through the learning process. Building on the working papers, recall was triggered where necessary by notes on the sheets and in the photo-reports. Unlike the practice in using more conventional methodologies, conclusions were not drawn out of the analysis, so much as out of the understanding which was obtained through the analysis.

The process of building up the policy began by identifying the decision taker which, on this occasion, was deemed to be the Government Commission. This was because such an identification would help in defining which decisions to focus upon, and in describing the choices made. What could be treated as a decision for one decision taker would, most usually, have to be treated as an uncertainty, or as the subject of an assumption, by another. At the same time the orientation of the commitment package was identified which, in this example, was '2½C'. (This happened to be one of the variations on the scenario involving regional concentration of landing points with free use of the railways for mainline distribution.) The need for identification of the orientation was that it was still not clear which of the short-listed orientations was going to be chosen eventually. Therefore, work had to be done on both in order to understand the consequences of each in policy terms.

Each combination of decision taker and orientation was written up on several sheets of paper. Then decision areas were written in and the policy choices noted (see Figure 7.10). Each row accommodated the various types of choice concerning that decision area where applicable, with cells left blank otherwise. Particular relationships between choices were noted with the use of arrows.

For example, in the case of the *Westerschelde* (at the bottom of Figure 7.10), the choice was for the use of the Walradar system in any case. But there was also considerable uncertainty about:

- the possibilities of sharing its financing with Belgium (uncertainty of type UR);
- and the priorities that had been established in the Walradar chain up to that time (uncertainty of type UV).

These were to be the subject of explorations. The former was then made the subject of future decision (to be made before 1 August 1983). The arrow across the bottom indicated that the results of research into the latter were to be used as the basis for alternative measures in the event that negotiations with the Belgians went badly.

Of course, the White Paper was not written in the half-day it took to put together the first full set of policy choices. But, the main policies were certainly structured and agreed in outline at that time. The complete document was then drawn up during the following weeks.

The basic policy was to discontinue the licensing of one terminal in the Rijnmond area and its associated pipeline, which had been planned to serve as the main form of inland transport. Instead, the development of a limited number of terminals was to be allowed. The pipeline would not be built and in its place a combination of improved barges and trains (run as single-freight, closed transport) were to be the preferred mode of bulk transport. Road transport was to be used only for more diffuse local distribution.

The commitment package framework survived throughout the process of finalization and its headings were used explicitly in the final published version of the White Paper. A summary of the more operational policy measures was listed under these headings, filling seven typeset pages. As it is impossible to quote all of them, a few typical policy statements from each heading have been selected to serve as examples.

A typical action was related to the development of Amsterdam as a landing point:

> 1.4 For the seaway approaching Amsterdam, for a distance of 2.5 km to the west and 3.5 km to the east of the locks, but excepting the locks themselves, approaching or passing LPG freighters is prohibited. This ban also applies from a distance of 2.5 km to the west of the America Harbour to the harbour itself.
>
> *Integrale Nota LPG* (p. 109)

As is often the case, the choice of this action was made in the face of considerable uncertainty and involved the making of assumptions, which could have serious consequences if they were to be proved wrong. In this case they were about the expected amount of shipping. A reasonable increase in traffic could have raised the danger significantly, and a contingency plan had to be designed to accommodate such an eventuality:

> 4.2 If a terminal is to be built in Amsterdam, a suitable safety zone for UG ships must be available. Should there be a substantial increase in imports, or in the number of shipping movements, then a refuge harbour should be built.
>
> *Integrale Nota LPG* (p. 115)

There were several actions concerning the handling of railway wagons in marshalling yards. For example:

> 1.10 In yards where UG pressure-vessel wagons are marshalled, the points in use must be so secured that they cannot be switched when one or more wagons are near or on them.
>
> *Integrale Nota LPG* (p. 114)

As was revealed by the analysis of uncertainty (see Figure 7.8), there was some doubt about the issue of marshalling, and this was reflected in policy statements which, in strategic choice terms, were explorations:

> 2.4 Research will be made into the risks in marshalling yards. The strength of LPG pressure-vessel rail wagons, especially in connection with potential leakages, will be investigated. The special equipment on these wagons, required to prevent, or at least considerably delay, a BLEVE[2] will also be looked into.
>
> *Integrale Nota LPG* (p. 110)

Typically, this was then linked to deferred decisions on a stronger policy:

> 3.5 The results stemming from 2.4, concerned with the construction of pressure-vessel rail wagons, will be applied internationally (R.I.D.) with the intent of incorporating them in international regulatory directives.
>
> *Integrale Nota LPG* (p. 114)

---

[2] A 'BLEVE' is a Boiling Liquid Expanding Vapour Explosion

The complete document, having been drawn up in draft form, then followed the more-or-less conventional six-month period of finalization. An extensive programme of consultation with other ministries and industry was undertaken. It was adapted and polished, and finally submitted to the Second Chamber of the Dutch Parliament.

Disaster Strikes Again

The LPG policy passed through its formal process of acceptance unopposed on 20 November 1984.

That very night there was a massive explosion and fire on the outskirts of Mexico City. Flames 100 metres high engulfed the area. At the source was one of the city's main gas distribution centres – including 80 000 barrels of LPG. Hundreds of people died and thousands were injured. Witnesses said that birds were fried in the air. Over 4000 homes were destroyed, and the suburb of San Juanico was no more (*The Times*, 21 November 1984). The news hit the newspapers in The Netherlands the next morning. If the LPG policy was going to be challenged, this would have been the time. But the reaction, unlike that after the accident in Spain six years earlier, was one of calm confidence. The policy, underpinned by the high level of consensus and commitment gained through the process, stood the test well.

Reflection, Commentary, and Conclusions

The story of the development of LPG policy in the Netherlands has continued to unfold, even though there was little of consequence to report in its first five years of operation. However, this case study, having been focused only on the use of strategic choice in that whole story, ends here. Thus it is at this point that it may be helpful to reflect on some of the lessons to be gained from the experience. The framework of considering the approach as technology, organization, process and products, introduced in the preceding chapter, provides the structure for this review. Commentary is provided, on reflection five years after the event, by people who were centrally involved in the project.

The Approach

The strategic choice approach was suggested at a point in the project when progress was almost at a standstill. Agreement was impossible even about which analytical techniques to use. Not only did those suggested have limited scope just as the risk analyses had – but each had the added disadvantage of being proposed by one of the participants, and thus tainted with their bias. The strategic choice approach overcame these difficulties. The 'tool-box' idea provided a wide range of techniques, concepts, and frameworks suitable for various aspects of the problem. What is more, it was introduced by independent consultants. However, this by itself was not enough. Formal analytical techniques cannot help people come to grips with the social aspects of an impasse. Thus two other elements of strategic choice played an important role:

- the cyclic model of the process that provided the initial breakthrough;
- the interactive style of working that provided a favourable context within which it could be applied.

In addition the approach offered an essentially different way of thinking about uncertainty. It was no longer seen as something to be worked against – to be eliminated or controlled. Rather it was seen as something to be worked with and managed creatively ('... the system of management of uncertainties played an important role ...' – Rene van Oosterwijk).

What is more, uncertainty is treated much more broadly within the strategic choice approach. Up to that time the focus had been almost exclusively on uncertainties about the physical context – those of type UE. It was only when strategic choice was introduced into the project that uncertainties of types UV and UR were brought into consideration. ('Very interesting was the handling of the inevitable uncertainties in the decision making: defining the uncertainties at stake, giving them a role in the decision making and giving them their own place in the policy ...' – Cees Moons.)

The Technology

The strategic choice approach is decision focused, thus providing a technology which is easily accessible to all concerned. The participants changed from concentrating on their perceptions of the system they were trying to manage. Instead, they focused on the decisions they were facing. ('These tools are effective in stimulating a process in which the energy of the actors is focused on a solution-oriented framework' – Bob van de Graaf.)

The Analysis of Interconnected Decision Areas (AIDA) allowed a logical approach to the identification of a focus, in place of intuition based on naturally partisan views. ('Also the relationship between problems became clear, as well as the lack of relationship through which it was possible to see how part-problems could be isolated' – Henk Waardenaar.)

AIDA also provided the means of handling the complexity presented by the interrelatedness between decisions. The number of alternatives under consideration at any one time was limited to only those which were feasible. ('The way in which alternative solutions were listed and worked out was also found to be useful' – Cees Moons.)

At the time of the LPG project, the strategic choice approach was less well developed to aid in the comparing mode of work than it is now. Some structure was used in the form of simple comparison tables. However, little else was provided other than the manner of writing everything on the wall to make the process more open. ('Strategic choice was less helpful in the "solution phase". Choosing is more of a creative process in which alternatives are combined to achieve an optimal result, rather than an analytical listing of possibilities' – Henk Waardenaar.)

Much of the early difficulty lay in the fact that an interdepartmental group, working on a policy problem, tends to work not as a team but as opponents in negotiation. While this cannot be totally changed, it was made much more manageable by the introduction of independent process consultants who operated in the role of facilitators. ('The success of the policy making in the LPG project, with its four competing government agencies, each with its own interests and views, owed much to the guidance of a more or less impartial third party' – Jan Jaap de Boer.)

But the strategic choice approach also provided a set of concepts, based on the management of decisions, which together formed a common framework for communication. Thus it proved extremely valuable as an aid in the many interactive sessions, which involved working not around a table, but on large sheets of paper on the wall – in most cases aided by the facilitators. ('Through this method all those involved obtained a clear and shared picture of the LPG problem' – Cees Moons.)

The Organization

At the time of the LPG project, many of the ideas about organization for strategic choice were in the early stages of development and were thus not applied as they would be now. However, they did provide a changed context which enabled partisan representatives to work jointly. ('Previously the discussion was usually influenced by misunderstandings, which caused feelings of fear in inter-ministerial discussions' – Cees Moons.)

In addition, the use of strategic choice promoted the development of more effective links with the 'home' organizations of the project group members. At the outset the primary interest of each lay in working with its constituency in its own field. Later their joint working became the primary interest. Consultations with their constituencies were selectively programmed, with strategic choice providing analysis and a common framework for communication. ('The team would generate solutions and would later present these to the various constituencies. Typically in this period there was a marked improvement in the social interaction among them' – Bob van de Graaf.)

The Process

One of the main contributing factors to the blocked process, which gave rise to the invitation to try out the strategic choice approach, was that the project group were adhering to a linear process. They were analysing one problem after the other, and trying to move from one decision to the next. ('The effect was like trying to get ahead by taking two steps back for every one taken forward' – Frans Evers.)

However, using the strategic choice approach, explicit recognition was given to the cyclic nature of any creative learning process, allowing progress to be made with provision for adaptation in the light of experience. With this the need for a sequence of complete negotiated agreements to each step could be overcome. ('The breakthrough came with the concept of the cyclic process. Making decisions, running through the whole problem, and coming back again. Making and re-making decisions until a consistent set was found' – Bob van de Graaf.)

The Products

The products of strategic choice are both visible and invisible, and based on the idea of incremental progress. For the visible ones, produced in the form of conventional documents, the commitment package provided a vital framework. It opened the way for decisions to be made with respect to time, under conditions of uncertainty and conflict. ('The most useful instrument in strategic choice, in my opinion, was the commitment package. In this way decisions were formulated so that the time element could be better taken into account. Commitments in the spirit of "we may agree that I am right now, but it may turn out later that you are right when certain occurrences become clear (e.g., through research and contingency plans)" could be clearly put into words' – Cees Moons.)

Joint commitment and mutual understanding were the principal invisible products. But they are, by their very nature, extremely difficult to demonstrate. In fact they were only experienced directly by those who were involved in the process, and even then they may only be recognized at some time in the future. ('The success of the policy-making in the LPG project with the competing government agencies, each with its own interests and views, ... depended in my view largely ... on the shared learning and use of the policy-making methods, on the shared information and mutual trust developed between all parties ...' – Jan Jaap de Boer.)

That the project was successful, at least in the eyes of the project group, can be seen from the commentary above. However, additional evidence can be found in the documents, especially in the White Paper itself – Appendix 4 of which is a description of the methodology, presented as part of the justification of the policy proposed.

What is more, in 1986 a retrospective study of five different environmental policy-making projects in the Netherlands was undertaken by Professor Dr R. Hoppe of the University of Amsterdam. He conducted an opinion survey of people concerned with the five projects from both inside and outside the Ministry. Two principal measures of quality were used:

- the degree to which the project achieved its goals;
- the standard of the policy document itself.

In these terms the LPG project was rated the best, with scores of 100 per cent on both measures.

Further confirmation comes, if any is needed, from the fact that since 1983 the strategic choice approach has been chosen for use on many other policy-making projects in The Netherlands. The issues have ranged from the ageing of the population to the highly polluted silt dredged from the Rhine estuary. It was used in, amongst other projects, the preparation of the National Environmental Policy Plan, which was put before the Second Chamber of the Dutch Parliament in 1989.

Acknowledgement

Photographs from the workshop on LPG policy are reproduced by courtesy of C.A. de Jong.

References and Bibliography

Government Documents

Rijksplanologischecommissie (RPC) (1982). *Scenarios*, RPC-LPG nr 116, Vergadering 26 Mei 1982, Den Haag.
Rijksplanologischecommissie (RPC) (1983a). *Opbouw en Selectie van Scenarios*, RPC-LPG nr 195, Vergadering 20 januari 1983, Den Haag.
Rijksplanologischecommissie (RPC) (1983b). *Opbouw en Selectie van Scenarios*, RPC-LPG nr 165, Vergadering 24 februari 1983, Den Haag.
Tweede Kamer de Staten-Generaal (1984). *Integrale Nota* LPG, Vergaderjaar 1983–1984, 18 233, nrs. 1–2, Den Haag.

Case Studies and Reports

de Jongh, A. and Hickling, A. (1990). *Mens en Beleid*, Stenfert Kroese, Leiden.
de Jongh, P. and Captain, S. (1999). *Our Common Journey; a Pioneering Approach to Cooperative Environmental Management*, Zed Books, London.
Environmental Resources Limited (1987). 'Case Study H: LPG Policy in The Netherlands', in *Risky Decisions: a Management Strategy*, ERL, London.
Gardenier, J. (1984). *New LPG Guidelines in The Netherlands*, Technical Report No. 23, ISSN 0111-2856, Town and Country Planning Directorate, Ministry of Work and Development, Wellington North, New Zealand.
van de Graaf, R. (1985). 'Strategic Choice in LPG Policy', in *Evaluation of Complex Policy Problems* (Eds A. Faludi and H. Voogd), Delftsche Uitgevers, Delft.
Hoppe, R. (1987). *Naar Prolessioneel Management in VROM-Beleidsvorming: Resultaten Enquete*, University of Amsterdam, Amsterdam.

Personal Communications

Many and various communications have taken place with members of the project team. Those quoted in the text are listed here in alphabetical order with their organizational affiliation at the time:

- Jan Jaap de Boer (Physical Planning arm of the Ministry of Environmental Affairs).
- Frans Evers (Environmental Hygiene arm of the Ministry of Environmental Affairs).
- Bob van de Graaf (Ministry of Economic Affairs).
- Cees Moons, (Environmental Hygiene arm of the Ministry of Environmental Affairs).
- Rene van Oosterwijk (Ministry of Transport and Public Works).
- Henk Waardenaar (Physical Planning arm of the Ministry of Environmental Affairs).

8 Robustness Analysis: Keeping Your Options Open

Jonathan Rosenhead

If you and a group of friends were going out to dinner together tomorrow, how would you choose which restaurant to go to? One approach would be to collect menus from all the restaurants in the vicinity, get each of your intended companions to rate each of the main courses on a suitable scale of utility, and then combine these evaluations to identify the restaurant expected to achieve the highest aggregate satisfaction of desire. *Alternatively*, you could engage as many of the group as are available in a discussion about the choice of venue. What restaurants have people visited or heard of which have a good reputation for their cooking? Are there types of food (fish? curry?) that particular individuals specially like or can't eat? The group could then select a restaurant, either by menu or by general type, which provides a spread of options broad enough to encompass their various tastes.

The fastidious among you will have noted that the first formulation is grotesquely oversimplified. What about starters? What about puddings? Don't we care about the wine list or the ambience? If we are going to take seriously the task of maximizing expected satisfaction, then this sketched approach can only be the starting point for an elaborate and sophisticated exercise. In fact, I rather doubt it will be complete in time for tomorrow's dinner.

Evidently the second approach makes fewer demands on data, on the quantification of preferences, and on mathematical analysis. But the distinctive grounds for preferring it are to do with its handling of uncertainty. It does not require as a precondition for any analysis the identification today of what dish each diner will wish to eat tomorrow. It is reasonable not to do so, since that question cannot be answered today (tomorrow's taste buds will be conditioned by a complex of internal and external events which cannot be anticipated) and so it should not be asked. Answers, if given, will be speculative, and any apparent optimum will be spurious.

The 'eating out' example can serve as an appetizing introduction (hors d'oeuvre?) to the field of application of robustness analysis. Robustness provides a way of supporting decision-making when there is radical uncertainty about the future, and where decisions can or must be staged sequentially. Its addresses the seeming paradox: how can we be rational in taking decisions today if the most important fact that we know about future conditions is that they are unknowable? It resolves the paradox by assessing initial decisions in terms of the attractive future options that they keep open. Some applications

Table 8.1 – Some robustness applications

Brewery location (US)
Chemical plant expansion (Israel)
Hospital location (Australia)
Regional health planning (Canada)
Oil field development (North Sea)

of robustness analysis are shown in Table 8.1. The approach may be used for conventional, behind the scenes analytic decision support, but its low-tech accessible character makes it particularly suitable for a participative workshop environment.

This chapter will outline the robustness approach, which is more a framework than a programmed sequence of operations. But first it will explore the reasons why planning under uncertainty is both important and difficult, and at the same time introduce the key elements which come together in robustness analysis.

Uncertainty

Uncertainty afflicts a wide range of problems a good deal more momentous than where tomorrow's dinner is coming from. Indeed it is an increasingly prevalent feature of, especially, advanced societies. However the word is used in so many different though related senses that some clarification is called for. Broadly, it applies to situations in which it is reasonable to lack confidence in potentially important aspects of the circumstances in which some decision(s) are called for. This can happen under conditions of

- *ignorance* – where particular knowledge is not available
- *unreliability* – where some information is of doubtful solidity, e.g., because of the credibility of its source
- *unknowability* – where certain information is in principle unobtainable.

John Friend has distinguished different categories of uncertainty (see Chapter 6 of this volume) depending on where the incompleteness of knowledge originates.

A concept related to uncertainty, and subject to equally diverse usage, is that of 'risk'. Until quite recently this conventionally referred to a decision with a number of possible alternative consequences, whose probabilities of occurring could be identified. Straightforward applications of this concept can be found in insurance, and in actuarial work. Now, however, the concept has expanded to justify books with titles such as 'The Risk Society'. It is argued that, although life has been hazardous throughout history, we have now entered on an age in which a) the unpredictable dangers to which we are exposed

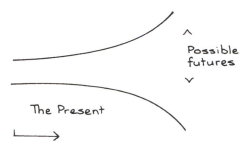

Figure 8.1 The trumpet of uncertainty

increasingly result from social activities rather than natural causes; and b) rather than accept the dangers passively, even fatalistically, we attempt to assess, reduce, even control them. Again, risk is increasingly seen not only as a threat, but also as a source of entre-preneurial advantage. When risk is used in this broader way, it connects directly with the notion of uncertainty we are discussing here.

Uncertainty is not the same as change. Some changes (tide heights; school populations five years ahead) may be predicted quite accurately. It is only unpredictable change, whether due to ongoing turbulence or to structural discontinuities rendering previous experience unreliable, which falls under the heading of uncertainty.

Uncertainty is significant for a decision situation if the range of variation of the imperfectly known feature is perceived to be large, if there is considerable sensitivity of benefits to the occurrence of the unpredicted, and if the cost of reversing a commitment once made is high. It is when the combination of these factors generates a wide possible variance in outcomes that uncertainty's invisible presence needs to be acknowledged and allowed for in any analysis. Such conditions are all too common. Town planners laying down infrastructure cannot predict whether future commercial development or population growth will justify it. Decisions on factory size will have different outcomes depending on the level of demand that materializes. Acquisition of new weapons systems may be caught in a budgetary squeeze some years down the road. A child who doesn't know what she wants to do when she grows up must nevertheless select subjects to study at school. And so on.

The future is necessarily a combination of the known and the unknowable. The pro-portion of the latter tends to rise as the time-scale extends, graphically represented by the 'trumpet of uncertainty' opening out into a wide bell (Figure 8.1). There is another sense in which time is against us. Things certainly seem to have been getting worse lately. With the growth in scale and reach of dominant institutions, developed societies are evidently approaching Emery and Trist's (1965) 'turbulent environment' – not only the decisions of individual units, but also the interactions between them, produce endemic unpredictability. Less developed countries, through their relationships of dependency, experience the backwash of this turbulence without articulated internal structures that can soften its impact. Unforeseen change is no longer the exception – we live at best with 'punctuated equilibria' (Evans, 1987). It is only the nature of the surprises that will be a surprise.

Uncertainty and Planning Methods

This everyday, commonplace observation has been routinely denied in practice by the planning methodologies that have been employed to guide society and its parts into the future. There are two alternative forms of denial. The first, dominant until the start of the 1980's, was for organizations to pursue long-range planning. For example, the National Health Service in Britain required local health authorities to draw up a strategic plan of how their services would look a decade ahead, and then approach it operationally in yearly stages. Large businesses developed elaborate corporate plans on much the same basis. Economic planning in the Soviet Union also followed this rigid 'master plan' approach. Not surprisingly, such plans became a burden on effective decision making as the unexpected diverged from the projected reality.

The second form of denial, a reaction to the over-inflated claims for long-range planning, was to retreat into a search for short-term advantage. Since the future was so unpredictable, and was more unpredictable the further ahead one tried to look, the answer (it was thought) was to concentrate on the short run. The entrepreneurial and opportunistic grasping of the immediate gain came to dominate any consideration of the longer term.

The first of these responses we may call 'rational comprehensive planning', and the second 'incrementalism'. The inadequacy of each can be brought home by analogy with a game of chess. Incrementalism proposes an opportunistic policy of short term gains – take what pieces you can now. A sure recipe for disaster against an even moderately skilful player. Rational comprehensive planning will propose, after long and deep analysis, that we should focus all our efforts on achieving mate with a combination of queen, knight, and passed pawn on square KB6 at move 39. Such a strategy would be impossible to operationalize in the opening moves, and rapidly prove irrelevant as the middle game develops (as it will) unexpectedly.

The rational comprehensive approach has been described as 'moon shot' planning. But in chess the target does not move in stately orbit – and life is far more complex than chess.

Forecasts and Futures

The fundamental problem with moon-shot planning is that it requires a knowledge of the middle- to long-term future which is, in principle, simply unobtainable. Sometimes

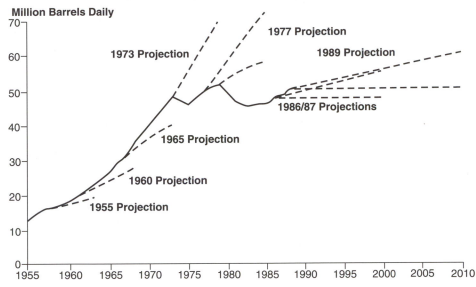

Figure 8.2 Estimates of world oil demand 1955–1989. Source: Hadfield (1991)

this certain future is merely assumed, in which case the assumption is that tomorrow will be essentially the same as today. Occasionally the formalistic procedures of the DELPHI approach are used – for surely the experts could tell us what the future will be like, if only they would agree. Most often the future is captured by means of a forecast, the projection of current trends.

It is tempting to retell here horror stories of forecasts their owners would rather forget. And in fact I have been tempted. Figure 8.2 shows the record of attempts by reputable and well-resourced organizations in the oil industry to forecast the world demand for oil over a 40-year period. But by themselves failed forecasts prove nothing: indeed they can be and are used by proponents of forecasting as evidence of the need for still more sophisticated forecasting. My argument is not that forecasts happen to be wrong, but that they are bound to be.

There are good reasons for believing that forecasts of any importance are inherently fallible. Our ignorance of what is happening *now* should not be underestimated. But this will be compounded by the succession of natural disasters, new discoveries, accidental conjunctures and conscious interventions that will lay their train across the future. Longer term or strategic planning cannot be firmly based on an attempt to predict what will happen, as this will be rendered infeasible by the purposeful interactions of a host of other human and social actors. A more limited task, of identifying a range of versions of what *might* happen, would be a modest and supportable basis for planning analysis.

Lee (1976) was early in advocating a mixed approach to forecasting in which regularities from the historical record are combined with various possible assumed structural changes. The value of this approach would not be that it would yield accurate forecasts, but rather that 'it focuses attention on the specification of different sets of reasonable, or even unreasonable but not ignorable, assumptions'. The Shell scenario approach does indeed operate on very much these lines (Wack, 1985). In this the uncertainty in the business environment is recognized by the development of a small number of 'scenarios' – each a coherent but contrasting picture of a future which the company might have to face. These scenarios are presented on a regular basis to senior management teams of national Shell companies, as part of a workshop-style meeting at which business strategy is established. This approach has now disseminated widely from Shell (van der Heijden, 1996).

Such scenarios, however, do not serve as inputs to further specified stages of a planning process. They function, rather, as informative background material of which managers should be aware while taking their decisions. Simply adopting a multi-future perspective still leaves us with a gap, that between information and commitment. What do we actually do, now?

Sequential Decisions

If one key to planning under uncertainty is the acknowledgement of multiple futures, the other is the recognition of a clear distinction between decisions and plans. I may plan in January to take a Mediterranean holiday in August, but my initial decision is to go to the local travel agent and collect brochures on a number of possible tourist centres. After further analysis I may from time to time take further decisions – to book a holiday, to pay for it, to insure my deposit, ... At each stage there remains an uncertainty whether the remaining stages of the plan will be implemented in the form originally envisaged, or at all. A letter from the bank manager, the illness of a close relative, growth of an insurrectionary movement – any of these and more could cause me to exercise my free will as a sequential decision-maker.

The distinction can be put more formally. A decision is a commitment of resources that transforms some aspect of the decision-maker's environment; the environment can be restored to its former condition, if at all, only by a further decision and at (at least) psychological cost. A plan consists of a foreshadowing of a set of decisions which it is currently anticipated will be taken at some time or times in the future, or an identification of an intended future state which necessarily implies such a set of future decisions. If a plan does not include within it decisions for implementation forthwith, then no commitment is made for the time being. The plan can in this case be revised or discarded without anything having been lost except time. But, of course, nothing has been gained either.

The distinction between 'plan' and 'decision' has been laboured at some length as it is crucial to an understanding of how rational decisions can be taken under uncertainty. The frequent practice of eliding their meanings, so that a plan is viewed as a commitment rather than a working hypothesis about future actions, causes both confusion and rigidity. Further, it concentrates attention, counter-productively, on trying to get the right *plan* – a mis-direction of intellectual resources since it is highly implausible that the plan as specified will ever be enacted. (If it is, through bureaucratic momentum, so much the worse.) A clear appreciation of the plan/decision distinction focuses analytic effort on getting the *decision* right, with the plan as a framework to ensure that the longer term is not sacrificed to short-term advantage. The appropriate visual aid for the uncertain planner is a pair of bifocals, enabling her to focus alternately on the horizon and on the terrain at her feet.

The decision/plan distinction is embodied in the Strategic Choice approach's concept of the 'commitment package' (see Chapters 6 and 7). Strategic Choice and robustness analysis have a shared concern with the management of uncertainty – indeed the two approaches have been used in conjunction (Friend and Jessop, 1969; Centre for Environmental Studies, 1970). The specific focus of robustness analysis is on how the distinction between decisions and plans can be exploited to maintain flexibility.

Flexibility and Robustness

There is more than one possible strategy when confronted by high levels of uncertainty. The very intensity of threat may elicit counter-productive reactions (such as those alleged of the ostrich). But there are alternative strategies even if we exclude the irrational. One might be to attempt to control the environment from which the uncertainty emanates. Another is to tighten up internal organization for quicker response when unpredicted change occurs. However, when none of these strategies is available, or in addition to them, ensuring flexibility may avoid untoward consequences. Indeed it may make it possible to take advantage of unexpected opportunities: the eventual manifestations of uncertainty are not always malign.

Once the unexpected has occurred it can be straightforward to see how policy or position should be modified. Such modification may, however, be impossible without damaging costs or sacrifice of other desiderata. How serious the consequences of change to meet the new conditions are will depend on how easily the previous posture can accommodate the necessary transformations.

Such flexibility may turn out to be available when demands on it are made. However, it is more prudent to attempt to engineer a high level of flexibility rather than to rely on lucky accidents. Liquidity (in financial management), versatility (of military forces –

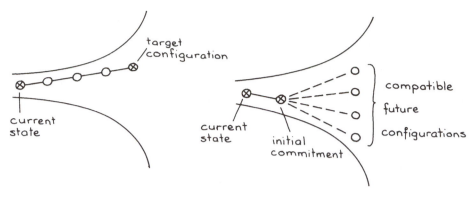

(a) Classical planning methodology   (b) Robustness methodology

Figure 8.3 Planning and the trumpet of uncertainty

Bonder, 1979), resilience (of ecological systems – Holling, 1973) and hedging (in the planning of investments) are all analytic tools developed in different planning environments to achieve a flexible capability.

'Robustness', and the analysis based on it, embodies a particular perspective on flexibility. It is concerned with situations where an individual, group or organization needs to make commitments now under conditions of uncertainty, and where these decisions will be followed at intervals by other commitments. With a robustness perspective the focus will be on the alternative immediate commitments which can be made, which will be compared in terms of the range of possible future commitments with which they appear to be compatible. Robustness analysis is a bifocal instrument.

The distinctive features of this perspective are brought out in Figure 8.3. Figure 8.3(a) represents schematically the classical 'planning-as-decision-making' approach: an optimal system for an assumed future state of the environment is derived, and the plan consists of the necessary decisions required to transform the current system into that target configuration.

The robustness methodology in Figure 8.3(b), by contrast, declines to identify a future decision path or target. The only firm commitments called for are those in the initial decision package – possible future commitments are of interest principally for the range of capability to respond to unexpected developments in the environment that they represent. (The term 'decision package' is used to indicate that initial commitments may come in integrated bundles.)

Graphical illustrations suggest but do not define a method. A more formal measure of the options left open is required, if alternative initial commitments are to be compared to see which is the more 'robust'. We will start with the most basic definition, and then enrich it.

Robustness analysis can be applied to situations, such as that illustrated in Figure 8.4,

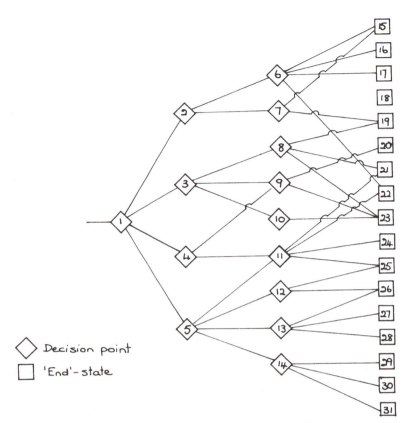

Figure 8.4 A three-stage planning problem

where it is expected that a number of decisions will be made in sequence. Commitment to an initial decision (or decision package) is needed now, and the effect of this initial decision and of the others that may follow is to generate a range of possible future configurations of the system that is being changed by the decisions. Generally only a limited time period (to the 'planning horizon') or a fixed and rather small number of sequential commitments will enter into consideration. Also there will be some threshold that can be agreed separating those configurations whose predicted performance is acceptable from those whose performance is expected not to be good enough. (All of this specification of the problem in any particular case will need to be elicited from or agreed by the problem owners.)

The robustness of any of the candidate initial commitments under consideration can then be defined as the ratio of the number of acceptable configurations that are 'reachable' from that commitment, to the total number of configurations which have been identified as having acceptable expected performance at the planning horizon. 'Reachable' means that there exists a sequence of subsequent available decisions that can take the system to that configuration. More briefly, the robustness of any initial decision is the number of acceptable options at the planning horizon with which it is compatible, expressed as a ratio of the total number of acceptable options at the planning horizon.

Clearly the robustness of any initial decision must lie between 0 and 1, since the number of acceptable configurations which are reachable can be no bigger than the total of acceptable configurations. The higher the robustness, the less the initial decision reduces the effective freedom to reconfigure the system in the future.

The definition of robustness given here is in its simplest form and begs a number of questions:

- isn't the choice of planning horizon and acceptability threshold inherently subjective and arbitrary?
- isn't it often the case that there are an effectively infinite number of possible future configurations?
- how can 'acceptability' be predicted if we adopt a multi-future perspective?
- what about situations where the tracing through of sequential decisions to form 'final' configurations is simply unrealistic?

Most of these questions can be met by appropriate answers, and two of them will lead on to extensions of the definition.

As to the planning horizon and acceptability threshold, their values are indeed necessarily subjective, but that does not mean arbitrary. They need to be established by those whose problem it is, based on their experience of the dynamics of the system that will be impacted by any decisions, together with its environment. These choices can be expected to reflect also the culture and organizational politics of the body or bodies that will control, steer or influence the evolution of the system through time.

There is another defence against the charge of arbitrariness. This is that the information provided by robustness analysis is on the *relative* flexibility of alternatives. Robustness scores, assessed as they are under consistent conditions, offer plausible flexibility rankings for the candidate decisions, and indeed make it possible to draw some broad conclusions about the orders of magnitude of differences in flexibility. They do not, it should be stressed, constitute absolute measures of flexibility, so they cannot be traded-off explicitly against other desirable characteristics – short-run performance, for example. Such balancing of incommensurable factors remains the province of human and social judgement, as it should.

Similar arguments apply to the second of the queries. The representativeness of any discrete set of configurations chosen to stand in for a continuum of future options needs to be guaranteed by the measured consideration of those whose problem this is, and who will have to take responsibility for the resulting decisions. But in any case the representative set chosen will be a common basis for the calculation of the robustness of all the initial commitments to be analysed, providing therefore a foundation for establishing the relative (but not absolute) flexibility which they maintain.

The first begged question to which this simple definition of robustness provides no answer is: Under what assumptions about environmental conditions has the assessment of 'acceptability' of future options been made? This will be addressed in the following section.

Multi-future Robustness

A system configuration, or a policy, which can perform very adequately under some circumstances might make no sense in another future. The simple version of robustness (in practice the first to be developed) is based on a single estimate of performance acceptability for each configuration, and so does not adopt an explicitly multi-future approach to planning.

A case can be made that this does not seriously undermine its usefulness. After all, a robust (under this definition) initial decision package does keep open a wide range of options which provide acceptable performance for one assumed state of the future. It is at least plausible that the more options kept open which are acceptable under the implicitly assumed future conditions, the more likely it is that one or more of them will prove to perform tolerably in the conditions which do in the end materialize. This is evidently not a rigorous argument. However, it is not unreasonable, and may be persuasive when time or resources for more extended analysis are lacking. At the least, a (single future) robust decision package can be expected to offer more directions for future development than would a conventional 'optimal' solution.

However, when there is time for fuller analysis this argument can be turned on its head. For a decision package that is in some sense 'multifuture robust' is yet more likely to offer worthwhile options for development than would a single-future robust commitment. Additionally, we will see, introducing a multi-future perspective has other advantages.

The extension of robustness analysis to the multi-future case is conceptually simple, but requires additional information inputs. We need, first, to identify a number, small enough to be manageable, of plausible future environments for the system. These should be distinctively different from each other, and be adequately representative of the relevant range of variation that knowledgeable stakeholders feel should be taken account of in arriving at any commitments. Then we need to agree assessments of the acceptability of configurations in each of these *'Futures'*. Then, using this information, the robustness of each candidate initial decision package can be calculated for each Future separately.

Single future robustness analysis, as defined in the previous section, provides a single number robustness score for each initial decision or decision package. Multi-future robustness analysis, by contrast, produces as many robustness scores as the number of Futures that it has been decided to work with. Instead of a relatively simple way of

	Future		
	F_1	F_2	F_3
d_1	1	0	0
d_2	0	0.9	0.8
d_3	0.6	0.6	0.6
d_4	0.8	0.8	0.3

Decision (left label spanning d_1–d_4)

Figure 8.5 An example of a robustness matrix

comparing the flexibility maintained by initial commitments ('which one has the highest robustness score?'), there is now a richer and more complex picture to analyse.

Consider the illustrative example of Figure 8.5, in which the robustness scores are displayed in a two-dimensional array or matrix, with each row showing the scores for a particular initial decision package across the range of possible Futures. The structured information displayed here is no use for giving an answer, but may be valuable in starting a discussion. In this example it is unlikely that decision package d_1, can be entertained; if futures F_2 and F_3 are regarded as of sufficient significance to be represented in the analysis, then the absence of any acceptable options at all under both these futures must be a crippling handicap.

However, other cases are less clear. Decision d_2 might look attractive if future F_1, was regarded as a relatively remote possibility. Further analysis and discussion might focus on this issue, including any leverage that could be exerted to prevent future F_1 from materializing. Decision d_3 provides reasonable all-round coverage. How important is it felt to be to have many alternative options *within* each possible future? Perhaps for a future regarded as less plausible, an insurance policy of maintaining at least one viable option will be regarded as adequate. Is future F_3 such a case in point? Then decision d_4 might have the edge. And so on.

This example should bring out the potential benefit of multi-future robustness analysis. This is not that it tells those who have the problem what to do – there will in any case be many other factors to consider. It is, rather, that it can initiate a process of reflection and research, aimed at clarifying participants' understanding of the nature of the predicament that confronts them.

Ways of Working with Robustness

The calculation of robustness scores between 0 and 1 is not an end in itself. Robustness analysis is rather a way of working which focuses attention on the possibilities (not probabilities) inherent in a situation. There is no single algorithm-like method, giving a prescription of which analysis to perform next. The analysis will be at its most productive when it responds successively to the unfolding shape of the problem situation – to both the logic of the complexities and uncertainties, and to the developing perceptions that the earlier stages of the analysis have helped to activate. Some of the variety of ways of bringing out the structure of interrelationship of threats, opportunities, and decisions will be illustrated in this section.

A hypothetical example will help explore some of the potential of the approach. Consider a situation in which decisions to transform a system of interest are expected to be made in a number of stages. Early decisions may foreclose certain future options; there may also be alternative decision routes to what is effectively the same system configuration. Figure 8.4 on page 189 illustrates such a case, with three stages to the planning horizon. We are poised at decision point 1. The choice to be made is not which of the 'end' states 15 to 31 should be selected, but which of the decision packages, leading to decision points 2 to 5, to commit to.

Suppose that those confronting the situation are happy to accept one view F_1 of the future of the environment of the system that concerns them. However, they feel that three categories (desirable/acceptable/unacceptable) rather than two are needed to characterize future performance. Their valuations are shown in Figure 8.6.

It would be possible to calculate single future robustness scores based either on the top category alone (two configurations) or on the top two categories combined (five configurations). However, one can effectively combine the two analyses by listing for each initial decision the numbers of desirable (D) and acceptable (A) options kept open, as in Table 8.2. On this basis initial decision 5 has a narrow edge.

Alternatively, it may be felt that the 'unacceptable' group is too broad, and should be subdivided into marginal, undesirable and catastrophic, as shown in Figure 8.7. This concern, about how disadvantageous some of the available options might be, is undoubtedly a factor in many situations. Why? Because those engaged in forward thinking about the system are less than certain that they will be able to determine all decisions that may be taken about it in the future. Otherwise they would only need to consider the number and variety of *good* options: with enough of these to hand, they would never have to choose a bad one. There would, therefore, be no reason to worry about them.

Lack of future control could be a concern where an opposing faction might come to power only a little way down the road. Or the decision makers might fear that negative options carelessly left open might be imposed on them by superior authority – for example, by governmental legislation or pressure. Attention to possible future bad outcomes could also make sense for the relatively powerless in a conflictual situation. Their leverage is limited – all the more reason for analysing current alternatives for the extent to which each curtails the scope for future distress.

This negative side of the robustness coin has given rise to the complementary concept of 'debility' (Caplin and Kornbluth, 1975). The debility of an initial decision is defined

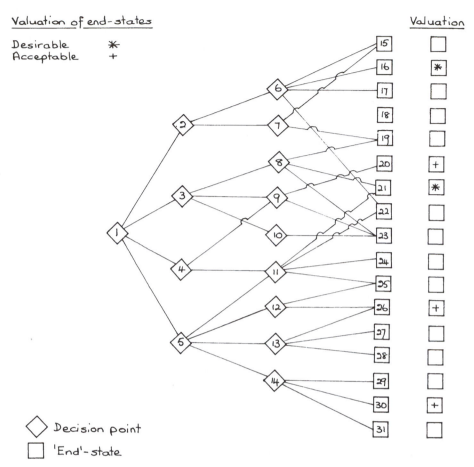

Figure 8.6 A three-stage planning problem with end-states valued

Table 8.2 – Preferred options left open by alternative decisions

Initial decision	Options left open		
	D	A	
2	1	0	
3	1	1	*Key*
4	1	1	D desirable
5	1	2*	A acceptable

*One option accessible by multiple routes.

as the number of unsatisfactory end-states (i.e., configurations) still attainable after an initial decision, expressed as a ratio of all such end-states. It broadens the scope of robustness analysis, as will be shown below.

The configuration valuations together with the structure of compatibility between configurations and initial commitments indicated in Figure 8.7 can be summarized, from a robustness analysis perspective, as in Table 8.3. This can be analysed in more than one way.

If only the preferred options (D and A) are taken into account, we have seen that

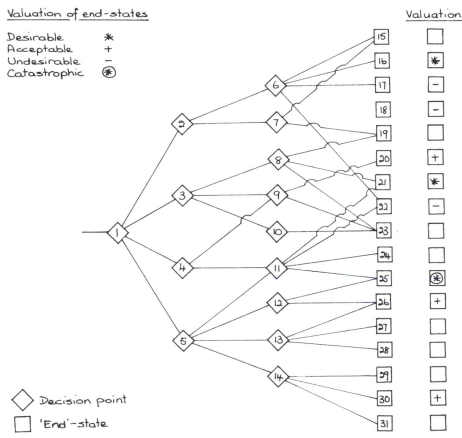

Figure 8.7 A three-stage planning problem – with revised end-state valuations

Table 8.3 – Preferred and non-preferred options left open by alternative decisions

Initial decision	Options left open				Key
	D	A	U	C	
2	1	0	2	0	D desirable
3	1	1	0	0	A acceptable
4	1	1	1	1	U undesirable
5	1	2*	1	1*	C catastrophic

*One option accessible by multiple routes

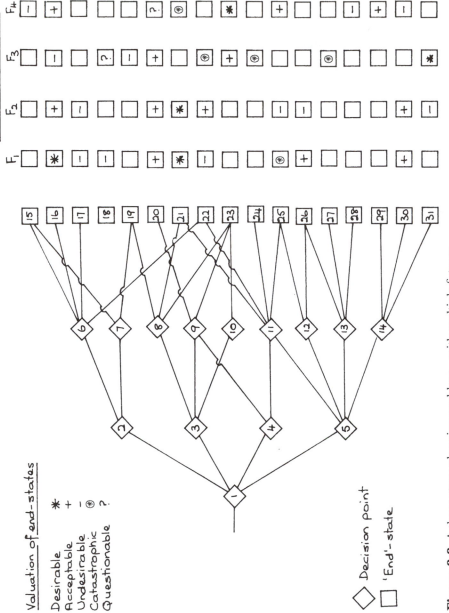

Figure 8.8 A three-stage planning problem – with multiple futures

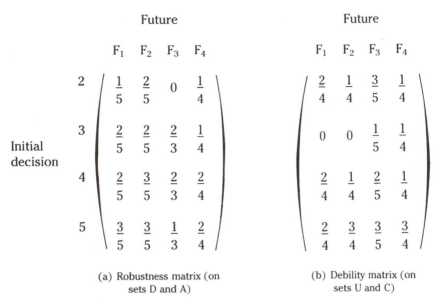

(a) Robustness matrix (on sets D and A)   (b) Debility matrix (on sets U and C)

Figure 8.9 Option maintenance analysis

initial decision 5 offers more future flexibility. But it also offers more opportunities than the others for eventual negative outcomes. If closing-off non-preferred options (U and C) is the sole criterion then initial decision 3 is a clear winner. If, as will be most usual, some balance between threat and opportunity is appropriate, then Table 8.3 provides simply-structured information to clarify the choices. Supplementary analyses can help to make the choice still clearer. For example, initial decision 4 can be discarded. It is dominated by decision 3, which keeps open identical preferred end-states, but has no compatible non-preferred options. Evidently in cases such as this, robustness analysis goes beyond a concern with keeping options open. Rather than option preservation we now have a broader focus on 'option management' under conditions of uncertainty.

So far, however, our example has been based on a single version of the future environment. If alternative futures can be identified (as in Figure 8.8, a four future case) then the analysis above can be extended further. For example, robustness scores based on the combined sets of desirable and acceptable end-states can be calculated, as shown in Figure 8.9(a). These indicate a clear flexibility advantage to initial decisions 4 and 5, but with decision 3 performing respectably. If we treat both 'undesirable' and 'catastrophic' end-states as unsatisfactory, the results are shown in Figure 8.9(b).

In contrast to robustness, it is low debility scores that are preferred. The superiority in this respect of decision 3 is evident. Whether this edge is sufficient to overcome the robustness advantage of decisions 4 and 5 is a matter for debate. The outcome will depend on perceptions of the plausibility of particular futures, and of whether sufficient control will be exercisable in the future to block off undesirable avenues left open by the current decision.

Sharp-eyed readers will have noticed some notation for a new concept in Figure 8.8: the 'questionable' end-state whose attractiveness or otherwise in some future is uncertain or disputed. The corresponding '?' signals an area for possible further research and discussion, if that valuation seems capable of influencing current decisions. This is evidently not the case for end-state 18 in future F_3 – the end-state is inaccessible from any of the initial decisions under consideration, so that it is possible valuation is an irrelevance. The '?' for end-state 20 under future F_4 might be more significant, as this end-state is consistent with initial decision 3. A positive valuation could make the argument for decision 3 look stronger.

The 'query' symbol to flag possible further investigations has been borrowed from the Strategic Choice approach (see Chapter 6). The query can be used quite generally – for example to condition links of accessibility between successive stages of the decision process.

This further dimension of uncertainty takes us back to the as yet unanswered fourth question about the definition of robustness, raised in an earlier section: what about situations where the tracing through of sequential decisions to form 'final' configurations is simply unrealistic? This question leads to an alternative approach we may call 'mode 2 robustness analysis'.

Mode 2 Robustness

There will be many planning situations in which uncertainties about links between stages become the rule rather than the exception. The time-scale may be too long for detailed causal connections and constraints to be convincing. The numbers of alternative decision paths may escalate beyond computational feasibility. And so on. Any of these conditions will rule out a method based on the elaborated sequential logic of the three-stage planning problem that has been used so far to illustrate ways of working with robustness.

This difficulty can be resolved by retrenching back to the basic minimal requirements for robustness analysis – the identifiability of initial decision packages, of alternative future states of the system subject to intervention, and of relations of compatibility between them. (Wong (1998) usefully terms this relationship one of 'attainability' from initial commitment to configuration.) These three components are sufficient to maintain the bifocal approach: that of assessing immediate commitments, but in terms of options left open for longer-term development.

There are various ways in which this form of analysis can be structured. (For one example in practice, see Best, Parston and Rosenhead, 1986). Perhaps the most useful is summarised in Figure 8.10.

(1) choose a future   **(2) identify a configuration**   **(3) identify initial steps**
                           which would work well in it   **towards configuration**

(5) check suitability of each   **(4) check compatibility of each**
configuration in each future   **commitment-configuration pair**

Figure 8.10 Mode 2 robustness analysis in outline

The information needed to perform mode 2 robustness analysis is generated in 5 stages, which are marked on the Figure:

1. Select one of the Futures. (Then stages 2 and 3 will be carried out for each Future in turn)
2. Identify one (or more) system configurations which seem particularly well-designed to operate in that Future. Each of the configurations generated in this way will thus operate harmoniously, and 'make sense' in at least one of the alternative Futures that the decision-makers see as relevant.
3. For each configuration generated at stage 2, identify one (or more) particularly suitable decisions or decision packages for initial implementation. That is, we are constructing a set of possible initial commitments, each of which earns its place in the list because it is a logical first step towards a configuration which has some reason to be considered
4. Having completed stages 2 and 3 for all the Futures, we now assess the attainability of each of the configurations generated at stage 2 from the state resulting from each of the commitments compiled at stage 3. *Non*-attainability will be recorded wherever the decision-making group regards the commitment as an implausible first step towards a particular configuration. It does not imply impossibility, but rather an inconsistency between that initial commitment and the developmental direction implied by a particular configuration
5. The circle can be completed by evaluating the acceptability of the expected performance of each configuration in each Future, just as would be done in mode 1 multi-future robustness analysis

Using this information it is possible to calculate, for a given Future, how many acceptable options (configurations) are kept open by (i.e., are attainable from) a particular initial commitment. This enables robustness scores to be computed in the usual way. We have been able to reach this result by substituting the commitment/configuration attainability relationship for the stage-by-stage tracing of paths required in mode 1.

Methodologies for Robustness

Much of the above discussion has proceeded, necessarily, in something of a vacuum. In order to demonstrate clearly the various technical possibilities, the issues involved in operationalizing the approach have been neglected. However, in the real world lists of candidate decisions or alternative futures cannot be summoned up by the magic words 'consider' or suppose'. There are two broad approaches, depending on the degree of active group participation in the activities of problem structuring.

The Established Methodology

The first application of robustness analysis occurred in the 1960's. This was a period in which analysis for decision support fell almost always into a 'backroom' mode. That is, analysts extracted information from databanks, collected some additional data them-selves, and retired to the backroom to analyse it. Interactions between analysts and the relevant decision-makers were often quite limited, and in any case were not prescribed by the methods then in use. Robustness analysis was at first employed in that vein, and the initial attempts to systematize it did not emphasize the participative potential offered by the intuitive appeal of 'keeping options open' combined with its mathematical sim-plicity. This initial representation will be summarized here, before moving on to the more participative version that has developed from it.

An early paper (Rosenhead, 1980b) has discussed some of the issues of operational-izing mode 1 robustness at some length. It is a possible reference for those who would like a more detailed presentation than can be afforded here. The version of the method-ology outlined in Figure 8.11 indicates one possible format for mode 2 robustness analysis.

Broadly the left-hand side of Figure 8.11 consists of input to the analysis, and the right-hand side presents the outputs from the analysis. The upper part is concerned with identifying initial decision packages. The lower part deals with possible future con-figurations of the system, and how they will behave in different futures.

That is the quick tour. A more informative trip might start with activities 3 and 4. Making sure that one is informed not only of the details of the existing system but also of confirmed changes that are in the pipeline is a wise precaution. Together they specify the 'impending system' (activity 8) – which will shortly be in existence independent of any decisions currently under discussion.

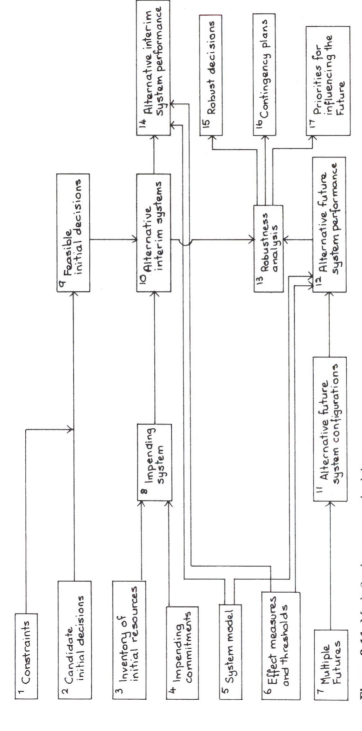

Figure 8.11 Mode 2 robustness methodology

1 Constraints

2 Candidate initial decisions

3 Inventory of initial resources

4 Impending commitments

5 System model

6 Effect measures and thresholds

7 Multiple Futures

8 Impending system

9 Feasible initial decisions

10 Alternative interim systems

11 Alternative future system configurations

12 Alternative future system performance

13 Robustness analysis

14 Alternative interim System performance

15 Robust decisions

16 Contingency plans

17 Priorities for influencing the Future

Possible initial decisions (activity 2) may be generated by a combination of methods. They may be inferred from configurations under consideration, as in the method of Figure 8.10; they may be proposed by participants in the decision-process or by other stakeholders; or they may be suggested by performance gaps revealed by comparative analysis. These elements will need to be composed into a manageable number of coherent alternative packages which make sense operationally and politically, and do not violate budgetary or other constraints (activity 1). Each of these alternative decision packages (activity 9) will impact on the impending system to give one possible version of the 'interim system' that will then function for some period (activity 10).

In general, and especially in public sector or multiple interest group situations, the performance on which systems will be assessed are multi-dimensional. For robustness analysis, this is reflected in the selection of one or more threshold levels – significant boundaries between less and more acceptable system performance (activity 6).

Robustness analysis is predicated on an ability to link decision to future consequences at some level of detail that can guide action. The system model (activity 5) organizes such understanding of cause-effect relationships. It may be a relatively sophisticated mathematical model – for example, the transportation method of linear programming used to simulate revised distribution patterns corresponding to alternative locations for an additional factory (Gupta and Rosenhead, 1968). Or it may be a comparatively simple accounting tool, balancing augmented health services against projected population forecasts (Best, Parston and Rosenhead, 1986). Indeed it may be possible to substitute expert judgement for explicit modelling, as we will see in the next section.

One further basic input to robustness analysis is the identification of future states of the environment within which the system may have to function (activity 7). The analysis will become unwieldy and over-theoretical if it attempts to employ more than a handful of sharply contrasting alternative futures. When analytic resources are limited, a single future may serve – either a status quo assumption or a simple trend projection. (The justification for this short cut has been discussed earlier.) Futures may be generated using the scenario approach already referred to, but other methods can be used. For example, the conventional DELPHI approach can only generate expert consensus on one future state; however, if DELPHI respondents are segmented (for example, using cluster analysis – Best, Parston and Rosenhead, 1986), then sub-groups can be liberated to produce contrasting futures.

Robustness analysis involves the matching of early commitments against differentially advantageous future system configurations under a range of plausible future conditions. In the version shown here, consistently with the schematic explanation of Figure 8.10, these configurations are generated by reference to particular identified futures (activity 11), and then each is assessed across the range of futures (activity 12). It is by testing the attainability of these configurations from alternative interim systems (from activity 10) that robustness analysis (activity 13) can proceed.

There is no single output of robustness analysis. It is a format for exploring certain aspects of planning problems under uncertainty, rather than a method for finding an answer. Some of the types of structured information which participants may hope to have by the time they quit the process are:

- a short list of possible decision packages rated in terms of their robustness against a variety of futures (activity 15).
- a prediction of the shorter term performance improvement to be expected from implementing each of these decision packages (activity 14).
- some guidelines as to what actions by other interests linked to the planning process would be more or less beneficial; these can serve as the basis for contingency plans, or for incentives to encourage mutually advantageous behaviour (activity 16).
- an assessment of which of the alternative futures the system, given its current condition and evolution, is particularly vulnerable to; this can focus lobbying or opinion-forming efforts on trying to influence the occurrence of futures which, in the light of current strategy, would present particular threats or opportunities.

This brief resume of the methodology is undoubtedly misleading. The presentation is both too elaborate, and not elaborate enough. It is insufficiently detailed because it does not specify the many necessary or possible interdependencies between activities. At an obvious level, relevant aspects of possible futures must feature in the system model. Less obviously, identified decision packages can be used to generate ideas for alternative futures, and vice versa. And so on.

The account of robustness methodology has been too elaborate, because it gives the impression of a prescribed and exhaustive process, a sequence of hoops which must each be negotiated in turn and with due deference. The reality of practice is quite different. Problems can be approached in an ad hoc fashion, skipping over apparently daunting procedures on the basis of common sense, and producing provisional insights on the backs of only a few envelopes. Analytic progress is as likely to provoke a re-examination of assumptions (with further analysis to follow) as to lead mechanically to a pre-ordained point of decision. The benefit of the process lies not merely (or principally) in the identification of robust decisions. At least as important is the achievement of the confidence necessary to take and live with those decisions. Robustness analysis and its associated technology can provide a framework for a debate in which that confidence is generated.

Participative Robustness Analysis

What I have called the established robustness methodology, described in the previous section, developed in repeated applications over many years. In the process its original 'backroom' format (analysis by analytic experts to produce recommendations for decision-makers) was transformed into the idea of robustness analysis as a framework for discussion and debate. This aspiration placed it squarely alongside the other problem structuring methods; and indeed the intuitive acceptability of its core idea (keeping

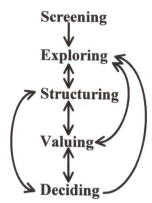

Figure 8.12 Phases of participative robustness analysis

options open) and the simplicity and transparency of its basic operations are conducive to its direct use by lay decision-makers. However the 'established methodology' provides no guidance on how robustness should be used in a workshop setting.

This section will describe in outline a *participative robustness methodology* appropriate for use in group situations. Although based on fewer applications than the established methodology, its format has been thoroughly recorded and analysed by Hin-Yan Wong (Wong 1998), on whose account this section substantially relies.

This methodology makes use of a variety of different modes of information collection and processing, and is structured into a number of phases. The phases are shown, diagramatically, in Figure 8.12. The diagram is structured linearly, indicating the direction of progress towards commitment. As indicated, however, reverse cycling is possible and even to be expected – discussion at any phase may reveal new options, add new criteria, suggest revisions to attainability, etc. The only exception is the screening phase, to which no return will normally take place.

The activities carried out within each phase can be summarized as follows:

- *screening phase* It is advisable before entering on any detailed work to establish whether or not robustness analysis is a suitable approach for those aspects of the problematic situation which stakeholders see as central. This should be carried out by confirming that sequential decisions are on the agenda, and that there are elements in the problem which map onto such key concepts as commitments, configurations, futures and attainability.
- *exploring phase* This phase is concerned with eliciting the information necessary to represent the problem within a robustness framework. Here most of the key aspects for a robustness analysis, identified in the screening phase as being present, are specified more closely – what decision alternatives are possible? what futures are relevant? which future configurations should be included? In addition the criteria for judging configuration performance need to be elicited.

- *structuring phase* Here the information surfaced in the exploring phase is connected up. A manageable number of coherent and representative initial decision packages are constructed out of the possible decision alternatives. And the attainability links between these decision packages and the identified configurations are established. The emerging structure should be reviewed – for example to ensure that it does indeed have sufficient richness to make flexible initial decisions possible.
- *valuing phase* In this phase the expected performance of each of the configurations incorporated in the problem structure is assessed. If the way in which performance is generated by the interaction of a configuration with a possible future context can be clearly specified, this valuation may be carried out using a quantitative model. In the absence of such a model, however, the subjective judgements of group members as to the rating of each configuration-context pairing on an ordinal scale can be employed. Where there is disagreement among the participants about configuration valuations, these different perspectives can be carried through to the final phase, where their differential effects on robustness scores can inform discussion. However the use of multiple perspectives and multiple futures together can produce combinatorial escalation, and requires great restraint in the number of perspectives and futures employed.
- *deciding phase* In addition to the information gathered and processed in the preceding stages, the satisficing levels to be employed on each dimension of performance need to be determined. This enables robustness scores of each decision package to be computed, for each of the futures under consideration, to serve as a framework for group discussion.

In any particular engagement using participative robustness analysis, there are design choices to be made about how much of this process will be carried out in the full group, and how much in other formats. The full range of format alternatives is a) backroom analysis; b) individual interviews; and c) workshop discussion.

In principle it would be possible for the entire process to take place in workshop sessions, as the simplicity of all the activities enables them to be performed with and by non-experts. This would ensure full ownership by the group of the developing problem representation. However the combinatorial nature of robustness analysis – decision packages matched against configurations to determine attainability, configurations tested on multiple performance dimensions in multiple futures (and perhaps multiple perspectives), etc – leads to a deal of repetitive work which can be quite time-consuming. Workshops sessions are expensive in the time of participants, and because of multiple diary constraints a decision to progress only in this mode will slow down the rate of progress. A principled compromise between full participation and the realities of time-economy will often be necessary.

To qualify as *participative* robustness analysis, the deciding phase must be carried out predominantly in workshop mode. Elsewhere, selective individual interviews may be used to elicit information more speedily and economically – notably in the screening and exploring phases. The role of workshops in these phases would then be to review, revise or confirm, and discuss the elicited material. Such events can be shorter than standard PSM workshops, no more than 2 hours as opposed to a half or whole day.

In the structuring and valuing phases, in particular, backroom activity by the consultants can make a major contribution to progress. This work can include the systematization of attainability information into 'attainability graphs' which render aspects of problem structure visually accessible, and the construction and deployment of quantitative valuation models. Once again, the outputs of this activity need to be validated by the group, with the possibility of stimulating new insights, if group ownership is to be maintained.

Participatory robustness analysis, then, is likely to be carried out somewhat differently in each engagement. The less elaborate is the formulation, the more participatory the process can be.

Discussion

Many of the general issues on the application of robustness analysis have already emerged in the preceding sections. More will be aired in the following chapter. Only three further aspects will be treated here.

First, the focus of this chapter has been on ways of managing the preservation of options using robustness analysis. It is therefore worth emphasizing that flexibility is a means, not an end in itself. Flexibility will almost always be one of a number of considerations, among which those who must live with the consequences of decisions will have to strike their own balance. Serendipity and symbiosis not withstanding, there will in general be a cost of some kind for the maintenance of flexibility.

Second, each extra available and acceptable option adds an equal amount to the robustness score, but that does not mean that each option has the same practical significance. Decisions need to be based on the actual options left open, as well as their number. The robustness score may be regarded as a convenient indicator of flexibility, but its calculation does not absolve one from the need to investigate its quality and significance.

Third, after robustness analysis it is not uncommon for the answer which has been reached to look quite unremarkable, even obvious. The reason is that effective robustness analysis does not just produce answers, it reformulates the way in which the problem situation is understood. If it is then impossible to recall why the situation previously seemed to be so confused and intractable, it is because the stakeholders (and consultants) have fought their way to an appropriate clarity.

References

Best, G., Parston, G., and Rosenhead, J. (1986). 'Robustness in practice: the regional planning of health services', *J Opl Res. Soc.*, **37**, 463–78.
Bonder, S. (1979). 'Changing the future of operations research', *Opns Res.*, **27**, 209–24.

Caplin, D.A. and Kornbluth, J.S.H. (1975). 'Multiple investment planning under uncertainty', *Omega*, **3**, 423–41.

Centre for Environmental Studies (1970). *The LOGIMP Experiment*, CES, London.

Emery, F.E. and Trist, E.L. (1965). 'The causal texture of organisational environments', *Hum. Relat*, **18**, 21–3.

Etzioni, A. (1968). *The Active Society: A Theory of Societal and Political Processes*, Collier-Macmillan, London.

Evans, J.S. (1987). *Strategical Flexibility. A Governance Principle for Punctuated Equilibria*, Menlo Park, California, mimeo.

Friend, J.K. and Jessop, W.N. (1969). *Local Government and Strategic Choice: an Operational Research approach to the processes of public planning*, Tavistock, London.

Gupta, S.K. and Rosenhead, J. (1968). 'Robustness in sequential investment decisions', *Mgmt Sci.*, **15**, 18–29.

Hadfield, P.D.S. (1991). From Scenarios to Strategy, Strategic Planning in Shell, Shell, London.

van der Heijden, K. (1996). *Scenarios: The Art of Strategic Conversation*, John Wiley & Sons, Ltd, Chichester.

Holling, C.S. (1973). *Resilience and Stability of Ecological Systems*, International Institute of Applied Systems Analysis, Laxenburg, Austria.

Lee, A.M. (1976). 'Past futures', *Opl Res. Q*, **27**, 147–53.

Rosenhead, J. (1980a). 'Planning under uncertainty 1: the inflexibility of methodologies', *J. Opl Res. Soc.*, **31**, 209–16.

Rosenhead, J. (1980b).'Planning under uncertainty 2: a methodology for robustness analysis', *J. Opl Res. Soc.*, **31**, 331–41.

Wack, P. (1985). 'Scenarios: uncharted waters ahead', *Harvard Business Review*, Sept–Oct., 73–89.

Wong, H.-Y. (1998). *Making Flexible Planning Decisions: Clarification and Elaboration of the Theory and Methodology of Robustness Analysis*, PhD thesis, University of London.

9 *Robustness to the First Degree*

Jonathan Rosenhead

Introduction

The literature on the practice of operational research abounds with, one might almost say consists of, accounts of decision making by large organizations. Reports of robustness analysis largely follow this pattern, dealing, for example, with breweries (Gupta and Rosenhead, 1968), chemical plants (Caplin and Kornbluth, 1975), and health systems (Best, Parston and Rosenhead, 1986). Reading between most of the lines, one can almost see the burly hard-nosed managers, waiting to be convinced before committing the sort of resources an individual worker cannot expect to earn with a lifetime of labour.

The subject of this chapter is quite different. She is, or rather was, a schoolgirl of fourteen. Her decisions would not cause concrete to rise or stock markets to fall. Her problem was – what subjects to choose for study leading to General Certificate of Education 'Ordinary Level' examinations.* But first, of course, she had to see that it was a problem.

There are a number of reasons for using this atypical (from an OR perspective) problem situation to illustrate the application of robustness analysis. One is precisely that this is unfamiliar territory. If one can erode restrictive stereotypes en passant, so much the better. But there are other factors also. One of these is the widely understood nature and limited complexity of Sarah's planning dilemma. This avoids the necessity of describing in detail the specifics of some system that is not the principal focus of attention, but only the vehicle for a journey at a different conceptual level. Another reason is that no complicated technique, be it linear programming or cluster analysis, was performed in even a subsidiary role in this application of robustness analysis. The ground is thus relatively clear, giving unencumbered vision of the target.

The case study that follows does not extract out the 'robustness analysis' bits from their context. What is described is an interactive process of attempting to shape and re-shape the recalcitrant material of real life, until we could work out what to do. Robustness analysis provided one important element of the structure we needed.

---

* Non-British readers may find some clarification of the public examination system in England and Wales helpful. Until 1988, when new arrangements came into force, the GCE was the nationally recognized qualification for those leaving school and/or hoping to enter further or higher education. Candidates for the Ordinary ('O') Level examination were typically about 16 years old. A candidate might take separate examinations in any number of subjects, though rarely more than ten in practice. Those wishing to continue formal education would then study, normally for two further years, for a more focused set of two or three Advanced ('A') Level examinations. Many pupils at or about 16 sat for a combination of GCE 'O' Level and Certificate of Secondary Education (CSE) examinations. Assessment at grade 1 of a CSE examination was regarded as equivalent to a pass in the same subject at GCE

In Loco Parentis

Sarah is my stepdaughter. In 1976, as for some years before and after, she formed part of the nuclear family which also included her younger brother Dominic, their mother Gillian, and myself. Relations between Sarah and myself were probably no better than average for step-parents and -children, which in turn are probably no better than the average for parents and their teenage offspring. However, communication was not completely impossible.

In the spring of 1976 Sarah was in the middle of her third year at Holland Park School, a state secondary school in a central London location, catering non-selectively for more than 1800 children with a broad range of academic abilities. We learnt from her, almost by accident, that she had been asked to choose the subjects she wished to study in the subsequent two years, and that she had in fact made up her mind. The subjects she could sit at GCE or CSE at the end of year 5 would be effectively restricted to those selected now.

I cannot now remember the details of Sarah's choice. However, there was a quite striking absence of subjects that appeared likely to give openings to rewarding jobs, more advanced education, or continuing intellectual stimulation. Subjects like photography, drama, home economics were there in plenty, but did not appear to represent any coherent alternative to more academic study. Few of the subjects led to GCE examinations, and some did not lead to CSE exams either.

In discussion with Sarah it emerged that a number of factors had influenced her list – her liking for particular teachers, the inherent interest of particular subjects, what other pupils were choosing, the need to fill up the list. We suggested to her that there might be other ways of deciding, that her choices now might have vocational implications as well as intrinsic interest. (This was not the precise language that we used.) It followed that she should think about the longer-term future as well as the next two years of study. However, it emerged that Sarah, like many (most?) children of her age had precious little idea what she might 'do' when grown up.

The problem was beginning to look like one of decision-making under uncertainty. There was a need to make commitments now, and the uncertainty about the future suggested that there might be a case for trying to keep options open. In view of my professional interest, I proposed to Sarah that we should see if we could work together to clarify her choices. She agreed to let me try.

The analysis that follows is the product of our work together. In the original published account (Rosenhead, 1978) I claimed that she committed only an hour or so of her time to the process. I now suspect that to be an underestimate – an hour for identifying her future career possibilities, yes, but as much or more again on explaining the method and discussing the results of the analysis. My own additional commitment amounted to a few evenings extracting relevant data on prerequisites for university courses from data sources compiled for other purposes. The whole procedure was over in about a week, as it had to be to meet the school's deadline.

Structured Choices

Holland Park School issued a booklet, Choices in the Fourth Year, from which the constraints on choice could be determined. English (leading to examinations in English Language and/or Literature) and Social Education were compulsory. Pupils in addition had to select one option from each of the six option lists in Table 9.1. All the subjects in one column would be taught at the same time, so that two choices from the same column would be infeasible. The risk of clashes ruling out desired combinations was reduced by the presence of more 'popular' options in two or even three option lists. Various other constraints might come into play – some subjects could accommodate only a limited number of pupils, and no subject would be taught unless at least 17 pupils opted for it.

Evidently this part of Sarah's problem was well and tightly specified. Even so, the number of possible option combinations (candidate initial decision packages) ran well into four figures.

The next step was to make some progress in identifying acceptable 'end-states' (or configurations). Sarah might not know what she wanted to do with any certainty or clarity, but that did not mean that she had no views. For example, there were plenty of things she definitely did not want to be – from accountant to veterinary surgeon.

A session spent with a book called Careers for Girls (Miller, 1975) added further definition. She and I went through the book, flicking through the alphabetically-organized pages from career to career. Some delayed us for only a matter of seconds, eliciting an instant negative from Sarah. Others caused a pause for reflection, followed by an ex-

Table 9.1 – Options list for 4th year study

Option 1	Option 2	Option 3	Option 4	Option 5	Option 6
Science Studies	Science Studies	Needlecraft	Geography	Science Studies	Mathematics
Physics	Biology	Metalwork	Science Studies	Chemistry	Geography
Spanish (contd.)	German (contd.)	Engineering	Electronics	Classical Studies	Music
History	German (beginners)	Home Economics	Human Biology	History	European Studies
Home Economics	Mathematics	Child care	Popular Music	Home Economics	Three from
Woodwork	Needlecraft	Environmental Studies	Technical Drawing	Woodwork	1. Electronics or Typing
Art	Metalwork	Photography	Photography	Art	2. Plastics or Dressmaking
	Engineering	Sport	French (contd.)	Home Furnishing and Maintenance	3. Cinematography or Embroidery
			French (beginners)		

(From Rosenhead (1978), reproduced with permission of the Operational Research Society.)

Table 9.2 – Desirable occupations

Definitely (Group A)	Quite (Group B)	Marginally (Group C)
Acting	Advertising	Agriculture
Broadcasting	Air Stewardess	Beautician
Film Production	Archaeology	Housemother
Interior Decoration	Art and Industrial	Medical Laboratory
Journalism	Design	Technician
Stage Management	Barrister	Music
	Dancing	Sociology
	Mechanical Engineering	Technician Engineer
	Fashion	
	Museum and Art Gallery	
	Photography	
	Psychology	
	Social Work	
	Window Display	

(From Rosenhead (1978), reproduced with permission of the Operational Research Society.)

pression of more or less guarded enthusiasm. In the end there seemed to be three levels of attractiveness, with the possible future occupations categorized as in Table 9.2. This format of categories emanated more from Sarah than from me. Indeed I had little idea how they might fit into the impending analysis. However, it seemed better to reflect Sarah's perceptions as fully as possible, rather than to impose an *a priori* structure based on analytic tractability.

There will be, for any individual, many intervening life events between 'O' levels and eventual career trajectory. These events might include 'A' levels, degree or other post-school studies, false starts in employment, career switches, etc. There is an indefinite number of stages, and of alternatives at each stage. Tracing through all possible life-paths was evidently a non-starter. Instead, the approach adopted was to explore the compatibility of particular careers with specific combinations of 'O' level subjects.

For this exploration I turned again to Careers for Girls. For each of the careers the book also listed both minimum qualifications and any necessary training. Some of these prerequisites were expressed in terms of 'O' or 'A' level results – either the total number or specific subjects required. Others were expressed as degree requirements, either for a vocationally related degree, or for a degree in one of a number of broadly relevant subjects. Where both types of prerequisite were provided for a single occupation, it was because there were two types of entry: graduate and non-graduate. For non-graduate entry, I decided to ignore 'A' level requirements, on the assumption that transfer between subjects after 'O' level would be feasible. The resulting summary of information bearing on Sarah's possible 26 future occupations is shown in Table 9.3. Needless to say, a number of heroic approximations, reducing the richness of the real world, were necessary to achieve this condensation.

Careers for Girls had taken us quite a long way. But it provided no mechanism for converting degree prerequisites into 'O' level requirements – though evidently 'O' levels

Table 9.3 – Prerequisites for desirable occupations

Occupations	No.	'O' level prerequisites							Degree
		Eng. Lan.	Eng. Lit.	French	Maths	Physics	Art	Other	
GROUP A									
Acting									
Broadcasting		√	√						Econ./Soc. Sci./ History/English
Film Production	3	√		√					
Interior Decoration	3	or Lit.							
Journalism	5	√							
Stage Management		√							
GROUP B									
Advertising	5	√							or English/Psychology
Air Stewardess		√			√			Geog.	
Archaeology								Latin	Archaeology
Art and Industrial Design	4	√							
Barrister									Law
Dancing						√			
Mech. Engineering	5	√			√	√			Mech. Eng.
Fashion	5	or Lit.			√ or Sci.				
Mus. and Art Gallery	4	√		√					or Art History/ Art and Design
Photography	4	√			√			1	
Psychology		√			√			arts	Psychology
Social Work	5	√			√ or Sci.				or Social Science
Window Display	4	√			√		√		
GROUP C									
Agriculture	4	or Lit.			√	√ or Sci.			
Beautician	3	√				√ or Sci.			
Housemother									
Med. Lab. Technician	4	√			√				
Music	5				√	√ or Sci.			
Sociology									Sociology
Technician Engineer	4				√				

(From Rosenhead (1978), reproduced with permission of the Operational Research Society.)

(as well as 'A' levels) are generally necessary to gain entry to universities. To effect this mapping I turned to the Compendium published by the Association of Commonwealth Universities (Committee of Vice-Chancellors and Principals, 1975). This copious volume listed all first degrees available at British universities, the general requirements for entry to each university, and the specific requirements for each course of study there. Of course, the degrees so listed were those to be offered in 1976–7. Though none of us had any idea in what year, if any, Sarah would commence university studies, we were all quite clear that she was not precocious enough to gain entry in the next six months. However, degree courses are not listed, because not decided, half a decade or more in advance. So the Compendium for 1976–7 was the best we could do.

A number of obstacles loomed up, obscuring the map. The first was that entry requirements for a particular course at a particular university were generally expressed in terms of a minimum number of 'O' levels, plus a specification of particular subjects at 'A' level. This obstacle was side-stepped by assuming that if a particular 'A' level was called for, then the pupil (that is, Sarah) would need to take the corresponding 'O' level.

It may seem obvious, with hindsight, that this flatly contradicts the assumption on 'O' level-'A' level transfer made for non-graduate entry requirements. However, it was not obvious at the time, nor has anyone commented on it since, although this application of robustness analysis to Sarah's education has received a good deal of public exposure.

Of course, one could produce rationalizations for differences in subject switching behaviour between those intending direct entry to an occupation and their university-bound contemporaries. But I cannot swear that I had such considerations in mind, because 1 cannot now remember. It is more plausible, however, to believe that the contrasting assumptions were made for reasons of convenience. Non-degree entry prerequisites were most commonly specified in terms of 'O' levels, while for degree entry 'A' level requirements predominated.

Such pragmatic considerations are not unreasonable in what must of necessity be rough-and-ready analyses. Both time and resources place constraints on the detail and sophistication of what can be achieved. So too does the need to keep the argument transparent, so that the logic can be appropriated by the client. In the end the effects of the questionable assumptions may well be swamped by other factors. The balance between completeness and convenience must, in general, be a matter for analytic judgement.

The other major obstacle in the way of converting university entrance conditions into 'O' level subject requirements was that universities were, and are, perversely different from each other. Consider law degrees. These were on offer from 29 universities. A sizeable minority required only four unspecified 'O' levels. However, the University of Warwick required five, and specified English Language, an arts subject, and Mathematics or a science. Other universities fell between these extremes. The same pattern of diversity recurred in all subjects.

How should this difficulty be tackled? One possibility would be to find the set of 'O' levels which would meet the requirements of all 29 universities – but the result would be so bulky a compilation of subjects as to make any child turn round and drop out. And in

Table 9.4 – 'O' level requirements for degree subjects

	No of Passes	Specified subjects	Coverage
Archaeology	4	English Language, Language	9/14
Art	4	English Language, Modern Language	7/15
Economics	4	English, Mathematics	32/40
Mechanical Engineering	4	English, Mathematics, Physics, Chemistry	27/34
English	4	English Language and Literature, French	20/31
History	4	English, French, History	22/34
Law	4	English	18/29
Psychology	4	English, Mathematics	23/36
Social Work	4	English, Mathematics	17/22
Sociology	4	English, Mathematics	24/29

(From Rosenhead (1978), reproduced with permission of the Operational Research Society.)

any case, no one needs to go to 29 universities. Another possibility would be to specify only enough subjects to make sure that at least one university would have her. After all, one is enough. But what if that one changes its admission rules, or changes the course? What if Sarah insists on moving out of London, or refuses to, or her grades aren't good enough? And so on. One is not enough.

The solution adopted was to start with the minimum requirement for a particular degree subject, and note how many universities it would gain access to. Then the effect on university accessibility of adding relevant possible 'O' levels to the minimum requirement, first one at a time, then in pairs, was explored. This process was terminated by the law of diminishing returns.

We can take law degrees as an example. Eight of the 29 courses required only four passes, subjects unspecified. Four passes including English would give access to eighteen of the courses, far more than any other single subject. The best single subject to add to English was Mathematics, and that garnered only a further two courses, raising the total to 20 out of 29. Further extensions of the 'O' level repertoire would produce only a dribble of additional universities in twos or ones. Moving to five 'O' levels adds a few more, mostly Scottish, universities, but only when three or more subjects are specified.

Evidently a very adequate range of future choice among law degrees could be achieved with four 'O' levels of which one is English. This was adopted as the 'O' level entry requirement for law. The requirements for all degrees relevant to Sarah's careers of interest, worked out in the same way, are shown in Table 9.4.

Coming to Conclusions

Tables 9.3 and 9.4 contain summary information about what Sarah would have to study to secure direct (non-graduate) or graduate entry to the possible occupations of her

Table 9.5 – Career accessibility in terms of key 'O' level combinations

Careers	Nil	French	Maths	Science	French/ Maths	French/ Science	Maths/ Science	French/ Maths/ Science	Other required Degree
Acting	✓	✓	✓	✓	✓	✓	✓	✓	
Broadcasting ⎱ or		✓	✓		✓	✓	✓	✓	History
Film Production ⎰		✓	✓		✓	✓		✓	
Interior Decoration	✓	✓			✓	✓		✓	
Journalism	✓	✓	✓	✓	✓	✓	✓	✓	
Stage Management	✓	✓	✓	✓	✓	✓	✓	✓	
Advertising	✓	✓	✓		✓	✓	✓	✓	
Air Stewardess		✓	✓		✓	✓	✓	✓	Geography
Archaeology		✓			✓	✓	✓	✓	Latin
Art and Ind. Design		✓		✓	✓	✓	✓	✓	
Barrister		✓		✓	✓	✓	✓	✓	
Dancing		✓	✓	✓	✓	✓	✓	✓	
Mech. Engineering							if Physics	if Physics	
Fashion			✓		✓	✓	✓	✓	
Mus. and Art Gallery		✓			✓	✓	✓	✓	
Photography ⎱ or	✓				✓	✓	✓	✓	Art
Psychology			✓	✓	✓	✓	✓	✓	
Social Work			✓		✓	✓	✓	✓	
Window Display	✓		✓	✓	✓	✓	✓	✓	Art
Agriculture				✓		✓	✓	✓	
Beautician		✓	✓	✓	✓	✓	✓	✓	
Housemother		✓			✓	✓	✓	✓	
Med. Lab. Tech.			✓	✓		✓	✓	✓	
Music		✓	✓	✓	✓	✓	✓	✓	
Sociology			✓		✓		✓	✓	
Technician Eng.			✓	✓		✓	✓	✓	

(From Rosenhead (1978), reproduced with permission of the Operational Research Society.)

choice. But to assist in her pressing present decision problem, further processing was necessary. The next stage was to turn the logic round. Instead of listing what subjects were required for particular occupations, we examined instead which occupations should be accessible with particular combinations of 'O' levels in her satchel.

The first step was to identify the key subjects out of which any 'decision package' of 'O' levels was likely to be constructed. Evidently the subjects that had featured prominently in Tables 9.3 and 9.4 more or less nominated themselves – English, French, Mathematics, a science. Table 9.5 displays for each possible career the decision packages of no more than four subjects that would give access to it. (Multiple decision packages give access to the same career because, for example, if Social Work entry is possible with 'O' levels in English and Mathematics, it is also possible with English, Mathematics, and any other subject or subjects.)

The rather precise information in Table 9.5 was, however, only achieved through a series of further assumptions, made for simplification or for definiteness. Where there were graduate and non-graduate entry routes, we required a set of 'O' levels which would give access to both. Where there were alternative degree routes, we took as entry requirements a set of subjects giving access to at least 50 per cent of the degree subjects. The number of 'O' level passes required was disregarded, on the assumption that any numerical shortfall could be made good in time. These were judgements made, effectively, by Sarah's mother and myself. There is no other justification for them than that they seemed reasonable at the time and that alternative assumptions could have been investigated in the same way.

From Table 9.5 it is now straight-forward to read off the careers rendered accessible by each decision package of 'O' levels. The number of careers in each attractiveness class maintained by each decision package is shown in Table 9.6. From this table one can, in effect, compute robustness scores for any subject combination at each of three satisfying levels. Thus if only 'Group A' careers are acceptable, 'English plus a science' has a robustness of 3/6; whereas if a career from any of the three attractiveness classes will do, the robustness of the same package is 10/26 (or 12/26 if Art is also taken).

However, there were more useful things to do with the tabular information. Investigation of possible patterns in the data soon showed that the addition of 'a science' gave little extra career accessibility in any case, and none at all within Group A. So the information was further simplified, as in Table 9.7, to show the coverage of possible careers provided by a reduced set of decision packages excluding 'a science'. Each of these sets of 'O' levels could then be checked against the timetable constraints of Table 9.1. Given the incomplete specification of Sarah's programme of study (no more than three subjects out of six), and their mainline nature, there were, of course, no timetable clashes.

Table 9.7 consists of 'management information' bearing on Sarah's education dilemma. It did not tell her, or us, what she should study. What it did do was provide the evidence on which a balance could be struck between the number of subjects to be selected for their career potential, and the number to be chosen for their current intrinsic interest. In discussion with her mother and myself, with the analysis described here as the

Table 9.6 – Numbers of careers made accessible by alternative subject combinations

	Career groups		
Subject combinations	Group A	Group B	Group C
English	3	3	2
English, French	4 (plus History, 5)	5 (plus Art, 6) (plus Latin, 6)	2
English, Mathematics	5	7 (plus Art, 9) (plus Geog, 8)	4
English, a science	3	4 (plus Art, 6)	3
English, French, Mathematics	6	9 (plus Art, 10) (plus Geog, 10) (plus Latin, 10)	4
English, French a science	4 (plus History, 5)	7 (plus Art, 8) (plus Latin, 8)	3
English, Maths, a science	5	7 (if Physics, 8) (plus Art, 9 or 10) (plus Geog, 8 or 9)	7
English, French Maths, a science	6	9 (if Physics, 10) (plus Art, 10, or 11) (plus Geog, 10 or 11) (plus Latin, 10 or 11)	7
Total in group	6	13	7

(From Rosenhead (1978), reproduced with permission of the Operational Research Society.)

Table 9.7 – Simplified information on career accessibility

	Career groups		
Subject combinations	Group A	Group B	Group C
English	3	3	2
English, French	4+	5+	2
English, Mathematics	5	7+	4
English, French, Mathematics	6	9+	4
Total in group	6	13	7

(From Rosenhead (1978), reproduced with permission of the Operational Research Society.)

focus, Sarah's position on her choice of subjects shifted. In particular she came to see the value of adding to the compulsory English both French and Mathematics – which she had previously doubted. We, for our part, saw more clearly that it was unnecessary to specify all six of Sarah's options on vocational grounds. Broad coverage could be achieved with a relatively small number of strategically selected subjects.

To English, French, and Mathematics Sarah added Art, Biology, History, and Photography on the basis of personal preference. This combination, as can be seen from Table 9.6, permitted access to all six careers from Group A, ten from Group B, and all seven from Group C. The three inaccessible careers from Group B were effectively excluded by her failure to choose Geography, Latin, and Physics, respectively.

Afterword

At the time of writing this chapter in 2001, Sarah is 38 years old. It might be thought appropriate, therefore, to ask what happened next, and later. In this concluding section I will attempt an answer, as well as pick out some features of the robustness analysis of her 1976 dilemma for further comment.

Life is full of uncertainties. Symbolic of this turbulence is that Sarah is no longer Sarah but Sas. More importantly, in terms of outcome, our analysis in the mid-1970s failed to take account of Mrs Thatcher or the then developing crisis of world capitalism. For Sarah/Sas's generation, even a job, let alone a career, proved to be a problematic notion.

What has transpired for Sas in educational/occupational terms is this. Her attempts in French and Mathematics proved unavailing, but she secured 'O' level or 'O' level equivalent passes in English Language, English Literature, Art and History, and in Sociology which she added to her studies extra-murally in Year 5. Sas decided to stay on at school, and studied for and achieved passes in 'A' level Sociology, Politics, and History. This qualified her for admission to degree-level studies, but she declined to apply; she entered instead on an extended period of introspection, personal crisis, and unemployment.

Organizing a women-only housing cooperative brought her eventually into contact with a housing association, which was itself part of a cluster of community work organizations operating with young people in West London. For the next eight or so years she worked for them, first as an outreach community worker, and subsequently in a variety of roles.

So, when the first edition of this book came out in 1989, I could write that Sas had ended up, for the time-being at least, in one of the Group B (quite attractive) careers she identified at age 14.* Which was really rather neat. However life is rarely so tidy. The voluntary organization for which she worked accidentally omitted to pay National Insurance contributions for its employees over an extended period, and this oversight produced an unmanageable debt. It was wound up. Sas has retrained as a plumber, and

---

*Alert readers might notice, by consulting Table 9.5, that this would appear to be an impossibility, without Mathematics 'O' level. The anomaly is, though, only apparent. Social work is a dual entry level career. Table 9.5 records the more stringent prerequisites for entry to be possible by both routes. Sas's non-graduate entry (see Table 9.3) did not require mathematics.

her business is now modestly blossoming. This was not an impulsive or unconsidered move; she had indeed expressed an interest in plumbing nearly 20 years before she took it up. Plumbing did *not* feature in the lists of possible careers she compiled in 1976 – because the source book (Miller 1975) which we consulted did not include it among its 'Careers for Girls'. Plumbing made its entry in the following edition (Miller 1978), retitled *Equal Opportunities: a careers guide for women and men.*

What has been happening to Sas since the moment of decision reconstructed in this chapter actually has precious little bearing on the validity of the method used. (A problem formulation does not stay fixed over 10 or 20 years – it represents the decision issues as perceived at a particular juncture.) I summarize it here principally to dispel any doubt which silence on the subject might otherwise have provoked. This one dimensional slice of life history does, however, both make a point and raise an issue. The point that it demonstrates is that it is virtually impossible to overestimate the richness of uncertainty, here relating both to unpredictable events and to future changes of preference. The valuable issue that it raises is: if the result of the analysis was to persuade Sas to study French and Mathematics, in both of which she failed to get 'O' level qualifications, wasn't the analysis a waste of time?

The answer is, I don't think so, and neither does Sas. It is not only decisions which emerge from the engagement between analyst and client. The process may be as significant as the product. In this case I believe the process of collaborating over her education choices may have contributed to a gradual improvement in our relationship. More significantly, Sas has stated on a number of occasions that the analysis of her 'O' level subjects was one of the turning points in her process of growing up. She came to see, not only that what she did now would affect her options in the future, but also that she could understand the connections well enough to make informed choices. It was a stage in feeling able to assume responsibility over her own life.

This empowering aspect of appropriate analysis is at least as important as any particular decisions that may emerge from it. Thus almost any educationalist or parent could have asserted to a child that English, French, and Mathematics are the three key 'O' level subjects. The result of our analysis was that Sas did not have to take this on trust. She understood why, so that the decisions became hers rather than ours. She could, in principle, have used the logic to explore the consequences of her subsequent educational decisions.

I am fairly sure that this did not happen at any conscious level. However, the basic logic was used again, and more than once. In 1980 Sarah's younger brother Dominic in turn confronted the choice of his 'O' level subjects, though with differences. English, Mathematics, Social Education, and a science were now all compulsory at Holland Park School, and the simultaneously timetabled options lists had shrunk to four in number. The school had reduced in size, and some option combinations (for example History with Physics) which had previously been possible were so no longer. The source book we used on careers was now titled *Equal Opportunities*, with some corresponding changes of content. But the principle difference was that Dominic was not Sarah.

Dominic was more academically oriented than Sarah. His career choices were similar in number to hers, but more tightly focused on 'professional' occupations. Furthermore, his preferences seemed to cluster them roughly into four groups (definite/likely/possible/unlikely), rather than three. Most significantly, he identified a first choice of subjects that gave us no qualms on vocational grounds. But he nevertheless had a problem. He doubted his ability to pass French and Mathematics, both of which were on his list. How crucial to his ambitions was success in these two examinations? A variant of the method developed for Sarah proved helpful. With this we were able to explore the reduction in career options resulting from failure to secure passes in either or both subjects. After passing eight 'O' levels well (but not French which he balked at) we used a further variant to examine the effects of alternative 'A' level choices.

Before this second bout with Dominic, however, I had worked with my niece Annabel on her choice of 'O' levels. She attended a nearby girls' public (that is, private) school with a high academic reputation. Her decision situation was different again. She was studying ten subjects, but the school would not permit her to be examined in so many. She had to find one, and preferably two, to drop. There was a lack of meeting of minds between herself and her parents on what should be sacrificed – Latin? Geography? Chemistry? Art? I was turned to by mutual agreement, as a possible way of breaking the log-jam. But in the end they resolved the issue themselves before the analysis had proceeded very far.

The main purpose of these digressions is not to introduce the reader to my extended family. It is, rather, to indicate the flexible nature of this approach to flexibility. Almost any relevant problem situation will present its own unique features. Only the very basic framework of sequentially and option preservation (or management) is common to all applications. Particular formulations of rich variety emerge out of the combination of objective circumstances, the subjectivity of the client, and the relationship between client and analyst.

Certainly the case study of Sarah's 'O' levels has features all its own. The methodology that we evolved in use is shown in Figure 9.1. Evidently this bears little overt resemblance to the generic methodology sketched out in Figure 8.11 of the previous chapter. Interpretation can, however, reveal some regularities.

Various activities in the generic model do not feature in the analysis of Sarah's problem. The identification of an impending system (activities 3, 4, 8) was unnecessary as there were no decisions in the pipeline. Multiple futures (activity 7) were not considered – the uncertainties being managed were of Friend and Jessop's type UV (uncertainty as to values) rather than UR (uncertainty in related decision fields). Alternative interim systems (activity 10) and their performance (activity 14) did not feature, as the initial decisions as to 'O' levels were only instrumentalities towards future careers. They did not define operating systems valued for themselves. Sarah had no illusions that she could influence the context within which her decisions would become operative (activity 17), nor did we develop contingency plans (activity 16) – though we did in Dominic's case. The remaining activities can be mapped loosely on to Figure 9.1 – but as the 'system

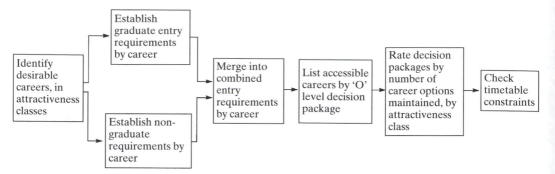

Figure 9.1 Methodology employed for Sarah's 'O' level choice

model' is of compatibility with desired careers rather than of acceptable performance, it connects rather differently. Robustness methodology, evidently, must be regarded as an enabling framework for both analyst and client, not a prescribed straitjacket.

The integral role of the model, evident in Sarah's case as in other applications of robustness analysis, links the approach clearly to the OR tradition. OR models can in general be used in two ways – as optimizing tools for recommending decisions which are in some sense 'best', or as option scanning devices. Robustness analysis has been used on occasions in the former mode (though with 'best' reinterpreted). In Sarah's case, however, the role of the model was clearly limited to the exploration of 'what if ...' questions about the consequences of alternative actions. Valuations of these consequences are excluded as external to the function of the model – they are the prerogative of the decision-maker.

The decision-aiding approach depends crucially on its accessibility to those whose problem it is. Sarah was, aged 14, the antithesis of the normal OR client, the technically qualified or experienced manager, accustomed to the depersonalized manipulation of capital or human resources. She, therefore, posed a particularly severe test for the transparency of the robustness approach, which it appeared to pass.

Sarah was an unusual client for OR not only in her youth and limited experience, but in her gender. Just how unusual was brought home to me when I submitted the original account of this work for publication in Britain's principal operational research journal. The paper was accepted for publication; but when the proofs arrived from the printers, I found that 'she' had everywhere been replaced by 'he'. Enquiry revealed that this was not an aberration of some deranged compositor. It was a deliberate act by the editor in compliance with the house style, which called for all decision-makers to be male. Publication without change of Sarah's gender was eventually agreed. But only on condition that a footnote be inserted, explaining that very similar methods would work for a boy.

This bizarre anecdote does bring out one aspect of the restricted nature of OR's traditional clientele, which has been commented on elsewhere (Rosenhead, 1986). This pervasive bias provoked the development of Community Operational Research (see Chapter 1), which aimed to redress the balance by focusing on analytic work with community groups. For this clientele, transparency of methods is at a premium. The relative accessibility of robustness analysis to Sarah suggests, therefore, that it could find a place in the repertoire of those practising community OR, as other problem structuring methods have done.

Militating against this are the practical and cultural obstacles to a community group, confronting pressing problems with minuscule resources, being able to detach itself sufficiently to address how the resolution of these immediate concerns might affect its future action space.

The link which I have made between Sarah's situation and that of community groups is not fanciful. They share a non-managerial status, and, in general, a lack of socialization into the ways of bureaucracy and processed knowledge. Community groups, too, exist to protect the interests of their members, with few resources to control except their own lives. Success for Community OR will depend on its practitioners' ability to establish committed relations with their clients; and to ensure that the analytic assistance offered is appropriate to their circumstances. Broadly such practitioners will need to eschew technical solutions in favour of the provision of illuminating structures. Within this context robustness analysis may yet have useful services to offer. It is no easy task to keep open the options of the weak in a hostile world.

References

Best, G., Parston, G., and Rosenhead, J. (1986). 'Robustness in practice: the regional planning of health services', *J. Opl Res. Soc.*, 37, 463–78.
Caplin, D.A. and Kornbluth, J.S.H. (1975). 'Multiple investment planning under uncertainty', *Omega*, **3**, 423–41.
Committee of Vice-Chancellors and Principals of the United Kingdom (1975). *The Compendium of University Entrance Requirements for First Degree Courses in the United Kingdom in 1976-7*, Association of Commonwealth Universities, London.
Gupta, S.K, and Rosenhead, J. (1968). 'Robustness in sequential investment decisions', *Mgmt Sci.*, **15**, 18–29.
Miller, R. (1975). *Careers for Girls*, Penguin, Harmondsworth.
Miller, R. (1978). *Equal Opportunities: A Careers Guide for Women and Men*, Penguin, Harmondsworth.
Rosenhead, J. (1978). 'An education in robustness', *J. Opl Res. Soc.*, **29**, 105–11.
Rosenhead, J. (1986). 'Custom and practice', *J. Opl Res. Soc.*, **37**, 335–43.

10 *Drama Theory and Confrontation Analysis*

Peter Bennett, Jim Bryant and Nigel Howard

Conflict and Cooperation

All the best plans – no matter now well thought-out or how pure your motives – encounter opposition. This is not necessarily because other people are pig-headed, stupid or malevolent (though they may be) or have hidden agendas and vested interests in frustrating progress (though they may have). Different people will naturally have different perspectives on any situation: they will approach it from different backgrounds, and perhaps from within different organizations.

This chapter introduces some ways of analysing situations involving several interested parties, each with a stake in what happens, and with some influence on events. Though they may not be in total opposition, they start by trying to bring about different outcomes. In that sense, they are in conflict. Such situations include not only obvious and spectacular events such as wars, strikes and riots, but also more mundane problems. Conflicts need not be destructive: they are faced by managers, administrators and council officers, for example, not just by politicians or generals. They are met in the everyday lives of friends and family, and not only when those relationships are going 'wrong'.

Whatever the setting, the key challenge for decision-making is that nobody has complete control of events. Each side must try to take into account the others' possible actions, while also trying to influence them (and knowing that they are also trying to predict and/or influence one's own choices). The potential therefore exists for threat, deceit, bluff and counter-bluff. However *conflict is hardly ever absolute*. Almost always, some common interests exist, and gains can be made by cooperating – or at least keeping conflict within limits. The methods introduced here apply in conditions ranging from comparative goodwill to outright hostility. They are based on an approach known as *Drama Theory*, which develops and extends the earlier *Theory of Games*.

The Theory of Games

The 'Game' Model

Game Theory provides a structure for understanding and analysing conflicts. It started life in economics (Von Neumann and Morgenstern, 1944) where it is still influential:

other applications range from international relations to biology. Nevertheless, it has always been controversial. This is partly terminology: calling something a 'game' can suggest that you are treating it as trivial, or just a matter of winning or losing – though in fact Game Theory implies neither of these. What it does is to structure situations in terms of:

- two or more *players*, who can be individual people, groupings such as committees or cabinets, or entities such as corporations or nations;
- *strategies* for each player, covering all possible courses of action.
- the possible *outcomes* of the game
- *preferences* for each player. These may be expressed quantitatively in terms of *utility scales*: however many models require only a *preference order* for each player, ranking outcomes between 'best' and 'worst'.

Preferences need not be selfish. Players may be altruistic or malevolent toward each other: their wants need not be for material things. They just have to be definable.

At one extreme, preferences may be exactly opposed, so that players can only gain at each other's expense. These are *zero-sum* games. At the other end of the spectrum, their aims may exactly coincide, in which case the problem is simply one of getting to the outcome everyone wants. Between the two extremes are games in which players' interests are in partial opposition, so that they may be torn between conflict and cooperation. These are known as *mixed-motive* games.

Whatever the players' preferences are, Game Theory analyses what happens if they act in pursuit of them. The simplest form of analysis assumes that everyone knows what the game is, but not each other's choice of strategy. Originally the main aim of analysis was to show how rational players *should* act. For some classes of game, most notably two-player, zero-sum games, this can be done convincingly. Even in situations too complicated to analyse completely – like the game of chess – the theory can throw light on what sort of solutions exist. However in the real ('mixed-motive') world of partial conflict, threats and promises, bargaining and negotiation, normative solutions are more difficult to find. Indeed, some results seem to cast doubt on the whole notion of rationality. Two very simple examples will help illustrate this

The Game of 'Chicken'

The game of 'Chicken' draws on an analogy with games played in cars or on motorcycles by Hell's Angels and the like. The two players – whom we shall here call Abe and Bea – drive straight toward each other, trying to demonstrate their bravery and nerve. The first to swerve is despised by the rest of the gang as a 'chicken'. Figure 10.1 shows choices and outcomes in the form of a matrix. In this very simple model, each player has just two strategies: 'swerve' or 'drive on', and four possible results are as shown in Figure

(a) Showing choices and outcomes

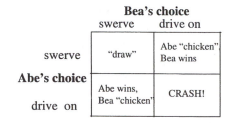

(b) Showing preference orders

Figure 10.1 Game of chicken

10.1(a). (A three-player game would have a 3-D matrix, and so on.) Figure 10.1(b) completes the model by adding preferences for each side, ranking them from 1 ('best') down to 4 ('worst'), and with those for Abe on the left in each cell. Note that our notation in this and the following chapter varies from traditional usage in game theory, where the most preferred outcome is given the largest ranking, as it seems to us more intuitive and understandable. The model assumes that each player wants to avoid being derided as a chicken, but would rather be a live chicken than a dead hero. Clearly, the two players cannot both win. But both can certainly lose: if neither backs down, they each end up in a head-on crash.

There is a tricky problem of choice here. Suppose you are Abe: you are trying to act 'rationally', and Bea knows this.

Being rational, you will swerve if you think Bea is not going to, since (3,1) is better for you than (4,4). Equally, you won't swerve if you think she is going to – (1,3) being better for you than (2,2). But if she knows that you are rational, she can work out that this will be your reaction. So she simply needs to communicate the intention not to swerve. The result: you swerve and she doesn't. This is her best outcome; it is certainly not yours. By contrast, if you 'irrationally' decide never to swerve, then provided *her* reactions are rational, you get your best outcome.

It may be objected that Chicken is just a silly game, which rational people should not play in the first place. However, it turns out that this problem is inherent in many situations. Being predictably 'rational' turns out, in general to mean being a sucker. People often face 'Chicken-like' decisions whether they want to or not: when a war looms, or a potentially disastrous strike, or divorce. Often, neither side wants such an outcome, but backing down first can entail real losses – not just loss of face, though this can matter in real life too. If so, the model tells us to expect a *race to establish commitment* (Schelling, 1960), each side trying to convince the other that it cannot or will not back down. 'Logical' tactics include tying one's own hands ('My own people wouldn't let me agree to this even if I wanted to'), deliberate impressions of irrationality, and displays of emotion and hatred toward the other side ('better dead than red'). These can be seen all too frequently, whether in everyday life or high politics.

Prisoners' Dilemma

This game derives from a story about two suspected criminals (say Alf and Bet) held in separate cells, each given the choice of confessing to armed robbery (and so implicating his or her partner) or maintaining silence. The authorities offer a deal. 'If you confess', Alf is told 'it will be better for you. If Bet has not confessed too, we'll see that she takes all the blame. She'll get 20 years, and you'll get a pardon for giving evidence against her. If she confesses too, you'll each get less than the maximum term – say 12 years. If neither of you confess, I admit we've not got the evidence to convict you for the robbery. But we will convict you for carrying illegal firearms – you'll each get 4 years. And by the way, you should know that we're offering Bet exactly the same deal.'

The resulting game is shown in Figure 10.2, firstly with the actual prison sentences and then with preference rankings, assuming each player wants to spend as little time in gaol as possible. (If they have other motivations, this leads to a different game.) Alf's preferences are shown on the left in each cell, with 1 as best for him. Trying to act rationally, he may reason thus:

> 'I'm not sure what Bet will do, but either way, I do better by confessing. If she stays silent, I get my best outcome ('1' instead of '2'). If *she* confesses, then by doing the same I at least avoid my worst outcome. Come to think of it, I can see that she faces the same problem: I must therefore expect her to confess too. Pity, but there it is.'

For each individual player, confessing pays off whatever the other does. So it surely seems rational for each to do so. But both then do worse than if they had acted 'irrationally' and stayed silent – 12 years in gaol instead of 4. Even if they earlier promised each other to stay silent if caught, there is no way of enforcing the agreement. Each would be tempted to double-cross the other, and both know it.

As with 'Chicken', the model has been applied to a wide variety of situations, in particular to arms races driven by distrust (e.g. Rapoport, 1960). In its multi-player form, it has also been used to analyse ecological issues, in which individual self-interest – e.g., in using up a resource – can lead to scarcity for everyone. Many laws and social

(a) Showing choices and years in gaol

Bet's choice

	silent	confess
silent	both get 4 yrs	Alf 20 yrs, Bet free
confess	Alf free, Bet 20 yrs	both get 12 yrs

Alf's choice (silent / confess rows)

(b) Showing preference orders

Bet's choice

	silent	confess
silent	2, 2	4, 1
confess	1, 4	3, 3

Alf's choice (silent / confess rows)

Figure 10.2 Prisoner's dilemma

rules can be seen as ways of resolving such dilemmas. For example, civil law helps parties to make binding commitments by imposing real costs on anyone defaulting. (Conversely, sometimes rules *prevent* actors from resolving Prisoners' Dilemmas – e.g., laws to stop companies colluding to fix prices.) Sometimes solutions are less formal: social cohesion can encourage value systems in which people prefer not to exploit each other. Real prisoners may have 'honour amongst thieves': they also tend to ensure that anyone 'squealing' suffers unpleasant consequences. All these factors can be modelled by modifying preferences, strategies or both.

Extending the Model

Though it is easy to recognize real situations somewhat akin to (say) Chicken or Prisoners' Dilemma, simple games leave out many important factors. To some extent, these limitations can be overcome by extending the game model in various ways. For example, simple Game Theory assumes that people see the world in the same way (the same 'game'). However it may be more realistic to say that decision-makers often see *different* games. This can be modelled using *games with incomplete information* (Harsanyi, 1968) or *hypergame analysis* (Bennett, 1977; 1980). *Multi-stage* models allow for linkage of choices over time using a series of linked games, the outcome of each influencing which game the players face next. (For example, some outcomes of an industrial relations negotiation might lead to a strike, this can be analysed as a separate game, and so on.) Games can also be linked in the sense of a given actor having to deal with several issues simultaneously. For example, negotiations can be analysed as 'two level games' (Evans *et al.*, 1993), in which leaders have simultaneously to negotiate with each other and maintain their own internal support.

From Games to Dramas

A Theory Built on Dilemmas

The above extensions to Game Theory (and others) allow a richer choice of models. But none of them removes the dilemmas for rational choice encapsulated in very simple games like Chicken and Prisoners' Dilemma. In both cases, players do better if they can undertake to act 'irrationally', against their own preferences. Analysts' responses to such dilemmas vary. Recognizing that rational choice can be problematic need not rule out constructing normative theory, and much mainstream work has continued in this direction (e.g. Binmore, 1987; Ordeshook 1989). An alternative view is that models are better seen in terms of helping to clarify the structure of the situation, complete with dilemmas and difficulties. The aim is then to provide insight into the decisions faced by the actors, how their choices interact, and what the implications are for bargaining, communication, and so on.

Drama Theory starts from this second interpretation of Game Theory, and builds on it. It seeks to analyse how conflicts change and develop over time, rather than just rational choice within fixed games. However these are not treated as separate matters. Rather, *conflict dynamics are often driven by the dilemmas of choice faced at any given time*. Thus drama theory offers a conceptual framework that actively encourages the exploration of deliberate change forced upon characters by the pressure of the dilemmas that they face. Responses to such dilemmas include emotion, preference change and generation of new options, along with the use of particular forms of argument. Though not part of rational choice, these responses are not random or arbitrary. Instead, they stem directly from the 'logic' of the situation.

Basics of Drama Theory

Drama Theory proposes an overall model of conflict and its resolution that can be summarized as follows:

- A drama unfolds as a series of *episodes* in which some of the parties (now termed *characters*) interact. Their actions influence not only the outcome of each particular episode, but also what happens next.

- Within each episode, there is scene-setting, build-up, climax and *dénouement*, a structure repeated on a larger scale for the drama as a whole.
- In the *build-up stage*, characters communicate, by word and/or deed. They may well start by simply exploring each other's (and their own) views, beliefs, aims etc. This may take a long time, or be over very quickly: the point is that at the end of this stage each character is advocating a particular *position* – a future that it wants the other characters to agree to or accept. Each character is also indicating what it will do if these wishes are not met, which we call that character's *fallback*.
- A key point is the *Moment of Truth*, at which the characters have succeeded in communicating definite positions and fallbacks to each other (and so have, for the time being, got over any problems caused by perceiving different games). Unless their positions are all compatible with each other, the characters try to get their way by threats and promises, backed up by persuasion and argument. However these influence attempts turn out to be problematic *because they rest on threats and/or promises to act against one's own preferences*. The emotional temperature rises, leading to....
- ... the *climax* of the episode. The paradoxes of rationality create specific forms of emotion and preference change, as well as generation of new options, involvement of other characters, etc.
- Some or all of the characters then take actions – as distinct from merely promising or threatening to do so – which move them into another episode.
- Through successive episodes, the characters reframe their views. An important part of this process is often the – perhaps reluctant – recognition of common interest. As a result, characters often start to take common actions to achieve their aims and may start to act as a single 'supercharacter' with a single position. (This process is always potentially reversible, though: it is important to look for sources of internal disagreement.)
- *Resolution* occurs on reaching an outcome that exhausts *both* rationality and emotion. There are no opportunities to do better within the current situation: nor are there any remaining dilemmas to trigger further transformations. (As will be seen, this idea can be given a quite precise definition.).

The principal aim of Drama Theory is to analyse real situations. But just as Game Theory can be used to analyse parlour games, it is often interesting to analyse scripted dramas – plays or novels – treating the characters as if they were real. Arguably, dramas that have 'lasted' have something important to say about human relationships, so their analysis can tell us something about life too. As with Game Theory, the basic model can be extended in various ways. For example, in many (real and scripted) dramas, one can discern different plots and sub-plots. These may run almost independently, or be highly intertangled. Dramas can often be seen happening simultaneously at many different levels, for example between and within groups and organizations.

Drama Theory models the interplay of rational choice, emotion and argument. In doing so it draws together existing insights into each of these, while offering some novel claims about how they are related (Bennett & Howard, 1996; Howard, 1999). The fundamental idea is that attempts to act rationally – to choose in accordance with current preferences – create dilemmas for characters. Consciously or otherwise, they are then driven to try to resolve them. This is where emotions and preference change come in: in this context emotions can be seen as the heat generated by the friction of preference change. Characters also bolster threats and promises with rational argument in the common interest and, when their own views change, use arguments that rationalize their new perceptions, both to themselves and to each other.

The rest of the chapter makes these ideas more concrete. In particular, we introduce the technique of Confrontation Analysis. This is both the mathematical underpinning for Drama Theory, and a useful method in its own right.

Confrontation Analysis: Setting Up A Model

Characters, Cards and Futures

Confrontation Analysis provides a way of structuring situations and identifying the dilemmas for different characters. From this, we can make predictions as to the sorts of responses liable to occur – though these are not mechanical and will make use of whatever is known about individual characters' personalities and values and about the wider social context. Confrontation Analysis provides a logical skeleton on which to put the relevant flesh. The method itself is designed to be as flexible and user-friendly as possible. Rather than considering whole strategies for each side, we build up combinations of binary (yes/no) options. This follows previous adaptations of Game Theory (Howard, 1971; 1989) and allows modelling to be done in easy stages, with options being added or modified as necessary. We often refer to options as *cards* that each side can play. (Though a partial reversion to 'game' terminology, this does correspond to a very widespread figure of speech.)

Different combinations of cards being played lead to different scenarios, or *futures*. In principle, even a modest number of available cards creates a large number of possible futures. Unlike earlier methods, however, Confrontation Analysis concentrates on the relationships between just a few of these, primarily the positions and fallbacks for each character. The starting-points for analysis thus become:

- the key *characters* (individual people, or groups or organizations, depending on the level at which the model is defined)
- the *position* being advocated by each character, defined in terms of *cards* to be played or not by *all* characters
- the *fallback* for each character, defined in terms of the cards played by that character alone. The *threatened future* is that in which every character plays its fallback cards.

A Card Table

All the elements just listed can be put together in the form of a *card table*. While this is illustrated more fully in the following Chapter, a simple example may be helpful here. This concerns a hypothetical (but realistic enough) confrontation between a rail operating company and a union representing part of the workforce. Let us suppose that:

> The company has proposed the introduction of a new rostering of shift work, which the union claims will lead to more inconvenient and antisocial working hours for its members. As a conciliatory gesture, the company has also said that it will review annual holiday arrangements to provide more flexibility. However the Union is not convinced that the new arrangements will be any better, and in any case they would not compensate for the proposed new rostering pattern. It has stated that it will accept the new roster only in conjunction with a substantial (5%) annual pay increase: currently the company is offering 2%. The Union is threatening to call a series of one-day strikes, and there has also been talk of an overtime ban. Failing agreement, the Company says that it will impose the rosters anyway, and withdraw the new holiday arrangements. Talks are currently stalemated.

Figure 10.3 shows a simple card table model of this situation.

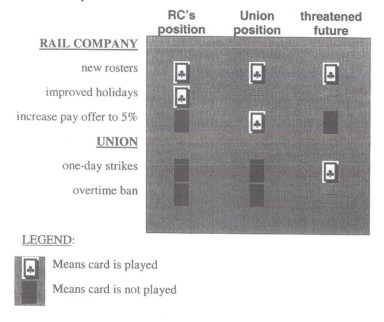

LEGEND:

Means card is played

Means card is not played

EXPLANATION:

Each column represents a particular future. The three futures shown here are the Rail Company's position, the Union position and the threatened future if no agreement is reached.

Figure 10.3 Card table for the rail dispute

There are two characters, 'Company' and 'Union', with cards defined directly from the description above. Three possible futures are shown, each drawn up as a column of cards played or not.

- *The Company's position* is that it should implement the new roster and the improved holiday scheme, and keep the pay rise to 2% (i.e. *not* raise the offer to 5%): the Union should accept this by not calling for strikes or an overtime ban. (We could add the further card 'accept Company's offer', but take this to be implied by lack of ban or strikes.)
- *The Union's position* (second column) is that the Company can introduce the new rosters if it also offers a 5% pay rise. The Union is indifferent to the holiday scheme, and the dash indicates that its position allows this to happen or not. If the Company improves its offer in this way, the Union will call off the strikes and not contemplate an overtime ban.
- Finally, the third column sets out the *threatened future* – i.e. the future in which there is no agreement, and both sides implement their fallbacks. The company unilaterally imposes the new rosters with only a 2% pay rise, and the Union calls the series of strikes. (At the moment, we suppose, the overtime ban is not an immediate threat. However it is not ruled out.)

Some Practicalities of Modelling

As will be seen in the next section, a great deal can be gained by considering the relationships between the above futures (and possibly a few others) in any given case. First, however, we offer some points to clarify exactly what is required in this first stage of modelling.

Defining 'position'

A character's position is whatever it is trying to convince the others to accept. It specifies a selection of cards to be played, typically including both demands on other characters, and some commitments of one's own. As in the everyday sense of the word, a position refers to a *public* stance: the character may or may not be *sincere* in intending to carry out its commitments. A common position may be held by two or more characters.

A position may consist of a *generalized* future – i.e., one in which some cards are left unspecified (like the holiday scheme in the Union's position). This is because not all options need be significant for that particular character, or it may be showing flexibility in order to pursue more important aims.

Fallbacks and the Threatened Future

A character's *fallback* consists of the cards it is threatening to play if its position is not accepted. Threats may range from physical violence to simply walking away from some proposed deal. Like a position, one's fallback is essentially a public matter: indeed it *must* be communicated (at least implicitly) to the other characters to have any effect. The character may not intend to carry out its threat: that is, it may be bluffing. In any case the *threatened future* is the scenario that would result from implementation of everyone's declared fallback.

Other futures

Though not essential to Confrontation Analysis, some other futures *may* also be of particular interest. For example:

- the *default future* – i.e., what will happen if the characters all carry out their present intentions.
- the *current status quo* – i.e., prior to any of the characters actually carrying out their intentions.
- *other potential resolutions* to the conflict – e.g., proposals made by a mediator, or alternative positions for any given character. Confrontation Analysis can help explore the potential viability of these.

The modelling process

Capturing a Moment of Truth, like any other modelling process, necessitates drawing boundaries around a focal area for analysis. This means making choices about which characters, which options and which futures to include in analysis – at least provisionally. There is no single 'correct' model. For example, we could have included more characters in the 'Rail Dispute'. Maybe the members of the Union have views of their own: they might vote down a strike call, or conversely start their own 'unofficial' action. Perhaps there are divisions within the Company management, some wanting to see a smoothly running service while others relish the prospect of a showdown with the Union. Other parties may have some influence, and so on. Such additional features can be brought in as modelling progresses, but there are great advantages to *starting as simply as possible*. In practice the modelling process usually a cyclical one. Insights generated by the modelling itself often encourage fresh formulations and suggest new boundaries for the analysis. Analysis itself helps to show which complications really matter, and are so worth keeping in the model.

Once a boundary has been chosen, starting with a few key futures makes Confrontation Analysis easier to apply (Bennett, 1998). Rather than having to make difficult judgements as to which options 'should' be included, we can start with the simple principle that *whatever is included in someone's position or fallback* should be included, and *nothing else need be.* Analysis thus builds on just those features that are most easily observable, making modelling much less of a 'black art'.

Dilemmas and their Implications

Introduction: the Six Dilemmas

Once characters recognize each other's stated positions and fallbacks, it can be proven that there are six (and only six) dilemmas that might beset any of them. This section outlines these dilemmas, and describes characteristic responses to them. First, one definition is needed:

> For any character C, a *potential improvement* is a move from one future to another that:
> • *can be made by C alone* changing its choice of cards, and
> • would leave C *no worse off* than before.

A potential improvement leads to a future at least as good for the character contemplating it, whereas an actual improvement leads to a better one. Though the distinction between the two does not always matter in practice, it is important in establishing the fundamental theorems of Drama Theory.

In what follows, we consider the six dilemmas in turn, grouped for ease of discussion. Each is first defined formally, considering just two characters A and B. However all the definitions generalize to dramas with any number of characters, and with any possible coalitions amongst them (Howard, 1999). We discuss typical responses to each dilemma, assuming (for the present) that characters try to overcome the dilemmas without abandoning their existing positions. These features are briefly illustrated, in most cases using different versions of the Rail Dispute example. In each case A is the character with the dilemma.

Cooperation and Trust

(i) Cooperation dilemma

Definition: A has a potential improvement from his own position

> This dilemma undermines cooperation in the Prisoners' Dilemma game, as discussed previously. If A advocates mutual cooperation, he will be tempted to defect from it. One possibility, of course, is that A's position is insincere, and that he has every intention of

double-crossing B. However it may also be that he genuinely wants to cooperate with B, but also is aware of the temptation to defect: in other words his dilemma may yet be unresolved. In either case, he will find it difficult to make his position credible.

(ii) Trust dilemma

Definition: B has a potential improvement from A's position

In this case, A's position is undermined by his knowledge that B would be tempted to move from it. He will thus have difficulty trusting B, even if she agrees to his position. This is also exemplified by Prisoner's Dilemma. If A proposes mutual cooperation, his own preferences create a cooperation dilemma, while his knowledge of B's presents him with a trust dilemma.

If two characters take the same position, these two dilemmas are simply mirror images of each other: if one side has a cooperation dilemma, the other has a trust dilemma. To overcome a cooperation dilemma requires A to demonstrate good faith. Depending on context, typical responses include displays of positive emotion toward B, commitments that bind A to his declared position (perhaps including early implementation of part of it), and rational arguments as to why such an outcome should be made to stick. Similarly, if A faces a trust dilemma he is liable to require some or all of these things from B. He may also look for ways of verifying compliance with her declared intentions and/or of retaliating quickly to punish any backsliding. (An alternative is a dramatic declaration of trust in B accompanied with strong positive emotions, in the hope that these will be reciprocated.)

In the Rail Dispute, for example, the Union would have a cooperation dilemma if it would be tempted to carry on with strikes even if the Company concedes the 5% pay increase. By the same token, the Company would have a trust dilemma if they believed this to be the case. Expanding on the second possibility, management might see the union leaders as troublemakers with some hidden agenda. Deprived of one pretext for a strike, they are likely to find another. How might the Union overcome such a perception? Displaying positive emotion is problematic in this case, given that it is also trying to make a threat credible (see below). However the possibility of a trust dilemma is an argument for at least moderating negative emotions of anger, contempt etc toward the other side. In terms of rational argument, the Union can stress how much it recognizes the need to work together in the future 'for the good of the industry' once this particular dispute can be fairly resolved. It can make public commitments to future cooperation that would be difficult or embarrassing to reverse.

Deterrence, Inducement and Threat

Whereas the two dilemmas above have to do with the credibility of promises, the next three have to do with threats. All therefore involve characters' fallbacks.

(iii) Deterrence dilemma:

Definition: B prefers the threatened future to A's position.

> Here, A's problem is that his fallback does not put B under any pressure to accept his position. She can do better by letting A implement his threat and living with the consequences.

In responding to such a dilemma, A has two basic ways forward. One is to move to a position more acceptable to B. This is discussed later. The other is to make the threatened future worse for B by inventing new and more damaging threats. Such a process is liable to be justified by negative emotions toward B and/or ethical arguments (e.g., that B's behaviour is so unacceptable that it's in nobody's interest – perhaps not even hers – that she should get away with it). In extreme cases, this can involve demonization of an opponent. Though often effective, such tactics carry the danger of provoking a similar reaction in response, leading to escalation of the conflict as both sides lose sight of anything they might once have had in common.

A deterrence dilemma could occur for either side in the Rail Dispute. For example, the Union would have this dilemma if faced with a 'militant' management who see a strike as losing the Company little while relishing a chance to combat the Union. If it is not prepared to modify its own position, the Union needs to invent (and justify) new threats. So it may well start to threaten the overtime ban explicitly, in addition to the one-day strikes, or perhaps an indefinite strike. It may attempt to gain support from other Unions. All this will be accompanied by negative portrayals of the Company management, dwelling on past grievances and alleged wrongs suffered at their hands.

(iv) Inducement dilemma

Definition: B's position is at least as good for A as the threatened future.

> This dilemma is exemplified by the 'Chicken' game. Against the threatened future of a crash, each player would actually prefer to give way and let the other win. Each therefore has difficulty in inducing the other player to concede.

(v) Threat dilemma

Definition: A has a potential improvement from the threatened future.

> If A's potential improvement consists of moving to B's position – as in the chicken game, for example – then it also gives him an inducement dilemma. However, threat dilemmas can also arise from potential improvements to other futures that are not in the character's position.

Even though they may coincide, the two types of dilemma play rather different roles, though both serve to undermine A's fallback. An inducement dilemma means that A will be tempted to accept B's position *during negotiations*. A threat dilemma means that if faced with implementing his fallback *after negotiations have broken down*, he would prefer not to do so. Rather than being tempted to accept B's position, he may be inclined to do something else altogether. B therefore has cause to suspect that A's stated fallback is merely a bluff that would not really be maintained.

Either dilemma could easily occur in the Rail Dispute. For example, the Company would face an inducement dilemma if the proposed strike would actually be very damaging to its finances. Its threat to introduce the new rosters unilaterally may then be seen as a bluff. Similarly the Union would be suspected of bluff if the threatened strikes would seriously damage its members' interests.

One common tactic is to demonstrate that one's own hands are tied, leaving one *no choice but to* carry out the threat. For example, the Union leaders can claim that their members would never accept a 'derisory' 2% offer even if the Union recommended them to do so. (The extreme case is the Chicken player who throws away the steering wheel just prior to impact. Unfortunately, both sides may do this at once!) Failing that, one can cultivate an impression of sheer bloody-mindedness. One important factor is often *reputation*: being known for never having backed down can be a great help in the next confrontation.

Like the deterrence dilemma, inducement and threat dilemmas generally provoke negative emotion and/or arguments in support of stern measures. However the underlying logic is quite different. Deterrence dilemmas are caused by having threats that would not be damaging enough. With an inducement or threat dilemma the threat would be damaging enough *if carried out*, but the intention to do so may be unbelievable. Conflating the two problems is all too easy for someone vaguely aware that a threat is 'not working'. One way round, this confusion will lead A to waste effort convincing B of his intention to carry out a threat she does not fear anyway. The other way round, it leads him to issue more and more extreme threats, each often less credible than the last ('I will do things so terrible that I've not even thought of them yet!'). This merely reinforces an impression of bluff and bluster.

Positioning

The sixth and final dilemma involves only the characters' positions, rather than the threatened future.

(vi) Positioning dilemma

Definition: A prefers B's position to his own

Here it appears illogical for A to press for his own position rather than B's.

At first sight, this might appear to be an odd situation – why does A not simply join forces with B? However, he might still have reason not to do so – for example if he believes B's position to be insincere or unattainable. Indeed A and B may have started out with a common position, but A now perceives no way of overcoming dilemmas posed by other characters and is arguing for a more 'realistic' alternative. The dominant emotion produced by such a dilemma is *irritation*. A will have some regret at having abandoned his original position – which he still prefers – and will resent having to keep on justifying his retreat to B.

This is not a dilemma easily illustrated by the Rail Dispute, but a real example may be provided by the reconvening of the Northern Ireland peace talks in 1997. The previous IRA cease-fire having broken down, the UK Government had been insisting that Sinn Fein (the Republicans' political wing) could not be admitted to new talks until at least some IRA weapons were decommissioned. This position had been shared by the mainstream Unionist parties. However in 1997, the (new) Government decided to allow Sinn Fein to be admitted without prior decommissioning. It seems implausible that the Government actually preferred this new position: rather, it seems to have decided that the old one was simply not going to work – an understandable conclusion given the dilemmas it entailed (Howard, 1999). The Unionists were naturally angered by this 'betrayal', while the Government spent much effort (with clear signs of irritation) attempting to justify the pragmatic break from its previous stance.

Preference Change

We have discussed the importance of emotion and preference change. Since each dilemma is created by a preference relation between possible futures, emotion linked to preference change is the immediate reaction to it, and may succeed in eliminating it. The sequence, roughly speaking, is as follows: experiencing a dilemma creates pressure to go against rationally grounded preferences; this causes emotion, in turn triggering attempts to rationalize (find good reasons for) the preference change. Demonizing an opponent is an example of such rationalization. If it succeeds, the new preferences are held without emotion; if partially successful, emotion may be needed to maintain them.

It is not always A's own preferences that constitute the dilemma. To get rid of A's trust and deterrence dilemmas, B's preferences need to be changed. But emotion projected toward B can still be helpful, whether A wants to convince B that his own preferences no longer constitute a dilemma or to influence B to change her preferences. In the first case, positive (or negative) emotion tend to make B believe that A's promises (or threats) will be maintained and will be carried out if called upon. In the second, case, negative emotion can make B think that, since A hates her, his fallback may be worse for her than she thought, while positive emotion can similarly make her think that A's promises may be worth more than she thought. Thus A's projected emotion can indirectly rationalize a change in B's preferences that eliminates A's deterrence or trust dilemmas.

Changes in Position

Preferences are not arbitrary. Perceived facts and accepted values underpin them. If the 'friction' these exert is too great, preference change will be impossible, and A's emotions, aroused to overcome this resistance, will disappear quite suddenly.

A may then resort instead to changing his own position – as distinct from trying to produce some change in B's. Changing position is a possible response to any of the dilemmas. The type and degree of change needed can be seen by analysing the dilemma in question. However a change of position – especially a conciliatory one – must also be made convincing to the other characters. They will often have reasons to suspect that the change is insincere and that the original position will be pursued given any opportunity. Credible changes require an appropriate emotional tone. They also need to be anchored in defensible arguments as to why change is desirable and/or necessary. It is worth noting two rough types of position change.

- One is the classic *compromise*, in which one party accepts some disappointment in order to move closer to agreement. This is liable to be accompanied by emotions of *resignation*. Supporting arguments are typically of the 'sour grapes' variety – the old position was not really that good, the dispute was not worth continuing, etc.
- Secondly, however, there may be creativity in devising new ways of resolving the conflict. Such creativity is (we argue) frequently stimulated by recognition of the dilemmas undermining existing proposals. These can lead to a reappraisal of the parties' values and needs, and whether these can be better met by expanding the range of solutions rather then treating current positions as a straitjacket (Fisher and Ury, 1983).

The second of these illustrates the key point that dilemmas can be stimulating – e.g. in prompting the search for win–win solutions – as well as problematic. This applies particularly to the deterrence dilemma. As noted already, this can trigger a response of demonization and conflict escalation. However a positive response *may* also be possible. Rather than making the threatened future worse, A may seek to find a better position, reaching out to and sympathizing with B's underlying needs. The arguments in favour of the change must, of course, be transparent and well-articulated if they are not immediately to be dismissed as a trick.

Irreversible Moves; Gratitude and Revenge

Changes in positions or preferences may be accomplished, not solely by emotion or rationalization, but by 'changing facts'. Israel has famously had a policy of 'changing facts' by building settlements on Arab land. Mrs Thatcher, having given in once to the miners, built up coal stocks so that, when the next strike came in 1983, her preference for the threatened future of sticking it out was enhanced. Thereby she eliminated an inducement dilemma by changing facts.

A warning notice should, however, be attached to irreversible moves. A character should be careful before making changes that pre-empt negotiations. This is because pre-emption can arouse strong feelings of gratitude or revenge. We are generally disposed to reward or punish good or bad things done to us, even though this can no longer have any encouraging or discouraging effect on actions that have already been taken. (Frank (1988) suggests that having such tendencies would make sense as an evolutionary strategy.) When handing out costly rewards or punishments that can have no effect on other characters' actions (since these are now in the past) we tend to be moved more strongly by emotion.

The next chapter ('The M&A Play'), contains an example of this. Here one player attempts to forcibly change the other's position by irreversibly playing a particular card. This move pre-empts negotiations between them, the intention being to leave the other side with 'no option' but to accept one's own position. However, this tactic fails to take the 'revenge factor' into account. Read the play to see what happens.

Deceit

As we have already hinted, *deceit* is always one possible response to a dilemma: emotion, preference change and irreversible moves can be faked; argumentation may be insincere. However faking is not cost-free, and does not remove the need to examine the logic of genuine change. Any situation in which deception is tempting is also one inviting disbelief. Credibility will require emotion and/or *supporting argument*. Getting angry to support a threat will change one's preferences. But so also will finding and rehearsing convincing arguments for carrying out the threat 'even if it hurts me too'. The original aim may be to convince others, but good arguments are liable to affect one's own beliefs. Similarly, faking of emotions is possible but not particularly easy (Frank, 1988), and success often depends on *self*-manipulation. The best way to appear angry is deliberately to work yourself into a rage: but then you are not immune to the effects.

Resolution of a Drama

When, in this model, is a conflict actually resolved? Drama Theory provides theorems about the overall development of the drama over a series of episodes (Howard, 1994; 1999). The most significant is the *theorem of the final state*, which concerns the circumstances under which a dramatic resolution of the conflict, free of all significant dilemmas is reached. It states that:

- if the cooperation, deterrence and inducement dilemmas are absent for all characters, *all must share a common position*
- this common position must be a *strict, strong equilibrium* – i.e., a future from which there are no potential improvements (for any individual character or coalition).

It also follows that no characters are affected by any of the other dilemmas: a common position precludes positioning dilemmas, while trust dilemmas are eliminated by the lack of potential improvements from it. (Strictly speaking, threat dilemmas can still exist, but are no longer relevant to characters' positions.)

A resolution in this sense provides both rational and emotional closure. Nobody can improve their lot within the situation as currently defined, while the lack of remaining dilemmas removes opportunities to transform the situation any further. However this does not mean that the ending need be a happy one: tragic endings can also exhibit this sort of closure. Hopes may have been destroyed rather than fulfilled. Nevertheless the drama has been fully played-out.

The ability to characterize a dramatic resolution mathematically is significant, not least in providing a natural stopping point for analysis. However no model is a complete description of the world it represents. In practice, the resolution may come unstuck through imperfect implementation (high-level agreements always leave many details to be resolved at lower levels, and they may not be). Some extraneous event may intervene, precipitating an entirely new drama.

To summarize, we have set out the six possible dilemmas of choice and the most significant responses to them. Each is named for what it makes difficult (the cooperation dilemma makes it difficult to cooperate, and so on). Identifying the dilemmas helps to pinpoint and understand the problems faced by each character in any given episode. Identifying the pressures acting within the current situation suggests how it is liable to change. As the drama unfolds, characters will encounter and deal with different dilemmas until a resolution is reached. The theory tells us what sort of properties such a resolution must have. In the final section below, we discuss various ways of applying this framework, and summarize what can be gained by doing so.

Using Confrontation Analysis

Process of Modelling

Modelling a confrontation is an art as well as a science. A broad 'scoping' process almost always makes a useful starting point: What is going on? Who is concerned? What's the core issue and what seem to be the 'bones of contention'? Asking questions like these provides a firm basis for more detailed modelling. From this it is a natural step to start constructing a list of the key characters. These can be selected from a longer list, perhaps developed through some form of stakeholder analysis (see e.g., Eden & Ackermann, 1998) or it may be easier to begin with a small core of 'obvious' characters and add others as the model is built up.

Finding and analysing dilemmas is both a predictive and a diagnostic process (Bennett, 1999). It is *predictive* in suggesting the types of tactics characters are liable to try, given what we know of their aims – always with the proviso that much will depend on individual character and social context. It is *diagnostic* in the sense that observing behaviour can suggest which dilemmas characters are grappling with. This can provide important clues as to their underlying motivations.

We have offered some modelling tips in the course of earlier discussion, some of the most important being summarized in Box 1 below. Analysis can be very 'quick and simple', e.g., modelling just one stage in an ongoing situation to understand better what is going on. Drawing up a card table and analysing dilemmas can certainly help achieve this. Much more elaborate modelling is also possible, e.g., linking dramas at several different levels throughout an organization. At its most ambitious, we can seek to track a drama through a whole series of episodes to a final conclusion, showing how different dilemmas arise and can be dealt with. Done for one particular character, this can generate a strategic plan for resolving (and creating) different dilemmas in turn, so as to steer the drama to a desired resolution. Howard (1999) discusses this process in the context of military peacekeeping operations. However care must be taken to explore the consequences of different assumptions – especially about how other characters might see the world. A good strategy will need to be both flexible and robust in the face of inevitable uncertainty: one benefit of analysis can be to show which uncertainties matter most.

Box 1: Tips for Setting up a Card Table

- Start by keeping the number of characters small: be alive to coalitions (characters acting in concert, who can be provisionslly amalgamated)
- Clearly fix the episode that you're modelling (choose one moment in time – e.g., the present – at which to fix characters, options and positions)
- Include characters' options in the card table, not their objectives (what they can *do*, not what they *want*)
- Include only cards that can still be played or not, not actions already taken (unless they can be reversed)
- Include only 'live' cards, representing something the presence or absence of which is insisted upon as part of some character's position

---

Having drawn up a card table model, the main point is to look for the dilemmas facing each character. Though it is possible to look for dilemmas in any order, it is often helpful to go through the following three steps:

- Start by 'settling' the threatened future. If this were really about to happen, would any of the characters be inclined to change their choice of cards? If so, this implies that they face a *threat* dilemma.
- Now consider all the characters' positions, together with the threatened future.

Preference comparisons between these futures will reveal any *inducement, deterrence* or *positioning* dilemmas for each character.
- Finally, consider each character's position as if it were really about to happen. Would any character be inclined to change its choice of cards? If so, we have a *cooperation* or *trust* dilemma.

Modes of Engagement

Barriers of terminology

Drama Theory and Confrontation Analysis can provide powerful research tools for those interested in conflict and its resolution. However the most interesting applications are generally those done with some more direct involvement in the situation. In seeking such involvement, care is needed with terminology. 'Drama' has fewer negative connotations than 'game', but can still suggest artificiality or 'staginess'. (Some existing uses of the metaphor (e.g., Goffman, 1959) focus on script-following behaviour rather than characters' choices: this has quite different implications.) Words such as 'confrontation' are obviously appropriate in some situations, but can sound too negative in some contexts ('there is no conflict in our organization'; 'we are *not* having a confrontation!').

In fact Drama Theory treats both conflict and cooperation as important and seeks to analyse conflict resolution. However this can take some explaining, perhaps because our culture makes too much of a distinction between conflict and cooperation. 'Win–win' techniques or philosophies are frequently contrasted with 'win–lose' ones. But 'winning' has no general scientific meaning in Drama Theory. There is nothing about the bare structure of a Drama-theoretic model that allows us to categorize outcomes as 'wins' for one or another player. How much it makes sense to talk about 'winning' depends entirely on the application you have in mind. What Drama Theory generally helps us to do is to find a resolution acceptable to all players – albeit perhaps after their objectives have changed. The eventual aim is thus to identify viable forms of collaboration. Certainly, achieving this may require confronting others as a step on the way. Nevertheless, 'collaboration analysis' may often be a helpful term, as 'confrontation analysis' risks confusing means with end.

Roles for analysis

Leaving points of terminology aside, the ideas set out here can be used in various forms of intervention (see Figure 10.4).

One already alluded to is *decision support* for a particular character. However modelling can also be used to bring different participants together during formal or informal

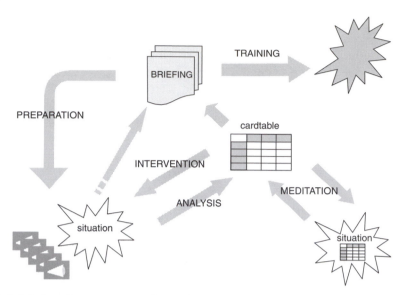

Figure 10.4 Modes of support in confrontation

mediation. For example, a card table can provide a powerful device for establishing a common framework for debate, then providing an ongoing record of a mediation process between them.

Confrontation Analysis can also feed into a range of 'off-line' applications. As rich summaries of complex situations, card tables can be used to structure *briefing material* to prepare those about to enter a particular arena. This will be helpful in managing changeover in personnel (a situation particularly common in a military/peacekeeping setting, as units are moved in and out). Computer-based systems exist which allow large amounts of contextual material to be attached to any element of the model, in plain text or other forms. Similar material can also be used in a more general training context. Here the aim is to impart some insights into the general nature of conflict and cooperation rather than to rehearse a specific situation. In either setting, briefings should build in the possible existence of different viewpoints, with the 'same' situation looking different to various characters. Separate card tables, with their own supplementary data, can be constructed, each specific to a particular viewpoint. In such use, individuals or teams playing characters in the drama use their subjective card table as a starting point for negotiating with others. This multi-perspective aspect, together with the structure provided by the card table, gives the framework advantages over more routine case materials or role-play instructions. Such exercises permit a surprising degree of realism, not because participants act out the superficial qualities of the 'real' characters, but because they gain a powerful appreciation of the pressures acting on them.

Returning finally to decision support, the characters in a real-life drama are the most obvious potential clients for analysis. However it can also help those with less power to affect events, but with a need to understand better what is happening. Examples might be someone affected by a quarrel between other family members, or a diplomat worried about a worsening dispute between two neighbouring countries. Sometimes, indeed, analysis can show that 'powerless' stakeholders have some potential influence after all, though of course this cannot be guaranteed. In any case the basic principle (as with other problem-structuring methods), is that problem-owners provide information about their situation. Analysts should help decision-makers and their advisors make the most effective use of their own knowledge and experience. Their primary roles are to ask pertinent questions, structure the information through modelling, and help draw out the implications of analysis.

Final comments

As with other methods, the *process* of modelling often has its own benefits. Important issues may be raised and resolved within a client group, and different areas of expertise synthesized. Assumptions tend to be more thoroughly discussed and explicitly laid out. The analysis itself can provide more specific benefits, for example by:

- suggesting some combination of options previously overlooked
- uncovering a crucial uncertainty about someone's preferences
- showing how an apparently powerful threat can be evaded or turned to advantage
- suggesting new routes to collaboration
- showing how one's own actions might trigger unexpected reactions in others.

Given a complex pattern of competing and common aims and interests, it is all too easy for 'sensible' actions to have quite unintended results, for unforeseen responses to be triggered or for opportunities to be missed. Analysis is no panacea. But it can improve the chances of making more effective choices.

References

Bennett, P.G. (1977). 'Towards a Theory of Hypergames', *Omega*, **5**, 749–51.

Bennett, P.G. (1998). 'Confrontation Analysis as a Diagnostic Tool', *Eur. J. of Ops. Res.*, **109**, 465–82.

Bennett, P.G. and N. Howard (1996). 'Rationality, Emotion and Preference Change: Drama-theoretic models of choice', *Eur. J. of Ops. Res.*, **92**, 603–14.

Binmore, K.G. (1987). *The Economics of Bargaining*, Blackwell, Oxford.

Bryant, J. (1997). 'The Plot Thickens: Understanding interaction through the metaphor of Drama', *Omega*, **25**, 255–66.

Eden, C. and Ackermann, F. (1998). *Making Strategy: The Journey of Strategic Management*, Sage, London.

Evans, P.B., Jacobson, H.K., and Putnam, R.D. (1993). *Double-Edged Diplomacy: International Bargaining and Domestic Politics*, University of California Press, Berkeley.

Frank, R.H. (1988). *Passions within Reason: The Strategic Role of the Emotions*, W.W. Norton.

Fisher, R.A. and Ury, W. (1983). *Getting to Yes*, Hutchinson.

Goffman, E. (1959). *The Presentation of Self in Everyday Life*, Doubleday, Garden City NY.

Harsanyi, J.C. (1968). 'Games with Incomplete Information Played by "Bayesian" Players', *Management Science (A)*, **159**, 320 & 486.

Howard, N. (1971). *Paradoxes of Rationality*, MIT Press, Cambridge MA.

Howard, N. (1989). 'The Manager as Politician and General: the Metagame Approach to Analysing Cooperation and Conflict', and 'The CONAN play', in *Rational Analysis for a Problematic World* (Ed. J. Rosenhead), John Wiley & Sons, Ltd, Chichester.

Howard, N. (1994). 'Drama Theory and its Relationship to Game Theory', *Group Decision and Negotiation*, **3**, 187–206 and 207–53.

Howard, N. (1996). 'Negotiation as Drama: How "Games" Become Dramatic', *International Negotiation*, **1**, 125–52.

Howard, N. (1999). *Confrontation Analysis: How to Win Operations Other than War*, CCRP, Department of Defense, Washington DC.

Howard, N., Bennett, P.G., Bryant, J.W., and Bradley, M. (1992). 'Manifesto for a Theory of Drama and Irrational Choice', *J. Opl. Res. Soc.*, **44**, 99–103 and *Systems Practice*, **6**, 429–34, 1993.

Ordeshook, P.C. (1989). *Game Theory and Political Theory: An Introduction*, Cambridge University Press, Cambridge.

Rapoport, A. (1960). *Fights, Games and Debates*, University of Michigan Press, Ann Arbor.

Schelling, T.C. (1960). *The Strategy of Conflict*, Harvard University Press (1st ed. 1960: revised edition with new preface, 1980), MA.

Von Neumann, J. and Morgenstern, O. (1944). *Theory of Games and Economic Behavior*, Princeton University Press (1st ed.), Princeton.

11 *The M&A Play: Using Drama Theory for Mergers and Acquisitions*

Nigel Howard

Introduction

This chapter illustrates how a large company's acquisitions team could use drama theory. It is a fictionalization of a real-world case, though not one in which drama theory was used in a client-interactive mode; published sources only were used in the analysis. Consequently, important details, such as would have been drawn out through interacting with a client, were unavailable. They have been extrapolated or invented.

The case may not therefore be a good guide to the real world example on which it is based. But it does illustrate the kind of problems encountered in mergers, acquisitions and alliances. To bring these out clearly, and to show the dynamics of a client-consultant relationship, it has been put in the form of a play.

Industry is undergoing global re-structuring through mergers and acquisitions. But these have a 50 to 80 per cent failure rate (as estimated, respectively, by Rankine (1998) and Dewhurst (1997)). Resources are being wasted on an epic scale.

Top-management teams dealing with acquisitions obviously need input from technical specialities, financial and legal. They also need a good strategic estimate of the synergy achievable from merging operations. But these considerations merely define the context of the basic problem.

The real problem is: how to get human beings with differing objectives to alter their objectives in order to be able to work together.

Because this is the problem, emotions are aroused. Love, hate and vehement rationalizations occur both during the acquisition process and in the post-acquisition phase, when managers try to realize synergies by merging operations. And this is why things go wrong. Acquisition teams often mishandle their own and others' emotions in the acquisition phase, giving managers a bad hand to play in the post-acquisition phase. Then, managers with a good or bad hand mishandle the 'political' process of merging operations.

Drama theory can be applied at both stages – the acquisition and the post-acquisition stage. Handling emotions in the acquisition phase is a 'unilateral' application of the approach. The player using a drama-theoretic tool would be one of the management teams involved. It would parse the dilemmas facing all players in order to construct a confrontation strategy – i.e., a plan for eliminating dilemmas in such a way as to bring about a resolution as close as possible to 'our' strategic objectives. The plan would incorporate financial and legal considerations. It would be based upon projected synergies, in that these essentially give the pot of value from which the team can offer handouts to persuade others to accept their solution.

The post-acquisition phase would be better handled as a 'multilateral' application. This is really a form of mediation. Top management now needs to analyse the dilemmas facing organizational players – the dilemmas arising from inter-divisional and other kinds of internal conflict – in order to discuss their resolution with the players themselves and take steps to remove them in the interest of all players.

This is a different way of proceeding. Unilateral analysis, done to benefit one particular player, is now inappropriate. First, other players are likely to object to unilateral analysis – even though, in benefiting one player, it arguably tends to benefit all – on the grounds that it benefits one more than the others. A more positive, defensible reason is that multilateral analysis can evoke more creative suggestions from organizational players as to how to eliminate dilemmas. It is a way for them to share and exploit each other's detailed knowledge of mechanisms for achieving or increasing synergistic gains. Thus it is a way of eliminating dilemmas that increases the acquisition's chances of success.

As discussed in the previous chapter, the tool used in such applications might better be called 'collaboration analysis' than 'confrontation analysis'. However, the tool used is really the same. For further examples of its use, together with a rather more detailed analytic description of how a real-world drama unfolds, the reader should go next to Howard (1999).

The Play

The boardroom of BDI (British Defence Industries) in a new office block near Farnborough. A flipchart with pens is at one end of the table. Enter Jim, the chairman, stocky and cross-looking. He is followed by Alex, Head of the Acquisitions Team, a quieter, more cerebral type.

JIM [*bellowing*]: A million *pounds?*

ALEX: Pounds. Yes, pounds, not dollars. Look, if the advice is right, it's worth it. They ran a Cray supercomputer to check out all the possibilities. Hence the cost. Under all possible assumptions, the result's the same: Stark'll come round.

JIM: According to game theory.

ALEX: Yes, we used game theory. Game theory works. Did you know, they used game theory to design the mobile-phone auctions...

JIM [*interrupting*]: ... that raised 22 and a half billion for the government. Yes, I know. But that's an auction, with sealed bids. In a sealed-bid auction, interaction between players is impossible. Have you heard of drama theory?

ALEX: No.

JIM [*sitting down and speaking quietly*]: I've just heard about it. Drama theory is a new development out of game theory. Basically, it's about how the players define the game prior to playing it. A guy at dinner last night – a drama theorist – told a story to illustrate the difference between drama and games. Now, Alex, please sit down and listen to the story. It worried me. I need reassurance.

ALEX [*sits down, bemusedly*]: Ok.

JIM: The story is called the Jerusalem taxi-driver[1]. Two professors, in Jerusalem for a conference, need a taxi to get from their hotel to the conference venue. They've heard that Jerusalem taxi drivers sometimes overcharge, so they use game theory. Instead of challenging the taxi-driver's estimate straight away, they wait till he's driven them to the conference centre. Then they offer him what they know to be the right fare. [*He stops and looks fixedly at Alex.*]

ALEX: Yes? So?

JIM: *Under all possible assumptions*, he'll take what they offer, right? He's driven them there, spent his time and petrol, can't get it back. He'll take what they offer, *down to one penny*.

ALEX [*after a pause*]: And what happens?

JIM: The taxi-driver presses a switch, locks the doors, drives them back to their hotel and dumps them. As drama theory – but not game theory – would predict.

ALEX [*thoughtfully*]: The taxi driver is mad as hell.

JIM: He's madder than hell.

ALEX: As is Stark, apparently.

JIM: My point.

ALEX: Oh, but Jim, look...

JIM: You see what I'm getting at. You can see why the story worried me. Now I've asked the guy – this drama theorist – to come and talk to us this morning. He'll be here any minute.

ALEX: That's why you dragged me here? [*Looking at his watch*]: I've got half an hour before lunch . . .

JIM: Alex, this is the future of the European defence industry. We must be sure we know what we're doing. The strategy is your responsibility, and I'm leaving it to you. But just listen to this guy. For half an hour.

They sit staring at each other.

ALEX [*finally*]: Ok. I'll listen. But tell me, who is this character? I mean, who employs him?

---

[1] The story is true, according to Dixit and Nalebuff (1991). This book is an excellent guide to game theory. As such it seems to a drama theorist to illustrate vividly how game theory can be misleading if applied to situations where 'pre-play communication' is allowed

JIM: He's a consultant, attached to some merchant bank, I believe. I forget which one. Apparently he's trying to persuade them to use drama theory as a tool for working interactively with people like us, people involved in mergers and acquisitions. So he's definitely looking at our kind of problem. Before that, I understand he was working for the military, looking at peacekeeping methods.

Alex *shakes his head doubtfully.* Jim's *personal assistant comes in, followed by* Nathan, *lean and intense looking.*

ASSISTANT: Mr Nathan Smith, to see you.

Assistant *leaves.* Jim *and* Alex *stand.* Jim *comes forward to introduce* Nathan, *while* Alex *stands looking at him with a frown.*

JIM: Nathan, good morning. Thanks for coming round. This is Alex Devon, who heads our acquisitions team. Alex, Nathan is the drama theorist I've been telling you about. I understand he's done work for the MOD and the Pentagon, designing systems for peacekeeping operations. [*To* Nathan]: Is that right?

NATHAN [*to* Alex]: That's it. The story is this. Generals are trained to fight wars, but nowadays they don't get many to fight. Instead, they're tasked with keeping the peace, making people democratic, that kind of thing. Drama theory is being tried out as a way of developing effective methods for that kind of operation.

JIM [*to* Alex]: Nathan believes the same methods might apply to acquisitions and alliances. [*To* Nathan]: As I understand it, your methods are basically game-theoretic, but you take emotions into account. You claim to be able to predict emotions ...

ALEX [*dismissively*]: I wouldn't think there's much point in that. Emotions are unpredictable. [*To* Nathan]: Look, the situation is this. We recently commissioned a game-theoretic analysis of an – er – important problem. We used DGI, Decision Gaming Inc – don't know if you've heard of them? [Nathan *shakes his head.*] Well, in any case, we've now started to implement the strategy their analysis – their game-theoretic analysis – recommended. Now I understand you have criticisms of this approach.

NATHAN [*carefully*]: It depends what kind of problem we're talking about. Game theory is certainly the right approach for some kinds of problem. The key question is whether or not the parties are trying to reach some kind of understanding with each other.

ALEX: Er – well, obviously the parties in this case are aiming for an understanding.

NATHAN [*quietly*]: Then game theory – if you take it seriously – could lead you astray.

They stand confronting each other. Jim *ends the silence.*

JIM: I suggest, Alex, that we ask Nathan to look at our problem. Let's hear what he has to say.

NATHAN [*turning his head from* Alex's *gaze*]: Now, you mean? Right away?

JIM: Is that possible? It's important for us.

NATHAN: I suppose so. I mean ... how long have you got? I'd need to ask a few questions. I could do a quick-and-dirty analysis, sufficient to let you judge whether you want to do a proper, full-scale job.

JIM: I think that's just what we need. We'll give you the rest of the morning. That should enable us to decide whether we want to go further. Don't you think so, Alex?

ALEX [*still gazing at* Nathan]: Just a moment. First, I'd like a better idea what this is all about. How do you mean to proceed?

NATHAN [*patiently*]: I mean to elicit from you, by my questions, what are the issues, *who* – i.e., which players – control them, and *how* they control them – i.e., which cards does each player hold. By playing or not playing its cards a player influences the issues. Then I mean to elicit the 'position' of each player – i.e., the solution it proposes, consisting of cards to be played and not played by each player.

ALEX: This is game theory! You're describing a game-theoretic model!

NATHAN: Absolutely. Drama theory relies on game-theoretic models. We model the situation as a game. The difference lies in what we do with the model. We don't try to solve the game as it stands. We ask – given that the players see the game in this way, what pressures are they under, through interacting over the game, to *redefine* the game, to *change* the game as they see it?

ALEX: Within game theory, they can't change it! The game models the situation they're in.

NATHAN: Exactly. But we're not within game theory! We're bursting out of the trap game theory lays for us! Game theory – as you know – confronts players with 'dilemmas' – like the prisoner's dilemma or the chicken dilemma. These are baffling paradoxes. They undermine rationality. They say it's rational to be irrational! Game theory traps us inside rationality when rationality seems not to be the answer.

ALEX: I know something about your game-theoretic dilemmas. But we have to stick to rationality in our analysis.

NATHAN: We do. Again, I agree with you. But the dilemmas aren't dilemmas just for the analyst, they're dilemmas for the players! Players confronting them become emotional, may behave *irrationally*. Drama theory is a rational theory about how *real* players (rational or irrational) behave when confronting game-theoretic dilemmas. Players think of ways to change the model so as to get rid of the dilemmas! They may change their preferences, or the options open to them – their opportunities. They may even add new players! They're driven to make these changes by the emotions (positive and negative) that the dilemmas produce in them. They rationalize their emotions by adopting a new, dilemma-eliminating definition of their situation.

JIM [*after a pause*]: You two may know what you're talking about. I'm afraid you've lost me.

NATHAN [*turning to him*]: Of course. I'm sorry. I suggest we start building the model, and analyse it. All will then be clear – at least in relation to your particular problem. [*Looking round*]: I see you have a flipchart. I'll need that. Ok, can you describe the problem to me?

Nathan *sits at the end of the table with the flipchart behind him and pulls over a notepad to take notes.* Alex *sits down to his right.* Jim *remains standing, his hands on a chair-back.*

JIM: You may have heard the recent announcement about our merger with Welland.

NATHAN: Aha! *That* problem . . .

JIM: Yes, that one. We took this move – really, we *bought* Welland from General Power – essentially as a way of breaking a stalemate in our negotiations with DA.

NATHAN: What was the stalemate?

JIM [*glancing at* Alex]: There were a number of issues. DA is owned one hundred per cent by Boss, whose chairman is Albert Stark. Stark wanted us to pay more, by upping the valuation of DA shares. In the end, we agreed to do that. But in exchange we wanted control. You see, our shareholding is distributed among a number of shareholders, so that a straightforward merger between BDI and DA would have meant effective control by Boss, because they own the whole of DA.

ALEX: Boss would have controlled the merged company, even though BDI would form the largest part of it! To get round this, our suggestion was that they accept non-voting shares. They agreed to accept some – but not enough to give us control. In the end, I suspect, they saw it as a question of whether Germany or Britain should control the European defence industry.

NATHAN: And they wanted it to be Germany . . .

JIM: Exactly.

NATHAN [*scribbling notes*]: Are they explicit about that? Or would they phrase the issue differently, if they were answering this question?

ALEX: Hm. Well, they do put it a bit differently. They talk about maintaining a balance to ensure that each nation's national interests are properly represented. But what they were proposing wasn't a balance. It was German control.

NATHAN: So: stalemate. Fine. But now – how would buying Welland break the stalemate?

ALEX: Buying Welland from General Power – who wanted to sell – was part of the overall plan for both sides. It made economic and commercial sense. The point is, that if we bought Welland first – before merging with DA – then the size of BDI-Welland would be such that we (the Brits) would have control of the merged entity. Or indeed, if the two deals took place simultaneously. So we suggested doing that to Stark . . .

NATHAN: . . . who didn't like the idea?

JIM: . . . who categorically refused to accept the idea! He agreed to buy Welland, yes. But only *after* the BDI-DA merger. That way, the company that bought Welland would be Boss-controlled: German-controlled. And it could buy Welland under a deal that maintained German control.

ALEX: We had a three-way meeting. Ourselves, Stark and Jack Dobson – he's MD of General Power, the company that owns Welland (till now). We and Jack Dobson wanted a three-way merger. But that would have meant the Brits, taken together, would have been in control. Stark wasn't having it. He ended the meeting and went on holiday.

NATHAN: Whereupon you did your game-theoretic analysis…

ALEX: … which told us, essentially, that if we just did it – just merged with Welland – then Stark would be faced with a *fait accompli*. We'd be making him an offer he couldn't refuse. Eventually he'd have to accept it. It made too much commercial and economic sense. The synergies were there.

NATHAN: I see. So you went ahead and did it. And Stark's reaction? No doubt he went through the roof.

ALEX [*looking uncomfortably at* Jim]: He went ape. So we understand. Bonkers.

NATHAN [*rubbing his hands delightedly*]: Great. Just great. Now I'd like to build a simple model of your *common reference frame* as you interacted with Boss … First, let's take the interaction before you came back with the suggestion that you should buy Welland …

Nathan *picks up a pen and turns to the flipchart. As he does so, the Narrator walks on stage and holds up his hand: all three characters freeze in position. The Narrator raises the top sheet of the flipchart, revealing Table 11.1.*

NARRATOR: Nathan now works with the other two to build a card-table model – shown in Table 11.1 – setting out the interaction as the players perceived it when Boss and BDI first ran into a stalemate. BDI's position (column *BDI*) was that it would pay the higher price Boss was asking (i.e., play the card *pay more*) if Boss would play *cede control*: both could then play *merge*. Boss's position (column *Boss*) was different. It wanted a merger at the higher price, but refused to *cede control*. The future that threatened if the players could not agree and therefore adopted fallback positions is shown as column *threat*: there would be no merger. This was also the *default* or 'present' future – the future that could be projected if present policies remained unchanged.

Jim and Alex accept this simple model as representing the players' 'common reference frame' at this point. Adding more details, they agree, would be useful for evaluating the different futures and estimating effects. But it would risk bringing in details not clearly known by the players to be known to each other, and known by them to be so known, … etc.

Nathan now proceeds to analyse the dilemmas in this model. To do so, he must ask questions about players' preferences between the columns in the table, and also about their preferences for playing/(not playing) the various cards shown as played (or not played)

Narrator *waves his hand, bringing the characters back to life, and walks off.*

NATHAN: So. Now let me ask – which of these two columns [*points to columns 'threat' and 'Boss'*] would be preferable for you, BDI? Which future would be better – to go ahead without a merger with Boss, or to merge in a way that gives them control?

ALEX [*after exchanging glances with* Jim]: I think we'd prefer no merger at all to a merger under Boss's control.

Table 11.1 – The stalemate between BDI and Boss

	BDI	Boss	threat	default
BDI				
merge with DA	♣	♣	□	□
pay more	♣	♣	□	□
Boss				
merge DA with BDI	♣	♣	□	□
cede control via non-voting shares	♣	□	□	□

LEGEND:

♣   Means card is played

□   Means card is not played

NATHAN: Let me be clear about that. I don't want a strategic preference – i.e., one based on the fear that expressing a preference for this column [*pointing to column 'Boss'*] might mean giving in to Albert Stark. Having that preference doesn't mean you have to give in! They might equally prefer your position to the threatened future! I want you to compare the two columns for their own sakes – for the sake of the futures they represent – as if they were the only two futures possible. [*As they look hesitant, he continues.*] Let's see, the only difference between your position (which you obviously prefer) and theirs is over the issue of control. Now you've said that Stark presents that not as a matter of German control, but of balancing different national interests. You could work on that to obtain safeguards . . .

ALEX: Oh, yes. He's offering safeguards. But they don't amount to the same thing as control.

JIM [*to Alex*]: Still, Nathan is right, I think. If those were the only two outcomes possible, we'd have to prefer their 'balance of national interests' to no merger at all.

ALEX [*conceding the point*]: It's true the sums come out in favour of it. And the government wants it.

NATHAN [*looking from one to the other*]: Ok? So I'll put you down as preferring their position to the threat. I'll indicate your preference ranking thus. [*In the row labelled BDI (i.e., the top row, containing no cards) he writes the figures that appear in Table 11.2: a figure 1 at the top of the column labelled 'BDI', a 2 in the column 'Boss', and a 3 in the 'threat' and 'default' columns.*] This says you most prefer your own position, theirs next and the *threat* future least.

ALEX: I assume these are preference rankings only. They don't show *degrees* of preference.

NATHAN: That's right. Just a preference ordering. Now these preferences mean you have an *inducement* dilemma. You're under pressure to accept the Boss position, given the threatened alternative ... [*They seem dubious about this. Nathan studies their expressions for a moment, then continues.*] But before drawing any conclusions from that, let's see what pressure *they* are under. [Alex *nods vigorously.*] Does Stark also have an inducement dilemma? Which does Boss prefer – your position [*pointing to column 'BDI'*] or the threatened future [*pointing to 'threat'*]?

ALEX [*earnestly, to* Jim]: By the same token, he's got to prefer our position. We can offer him safeguards to offset their fears about British control. In fact, we've done so. And the German government is just as keen on an integrated European defence industry as ours – if not more so. And the Germans pay more heed to their government than we do.

JIM [*to* Nathan]: That's correct. All of it.

NATHAN: Then they have an inducement dilemma to match ours! By the way, from what you're saying I think that later we might enlarge this model to include the two governments, just to check on some of the assumptions that seem to be behind it. But first, let's finish analysing this model. What other dilemmas are there? Let's see ... We've found that both players have *inducement* dilemmas. This means that neither one has a *deterrence dilemma* – i.e., neither of you is unable to pressure the other to accept your position.

ALEX [*sharply*]: What's that?

NATHAN [*patiently*]: Dilemmas are the difficulties players find in getting their way. A dilemma is a weakness in the bargaining hand I have to play. One kind of weakness, as I've said, is that I may be under pressure to accept your position. That's an inducement dilemma. Another possible weakness – a deterrence dilemma – is that you may be under no pressure to accept my position ... You prefer the threat future! In that case, whether or not my threat is credible, it's inadequate! If I have a deterrence dilemma and want to stick to my position, I must either make my position more attractive to you or make the threat future worse for you ...

ALEX: I can see that.

NATHAN: Now these two dilemmas can't exist together, in the sense that if I have an inducement dilemma, I am under pressure to accept your position, so you can't possibly have a deterrence dilemma. My having an inducement dilemma is the same as your *not* having a deterrence dilemma.

ALEX [*slowly*]: Fine.

NATHAN: Let's see, what's next? The next thing is that neither of you has a *positioning* dilemma. Neither of you prefers the other's position to its own – which is a difficulty that may arise when a player considers another's position to be attractive, but unrealistic.

ALEX: Unrealistic? In what way?

NATHAN: Through suffering from a deterrence dilemma! For example, suppose we agree that X is the best policy, but it can't succeed because the production department will never buy it. Seeing this, I support policy Y. You, however, insist on sticking to X. Then I have a positioning dilemma. My reaction: I get irritated with you.

JIM [*laughing*]: I could give you some examples of that!

ALEX [*frowning hard*]: Ok, so what other dilemmas are there?

NATHAN: Well, it seems to me that neither of you has a *threat dilemma* either; that is, neither of you would be tempted to move *unilaterally* from the threatened future, if it were to be implemented . . . No, you wouldn't, because a merger would require you to move together, and the other cards are meaningless without a merger.

ALEX: What would a threat dilemma mean?

NATHAN: It would mean you're probably bluffing. You have a threat dilemma when you'd rather not carry out the threatened future, if it came to it – i.e., you'd rather not do what you said you'd do if your position was rejected. [Alex *nods*.] Now – *trust* and *cooperation dilemmas*? No need to worry about them, since either of these positions, once both sides agreed to it, would be fixed by binding, legal contracts. [*To* Alex.] I have a trust dilemma if I can't trust you to carry out my position, even if you agree to it. A cooperation dilemma is the same kind of thing from another point of view: I have a cooperation dilemma if you couldn't trust me to carry out my own position, even if you agreed to it.

ALEX: These sound like the prisoner's dilemma . . . I can't trust you, you can't trust me . . .

NATHAN: Exactly! They're different aspects of that dilemma.

ALEX: Ok, but game theorists know all about the prisoner's dilemma. If I'm in a prisoner's dilemma type situation, I have to watch out. What do you have to say about the prisoner's dilemma that's different or new?

NATHAN: Trust and cooperation dilemmas, like the other dilemmas, trigger emotional reactions. In their case, the emotion is positive – I have to either convince you that I can be trusted, or convince you to become trustworthy. Positive, cooperation emotion triggers off a search for ways to ensure trustworthiness, or else changes people's values so that they become both trusting and trustworthy.

Alex *simply stares at him*.

NATHAN [*turning to* Jim]: Right – so it seems these two inducement dilemmas are the *only* two dilemmas in this model.

JIM: And what does that mean?

NATHAN: It means a tug-of-war consisting of rational/emotional arguments and shifts of position. Each of you is trying to get the other to give up its own position and accept yours. The rationale underlying it all is this. If either of you can credibly present your preferences as having changed so that you now prefer the threatened future to the other's position, then the other's position becomes unrealistic. Hence (provided the other's preferences have not undergone a corresponding change) – the other will accept your position.

ALEX [*keenly*]: What if we simply make their position impossible? Then they'll have to accept ours.

NATHAN: Er – yes. Presenting arguments or taking action to make their position seem impossible is another way of doing it. [*Resuming his exposition*]: So, facing these dilemmas, each side will experience two kinds of emotion. Negative emotions (anger, defiance, etc) help us find reasons to prefer the threatened future to the other's position, or to reject their position as impossible. Positive emotions (such as empathy, or willingness to cooperate) help us to combat the other's negative reasons. They help us find reasons why the other side should go on preferring our position to the threatened future.

JIM: Reasons? What kind of reasons do you have in mind?

NATHAN: Principles. Mission statements. Pressure from others, such as your own government or clients. Or different commercial prospects. But even different commercial prospects are not a simple matter of objective calculation. Even when you're adding up figures, emotion precedes reason. It gives you a case you want to prove. You then research facts in order to try and prove your case.

JIM [*puzzled*]: 'Emotion precedes reason' isn't normal consultant-speak. It's not very scientific, is it?

NATHAN [*quietly*]: Actually, it is. It's the heart of scientific method. Science doesn't progress by scientists 'objectively' viewing all the facts. What facts? How would they select the facts to view? It progresses by scientists coming up with a theory they'd like to prove, then questioning the facts to see if it can be upheld.

ALEX [*breaking in*]: Ok. But when we confronted Stark, we found that arguments and reason weren't getting us anywhere. So we took other measures. *We made their position impossible.*

NATHAN [*looking thoughtfully at him*]: I see. Yes. You bought Welland. That's what you did, isn't it? Let's put that card on the table.

As Nathan *picks up the pen and approaches the flipchart, the* Narrator *steps forward, holds up his hand and freezes the characters in position. He then lifts the top sheet of the flipchart to reveal Table 11.2.*

NARRATOR: Nathan now learns from Alex and Jim that in their last confrontation with Boss, BDI introduced the card '*buy Welland*' and made playing it part of BDI's position. [Narrator *points to 'buy Welland' card in the 'BDI' column.*] In other words, BDI proposed, as a way of getting round the control problem, that rather than ask Boss to *cede control via non-voting shares* [*pointing to last cell of 'BDI' column*], BDI would *buy Welland*, either separately or as part of a merger agreement, and so effectively allow control of the merged organization to go to BDI. Stark rejected this, insisting on Boss's original position. He agreed that to *buy Welland* made commercial sense, but it should be done only after the merger – and not therefore by BDI alone, but by the BDI-Boss merger.

Table 11.2 – Introducing the card 'buy welland'

	BDI	Boss	threat	default
BDI	1	2	3	3
merge with DA	♣	♣	☐	☐
pay more	♣	♣	☐	☐
buy Welland	♣	☐	♣	☐
Boss	2	1	3	3
merge DA with BDI	♣	♣	☐	☐
cede control via non-voting shares	☐	☐	☐	☐

Thus the new positions were as in the first two columns of the table … Nathan also learns that during the meeting with Stark, *buy Welland* implicitly became part of BDI's fallback position [*pointing to the 'buy Welland' card in the threat column*], hence part of the threatened future.

Narrator *leaves the stage, waving his hand and bringing the characters back to life.*

NATHAN [*pointing to the 'buy Welland' card in the threat column*]: Ok, so that card is now played as part of the threatened future because Stark must have believed, at your last meeting, that you *would* play it if the merger negotiations broke down.

JIM [*carefully*]: He would have believed that. But at our last meeting, negotiations hadn't broken down. We expected to carry on. We agreed to go away and reconsider, on both sides.

NATHAN: I see. That's an important point … But let's do things in order. We've established that Stark realized that you would play this card if negotiations did break down. Next – these preference rankings. They remain the same, I believe. Both sides still preferred the other's position to the *threat* column.

ALEX [*loudly, coming forward and picking up a pen*]: And that's the whole point. Because we were under pressure to accept their position, they were refusing to accept ours! As you've pointed out, that was the problem. So we thoroughly checked the situation out, using game theory. Then we cut the Gordian knot. We *played* the 'buy Welland' card – irreversibly. Let me show you what that means in terms of your card table.

The Narrator *steps forward, waves his hand to freeze the characters in position, and turns up Table 11.3 on the flipboard. Then he steps back and waves his hand to bring them back to life.*

ALEX [*stepping back and laying down the pen*]: We fixed the 'buy Welland' card at 'played'. So their position became impossible – deleted from the table. [*To Nathan.*] That's right, to delete it, isn't it? You can't continue to have an infeasible column on the card table?

Table 11.3 – The card 'buy welland' is fixed, deleting the column 'boss'

	BDI	Boss	Threat	default	
BDI	1	2	3	3	
merge with DA	♣	♣	☐	☐	■
Pay more	♣	♣	☐	☐	■
buy Welland	♣	☐	♣	♣	
Boss	2	1	3	3	
Merge DA with BDI	♣	♣	☐	☐	■
cede control via non-voting shares	☐	☐	☐	☐	■

NATHAN: No, you can't. That's right.

ALEX: And so the only position still available is ours. They'll have to accept it. Our game-theoretic analysis shows they're bound to come round. They prefer our position to 'no merger'.

NATHAN: You did all that without telling them? Let me see if I've got this right ... At your last meeting, you discussed playing the 'buy Welland' card – but you didn't tell them that upon leaving the meeting you'd do it, *unilaterally and irreversibly*.

ALEX: Er, no, we didn't tell them. We hadn't yet used game theory to analyse the situation. [*To* Jim]: What would have been the point in telling them? – it would only have raised the temperature.

NATHAN [*grimly*]: And I suppose the temperature wasn't raised when you did it pre-emptively, without giving them a chance to reason with you ...

JIM: The temperature's certainly been raised!

ALEX [*impassively*]: Sure it has. But they'll come round in the end.

NATHAN: In saying that you're assuming that their preferences, value systems, ways of assessing the situation, are fixed – can't be altered under the pressure of emotion ...

ALEX: Yes, we're sticking to that assumption. Stark is tough. He uses emotion to get his way. But he's a professional. He's not going to let emotion affect his assessment of the bottom line.

NATHAN: Let me explain to you about retrospective emotion – the emotions of gratitude and revenge ...

ALEX [*interrupting*]: Look, even by your standards he's bound to come round. You say that emotion is created by dilemmas. But we've eliminated the dilemma. The choice he's faced with now is very simple. He accepts a merger with an enlarged BDI – a

BDI that's bought Welland – or no merger at all. Economics and politics both say he prefers the merger with an enlarged BDI.

JIM: Just a moment, Alex. Nathan, what were you saying about gratitude and revenge?

NATHAN: The theory is this. Suppose another player *pre-empts* you – i.e., takes action to irreversibly alter the common reference frame before you've finished interacting over it. At the extreme, their frame-altering action may have been taken before you've even *begun* to interact. Then you feel an emotional urge to *actually* reward or punish them in the way you would have *promised or threatened to*, if you'd had the chance. You feel this urge all the more strongly because it's irrational! The action that you needed to induce or deter has been irrevocably taken! For example, suppose someone rescues your child from drowning. Emotionally you want to reward them by giving them all or more than you *would have* offered – if you'd had the chance – to *induce* them to save the child. That's gratitude. We need to feel this emotion so that others may know they'll be rewarded for rescuing our children. Evolutionarily, those that acted out of irrational feelings of gratitude survived better – or their children survived better – than those that didn't.

JIM [*listening intently*]: Ok. That's gratitude. What about revenge?

NATHAN: That's evoked when someone takes action you would have wanted to deter. That's the feeling of the Count of Monte Cristo, who dedicates his life to avenging his wrongful imprisonment, when he was young. Why? His imprisonment is a fact. It's in the past. Now he's free. What good does it do him to take revenge? The answer is – that's the objective he set himself. Why? Because he felt such a deep emotion of vengefulness that it caused him to redirect all his life's ambitions.

JIM: And you're saying we can apply this to Stark? By taking this unilateral action – buying Welland – we pre-empted him. So emotionally he will want to take the action he was threatening to take to deter us?

NATHAN: I'm afraid so. Not only Stark personally, but all those that shared his aims. His team. The German government, perhaps, if they were part of his coalition (something we really should look at). What's likely to happen is that they'll try to reformulate their whole strategy for the European defence industry so that it excludes a merger with BDI. Notice: that doesn't mean their new strategy, once they've worked it out and rationalized it, will be irrational. The Count of Monte Cristo didn't behave irrationally, given his objectives. He planned and carried out his revenge with utmost rationality. Similarly the Germans will try, using the most rational means, to find a coherent, profitable, politically sound strategy *that excludes BDI*. Once they've found it, they'll be able to produce every kind of good reason for pursuing it – while feeling all the time a nice, warm, well-hidden feeling of gratified revenge.

JIM: What if they can't find a coherent, rational strategy that fits the bill?

NATHAN: We'll have to see. They may not be able to – in which case they'll come back to you in the end. But they'll do their best to find one.

ALEX [*looking at the floor*]: There are two other alternatives for them. An alliance with the Americans. There, they're handicapped by comparison with us because the US government feels more secure with us, defence-wise. Still, they might try. The other alternative . . .

JIM: . . . is to build on the usual Franco-German axis. Bring in other partners – the Italians, the Spanish – having built a Franco-German alliance. If they offered that to the French, leaving us on the outside, I guess the French would be willing, in return, to bite the bullet and privatize their defence industry.

A pause while Jim *and* Alex *stand looking at each other.*

ALEX: Maybe . . .

NATHAN: Our next step might be to look at that...

ALEX [*with sudden determination*]: No. The fact is we've looked at all these factors, exhaustively, in our game-theoretic assessment. These models [*waving his hand at the flipchart*] are altogether too simple. There are no calculations underlying them. We've looked at all the questions they raise in far more detail.

NATHAN: Including the emotional factors?

ALEX [*angrily*]: Emotions! I assure you, Stark is a professional.

NATHAN: I think you underestimate the need for professionals to have and act upon emotions. An effective politician or businessman *must* act upon rationalizations of gratitude and revenge. Mrs Thatcher, for example, never forgot her friends or her enemies. But she always had good, current reasons for not doing so. Chancellor Kohl – the same. I'm sure it must be true of Stark.

ALEX [*contemptuously*]: An effective businessman assesses the constant factors – commercial or political – that need to be considered in assessing different outcomes. He does not allow emotion to cloud his judgement.

NATHAN: Listen – may I tell you a story? [*He looks from one to the other. As they do not answer, he continues*]: One author[2] illustrates the point we are arguing about as follows. He was at a rock festival when he saw a hippy sitting on a bank, drugged out of his mind. A dog came up and sniffed at him. Somehow, by the smell, he could tell the hippy had *no revenge* in him. So the dog lifted its leg and peed on him.

He looks at *Jim*, then at *Alex*. They gaze blankly at him.

NATHAN: The dog was right! The hippy just sat there and let it happen. Now you or I – normal people – would have leapt up and kicked the dog. Why? It's already peed on us (let's suppose). By kicking it we merely risk hurting our foot. It's quite irrational. But *you'd better be a normal person, in whom a dog can smell irrational revenge* – or all the dogs in the block will pee on you.

JIM: So – how do you apply this?

---

[2] See Frank (1988). Another true story, apparently

NATHAN: Just to make the point, once more, that a politician or businessman needs to be a real person, given to projects of gratitude or revenge, rather than a calculating robot with fixed objectives. It's a mistake to think that a robot would do better. A robot will just get peed on! I'm again addressing the point about professionalism. If Stark and the other Germans involved are effective professionals, so much the more reason to fear that they'll find a strategy for European defence integration that excludes BDI!

ALEX [*looking at his watch*]: I'm afraid, Jim, that I can't spend any more time on this. It's been very interesting. It's worth looking at new techniques that come along. But I'm satisfied that we've already covered all the factors this has brought up. All, at least, that actually mean anything.

JIM: Are you satisfied that Stark will come back to us?

ALEX: Yes.

They stand looking at each other.

NATHAN [*shrugging his shoulders and turning away*]: I'm not.

The Narrator *comes forward waving his hand, so that the characters freeze in place.*

NARRATOR [*addressing the audience*]: What do you think? Will Alex be proved right – or will Nathan's fears turn out to be justified?

Postscript

The analysis fictionalized here was done in January 1999. On March 6th, the *Economist* reported as follows: 'BAe [the British defence giant] seems to have underestimated the hostile reaction from DASA and the German defence establishment, although the firm had been warned about it by Britain's prime minister, Tony Blair. BAe's chief executive, John Weston, has been virtually shunned in German defence circles... [But] the jilted Germans are not sitting around sulking.'

The report goes on to describe German efforts to link up with the US defence in-dustry, adding 'This is all a huge pain for the governments of France, Britain, Germany and Italy. At the end of 1997 they announced a grand design for the creation of a Euro-pean Defence and Aerospace Company (EDAC), big enough to cope with America's giants.'

European governments' pain had eased by July 2000, when the European Aeronautic Defence and Space company (EADS) was launched. By this time the Germans had failed to link up with the Americans. They had instead resolved problems over French government share ownership and linked up with the French. EADS comprised a union of German, French and Spanish firms, soon to be joined by Italians. BAe was left on the outside, linked to EADS only through specialist joint ventures.

Control of the European defence industry is now with the Germans and French. BAe has had to seek alliances and acquisitions in the US. Ironically, it has succeeded with these. It may have done better on its own than it would have done in an Anglo-German merger. This was not, however, the view it took at the time.

Our forecasts of the future are usually wrong. We must, however, make them in order to plan and form alliances.

References

Dewhurst, J. (1997). *Buying a Company: The Keys to Successful Acquisition*, Bloomsbury, London.
Dixit, A. and Nalebuff, B. (1991). *Thinking strategically*, W.W. Norton, New York.
Frank, R. (1988). *Passions Within Reason*, W.W. Norton, New York.
Howard, N. (1999). *Confrontation Analysis; How to Win Operations Other Than War*, CCRP, OASD(C3I), Pentagon, Washington DC. Available from www.dodccrp.org
Rankine, D. (1998). *A Practical Guide to Acquisitions*, John Wiley & Sons, Ltd, Chichester.

12 *An Overview of Related Methods: VSM, System Dynamics, and Decision Analysis*

John Mingers and Jonathan Rosenhead

Introduction

Any book is of finite size, and the topics of books are generally selected from an approximately continuous field. Where ever one draws a line round the subject matter, there are subjects on the other side of the exclusion line which could almost as easily have been selected for inclusion. This chapter provides much shorter summaries of some of those methods which are, at the very least, near neighbours of PSMs.

The characteristics of PSMs include – an orientation to group working, a basis in transparent model representation of the problematic situation, and an iterative and interactive mode of working. The extent to which the methods described here (the viable systems model, system dynamics, and participative variants of decision analysis) match these characteristics is a matter for debate – not least between the editors of this volume. However what is clear is (i) that readers who wish to know about PSMs will in many cases also be interested in a further range of methods which bear so strong a resemblance; and (ii) that such knowledge will also be of value since these methods are not infrequently used in combination with PSMs. This topic of the combination of methods will be addressed in the following chapter.

The Viable System Model (VSM)

The viable system model (VSM) is unlike other methods described in this book as it is not in itself a methodology or process for problem structuring or interventions. Rather it is an abstract model or generic blueprint for helping to design the structure of an organization. Its main tenet is that for an organization to be *viable*, that is to be able to survive within a changing environment, it must undertake particular activities and there must be certain relations between them. The model itself is at a very general level and so can be implemented in many different ways. The VSM has been developed after studying how human beings are organized as viable systems, based on the principles of cybernetics

(Beer 1966; Beer 1972; Beer 1979; Espejo and Harnden 1989). It is analogous to an abstract design for a house that specifies what there must be, e.g., cooking area, living area, etc., and specifies important principles of design based, for example, on ergonomics.

Fundamental Principles – Viability, Variety and Cybernetics

Cybernetics is a term coined by Norbert Weiner (1948) to refer to 'the science of communication and control in the animal and the machine'. It is concerned with how complex systems can control and regulate themselves through feedback processes that rely on information and communication. This is central to the question of whether a system – be it organism or organization – can remain viable, i.e., survive, within a particular environment. Viability implies the necessity of a structural connectivity between components that allows it to adapt and become successfully coupled to its environment. This in turn brings in questions of *identity* – what is the 'it' that is surviving? In the organizational context this immediately raises strategic questions such as: What are we? What do we do? What are our boundaries? We should not assume that there are definitive answers to such questions when we build VSM models – rather the modelling process should be seen as establishing some temporarily acceptable conventions that may be useful within organizational conversations.

An organization exists within, and is coupled to, an environment. The organization can be seen as undertaking various activities or operations with respect to the environment – its *primary activities* that produce it, and determine its identity. To survive, however, the organization must be able to regulate these activities and, if necessary, change them. That is, the activities must be *managed*. These are the three essential elements of the VSM – environment, activities, and management, each embedded within the other. The fundamental problem from a cybernetic viewpoint is how to manage *complexity*? Complexity is a tricky concept to define, but it is clearly related to *variety* – the number of states or behaviours that a system can exhibit. There is a fundamental law of cybernetics, formulated by Ashby (1956, p. 207) as the Law of Requisite Variety: 'only variety can destroy variety'. This means that for one system to be able to effectively control or regulate another it must have a similar degree of variety. The problem is clear – the environment will have enormously more variety than the organization, which in turn will have much more variety than the management. The organization can never be aware of, let alone respond to all possible occurrences of requirements of the environment, nor can management ever know every detail of all its employees and activities.

What occurs in practice is that variety is *engineered*, either consciously, or more likely unconsciously. The high variety is necessarily reduced or *attenuated*, while the low variety controller is *amplified*, as shown in Figure 12.1.

Variety attenuation can happen in many ways; perhaps the most common deliberate technique is filtering – only paying attention to totals, averages, yearly figures etc. The greatest *unconscious* attenuator of variety is of course *ignorance*. It is often, also, the most

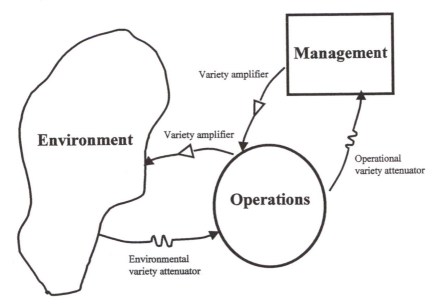

Figure 12.1 Variety attentuation and amplification

lethal. From the other side, an effective organization must amplify its own, and its management's variety – it must generate a richer range of possible actions. In fact, the point is not so much *absolute* variety, but *requisite* variety – there must be a satisfactory balance between the attenuated variety of the environment and the amplified variety of the organization. The system must be designed so as to *absorb* variety with its own. This leads to one of the major premises of VSM – the need for an appropriate balance between central control and peripheral autonomy. Clearly management will find it hard to match the variety of the operational organization, let alone the outside environment, and so it has to allow its operating units autonomy in order to absorb environmental variety. As a final point, computers and information systems are one of the greatest potential tools available to us for both attenuation and amplification yet in many cases they work in precisely the wrong way – presenting us with vast amounts of unnecessary information, and then restricting our range of responses.

The VSM – Systems One to Five

The heart of the VSM is a description of five different functions that need to occur in all viable systems. We have so far distinguished between the primary activities that an organization does, to be what it is, and the management of those activities. These primary activities constitute the System One (*Operations*) of the organization but we need to be very careful in deciding precisely what they are. It is wrong simply to look at a list of Departments or an organization chart – we have to distinguish between the primary activities, *which are viable systems in their own right*, and the secondary activities that support them. A second fundamental premise of VSM is the notion of *recursion*. Viable systems are embedded within viable systems. A university is a viable part of the education system but itself consists of departments that could be viable, and within them courses. The test is, could this activity in principle be taken out of the organization and have its own separate existence? If so, it is a primary activity. If, however, it only exists to support another activity then is in not viable. Thus activities such as accounting, information systems, personnel, and even sales and marketing are generally *not* primary activities since they would have no *raison d'etre* without a product or service.

The concept of recursive or nested viable systems implies that we have to consciously choose the level of our analysis – what Beer calls the *system in focus*. And, at the same time we should be aware of other levels, in particular the levels immediately above and below the system in focus. Figure 12.2 shows how the System One of our system in focus itself consists of several viable systems, each with their own management (the square boxes).

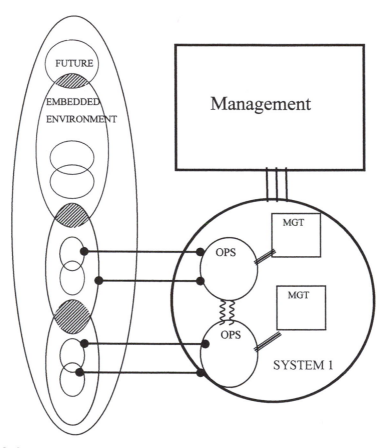

Figure 12.2 System Ones of the System in Focus

Each of these systems will interact with distinct (or perhaps overlapping) parts of the environment and is likely to have a variety of possible interactions between themselves. For instance, the primary activities could be sequential as in a complex production process, or the different stages of an educational system; they could be divided geographically as in different sales or administrative regions of the same organization; they could simply differ in terms of products but with the same population of customers and wholesalers as in a supermarket. In analysing an organization, consider each of its System Ones in terms of all of their interactions with their environments – what are the possible or actual variety attenuators and amplifiers? Do they balance variety effectively?

The different types of structural relations between the System Ones can be recognized within the model but the potential problem that can occur is in co-ordinating or orchestrating their interactions so as to avoid oscillations or clashes. This is the function of System Two – *Co-ordination*. Examples of Systems Twos are: production planning, timetabling and scheduling, project networks, safety codes, and house styles. These are shown in Figure 12.3 as the linked triangles. Such mechanisms do (or should) exist

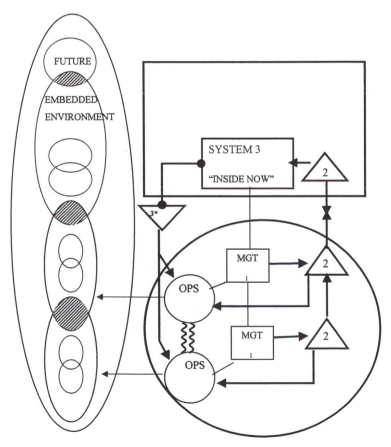

Figure 12.3 System Three – Control

between each System One, as well as at the management level which is able to view the operational system as a whole. The importance of System Two obviously varies with the degree of linkage of the System Ones but it is often under-estimated or even ignored. It should not be confused with management since its purpose is not to control, but to facilitate and smooth.

So far we have not looked into the box labelled 'Management' that deals with the whole of the System One in focus. If we do we find that it is necessary to manage both the internal environment of the organization, the 'inside and now', and the outside environment – especially the future, the 'outside and then'. These two activities are System Three (*Control*) and System Four (*Intelligence*).

System Three is in overall control of all the various System Ones as well as being responsible for the co-ordination function of System Two. Its primary purposes are: to communicate the organizational policy for System One and ensure that it is implemented; allocate resources between the various activities; and monitor actual performance. Of these, the most fundamental is the 'resource bargain' which is at the heart of the balance between control and autonomy. Which activities are to be undertaken and which not? What resources will be made available to support these activities? What are the expectations about performance and how will they be monitored? Once agreements on these matters have been reached, the day-to-day managing of the lower-level activities can be passed down and given their due degree of autonomy. The System Ones will operate within the parameters of the organization – legal, ethical, cultural, environmental – as specified by System Three, and will be accountable to System Three for its results.

These three forms of interaction – the resource bargain, accountability, and corporate identity – will involve considerable amounts of variety attenuation and amplification. This generates a significant potential control problem for System Three. As it stands it has to rely exclusively on information generated by System One to understand what is happening in System One. This information will be of a very attenuated nature and it would precisely go against the whole point of autonomy if System Three were to attempt to regularly scrutinize the day-to-day happenings in System One. The question is then, how can System Three know that it is getting accurate and adequate information from System One? The answer is this it is necessary for System Three to look directly into the operations of System One, but only sporadically, not continually or routinely. This is what is conventionally called *Audit* and within VSM is known as System Three*.

If System Three controls the internal environment, of equal importance is a system to monitor the external environment, especially with regard to the future. It is important to be clear that this function – System Four – is not the same as the interactions with the environment carried out by the various System Ones. These latter interactions will only be partial subsets of the whole environment faced by the system in focus, and importantly they will reflect only the current activities. Many, many organizations have failed because they have not foreseen the changes that make their current operations redundant. There will be, of course, System Fours *within* System Ones at lower levels of recursion but these will have a more restricted and specific set of concerns. That is not to say that the System Fours at different levels do not communicate with each other and may well thereby learn things of importance for themselves.

System Four (*Intelligence*) is concerned with outside developments, now and in the future, that are relevant to the organization and possible organizational responses to these. This makes it different to the other systems in that it must be aware of, or *have some model of*, the system in focus *as a whole*. This makes it essentially self-referential, for its model must of course include itself. System Four stands at a cross-roads within the organization – it mediates between the outside and the inside, and also communicates important information vertically between Systems Three and One and the policy maker System Five. Its primary function can be seen as one of adaptation – stimulating and bringing about change in response to developments in the environment, as opposed to System Three's function of maintenance and control.

This makes the relationship between Three and Four of primary importance, as shown by the large arrows linking them in Figure 12.4. Too much emphasis on System

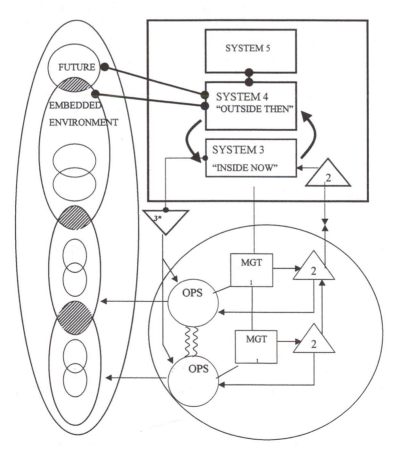

Figure 12.4 System Four (Intelligence) and System Five (Policy)

Four and the future as opposed to day-to-day operations can lead to the collapse of the organization as it is now, while too much concern for internal efficiency can lead to excellent products that have no future.

Finally, we reach the end of the model – the closure of the system – System Five (*Policy* or *Identity*), where the buck stops. System Five, which could typically be the Board (not the chief executive), sets the overall policy and ethos of the organization; it also ensures that the organization has an identity and that this is known and acted upon. This is where we started the model – what are the primary activities that produce the organization and thereby its identity? Beyond that, System Five is necessary to arbitrate in the debates and conversations between Systems Three and Four, and ultimately to determine which of the various futures for the organization will be enacted. It also has a representative function, representing the whole of the system in focus to itself and to outside and wider systems. Finally, it needs to be available to recognize and take action in extreme situations. The organization itself, with its various filters and balances, may well appear to System Five to be functioning unproblematically and so it is necessary for there to be signals, out of the normal channels, that will alert it to the unusual. Beer terms these signals *algedonic*, meaning 'to do with pain and pleasure'. We can see the currently ongoing problems of Marks and Spencer as a failure of System Four to understand developments in the market, and a failure of the algedonic system to alert the board in time.

This brings us to Figure 12.5 which shows the whole of the VSM, including the recursive embedding of the whole model within each System One.

VSM in Practice

The basic model can be used in two ways – for *diagnosis* – by mapping a particular organization on to it to discover weaknesses and problems, and for *design*, in order to construct a more effective structure. It can be used on its own, perhaps within a methodology such as that of Beer (1985) or Espejo, Schumann *et al.* (1996), or is often combined with other approaches such as SSM (see Chapter 13).

All of Beer's books contain many examples and illustrations but the following give case studies of its use by other people:

*   Chapters 5 to 11 of *The Viable Systems Model* (Espejo and Harnden 1989) each contains a detailed case study covering, for example, broadcasting, manufacturing companies, and a training network.
*   A special issue of *Systems Practice* **3**(3), 1990 is devoted to the VSM.
*   The following are illustrations of its use combined with other methods in a multimethodology – Leonard (1997), Ormerod (1998), Gill (1997).

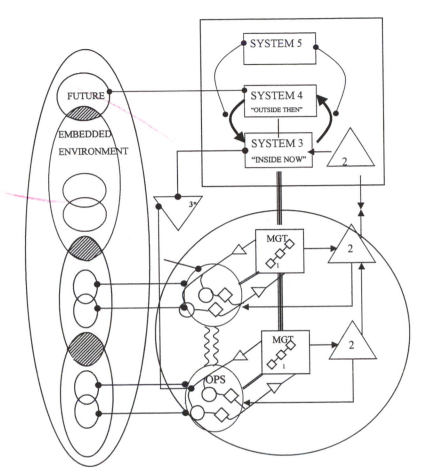

Figure 12.5 The VSM as a whole

When used in diagnosis mode, the following are some of the common problems found within organizations:

- System 1 is not treated as sufficiently autonomous and so cannot deal with its own local variety.
- Systems 2–4 see themselves as autonomous in their own right whereas they are really secondary to system 1.
- The functions of some subsystems are often not performed, especially System 2 – coordination, and System 4 – intelligence.
- System 4 is weak because it is seen as a staff (rather than line) function. This may lead System 5 to collapse into System 3 and just undertake control functions.
- System 5 may not be creating a strong enough identity and representing the whole system to its wider systems.

• Information and transmission channels are not appropriate or rapid enough. They may amplify or attenuate variety in the wrong directions – e.g. many information systems.

System Dynamics

The basis of system dynamics (SD) was developed in the late 1950s by Jay Forrester (1961) and was initially called 'industrial dynamics'. It reflected his view that the dynamic behaviour in terms of growth and stability of industrial systems, whether individual organizations, supply chains, or whole industries, resulted from underlying structures of flows, delays, information, and feedback relations. Like the VSM, it drew its inspiration from the pioneering work in cybernetics. Its approach was to develop a mathematical model of the relations between the various components of a system, expressed in difference equations, and then run the model as a form of simulation on a computer. Forrester's work was further developed within wider contexts – e.g., the development of cities (Forrester, 1969) and eventually models of the industrialized world (Forrester, 1973). But it remained somewhat marginal until the 1990s when the advent of good quality graphical software (e.g., *iThink* and *Powersim*), and the popularity of Peter Senge's (1990) work on learning organizations generated a resurgence of interest. There are excellent modern introductions to SD by Sterman (2000) and Vennix (1996).

Fundamental Principles – Counterintuitive Behaviour, Feedback, Dynamic Complexity

One of the most common experiences in trying to manage a situation is that one's actions turn out to make things worse either by generating some form of resistance or adaptation, or by creating a new and often worse problem. Low nicotine cigarettes lead to more being consumed; flood prevention measures like dams often lead to more severe flooding; building new motorways leads to even more congestion and so on. These *counterintuitive* behaviours result from the *systemic* nature of relations – system components are related to each other in multiple, complex ways; cause and effect are not localized but often distant in both space and time; and chains of influence are not linear but circular leading to positive and negative feedback.

In fact, the behaviour of systems is seen as resulting not from the nature of the components themselves but from the relations between components. More precisely, from the interactions between the only two possible types of *feedback* processes, positive (self-reinforcing) and negative (self-correcting, balancing)[1]. Positive feedback occurs when an increase (decrease) in one period leads, through other factors, to a further increase

---

[1] Note that in SD 'negative feedback' simply means a process where the value of a variable in one period is negatively related to its value in a previous period. In classical cybernetics, negative feedback usually implies 'error-controlled' feedback, that is where the difference between an actual and a desired state is fed back to control a system as in a thermostat

(decrease) in a later period. For instance, an increase in the weapons held by country A leads to an enemy country B increasing its weapons, which pressures A into increasing even more (Figure 12.6a). Conversely, of course, a decrease would tend to lead to further decreases (or at least lower increases). Reinforcing feedback generates a dynamic behaviour of exponential growth or decay. Negative feedback occurs when an increase (decrease) in one period leads to the opposite, a decrease (increase) in later periods. This has stabilizing effects counteracting the initial change. For instance, producing more weapons requires a greater share of a country's wealth, and so will lead to pressure against further increases (Figure 12.6b). Balancing feedback generates a stable dynamic behaviour.

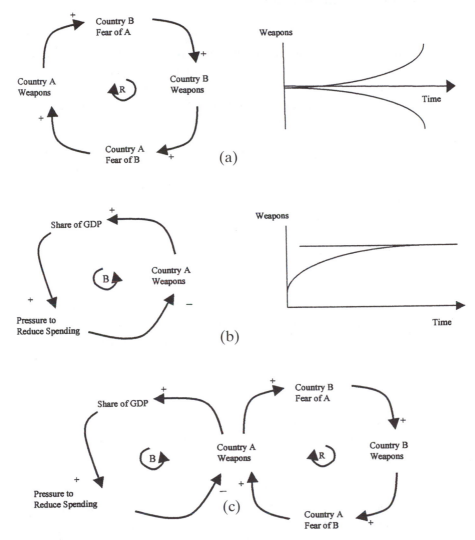

Figure 12.6 Balancing and Reinforcing Feedback

Ultimately, all positive feedback loops must be controlled by negative feedback for there can never be ever-lasting explosive growth, and the *dynamic complexity* of the behaviour of systems is the result of the relative strength of reinforcing and balancing loops over time (Figure 12.6c). Note that there is a contrast between *dynamic* complexity and *detail* complexity; the latter referring to the number of components and relations within a system. Systems with little detail complexity can nevertheless display dynamic complexity, e.g., a magnetic pendulum moving in several magnetic fields, and *vice versa*, e.g., a clockwork watch.

Developing System Dynamic Models

SD models are generally developed for clients within organizations in order to explore and explain some dynamic feature of the situation that is undesirable, or to provide a tool (often called a 'flight simulator' or 'microworld') for training and learning purposes. Table 12.1 shows an outline of the steps in developing an SD model adapted from Sterman (2000), variants can be found in Vennix (1996) and Lane and Oliva (1998). Four points should be made about the process generally:

- It is iterative – models go through continual development, testing, and refinement.
- The process occurs in close cooperation with the client – indeed the process is often one of making explicit the client(s) own *mental model* of the situation. There is, in fact, some debate about what exactly a SD model is modelling. Is it a relatively objective representation of the world, or is it really a model of peoples' beliefs about the world? A range of views are discussed by Lane (1999; 2000).
- Modelling is always embedded within a social and organizational context. There must be continual iteration between the virtual world of the model and learning in the real world.
- In most cases the main point of the whole process is not the construction of an accurate model for *predictive* purposes, for this would be impossible. It is rather the *learning about the situation* generated through the development and use of the model(s).

Problem articulation

This stage is common to all OR interventions and is really what this whole book is about – problem structuring. However, there are aspects particular to developing an SD model. The prime purpose of SD is to be able to explain dynamic behavior in terms of a causal model. This focuses on:

- The time frame – both historical and in the future. It must be long enough to display the behaviour of concern, but not too long so that its detail is lost.
- The boundary to be considered in terms of factors/variables to be included. This

Table 12.1 – System Dynamics Modelling Process. Adapted from (Sterman, 2000).

Problem Articulation	Structuring the problem; determining the main variables, bounding the scope; specifying the time frame; defining the reference mode – 'typical' behaviour
Formulation of Dynamic Hypothesis	Develop maps/causal-loop/influence diagrams of the relations between the factors; identify the main feedback structures; generate hypotheses explaining the behaviour in terms of the feedback processes.
Formulation of Simulation Model	Generate a representation in terms of stocks and flows; estimate all necessary relationships and parameter values; develop a computer model and test for consistency.
Testing and Validation	Comparison with reference mode; robustness under extreme conditions; sensitivity to parameters, initial conditions.
Using the Model – Policy Design and Evaluation	Specify possible scenarios; develop alternative strategies and policies; do what-if analyses; check sensitivity and interaction of policies; use for training.

decision is always relative to the particular purpose of the model – what to include and what to exclude is crucial for overall success. There is often a desire for the modeller to create a comprehensive model of everything but this is quite counter-productive – the model should be no more detailed than is necessary for its purpose.
• The 'reference mode' of behaviour. That is the typical behaviour, either unwanted or desired, that the model needs to be able to reproduce.

Formulating a dynamic hypothesis

This is in many ways the most important stage of the process as it is where the main causal modelling occurs. The result is a *qualitative* model of the variables and their re-lationships such that the reference mode dynamic behaviour can be explained *endogen-ously*, that is purely within the model rather than depending on external factors. The model is, of course, an hypothesis – it is always provisional and subject to development or even abandonment as learning about the situation develops.

There are several tools, especially particular types of diagrams, that are used at this stage. The most common is a causal loop diagram (CLD), also sometimes known as an influence diagram or multiple-cause diagram. Other diagrams, e.g., a model boundary chart or a subsystem diagram are described by Sterman (2000). A CLD consists of factors or variables that are joined by arrows showing the causal links between them (see Figure 12.7a). Each arrow must be labelled with a '+' or '−' to show the direction of causation, that is how the dependent (Y) variable responds to a change in the in-dependent (X). A positive link means that if X increases (decreases) Y will be larger (smaller) than it would otherwise have been. Thus in Figure 12.7a an increase in the number of hare births increases the hare population; an increase in the birth rate increases the number of births. A negative link means that if X increases (decreases) Y will be smaller (larger) than it would have been. Thus an increase in deaths reduces the population.

A CLD is intended to identify the causal or feedback loops that involve several variables, as described above. Each loop that is identified should also be labelled as reinforcing (positive) or balancing (negative) – some people use R and B, others + and –. In Figure 12.7a, there is a reinforcing loop between number of births and population size since both causal links are positive. This loop interacts with a balancing one

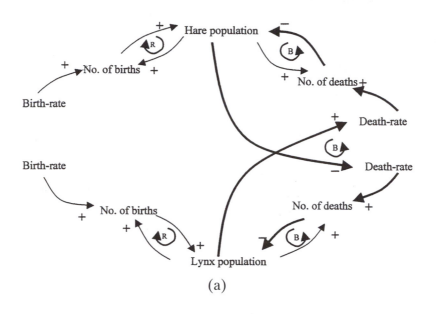

(a)

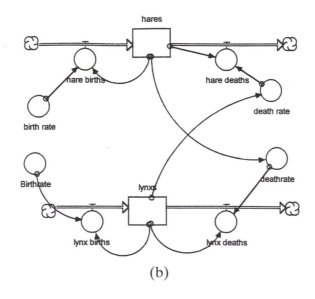

(b)

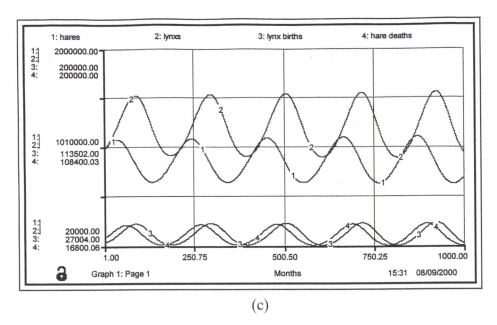

1: hares   2: lynxs   3: lynx births   4: hare deaths

(c)

Figure 12.7 (a) causal loop diagram for competing populations; (b) Stocks and Flows Diagram; (c) typical output from SD software

between population size and number of deaths: as population rises there are more deaths which in turn reduces population. In this classical predator-prey model there are also feedback loops between the two species which need to be traced out. The greater the lynx population the greater will be the hare death rate and this will reduce the hare population. Eventually the reduced source of food for lynxes will lead to more of them dying and start reducing the lynx population which will in turn allow the re-growth of the hare population, thus starting the cycle again. Thus, in this very simplistic scenario the cyclical changes in the size of two competing populations can be generated through the causal structure embodied in the CLD.

The next stage of the process may be to develop the qualitative CLD into a quantitative model that can actually be simulated on a computer. The 'may be' is because many studies do not actually proceed on to a simulation, either because the development of the CLD has generated sufficient learning or because there is insufficient good quality information to produce a useful simulation (Lane, 1994; Wolstenholme, 1999b). Within the context of problem structuring for messy situations the development of an actual computer model is quite rare. One useful result of CLDs is the identification of 'systems archetypes' (Senge, 1990; Lane, 1998). These are patterns of feedback loops and resulting behaviour which are observed very commonly in practice – for example, 'success to the successful' where two activities compete for the same resource, the result being that one gets stronger and stronger at the expense of the other.

Formulation of a simulation model

Clearly we cannot cover in any detail the process of constructing a real SD simulation model – see (Forrester, 1968; Roberts *et al.*, 1984; Coyle, 1996; Vennix, 1996; Sterman, 2000) – but there are two main steps: transforming the CLD into a 'stocks and flows' diagram (SFD), and then estimating all the model relationships and parameters.

Stock and flows, together with information and control, are really the foundations of SD modelling. A stock is the level of a variable at a point in time. This level is changed by inflows and outflows which in turn are controlled by rates of flow or 'valves'. Stocks are not necessarily physical – there can be stocks of memories, beliefs or ideas. They can be thought of as the structure of the system – if a snap-shot is taken at a point in time, what are the important aspects of the system that can be counted or measured? Stocks are shown as rectangles and flows as pipes with valves (Figure 12.7b). The ends of the pipes which are shown as clouds denote the chosen boundaries of the model. The other features are arrows that denote information and control, and auxiliary variables that might be parameters or values calculated from other variables.

Figure 12.7b shows the CLD translated into an SFD; in this case one is very similar to the other. The two stocks are the numbers of hare and lynx, with the inflows and out-flows being births and deaths. The causal loops are largely shown by the control arrows. Arrows from the stock of hares go to the flows of births and deaths, while the interactions between the species are shown by the arrows from stock of lynxs to death of hares for example. The diagram itself can easily be created using the icons available in current graphical software but what is important is what is behind the diagram, that is a mathematical formulation of all its relationships. Some will be quite obvious, e.g., $\text{population}_{t+1} = \text{population}_t + \text{births}_t - \text{deaths}_t$. Others will require empirical estimation or expert judgement and may lead to an expansion of the CLD into much greater detail. For example, the lynx/hare death relation might involve specifying the average number of kills per lynx depending on the density of hares, type of terrain, and availability of other types of prey. The software allows relationships to be specified as functional equations or as estimated empirical relationships. Figure 12.7c shows examples of the graphical output that can be obtained from software such as *iThink*.

Testing and validation

In many ways, validating and testing the model is not a separate stage but goes on throughout the process of model building. It can be seen as both a technical process in terms of the internal and statistical reliability of the model, and also as a social process where the prime consideration is the learning and confidence generated for the client (Lane, 1999). We can distinguish between *reliability* and *validity*. Reliability concerns the internal consistency of the model – does it make sense and does it produce consistent results from one run to another? Validity concerns its external relationship – does it reproduce the behaviour that it is supposed to? Some of the main techniques of validation are:

- Replicating the reference mode of behaviour if it was possible to specify one. In practice the model will rarely match the behaviour exactly as it is inevitably a simplification of the world, but it is important to identify and then explain any anomalies. This indeed can be a valuable part of the learning process.
- Testing the model under extreme conditions. It is very easy to develop a model that provides plausible output under typical conditions but which actually has underlying flaws or is inconsistent. One way of discovering this is to test it under conditions that would never actually occur – for instance zero energy input or billions of orders and see whether it does behave as it should.
- Investigating the sensitivity of the model to its parameters, initial conditions, and relationships by varying them in a systematic way. This will show which ones have a particularly significant impact on the results and may therefore be important policy levers.

Using the model

Once the model has been tested and both modeller and client have confidence in its reliability and validity then it can be employed in various ways. One common way is to use it like a flight simulator for training purposes, to put managers in difficult situations and see how they would react and what the consequences would be. It can also be used to explore the consequences of different scenarios for the future. This might just involve minor changes to the parameters or major changes to the whole feedback structure. Equally, the model can be used to test different policies or strategies within the same environmental conditions.

System Dynamics in Practice

There are many examples of CLDs and SD models in the text books already referred to. Also the various software packages that come with a wide selection of ready-built models. Morecroft and Sterman's (1994) edited book contains several case studies as well as theoretical and practical discussion. There is a special issue of the *Journal of the Operational Research Society* (**50**(4), 1999) on SD that also has a variety of case studies as well as more general overviews. The following are recently published case studies: Gonzalez-Busto and Garcia (1999); McCray and Clark (1999); van Ackere and Smith (1999); Wolstenholme (1999a); Bajracharya, Ogunlana, and Bach (2000); Dangerfield and Roberts (2000); and Lane, Monefeldt, and Rosenhead (2000).

With regard to the use of SD within multimethodology, it is probably most often combined with SSM (Cavana *et al.*, 1996; Coyle and Alexander, 1997) and with cognitive mapping, which is closely related to CLD (Eden, 1994; Ackerman, Eden, and Williams, 1997; Bennett *et al.*, 1997).

Decision Conferencing

Decision Conferencing is a workshop-based process which bears, at the very least, a close resemblance to the methods described in the previous ten chapters. Its aims have been described as the achievement of shared understanding, the development of a sense of common purpose, and the generation of commitment to action (Phillips, 1989). It operates in workshop mode employing an independent, impartial facilitator. And it makes use of real-time expert modelling, usually computer-based, to achieve its aims. Most of these are propositions to which proponents of PSMs could happily sign up. (There might be some sensitivity about the word 'expert', with its possible connotation of exclusivity, and about the reliance on computers.) The difference, however, lies in the types of models commonly deployed in Decision Conferences.

Origins of Decision Analysis

Here we need to track back to an earlier period in the history of modelling in support of decision-making. In the 1960's a way was developed of formalizing the choice between decision alternatives when there was uncertainty about future events which affected their consequences (Raiffa and Schlaiffer, 1961; Howard, 1966; Raiffa, 1968). This was most commonly represented as a branching decision tree, and the consequences were taken to be a one-dimensional performance measure (often in practice traded-off and expressed in cash terms). The developments of this approach are known as decision analysis; for full accounts see French (1986; 1989), Watson and Buede (1987), and Goodwin and Wright (1998).

This formulation was extended by Keeney and Raiffa (1976) to allow for there to be multiple criteria, and the approach developing from this innovation became known, not surprisingly, as multi-criteria decision analysis (MCDA) – though multi-attribute utility theory (MAUT) is a more precise name. One of the features of this approach was an interest, not only in the branching tree of decisions, but also in the hierarchy of objectives held by the decision maker. That is, a 'value tree' is constructed, with the most general objectives at the top, each of which is subdivided into components, which may again be subdivided etc. It becomes necessary, therefore, both to weight the components against each other at each level, and to score any alternative action on each of the most basic sub-components of the tree. The formulation may or may not involve establishing the probabilities of outcome, and their incorporation into the calculations. For a full treatment of MCDA, see Belton and Stewart (2001).

The information that is needed for these models can impose considerable demands on the decision-maker, and there are now a wide range of alternative methods which tackle this problem in different ways – see DETR (2000). All of these variants are most often used in the traditional manner, with expert analysts eliciting information, operating on it, and reporting results to clients. The details of their different mathematical formulations are not the issue from the stand-point of this book. What is relevant is the fact that they can in many cases be used in participative mode. This mode is known as 'Decision Conferencing'.

Workshop-based Decision Analysis/MCDA

There is an absence of full-length descriptions of Decision Conferencing – accounts are often a few paragraphs to a few pages either within a description of Decision Analysis/MCDA more generally, or as preface to a case study (Phillips, 1989, 1990; Watson and Buede, 1987). However the general structure of a Decision Conference is quite clear, and in most respects similar to that of a PSM workshop.

The conference itself will last two or exceptionally three days, and be located away from the participants' workplace. Sometimes there may be a sequence of conferences held at intervals. All the key players need to be present, and the conference is run by a team of two or more facilitators. Generally the lead facilitator will meet the chief client in advance to ensure that the issue is appropriate, and to set expectations.

At the conference itself there will be broadly three phases – of formulating the nature of the problem, of model building, and of exploring its implication for decision. Belton and Stewart (2001) call these phases problem structuring, model building, and using the model to inform and challenge thinking.

Belton and Stewart's first phase, problem structuring (sometimes called 'problem framing'), is concerned with the identification of the problem or issue – who are the stakeholders, what are the goals and values, the alternative courses of action and constraints, what are the relevant environment and the prevalent uncertainties? There is an evident convergence here with PSMs, and indeed there is growing experience of the use of PSMs to assist with the framing phase (Belton, Ackerman and Shepherd, 1997; Bana e Costa *et al.*, 2001).

There is no firm line between the second and third phases. There is general agreement that the model is not 'an objectively faithful representation of the problem' (Watson and Buede, 1987), and that its role is not as a finished object to be used to identify optimal solutions. Rather it serves as a vehicle for the ongoing discussion of issues between the parties. Phillips (1990) emphasizes that the model is a rough one constructed rapidly; it is explored in detail only in so far as the differences seem to matter. Modifications are proposed and tried out successively; re-weightings and re-scorings are conducted, which often demonstrate their negligible impact on the model's outputs.

The initial output of a model may not be in agreement with the group's intuitive preferences. In this case both the model and the intuition are challenged, which may surface tacit objectives or generate new options. This process continues until the group accepts the developed model's implications for commitment.

What distinguishes the analytic dimension of different decision conferences from each other is the particular structure of model that is used. What distinguishes decision conferences as a whole from the PSMs described previously is the nature of decision analytic/MCDA models as a category.

As regards differences between models, they may arise from the nature of the problems that they are designed to address, from the process of elicitation and re-processing of information which is adopted, from the software being used, or some combination of these dimensions. Thus, for example, the well-known HIVIEW and EQUITY software packages cater, respectively, for problems of choosing between alternatives, and of allocating resources. Other multi-purpose software explicitly within the MCDA tradition includes V·I·S·A (Belton and Vickers, 1990) and MACBETH (Bana e Costa and Vansnick, 1999).

These factors make for a great deal of variety within the field. However it is what these various formulations within decision analysis/MCDA have *in common* that gives decision conferencing certain aspects that are distinctively different from the PSM workshop process. Evidently the mathematical expression of their problem will not, in general, be comprehensible to the group members. Therefore there is considerable reliance on software that can improve transparency by demonstrating diagrammatically the implications of the formulation, and of any changes to it that are under consideration. The mathematics does its work behind the scenes; group members accept the implications through a combination of the transparency that is achievable, and trust in the computer and in the facilitators.

This feature becomes especially prominent in Belton and Stewart's second, model building, phase. While there are differences in individual style, it is not uncommon for the lead facilitator and the computer and the computer display projected onto a large screen to take centre stage in a way that would be extremely rare in a PSM workshop. Indeed on occasion the technical demands of real-time modelling can be intense. Watson and Buede (1987) suggest that a team as large as four may be needed – one to facilitate, and the others to operate the software, take notes, and assemble summary documents and visual aids. Quite commonly the decision conference takes place in a sophisticated purpose-built facility with room for twelve participants at a circular table, and enclosed by whiteboards, screens with back-projection etc. There is thus a sharp contrast with the ambience (no fixed furniture, low tech, blu-tack) that characterizes the typical PSM workshop for most of the methods described in this volume.

It might appear that Decision Conferencing's reliance on models that quantify objectives and combine them onto a single dimension would place a significant ideological and practical barrier between these two approaches. In practice Decision Conferencing is commonly used in an exploratory and non-optimizing way, so that what unites Decision Conferencing and PSMs is on balance at least as extensive as what separates them.

References

Ackerman, F., Eden, C., and Williams, T. (1997). 'Modeling for litigation: mixing qualitative and quantitative approaches', *Interfaces*, **27**, 48–65.

Ashby, W.R. (1956). *An Introduction to Cybernetics*, Chapman Hall, London.

Bajracharya, A., Ogunlana, S.O., and Bach, N.L. (2000). 'Effective organizational infrastructure for training activities: a case study of the Nepalese construction sector', *System Dynamics Review*, **16**, 91–112.

Bana e Costa, C.A., da Costa Lobo, M.L., Ramos, I.A., and Vansnick, J.C. (2001). Multicriteria Approach for Strategic Town Planning: the Case of Barcelos, Working Paper 36, Department of Operational Research, London School of Economics, London

Bana e Costa, C.A. and Vansnick, J.C. (1999). 'The Macbeth approach: basic ideas, software, and an application', in *Advances in Decision Analysis* (Eds. N. Meskens and M. Roubens), Kluwer Scientific, Dordrecht.

Beer, S. (1966). *Decision and Control*, John Wiley & Sons, Ltd, London.

Beer, S. (1972). *Brain of the Firm*, John Wiley & Sons, Ltd, Chichester.

Beer, S. (1979). *The Heart of Enterprise*, John Wiley & Sons, Ltd, Chichester.

Beer, S. (1985). *Diagnosing the System for Organizations*, John Wiley & Sons, Ltd, Chichester.

Belton, V., Ackermann, F., and Shepherd, I. (1997). 'Integrated support from problem structuring through to alternative evaluation using COPE and V·I·S·A', *Journal of Multiple Criteria Decision Analysis*, **6**, 115–30.

Belton, V. and Vickers, S.P. (1990). 'Use of a simple multi-attribute value function incorporating visual interactive sensitivity analysis for multiple criteria decision making', in *Readings in Multiple Criteria Decision Aid* (Ed. C.A. Bana e Costa), Springer-Verlag, Berlin.

Belton, V. and Stewart, T.J. (2001). *Multi Criteria Decision Analysis an integrated approach*, Kluwer, Amsterdam.

Bennett, P., Ackerman, F., Eden, C., and Williams, T. (1997). 'Analysing litigation and negotiation: using a combined methodology', in *Multimethodology: The Theory and Practice of Combining Management Science Methodologies* (Eds. J. Mingers and A. Gill), pp. 59-88, John Wiley & Sons, Ltd, Chichester.

Cavana, R., Lee, M., Bennet, J., and Taylor, R. (1996). 'Possum and gorse control on a farm woodlot: a system dynamics approach', *Asia-Pacific J. Operational Research*, **13**, 181–207.

Coyle, R. (1996). *System Dynamics Modelling*, Chapman Hall, London.

Coyle, R. and Alexander, M. (1997). 'Two approaches to qualitative modelling of a nation's drug trade', *System Dynamics Review*, **13**, 205–22.

Dangerfield, B.C. and Roberts, C.A. (2000). 'A strategic evaluation of capacity retirements in the steel industry', *J. Opl Res. Soc.*, **51**, 53–60.

DETR (2000). *Multi-Criteria Analysis: a manual*, Department of Environment, Transport and the Regions, London.

Eden, C. (1994). Cognitive mapping and problem structuring for systems dynamics model building, Dept. of Management Science Working Paper 94/6, Strathclyde University, Glasgow.

Espejo, R., and Harnden, R. (1989). *The Viable Systems Model: Interpretations and Applications of Stafford Beer's VSM*, John Wiley & Sons, Ltd, Chichester.

Forrester, J. (1961). *Industrial Dynamics*, MIT Press, Cambridge, MA.

Forrester, J. (1968). *Principles of Systems*, MIT Press, Cambridge.

Forrester, J. (1969). *Urban Dynamics*, MIT Press, Cambridge, MA.

Forrester, J. (1973). *World Dynamics*, MIT Press, Cambridge, MA.

French, S. (1986). *Decision Theory: An Introduction to the Mathematics of Rationality*, Ellis Horwood, Chichester.

French, S. (1989). *Readings in Decision Analysis*, Chapman and Hall, London.

Gill, A. (1997). 'Managing a Virtual Organization', in *Multimethodology: Theory and Practice of Combining Management Science Methodologies* (Eds. J. Mingers and A. Gill), pp. 153–83, John Wiley & Sons, Ltd, Chichester.

Gonzalez-Busto, B. and Garcia, R. (1999). 'Waiting lists in Spanish public hospitals: A system dynamics approach', *System Dynamics Review*, **15**, 201–24.

Goodwin, P. and Wright, G. (1998). *Decision Analysis for Management Judgement* (2nd ed.), John Wiley & Sons, Ltd, Chichester.

Howard, R. (1966). 'Decision analysis: applied decision theory', in *Proceedings of the Fourth International Conference on Operational Research* (Eds. D.B. Hertz and J. Melese), pp. 59–71, Wiley-Interscience, New York.

Keeney, R.L. and Raiffa, H. (1976). *Decisions with Multiple Objectives*, John Wiley & Sons, Inc, New York.

Lane, D. (1994). 'With a little help from our friends: how system dynamics and "soft OR" can learn from each other', *System Dynamics Review*, **10**, 101–34.

Lane, D.C. (1998). 'Can we have confidence in generic structures?', *J. Opl Res. Soc.*, **49**, 936–47.

Lane, D. (1999). 'Social theory and system dynamics practice', *European Journal of Operational Research*, **113**, 501–27.

Lane, D. (2000). 'Should system dynamics be described as a "hard" or "deterministic" systems approach?', *Systems Research and Behavioural Science*, **17**, 3–22.

Lane, D.C., Monefeldt, C., and Rosenhead, J.V. (2000). 'Looking in the wrong place for healthcare improvements: A system dynamics study of an accident and emergency department', *J. Opl Res. Soc.*, **51**, 518–31.

Lane, D. and Oliver, R. (1998). 'The greater whole: towards a synthesis of system dynamics and soft systems methodology', *European Journal of Operational Research*, **107**, 214–35.

Leonard, A. (1997). 'Using models in sequence: a case study of a post-acquisition intervention', in *Multimethodology: Theory and Practice of Combining Management Science Methodologies* (Eds. J. Mingers and A. Gill), pp. 105–26, John Wiley & Sons, Ltd, Chichester.

McCray, G.E. and Clark, T.D. (1999). 'Using system dynamics to anticipate the organizational impacts of outsourcing', *System Dynamics Review*, **15**, 345–73.

Morecroft, J. and Sterman, J. (eds.) (1994). *Modelling for Learning Organizations*, Productivity Press, Portland.

Ormerod, R. (1998). 'Putting soft OR methods to work: the case of the business improvement project at Powergen', *European Journal of Operational Research*, **118**, 1–29.

Phillips, L. (1989). 'People-centered group decision support', in *Knowledge-based Management Support Systems* (Eds. G. Doukidis, F. Land, and G. Miller), pp. 208–24, Ellis Horwood, Chichester.

Phillips, L.D. (1990). 'Decision analysis for group decision support', in *Tackling Strategic Problems: the role of group decision support* (Eds. C. Eden and J. Radford), pp. 142–50, Sage, London.

Raiffa, H. (1968). *Decision Analysis*, Addison-Wesley, Reading, MA.

Raiffa, H. and Schlaifer, R. (1961). *Applied Statistical Decision Theory*, Harvard Business School, Cambridge, MA.

Roberts, N., Andersen, D., Deal, R., Garet, M., and Shaffer, W. (1984), *Introduction to Computer Simulation*, Productivity Press, Portland.

Vennix, J. (1996). *Group Model Building: Facilitating Team Learning Using System Dynamics*, John Wiley & Sons, Ltd, Chichester.

Senge, P. (1990). *The Fifth Discipline: The Art and Practice of the Learning Organization*, Century Books, London.

Sterman, J. (2000). *Business Dynamics: Systems Thinking and Modelling for a Complex World*, McGraw-Hill, New York.

van Ackere, A. and Smith, P.C. (1999). 'Towards a macro model of National Health Service waiting lists', *System Dynamics Review*, **15**, 225–52. *Systems Dynamics*, John Wiley & Sons, Ltd, London.

Watson, S.R. and Buede, D.M. (1987). *Decision Synthesis: The Principles and Practice of Decision Analysis*, Cambridge University Press, Cambridge.

Weiner, N. (1948). *Cybernetics: or Communication and Control in the Animal and the Machine*, MIT Press, Cambridge, MA.

Wolstenholme, E. (1999a). 'A patient flow perspective of UK Health Services: Exploring the case for new "intermediate care" initiatives', *System Dynamics Review*, **15**, 253–71.

Wolstenholme, E. (1999b). 'Qualitative vs quantitative modelling: the evolving balance', *J. Opl Res. Soc.*, **50**, 422–28.

13 *Multimethodology – Mixing and Matching Methods*

John Mingers

Introduction

Most of this book is concerned with exploring particular, generally 'soft', problem struc-turing methods. This chapter, however, is not about a single method(ology) but about the possibility of combining together different methods, or parts thereof, within a par-ticular organizational intervention. Different types of methods, such as hard and soft, focus on particular aspects of the very complex world which decision-makers have to deal with. Therefore, employing more than one method in combination will help to address the different levels and dimensions of a problematic situation.

At its simplest, *multimethodology* just means employing more than one method or meth-odology (I will generally talk of 'methods' but some approaches, e.g., SSM, are referred to as 'methodologies'*) in tackling some real-world problem. For instance, one could be using SSM but feel that some cognitive mapping might be useful in understanding how certain managers are thinking. Or one could use SSM as a whole to gain agreement on desirable changes, and then build a simulation model to help implement them. Or you could do some cognitive mapping and then develop this into a causal-loop diagram and ultimately a system dynamics model. It is often sensible, especially for beginners, to use one main or overall methodology, such as SSM, and then augment it by bringing in techniques from others. Alternatively, one can use several whole methodologies to address different parts of the problem situation. The most ambitious approach is to link together different parts from several methodologies, creating a design specific to the particular situation.

Why Should We Bother?

There are three main arguments in favour of multimethodology. The first is that real-world problem situations are inevitably multidimensional. There will be physical or material aspects, social and political aspects, and personal ones. Different approaches tend to focus attention on different aspects of the situation and so multimethodology is

---

* Many terms you will come across can be used with different meanings. I have included a glossary at the end to explain how I will be using them in this chapter

necessary to deal effectively with the full richness of the real world. The second is that an intervention is not usually a single, discrete event but is a process that typically proceeds through a number of phases, and these phases pose different tasks and problems for the practitioner. However, methodologies tend to be more useful in relation to some phases than others, so the prospect of combining them has immediate appeal, combining a range of approaches may well yield a better result. Third, combining different methods, even where they actually perform similar functions (such as cognitive mapping and rich pictures) can often provide a 'triangulation' on the situation, generating new insights and providing more confidence in the results by validating each other. The next section will look at each of these points in more detail.

The Multi-Dimensional World

Adopting a single approach is like viewing the world through a particular instrument such as a telescope, an X-ray machine, or an electron microscope. Each one reveals certain aspects of the world but is completely blind to others. Although they may be pointing at the same place, each instrument produces a different, and often seemingly incompatible, representation. These very general ways of looking at the world are sometimes called paradigms. In adopting only one paradigm you are inevitably gaining only a limited view of a particular real-world situation – for example, attending only to that which may be measured or quantified; or only to individuals' subjective meanings and thus ignoring the wider social context. This argument is a strong one in support of multi-paradigm interventions suggesting that, ideally, it is always wise to utilize a variety of approaches.

To explain more clearly the main dimensions of a problem situation, a framework developed from Habermas (1984; 1987) is shown in Figure 13.1. It suggests that it is useful to distinguish our relations to, and interactions with, three worlds – the material world, the social world, and the personal world.

Each world has different modes of existence, and different means of accessibility. The material or physical world is independent of human beings. It existed before us and would exist whether or not we did. We can shape it through our actions, but ultimately we are always subject to its laws. Our relationship to this world is one of *observation* rather than *participation* or *experience*. But we must always be aware of the limitations of the observations we make. They will depend on the particular theories and beliefs we hold, and the measuring instruments and processes of data collection that we employ. We can characterize this world as objective in the sense that it is independent of the observer, but clearly our observations and descriptions of it are not.

From this material world, through the process of evolution, human beings have developed the capability for language and thus the possibility of communication and self-reflection. This has led to the social and personal worlds. The personal world is the world of our own individual thoughts, emotions, experiences, values and beliefs. We do

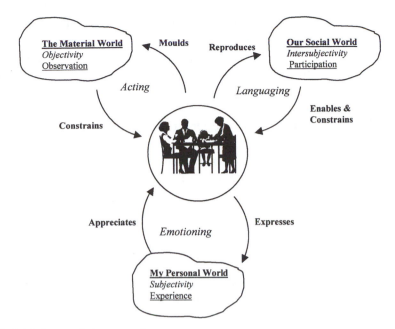

Figure 13.1 Habermas' three words

not observe it as outsiders, but each *experience* it. This world is subjective in that it is generated by, and only accessible to, the individual subject. We can aim to express our subjectivity to others and, in turn, appreciate theirs.

Finally there is the social world that we (as members of particular social systems) share and *participate in*. Our relation to it is one of intersubjectivity since it is, on the one hand, a human construction, and yet, on the other, it goes beyond and pre-exists any particular individual. It consists of a complex layering of language, meaning, social practices, rules and resources that both enables and constrains our actions and is reproduced through them.

Thus, any real-world situation into which we are intervening will be a complex interaction of substantively different elements. There will be aspects that are relatively hard and observer-independent, particularly material and physical processes, which we can observe and model. There will be aspects that are socially constituted, dependent on particular cultures, social practices, languages, and power structures, which we must come to share and participate in. Finally, there will be aspects that are individual such as beliefs, values, fears, and emotions that we must try to express and understand.

Intervention as a Process

The second argument is that intervention is not a discrete event but a process that has phases or different types of activities predominating at different times. Particular methods and techniques are more useful for some functions than others and so a combination of approaches may be advantageous to provide a successful outcome. To help design an intervention in practice it is useful to have some categorization of the phases of a project, against which the strengths of various methodologies can be mapped. The following four phases have been identified (Mingers and Brocklesby, 1997):

- **Appreciation** of the situation as experienced by the practitioners involved and expressed by any actors in the situation. This will involve an initial identification of the concerns to be addressed, conceptualization and design of the study, and the production of basic data using methods such as observation, interviews, experiments, surveys, or qualitative approaches. Note that this cannot be an 'observer-independent' view of the situation 'as it really is'. The practitioners' previous experience and their access to the situation will condition it.
- **Analysis** of the information produced so as to be able to understand and explain why the situation is as it is. This will involve analytic methods appropriate to the goal(s) of the intervention and the information produced in the first stage. Explanation will be in terms of possible hypothetical mechanisms or structures that, if they existed, would produce the phenomena that have been observed, measured, or experienced.
- **Assessment** of the postulated explanation(s) in terms of other predicted effects, alternative possible explanations, and consideration of ways in which the situation could be other than it is. Interpretation of the results, and inference to other situations.
- **Action** to bring about changes, if necessary or desired.

Put crudely, these phases cover: What is happening? Why is it happening? How could the situation or explanation be different? And, what shall we do? See Figure 13.2.

At the beginning of an intervention, especially for a practitioner from outside the situation, the primary concern is to gain as rich an appreciation of the situation as possible. The next activity is to begin to analyse why the situation is as it appears, to understand the history that has generated it, and the particular structure of relations and constraints that maintain it. Next, in cases where change to the situation is sought, consideration must be given to ways in which the situation could be changed. This means focusing attention away from how things are, and considering the extent to which the structures and constraints can be changed within the general limitations of the intervention. Finally, action must be undertaken that will effectively bring about agreed changes. We should emphasize immediately that these activities are not to be seen as discrete stages that are enacted one by one. Rather, they are aspects of the intervention that need to be considered throughout, although their relative importance will differ as the project progresses. Equally, different projects will place their emphasis at some stages rather than others.

It is clear that the wide variety of methods and techniques available do not all perform

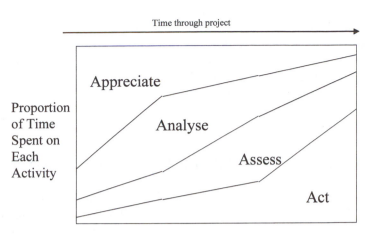

Figure 13.2 Phases of intervention

equally well at all these phases. To give some brief examples: collecting data, carrying out questionnaires and surveys, developing rich pictures and cognitive maps, and employing the twelve critical systems heuristics (CSH) (Ulrich, 1991) questions all contribute to finding out about the different aspects of a particular situation. Whereas building simulation or mathematical models, constructing root definitions and conceptual models, using role-playing and gaming, or undertaking participant observation helps to understand *why* the situation is as it is, and to evaluate other possibilities.

It should be noted here that, however *desirable*, there are concerns about how *feasible* multimethodology is. Questions have been raised about the skills and knowledge it requires of the practitioner, the philosophical and conceptual problems of combining methodologies from different paradigms, and the cultural and organizational barriers to a radical pluralism of method. These concerns are addressed in Mingers and Brocklesby (1997) and Munro and Mingers (2000).

Triangulation of Results

There are other advantages to combining methods (Tashakkori and Teddlie, 1998) – i) triangulation – seeking to validate data and results by combining a range of data sources, methods, or analysts; ii) creativity – discovering fresh or paradoxical factors that stimulate ideas and solutions; and iii) expansion – widening the scope of the study to take in other aspects of the situation that may be of importance. One approach is to use a variety of methods to carry out a similar function – for example using rich pictures, cognitive maps, and CSH questions to appreciate a situation; doing a simulation and then using queuing theory as a rough check; or using drama theory and strategic choice to consider different ranges of options. The other is to use some quite different method to get a new insight on the problem. For example, having developed a particular model or even proposed solution, challenge it with the CSH questions, or perhaps SSM using an antagonistic Weltanschauung. Another idea is to take a particular method and then use it in an unusual way. For example, instead of assuming an LP is an objective model of some aspects of reality, treat it like a cognitive map and develop several incorporating different assumptions and values (Mingers, 2000).

Frameworks to Help in Designing Multimethodologies

So far, we have shown that there can be many benefits in combining methods together, both to deal with different dimensions of a situation and because of the different phases of an intervention. But, given that there are many, many different methods and methodologies, how should an analyst choose which to use in a particular intervention? In this section several frameworks will be presented that can help the practitioner to design a multimethodology suitable for a particular situation. They will be incorporated into a general description of a design process in the next section.

The Context of Practical Interventions

The general context for the use of multimethodology is the purposeful engagement of an agent(s) with some aspect of their social or organizational world. Checkland interprets such situations in terms of two notional systems, a *problem-solving system (PSS)* and a *problem-content system (PCS)*. The use of multimethodology clearly lays extra emphasis on the various methodologies and techniques available, and so a framework with three systems, and the relations between them, is more useful as shown in Figure 13.3.

The Intervention System (IS) consists of the particular people engaged with the Problem Content System (PCS), and possibly being ordinarily part of it. And the Intellectual Resources System (IRS) consists of those frameworks of theories, methodologies, and techniques that could potentially be relevant to the problem situation, although not necessarily within the practitioners' current repertoire.

More important from the point of view of multimethodology are the relationships (labelled A, B and C in Figure 13.3) *between* these notional systems – those between agents and methodologies/techniques (A), those between the agents and the situation (B), and those between methodologies/techniques and the situation (C). It is these relationships that are unique to a particular intervention and it is consideration of these that will guide the agents in their methodology choices. Some of the important dimensions of these relations can be highlighted in a series of questions. These are shown in Table 13.1. Of course, these relationships are not independent of each other. For example, in considering relation A, what methodologies the agent might use, it is also necessary to consider (B) the agent's relationship to the situation (e.g., am I expected to be a facilitator or an

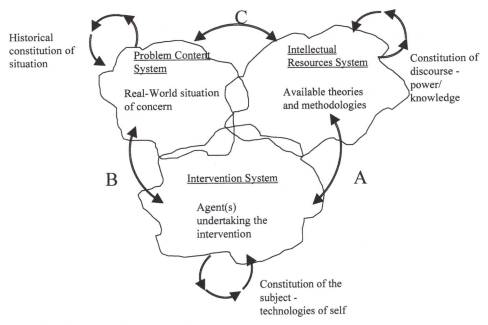

Figure 13.3 Context of an intervention

expert?), and (C) the relation between methodologies and the situation (e.g., does the organization have any experience of this particular methodology?).

These three worlds and the relations between them constitute the context for an intervention. Consideration of these sorts of issues will determine both the initial actions taken and the planning or design of the intervention as a whole. During an intervention they both condition, and change in response to, what happens. Thus they serve as continual reference points for the process of critical reflection that is necessary to structure the methodological choices made during the process.

A Framework for Mapping Methods

Given that the main argument of this chapter is the potential advantages of combining together different methods, it is necessary to provide some way of characterizing them so that a practitioner can use them in an informed way. The framework described next allows methods to be mapped in terms of the different aspects of a situation that they can deal with. In the earlier section on the desirability of multimethodology two important features of interventions were described – their multidimensionality and the different types of activity that need to be undertaken. Combining these two factors produces a grid (see Table 13.2) that can be used to map the characteristics of different methodologies to help in linking them together.

The logic of this framework is that a fully comprehensive intervention needs to be

Table 13.1 – Critical questions concerning the context of an intervention

A) Relations between practitioner(s) and intellectual resources

- What is my level of critical awareness/understanding of potential methods?
- What is my experience and skill in using them?
- What is my personality/cognitive style comfortable with?
- To what extent can I work in varied paradigms?
- Nature of relation B) – intervention system to problem content system – e.g., what might I be able to use in this situation?
- Nature of relation C) – problem content system to intellectual resources system – e.g., what methods might be relevant to this situation?

B) Relations between practitioner(s) and problem situations
- What has initiated this engagement?
- What, if any, is my history of interactions in regard to this situation?
- What are my commitments to various actors in the situations?
- Who do I see as clients/victims/problem owners, etc.?
- What resources and powers do I have?
- Nature of relation A) – intervention system to intellectual resources system – e.g., what methods am I experienced in that may be useful? What might I have to learn?
- Nature of relation C) – problem content system to intellectual resources system – e.g., what methodologies may or may not be seen as legitimate here? What methods have they experienced?

C) Relations between problem situation and intellectual resources
- What is the culture of the organisation/situation with regard to methods?
- What is the history of past methods use?
- What methods are likely to be useful in this situation, given the particular tasks or concerns initiating the intervention? For example, is the task technical or strategic, well-defined or messy, uncontentious or political?
- To what extent are the values embedded in the methods appropriate to the situation?
- Nature of relation A) – intervention system to intellectual resources system – e.g., will the agent's experience allow the use of a particular method here?
- Nature of relation B) – intervention system to problem content system – e.g., does the practitioner's history with this organisation suggest particular methods?

Table 13.2 – A Framework for mapping interventions and methodologies

	Appreciation of	**Analysis of**	**Assessment of**	**Action to**
Social World	Roles, norms, social practices, culture and power relations	Underlying social structures	Ways of changing existing practices and culture	Generate enlightenment of social situation and empowerment
Personal World	Individual beliefs, meanings, values, and emotions	Differing Weltanschauungen and personal rationalities	Alternative conceptualizations and constructions	Generate understanding, personal learning and accommodation of views
Material World	Material and physical processes and arrangements	Underlying causal structures	Alternative physical and structural arrangements	Select and implement best alternatives

concerned with the three different worlds – *material, personal,* and *social* – and the four different phases of an intervention – *appreciation, analysis, assessment,* and *action.* Thus each box generates questions about particular aspects of the situation/intervention that need to be addressed. Such questions cannot be answered purely objectively, that is independently of the agents involved. Rather they should provoke ongoing debate, construction and reflection amongst the actors participating in the intervention from which decisions about the methods to be used should emerge.

This framework can be used in a number of ways. First, it is possible to look at particular methods, mapping them on to the framework to see to what extent they address these questions, and to appraise their relative strength in each box. Figure 13.4 shows a tentative mapping for a number of well-known methodologies:

For example, SSM mainly contributes to exploring the personal dimension and is particularly strong (darker shading) for analysis and assessment. The underlying philosophy of SSM emphasizes the importance of individual actor's viewpoints and makes such perspectives explicit within root definitions and conceptual models. In doing this, it contributes to an *analysis* of the situation – i.e., to revealing how surface appearances can be explained in terms of differing, and often implicit, worldviews. Moreover, the emphasis within SSM on exploring a range of root definitions, sometimes new to the situation, and on separating the world of conceptual thinking from the real-world, contributes to the *assessment* of alternatives. SSM also has some techniques for appreciating the social dimension (analysis 1, 2 and 3), and recognizing the material dimension within Rich Pictures.

Strategic Choice also covers the full range of intervention activities, and is strongest for *assessment* and *action* (its designing and choosing modes). The idea of a *commitment package* has been usefully combined with several other methodologies. But, I would argue, Strategic Choice is not aimed so much at generating and exploring a diversity of individual viewpoints (i.e., the personal world), but more at generating commitment to a particular viewpoint, hence its location across the personal/material divide. VSM is seen as relating essentially to the material and social (organizational) worlds, providing a model of viable organizational structure based on an objectivist analysis of biological organisms. It thus has power to analyse weaknesses and suggest effective alternatives. It has almost nothing to offer, however, in terms of individual actors within a problem situation. Cognitive mapping and SODA have strengths in appreciating and analysing individuals' patterns of belief, and in gaining commitment to action (through merging maps), but is weak in assessing possible alternatives.

The second use of the framework in Table 13.2 is in the design of a particular intervention. Here the focus is on the individual boxes. The practitioner can ask which of the boxes are of most importance for the particular intervention. In theory, of course, all are relevant but in practice limitations of time, resources, and competence, and the actual problem of concern may well make it necessary to focus most of the attention on only certain aspects of the problem space. Then, for each of the boxes in focus methods can be chosen that are particularly strong in those areas.

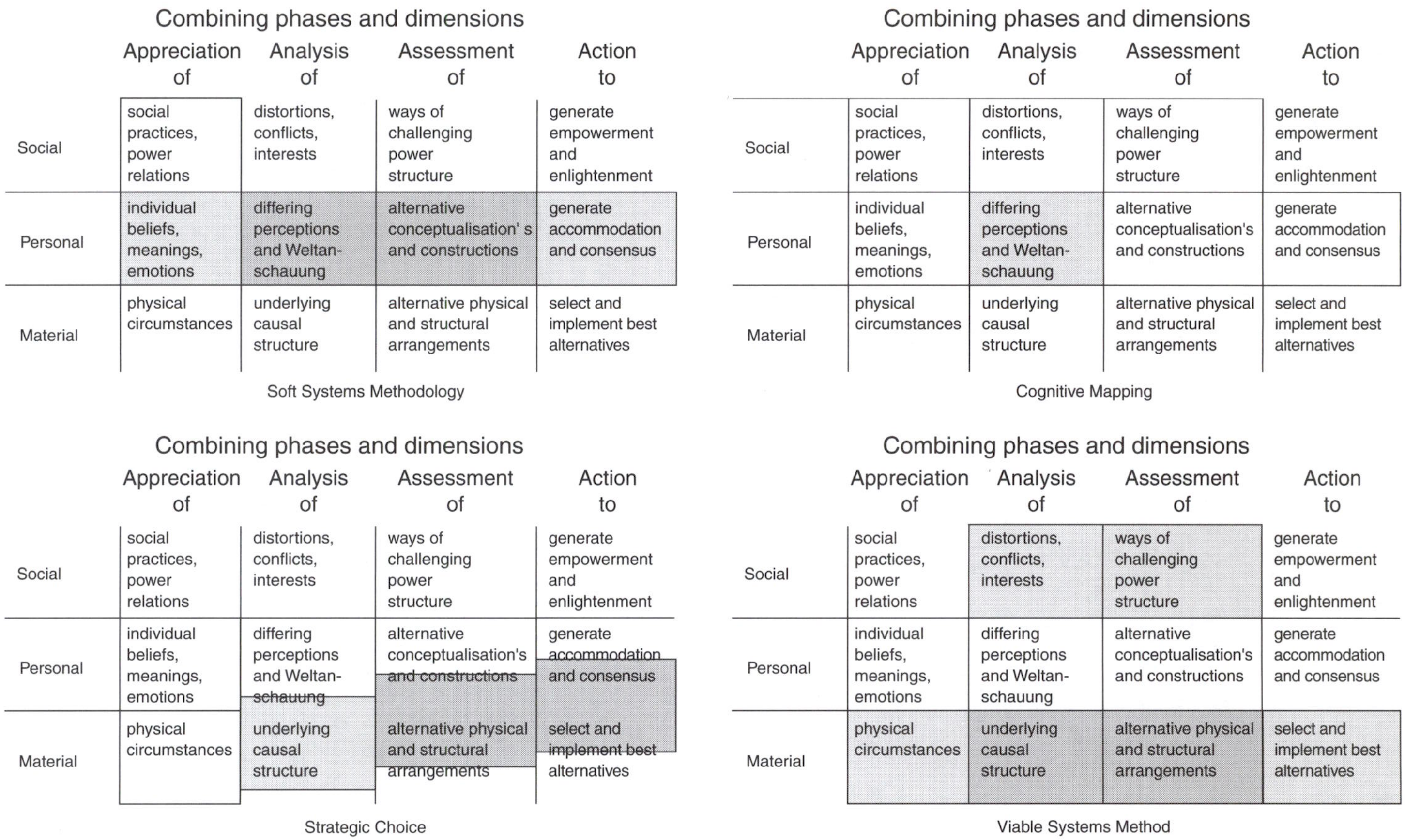

Combining phases and dimensions

	Appreciation of	Analysis of	Assessment of	Action to
Social	social practices, power relations	distortions, conflicts, interests	ways of challenging power structure	generate empowerment and enlightenment
Personal	individual beliefs, meanings, emotions	differing perceptions and Weltan-schauung	alternative conceptualisation's and constructions	generate accommodation and consensus
Material	physical circumstances	underlying causal structure	alternative physical and structural arrangements	select and implement best alternatives

Soft Systems Methodology

Combining phases and dimensions

	Appreciation of	Analysis of	Assessment of	Action to
Social	social practices, power relations	distortions, conflicts, interests	ways of challenging power structure	generate empowerment and enlightenment
Personal	individual beliefs, meanings, emotions	differing perceptions and Weltan-schauung	alternative conceptualisation's and constructions	generate accommodation and consensus
Material	physical circumstances	underlying causal structure	alternative physical and structural arrangements	select and implement best alternatives

Strategic Choice

Combining phases and dimensions

	Appreciation of	Analysis of	Assessment of	Action to
Social	social practices, power relations	distortions, conflicts, interests	ways of challenging power structure	generate empowerment and enlightenment
Personal	individual beliefs, meanings, emotions	differing perceptions and Weltan-schauung	alternative conceptualisation's and constructions	generate accommodation and consensus
Material	physical circumstances	underlying causal structure	alternative physical and structural arrangements	select and implement best alternatives

Cognitive Mapping

Combining phases and dimensions

	Appreciation of	Analysis of	Assessment of	Action to
Social	social practices, power relations	distortions, conflicts, interests	ways of challenging power structure	generate empowerment and enlightenment
Personal	individual beliefs, meanings, emotions	differing perceptions and Weltan-schauung	alternative conceptualisation's and constructions	generate accommodation and consensus
Material	physical circumstances	underlying causal structure	alternative physical and structural arrangements	select and implement best alternatives

Viable Systems Method

Figure 13.4 Mapping particular methods

Some caveats are in order in using the framework. First, it is not intended that methodologies be slotted into particular boxes in the manner of Jackson and Keys' (1984) system of systems methodologies. Rather they are mapped across all the different areas to which they can contribute. Second, clearly the precise placing of a particular method or methodology is debatable. I would be happy for further debate to result in the scope of methodologies being widened on the framework subject to them not becoming so wide that the framework is no longer of use in discriminating between them.

Partitioning/Decomposing Methodologies

One approach to multimethodology is that of linking together *parts* of methodologies (rather than combine whole ones), possibly from different paradigms. This requires detailed study of the different methodologies to see where fruitful links can be created, but is in any case dependent on the idea that techniques or methods can be detached from one methodology and used in another. Generally, such a transfer will conserve the original function, for example, using cognitive mapping within SSM to explore actors' viewpoints. However, it is possible to transfer a methodology or technique into a setting that makes different paradigm assumptions. For example, system dynamics models are usually seen as hard or positivist, being possible models of *external reality*. However, they could be used in an interpretive way, as models of *concepts*, i.e., as models of how things might be from a particular viewpoint in a similar way to cognitive maps.

This linking process requires that methodologies be decomposed or partitioned in some systematic way to identify detachable elements and their functions or purposes. It is proposed this can be done in terms of distinctions between underlying principles (*why*), methodological stages (*what*), and techniques (or methods) (*how*). The primary focus of a methodology is its stages – a conceptual account of what needs to be done. These are justified by the underlying philosophical principles and actualized by a set of activities or techniques within a methodology. The techniques may be complementary to each other in that several must occur, or they may be substitutes, any one being potentially satisfactory.

It seems potentially possible to detach pieces of a methodology either at the level of techniques or at the higher level of methodological stages. The former is more straight-forward and is particularly useful when enhancing a whole methodology (e.g., SSM) with techniques from another (e.g., cognitive mapping). Whilst a technique does have a particular purpose or output, this needs to be interpreted within the context of the methodological stage that it realizes. Thus in moving a technique from one methodology (and possibly paradigm) to another, its context and interpretation may be changed. To take one of the examples above, if a system dynamics model is built as part of a hard methodology its context will lead to the results being interpreted as a model of reality. If it is detached and used within a soft setting it will be interpreted as a model of a notional system or concept. The model-building process will be essentially the same, although the previous stage of generating inputs to the model will be different.

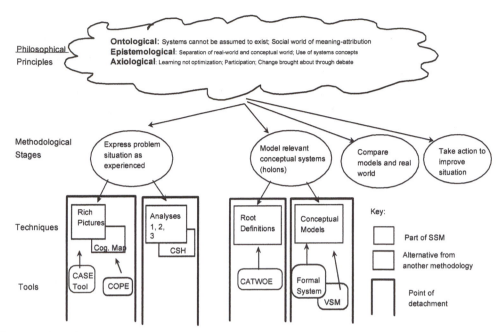

Figure 13.5 Decomposing SSM

Figure 13.5 shows a decomposition of SSM and concentrates on the stages concerned with expressing the real-world situation and with modelling relevant conceptual systems. Each of these stages has particular techniques that help accomplish them, for example, rich pictures and analyses 1, 2 and 3 for expressing the situation. Some techniques may have lower-level tools such as CATWOE or a computerized system for drawing rich pictures (CASE tool). It is these techniques (and their lower level tools) that can be disconnected from the methodology, as shown by the thick lines, and used in other contexts within other methodologies. The figure also shows how techniques can be imported into the methodology, for example, cognitive maps (and the associated computer tool COPE) instead of, or as well as, rich pictures; Ulrich's (1991) critical systems heuristics (CSH) as a complement to Analysis 3; or a viable systems model (VSM) (Beer, 1985) to aid development of a conceptual model.

The main emphasis in Figure 13.5 is on the disconnection of techniques from their 'home' methodology. The second possibility mentioned above, of detaching at the higher level of stages, is possible and occurs in both methodological enhancement (adding a stage to another methodology that is deficient) and multimethodology (combining various stages to construct a new, ad hoc, methodology). It is, however, more problematic, particularly in the multi-paradigm case since the stages are more strongly related to their philosophical paradigm. For example, 'Modelling relevant conceptual systems' clearly expresses the soft rather than the hard view of model building.

The Process of Multimethodology Design

The design of multimethodology interventions occurs in two stages: at the initiation of a project a broad plan will be specified detailing what combination of methods and techniques may be used in the light of the questions outlined in Table 13.2. Then, as the project proceeds, there will be a continual monitoring process of reflection and design to adjust the activities in the light of actual occurrences both internal and external to the project. The balance between these two may differ – some projects may be well-specified in advance, while others may be deliberately left to evolve as the project develops – but it is important to maintain a clear mental distinction between the ongoing design of the project and its actual operation, as Figure 13.6 shows.

The two lower cylinders show the ongoing process of the intervention in which the practitioner(s) take action in the problem content system. The fact that the two circles are not contiguous represents the fact that both systems have lives of their own outside, but conditioning, the intervention. The upper cylinder shows the metalevel activities of *reflection* and *design* that appreciate and respond to the intended and unintended consequences of previous actions by specifying the next steps to be taken and methods to be used. There are four key sub-activities:

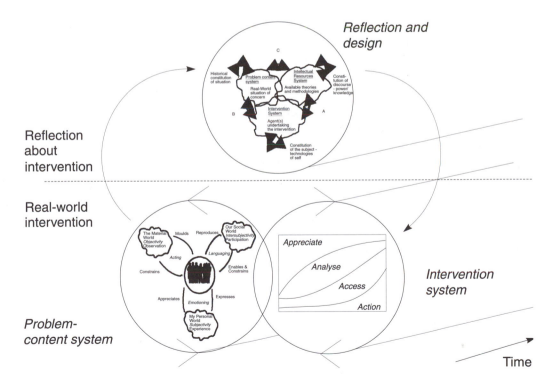

Figure 13.6 Multimethodology Process

Table 13.3 – A illustrative multimethodology design

	Appreciation of	Analysis of	Assessment of	Action to
Social World	Critical Systems Heuristics – 'Is' SSM – Analysis 1, 2,3		Critical Systems Heuristics – 'Ought' Viable Systems Model	
Personal World	SSM – Rich Pictures	SSM – RDs and CMs Cognitive mapping	SSM – RDs and CMs	Strategic Choice – commitment package
Material World	SSM – Rich Pictures Data production and statistical analysis		Viable Systems Model	

Reflection:
- *Review* the current situation.
- *Determine* which areas of the problem situation currently need addressing.

Design:
- *Understand* what methods or techniques could possibly be useful.
- *Choose* the most appropriate to use in relation to the project context as a whole.

These sub-activities are posed here at a rather general level, but the frameworks described above have been developed to assist in undertaking them. The following points will be illustrated later by considering the interventions described by Richard Ormerod in Chapter 10.

At the start of the intervention especially, attention must be paid to the general context – PCS, IS, and IRS (Figure 13.3) and the list of critical questions (Table 13.1) should be used to help produce a set of feasible methodological choices. These will reflect the nature of the task to the extent that it can be defined, the organizational context, and the knowledge and experience of the practitioners. This initial consideration may suggest only one or two possible methods, or it could leave open a wide range. To help narrow this choice down, it is useful to consider the different dimensions of the problematic situation – material, social, and personal (Figure 13.1), and the different stages of a project – the 4 A's (Figure 13.2) and the methods or techniques that may be particularly useful at each phase. These last two aspects can be considered together using the framework for mapping methodologies (Table 13.2). One could then end up with a selection of methodologies, or their parts, mapped onto the framework, showing how they will fit together within the project as a whole. An example of such a multi-methodology design is shown in Table 13.3.

This should not be seen as a generic multimethodology design, but simply one that could be suitable for a particular intervention. In this example, several methods are used in the first, Appreciation, phase – SSM rich pictures and analysis 1, 2,3, CSH 'is' questions, and some data production and analysis. In the Analysis phase, cognitive mapping and SSM conceptual modelling are used to make sense of the information produced in the first phase. Consideration then turns to Assessing various possible alternative solutions using conceptual modelling again, the viable systems model for organizational design, and the CSH 'ought' questions. Finally, as the project moves to the Action phase, a strategic choice type commitment package is agreed.

With an understanding of the issues that need to be addressed at a particular point in time and an appreciation of the contribution that various methods and techniques can make, the methodology choices can be made and put into action. However, the final decision about which methods and techniques to use brings us back to the individual practitioner (or team) for it is ultimately their choice (in negotiation with the client), and it will necessarily and appropriately reflect their personal skills, experience, values, and personality. Some might argue objectivity requires that the nature of the task, rather than the analyst, should determine the choice of approach. But from the multimethodology perspective this is impossible both philosophically and practically. Philosophically because, as Ackoff (1977) has said, objectivity can only be the result of many subjectivities: it is value-full not value-free. Practically, because individuals' skills and experience actually matter in their choices of method. Everyone is not equally competent across a wide range of quantitative and qualitative approaches, and we all tend to have our own favourites with which we feel most comfortable. It is often more effective to use a somewhat inappropriate method well than an appropriate method badly. In the longer term it is important that practitioners review their range of knowledge and skills and develop their methodological competence (Ormerod, 1997).

What is Happening in Practice?

In this final section we will flesh out these rather abstract ideas by briefly considering the two interventions described by Richard Ormerod in Chapter 10, and then discussing more generally the use of multimethodology in the practitioner world based on an empirical survey and a literature review.

Sainsbury's and PowerGen Examples

These two interventions were carried out independently of the frameworks outlined in this chapter, but nevertheless exemplify many of the points very well. In both examples we can see the two stage process of design – a preliminary, and here quite well defined, decision about which methods were to be used, and then a continual reflective adjustment of the design as events unfolded. These decisions were made in the light of the requirements of the organizational and project contexts as well as the practitioner's expertise and experience. As can be seen, particularly in PowerGen, the process needed to be quite creative, not just a slavish following of methodological stages. The decision to base the project around senior management participation required agreement from the company, and also determined to a large extent the possible methods to be used. It is interesting that commitment to participation at PowerGen was not at first forthcoming and had to be generated later in the project. The importance of context, and the interaction between problem content system, intervention system, and intellectual resources system (Figure 13.3) is clearly shown.

In both cases the intervention was guided by an overall methodology, Ackoff's interactive planning, and then various other methods were brought in at particular stages. In terms of different types of multimethodology this is an example of methodology enhancement at two levels – interactive planning is enhanced by other methodologies (cognitive mapping, SSM, strategic choice) which are themselves further enhanced (e.g., Porter's five forces and VSM). Ormerod's description of the phases of the Sainsbury's project is very similar to the phases outlined in this chapter, and the sequence of methodologies – cognitive mapping for appreciation, SSM for analysis and strategic choice for assessment – fits well with the mapping presented in Figure 13.4. The majority of the methods used were soft, fitting mainly into the personal and social dimensions of the situation, but harder, quantitative, techniques were also employed, particularly in the evaluation of various proposals.

Survey and Review

Munro and Mingers (2000) have recently carried out a survey of OR and systems practitioners to discover the extent of multimethodology use, and the particular combinations of methods that work well together. 64 respondents gave details of 163 different interventions each employing a combination of methods. Tables 13.4 and 13.5 list the most popular combinations occurring in pairs and in threes (sometimes combined with other methods as well).

Actual examples of multimethodology use do show particular combinations that work well together. Some of the main points of interest are:

- SSM is used extensively as a methodology that can be combined with many others. SSM itself is very flexible and can be used to structure the whole intervention. It is often used as the dominant method augmented by other techniques. It has been used extensively in information systems development (Stowell, 1995) both as a 'front-end' to harder, structured systems analysis techniques, and as the controlling method throughout the systems development.
- Cognitive mapping is a general approach to capturing peoples' thinking about particular complex issues and as such is compatible with many other methods. It is particularly synergistic with systems dynamics, as a map can be converted into an SD model; and it is also often used in the early stages of SSM to enhance the appreciation of the problem situation. It has also been used with strategic choice, decision analysis, and Delphi.

Table 13.4 – Most popular pairs of methods

Method 1	Method 2	Frequency
Simulation	Statistics	13
Forecasting	Statistics	9
SWOT/PEST	SSM	9
Simulation	SSM	8
Influence Diagrams	SSM	8
Strategic Choice	SSM	8
Critical Systems Heuristics	SSM	7
SSM	Interactive Planning	7
SSM	Cognitive Mapping	7
Statistics	SSM	7
VSM	SSM	7
Maths. Modelling	Statistics	7
Maths. Modelling	Simulation	7
Structured Analysis & Design	SSM	6
Maths. Modelling	Heuristics	5
Decision Analysis	Strategic Choice	5
Decision Analysis	Cognitive Mapping	5
Statistics	Cognitive Mapping	5
Influence Diagrams	VSM	5
Influence Diagrams	SSM	5
Strategic Choice	Cognitive mapping	5
Interactive Planning	CSH	5
Strategic Choice	Interactive Planning	5

Table 13.5 – Most popular triads of methods

Method 1	Method 2	Method 3	Frequency
Strategic Choice	SSM	Interactive Planning	4
Maths. Modelling	Simulation	Statistics	3
Maths. Modelling	Simulation	Heuristics	2
Statistics	Influence Diagrams	Cognitive Mapping	2
Statistics	SWOT	SSM	2
Statistics	SSM	Cognitive Mapping	2
Statistics	Project Networks	Forecasting	2
Statistics	Forecasting	Inventory	2
SSM	VSM	Strategic Choice	2
SSM	VSM	TSI	2
SSM	VSM	CSH	2
SSM	Interactive Planning	CSH	2
SSM	Scenarios	CSH	2
Cognitive Mapping	Delphi	Scenarios	2
Hypergames	Delphi	Scenarios	2
Cognitive Mapping	Delphi	Systems Dynamics	2
Cognitive Mapping	Decision Analysis	Strategic Choice	2
Cognitive Mapping	Influence Diagrams	Systems Dynamics	2

- Strategic choice can also be combined with SSM, particularly in the later stages of an intervention when decisions about, and commitments to, action are being negotiated.
- The viable systems model (VSM) is useful where organizational change is concerned, as it focuses attention on the necessary structural and communicational features of an effective organization.
- Hard methods are combined together, e.g., mathematical modelling, simulation and statistics, but it is rare to mix hard and soft. This may well reflect the practitioners' skills and predilections rather than a lack of potential success.

A survey of the literature has also been undertaken (Mingers, 2000) to discover reported practical applications of problem structuring methods in general, and multimethodology in particular.

Conclusions

This chapter argues that modelling and analysis of the kind which is provided by operational research and the systems approach is being enhanced through the development of a range of soft problem structuring methods that address the qualitative, people-centred issues that are always present in real-world intervention. The main proposal is that these soft methods and techniques should be used in combination, both with themselves and with more traditional quantitative modelling, to yield a richer form of multimethodology. The main contribution of the chapter has been to outline a process for designing a multimethodology together with frameworks that can help link methods and techniques.

Further work can be expected to contribute to the practical use of multimethodology. In particular:

- More case studies showing both the successful and the less successful mixing of methods.
- Empirical and theoretical analysis of how particular methods can best be decomposed, and which combinations are most fruitfully linked.
- Consideration of the importance of the personal characteristics of the practitioner in both choosing and using multiple methods. In particular, how difficult is it for individuals to work across paradigms combining technical, quantitative analysis with soft facilitation skills?
- Consideration of the impact of project teams (rather than individual practitioners) on multimethodology. How do the benefits (such as a wider range of skills and experience) compare with the costs (e.g., possible disagreement about which methods to use)?

Glossary

This section will clarify a set of terms (e.g., methodology, method, technique) that is used throughout the chapter. Words such as 'paradigm', 'methodology', 'method', and 'technique' are open to many interpretations so while I shall endeavour to use the following definitions consistently it must be recognized that these are not claimed to be the 'correct' ones, and that inevitably some latitude will be required in applying them across a variety of areas.

Methodology, Method, Technique

Interventions and research are conducted by undertaking particular activities such as building a simulation model, doing cognitive mapping, developing root definitions and conceptual models, or administering and analysing a survey. These basic activities will be termed *methods* or *techniques*, using these words synonymously. They are generally well defined sequences of operations that, if carried out proficiently, yield predictable results. However, there is often a confusion between the terms 'method' and 'methodology'.

For this chapter it is useful to distinguish three usage's of the term *methodology*.

i) The most general meaning is 'method-*ology*' meaning the study of methods. One might use this meaning to refer to a course in OR Methodology that covered a whole range of different methods.
ii) The most specific meaning is when talking about 'the methodology' of a particular project. In this sense the term refers to the actual method(s) or technique(s) used and thus every project has its own, individual, methodology.
iii) The third usage is a generalization of the second. Particular combinations of methods occur many times in practice, or are deliberately designed *a priori*, and come to be called 'a methodology'. Examples are Soft Systems Methodology, SODA, and Strategic Choice.

Using the term in this third way, 'a methodology' is more general and less prescriptive than a method. It is a structured set of guidelines or activities to assist in undertaking interventions or research. It will often consist of various methods or techniques, not all of which need be used every time. This chapter is generally concerned with combining research *methods* or *techniques*, but it is also possible to combine these more generic *methodologies*.

Paradigm

Methodologies, and therefore methods, make implicit or explicit assumptions about the nature of the world and of knowledge. It has been conventional to call particular combinations of assumptions *paradigms*. A paradigm is thus a construct that specifies a general set of philosophical assumptions covering, for example, *ontology* (what is assumed to exist), *epistemology* (the nature of valid knowledge), *ethics* (what is valued or considered right), and *methodology*. In simple terms, we can say that a methodology specifies *what* to do, a paradigm defines *why* this should be done, and a method or technique provides a particular *how* to do it. There can only be a relatively small number of paradigms existing within a discipline at one time although there may be different ways of classifying them. This chapter uses the idea of different paradigms to emphasize the desirability of combining together methodologies that have distinctively different assumptions, but does not thereby wish to remain wedded to the particular paradigm boundaries that exist at the moment. To fit in with current literature, I will generally refer to three – hard or positivist, soft or interpretive, and critical.

Types of Multimethodology

The essence of multimethodology is to utilize more than one methodology or part thereof, possibly from different paradigms, within a single intervention. There are several ways in which such combinations can occur, each having different problems and possibilities. Broadly, we can distinguish the following:

* *Methodology combination*: using two or more whole methodologies within an intervention.
* *Methodology enhancement*: using one main methodology but enhancing it by importing methods from elsewhere.
* *Single-paradigm multimethodology:* Combining parts of several methodologies all from the same paradigm.
* *Multi-paradigm multimethodology:* as above, but using methods from different paradigms.

References

Ackoff, R. (1977). "Optimization + objectivity = opt out", *European Journal of Operational Research*, **1**(1), 1–7.
Beer, S. (1985). *Diagnosing the System for Organizations.* John Wiley & Sons, Ltd, Chichester.
Habermas, J. (1984). *The Theory of Communicative Action Vol. 1: Reason and the Rationalization of Society*. London, Heinemann.
Habermas, J. (1987). *The Theory of Communicative Action Vol. 2: Lifeworld and System: a Critique of Functionalist Reason*. Oxford, Polity Press.
Jackson, M. and Keys, P. (1984). 'Towards a system of system methodologies', *Journal of the Operational Research Society*, **35**(6), 473–86.
Mingers, J. (2000). 'Variety is the spice of life: combining soft and hard OR/MS methods', *International Transactions in Operational Research*, **7**, 673–91.
Mingers, J. and Brocklesby, J. (1997). 'Multimethodology: towards a framework for mixing methodologies', *Omega*, **25**(5), 489–509.
Munro, I. and Mingers, J. (2000). The use of multimethodology in practice – results of a survey of practitioners. Warwick Business School, Coventry.
Ormerod, R. (1997). 'Mixing methods in practice: a transformation-competence perspective', in *Multimethodology: Theory*

and Practice of Combining Management Science Methodologies (Eds. J. Mingers and A. Gill), pp. 29–58, John Wiley & Sons, Ltd, Chichester.

Stowell, F., (Ed.) (1995). *Information Systems Provision: The Contribution of Soft Systems Methodology*. McGraw Hill, London.

Tashakkori, A. and Teddlie, C. (1998). *Mixed Methodology: Combining Qualitative and Quantitative Approaches*. SAGE Publications, London.

Ulrich, W. (1991). 'Critical heuristics of social systems design', in *Critical Systems Thinking: Directed Readings* (Eds. R. Flood and M. Jackson), pp. 103–15. John Wiley & Sons, Ltd, Chichester.

14 *Mixing Methods in Practice*

Richard Ormerod

Introduction

In the 1980s Sainsbury's was the leading supermarket chain in the UK. After over 10 years of consistent growth in revenues and profits they were lauded by investors, customers and business observers alike. They were proud of their history, their current success and their acknowledged retail capabilities. In 1988, believing that their investment in IT had played a major role in their success to date and keen to build on their advantages, they decided to engage management consultants to lead an initiative to develop a new information systems strategy.

At the end of 1993, three years after the privatization of the UK electricity industry, PowerGen, one of the electricity generation companies that emerged, took stock of their position. They concluded that they would aspire to be the best power generating company in the world. But how would they know whether they were meeting their aspiration? In an attempt to define and measure the 'best in the world' they decided to initiate a bench-marking exercise and to engage an external consultant to help them do it.

In the previous chapter John Mingers has summarized the current state of the theory of mixing methods. In this chapter, to illustrate the use of multiple methods in a single intervention or project, I am going to describe two separate cases, the Sainsbury's case (1989) and the PowerGen case (1994). In each case I was the lead consultant responsible for designing the process of intervention and implementing it. In fact, the cases are really stories told from a personal point of view; others involved would tell different stories, each highlighting a different aspect, some more enthusiastic, some less. A personal story inevitably includes biases, idiosyncrasies, and choices. Few involved would lay such emphasis on the methodological choices made during the projects, but that after all is what this book in general, and this chapter in particular, is about. Nor can I claim that the methodological choices I made were in some sense the right ones or indeed had the best outcomes; who knows what might have happened if some other path had been followed. I have, however, chosen these two because several methodologies were used in each, because the results were implemented, and because those involved generally felt the projects were successful (a necessary but insufficient test of the success of the approach). I can also claim some success for the originators of the methods I used. I found the approaches helped me, and more importantly the participants, to shape and analyse the problem we faced. We found them useful in practice.

As other authors in this book emphasize, reality is messy. To make the account intelligible (both for the author and the reader) a certain amount of mental tidying up and selectivity has to occur. Both projects lasted over 6 months and each had many twists and turns, diversions and alarums of one sort or another. I have tried to stick to the main story, concentrating on events that had an impact on methodological choice.

The two cases depict very different situations in terms of the particular industries and their context (supermarket retailing; power generation), in the objectives of the projects (information systems strategy; business improvement), and in the people affected (the whole company at Sainsbury's; the head office at PowerGen). I was the common factor in both cases. I was keen to use a participative approach in general and soft OR methods in particular. However, in consultancy the desire to achieve the aims of the project always dominates. I also provide a link between the two projects, using as I did the experience of Sainsbury's (and of some mining projects in South Africa) to design and run the PowerGen project; the two projects both lie within the same 'strand of practice' (Corbett *et al.*, 1993).

Designing an Approach for IS Strategy Development at Sainsbury's

In pitching for the consulting job at Sainsbury's, PA Consulting Group, the company I worked for, was the underdog. We had never worked with Sainsbury's before and there were three other competitors, each of whom was already engaged in consulting jobs within Sainsbury's. To win, we felt we had to do something different, exciting, creative, even visionary. My colleagues in the sales team were particularly keen on this, but I had the somewhat daunting task of turning these ambitions into something practical. I had previously developed a number of information systems strategies for clients as varied as banks, manufacturing companies and government departments. Given that the overall aim of the project was to develop an information systems strategy which would identify opportunities for investment and prioritize them, the overall shape of the project was not difficult to sketch out. I opted for an approach broken into five phases based on my experience of developing IS strategies in different contexts:

Phase 0   Project Initiation
- Formation of a Steering Committee
- Formation of a Task Force
- Formation of an Advisory Group
- Produce a detailed project plan

Phase 1   Business Imperative
- Identify primary activities
- Identify support activities
- Identify strengths and weaknesses

- Examine customer service
- Understand the competitive strategy
- Understand the values
- Identify the mission

Phase 2   Future Systems
- Identify points of IT leverage
- Identify candidate systems for investment
- Analyse the consequences

Phase 3   Evaluation
- Establish criteria
- Debate significance
- Analyse sensitivity and risk
- Determine priorities

Phase 4   Strategy
- Agree direction
- Identify implications
- Agree vision of the future
- Determine systems architecture
- Draw up resource plans
- Establish the implementation schedule
- Make budget projections

This was fairly conventional except for the Phase 0 which emphasized the Formation of the Steering committee, the Task Force and the Advisory Group. The novelty was to lie in the roles of these groups, the freedom the Task Force in particular would be given and the support they would receive from new techniques. Initially I had no idea what these techniques might be but I was determined that the approach would be participative. This determination arose from the company's desire to place users (as opposed to the IT professionals) at the centre of the systems strategy development and from my own experience of applying non-participative approaches. The Phases map quite well onto the phases subsequently suggested by John Mingers in the previous chapter: Appreciation (Phase 0), Analysis (Phases 1 and 2), Assessment (Phase 3), and Action (Phase 4).

On previous strategy development exercises I had taken a conventional approach. Key people were interviewed, data was gathered and analysed, a report was written, conclusions reached. I stood at the centre of the process from the initial interviews to the final presentation of the recommendations. In the process I became committed to a particular course of action and I had to persuade decision-makers to adopt it. The decision-makers in turn had to motivate their line managers to implement the strategy. In the past I had been fortunate in that my recommendations had usually been adopted and implementation had ensued. However, it was a precarious business and a good deal

of guessing as to what might be acceptable or indeed feasible was involved. A participative approach seemed to me to be altogether more attractive. If decision-makers and
line managers could be persuaded to engage in the formulation of the strategy, they
would own the outcome and be committed to implementation. They would ensure the
strategy was acceptable and feasible. This would occur whether or not I had become
committed and whether or not I was persuasive. I was convinced a participative approach
could form the basis for the sort of novel, creative approach, which everyone wanted.
The search was therefore on to find methods to support a participative approach.

Some Fixed Points

In any intervention there are a number of fixed points or constraints that influence the
design. The key requirement is that a practical and desirable strategy comes out of the
project. This implies engaging in data gathering, analysis and reporting activities as set
out in the *Phases* above. Elapsed time and the cost of the consulting support are two
obvious constraints. Availability of management input is another. In this case I obtained
agreement that the Task Force members would dedicate up to two days per week to the
project. The members of the Steering Committee were prepared to meet intermittently.
They needed to be comfortable with the process and make sure that the company's
strategy was correctly understood and supported by the new IS strategy.

Another crucial point as far as the company was concerned was that the users should
be at the centre of the strategy development and that the IT professionals in the
company should also have an appropriate role. This gave rise to the requirement for a
Task Force and an Advisory Group (of the IS professionals) each with a distinct role.
Overall the constraints were not too onerous. This is not always the case. When running
similar exercises at remote mine sites in South Africa time and travel were major issues.

Choosing Methods to Support a Participative Approach

When looking for methods to support the intervention, I was immediately attracted to
the 'interactive planning' paradigm advocated by Ackoff (1979a, b). In his papers Ackoff
makes a number of assertions which immediately resonated with the type of project I
had in mind:

> '... there are no experts when it comes to answering the question: what ought a system to
> be like? Here every stakeholders's opinion is as relevant as any other's.'

> 'Because engaging in such design is fun, participation is not hard to get.'

> '... idealized design facilitates the incorporation of the aesthetic values of the stakeholders
> into its planning.'

'... participation in idealized design tends to generate consensus among the participants.'

'... idealized design mobilizes its participants into a crusade in pursuit of its product.'

'... idealized design releases large amounts of suppressed creativity and focuses it on organizational development.'

'... the idealized design process expands its participants' concept of feasibility.'

All this seemed to fit well with the idea that strategy was about first creating a vision and then making it happen. It also seemed to chime in with the ideas of other commentators who wrote about creativity, action learning, exceptional performance and superteams. Thus out of i) the requirement for an IS strategy, ii) the desire to place users at the centre of the assignment, and iii) our desire to offer something that was creative and novel, the idea of developing the senior line managers into a 'superteam' was born. The motivation for managers to perform in this way would be provided by i) the excitement of creating the companies future (Ackoff's paradigm), ii) the intellectual challenge of getting to grips with the issues (supported by frameworks and methods yet to be determined), and iii) the injection of some lightness and fun into the proceedings (good facilitation).

I was not, however, at the time aware of any detailed guidance as how to conduct an investigation under Ackoff's interactive planning paradigm. I therefore explored the possibility of using other methods in this role. My list included some methods from the OR literature (cognitive mapping, soft systems methodology, viable systems model, decision conferencing, strategic choice, strategic assumption surface and testing, and critical systems heuristics) and some from my systems strategy experience (BIAT 7 questions, entity-relationship diagrams, functional models, Porter value chain analysis, Mintzberg's organizational models). This was clearly a mixture of apples and oranges and so I developed some criteria to inform my choice. These were that the approach should support:

1.   *Learning:* strategy and planning is an organizational learning process;
2.   *Interpretation:* it is management's task to state and develop their interpretation of the company and its environment;
3.   *Participation:* the active participation of management is essential to give commitment and ownership;
4.   *Pluralism:* diverging interests between groups have to be accommodated;
5.   *Adaptation:* organizations are complex, open and adaptive systems.

The four methods that seemed to best meet the criteria were:

• Cognitive mapping
• Soft systems methodology (SSM)
• Strategic choice analysis (SCA); and
• Strategic assumption surface and testing (SAST).

Each method has associated with it a process for engaging participants with a facilitator assisting. Each envisaged the participants themselves structuring the problem and seeking alternatives, the facilitator playing a neutral role. These seemed ideal but which one or ones to choose?

I rejected the use of SAST as it involved creating conflict between participants, an approach that, in my mind at least, didn't fit easily within interactive planning with its emphasis on reaching consensus. The other three, however, all looked potentially usable. I then considered how each method would support each of the different phases of the project. It seemed to me vital that *Phase 1, Business Imperatives* should include a lot of listening to senior executives of the company. Sainsbury's were clear that the systems strategy had to support their current way of doing business and their future strategy. Task Force members (16 senior line managers) and Advisory Group members (senior managers drawn from the IT department) needed to develop an understanding of the current business and strategy. Board members of large companies choose their words carefully and cognitive mapping seemed ideally suited to a process of careful recording and analysis of what was said. The rich pictures used in SSM seemed too crude to catch the nuances of the spoken word. SCA assumes that options already exist to be shaped and evaluated; it does not include the generation of options in the first place.

In *Phase 2, Future Systems*, I envisaged that the Task Force would be split into groups to investigate different parts or aspects of the business. Senior managers are not generally equipped with consulting skills. I needed an approach, which would support but not constrict them in their investigations. I envisaged them gathering information, debating the issues, capturing aspects of what they found in models, and generating new ways of doing things with the support of IT. SSM struck me as providing a robust model to support this crucial investigatory stage of the project. The worry was whether senior managers would submit themselves to being trained in the method and whether they would stick with it once they were let loose on the business. Cognitive mapping seems best suited to understanding how people think about things rather than going out, observing and gaining new insights. SCA seemed more suited to choosing what to do, than to supporting a process of inquiry and sense-making.

In *Phase 3*, Evaluation, all the possibilities generated in *Phase 2* needed to be evaluated and prioritized. Neither cognitive mapping nor SSM directly support a decision process whereas SCA concentrates on evaluating and choosing from a set of given possibilities. Thus SCA was chosen to support *Phase 3*.

Thus I determined that different methods were to be used in each of the *Phases 1, 2 and 3*. The methods were not to be integrated, the only connection being that the outputs of an earlier phase become the inputs to a later phase. Some of the other methods would also come in useful, but my overall design was to use cognitive mapping, soft systems methodology and strategic choice analysis within the interactive planning paradigm as shown in Figure 14.1. There was a natural flow to the methods. Cognitive mapping and SSM allow wide ranging debates and encouraging the recognition of conflicting points of view. Strategic choice provides a mechanism for closing down the debate and

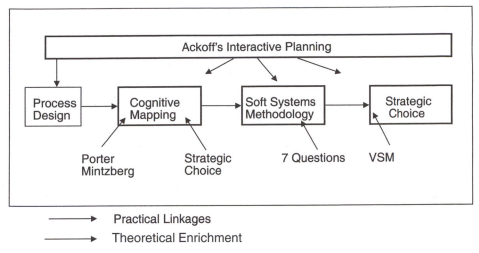

Figure 14.1 Linkages between methods

reaching decisions. Each phase would last a couple of months giving time to introduce participants to each method in turn.

Using the Methods in Practice at Sainsbury's

The application of methods is seldom as clean cut as the design might imply. Decisions have to be taken along the way. At anytime a method could be dropped or another taken up as circumstance dictated and there was a real possibility that the Task Force would not take to the methods at all. In fact, the Task Force members did take to the methods, which as a result became central to the project.

Cognitive mapping was successfully used in *Phase 1*, although in a slightly different way from that envisaged by the authors of the Strategic Options Development and Analysis (SODA) process. In this case the maps were used to transfer the Board's under-standing of the business strategy to the Task Force members. Figure 14.2, for instance, shows an exploration of the interrelation between company objectives. In a series of workshops maps were used to debate strategy and identify areas for further investigation (akin to the 'shaping' mode of SCA).

In *Phase 2* the members of the Task Force were trained in the use of SSM for a day and then four cross-functional teams spent six weeks investigating their chosen area of the business. The investigation was conducted entirely using SSM, following the step-by-step method, using rich picture, CATWOE, conceptual, real/ideal, desirable/feasible models. No new tools were introduced. Help was given with the method if sought. Inter-mediate workshops were held to discuss progress, problems and overlaps. The main

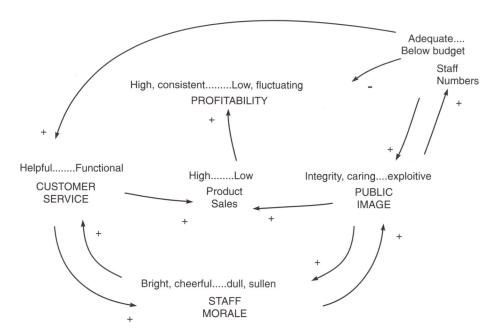

Figure 14.2 A cognitive map showing the interrelationships between objectives

difficulty the participants encountered was in choosing and defining the transformation. They had to struggle, which was probably a good thing. The main downside of placing the method in the hands of the participants was that they were not particularly consistent or rigorous in the way they used the approach.

Figure 14.3 shows one of the diagrams the Task Force produced. The issue was the exponential growth of customer complaints. Complaints could be made at any point in the organization and handling the complaint could involve Sainsbury's retail managers, its scientists and buyers, and the supplier's product experts. Customers could then inquire, again at any point in the organization, where the complaint had got to and when it would be resolved. To deal with all the inquiries it seemed that a case tracking system accessible anywhere in the organization would help. Finally, armed with such suggestions, the Task Force members themselves presented the results to the Steering Group.

In *Phase 3* the idea was to apply the comparing and evaluating modes of the SCA approach. However, for the comparison element the Steering Group was keen that a quantitative approach should be taken to guide the choice. To respond to this the quantitative prioritization framework shown in Figure 14.4 was developed from the qualitative approach of SCA. Each candidate system was evaluated in terms of the hard and soft costs and benefits and an assessment of business and technical risks. In addition two concepts that had developed out of the cognitive mapping in *Phase 1* were applied. The first, potential for leverage, considered whether the improvement envisaged applied

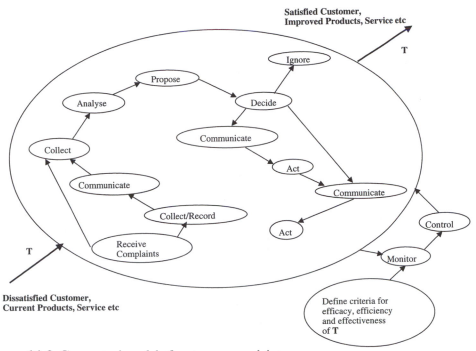

Figure 14.3 Conceptual model of customer complaints

internally to Sainsbury's or whether it also has a negative effect on competitors in a zero sum game (by, for instance, taking a customer away from a competitor). The second, potential to sustain, assessed the sustainability of any competitive advantage sought. The costs and benefits were estimated in monetary terms with the additional factors causing these to be increased or reduced. Thus the final outcome, the priority, was derived from the relationship between the adjusted cost and adjusted benefits. The approach in Figure 14.4 is, in effect, a multi-criteria decision scheme. Such an approach, which is quantitative in nature, is a 'hard' approach. Thus both 'soft' and 'hard' approaches were deployed in the project. In addition in *Phase 3* an attempt was made to use the Viable Systems Model. My idea was to use the VSM model as a quality check to make sure all the elements were present in the company to achieve viability. It proved time consuming and not obviously useful given that Sainsbury's clearly was viable. This was perhaps a model-too-far in this instance and the idea was dropped. This had nothing to with the qualities of the model, so I resolved to try to use it again in some future project (see the PowerGen case that follows later in the Chapter).

In *Phase 4, Strategy,* the candidate systems with a high priority were grouped into larger projects, which we termed initiatives, taking account of technical dependencies (for instance, project B requires project D to be built first because B uses data created in D) and the need for consistency. Each initiative was allocated to a Board Member to sponsor the implementation. The process of grouping and scheduling derived from the

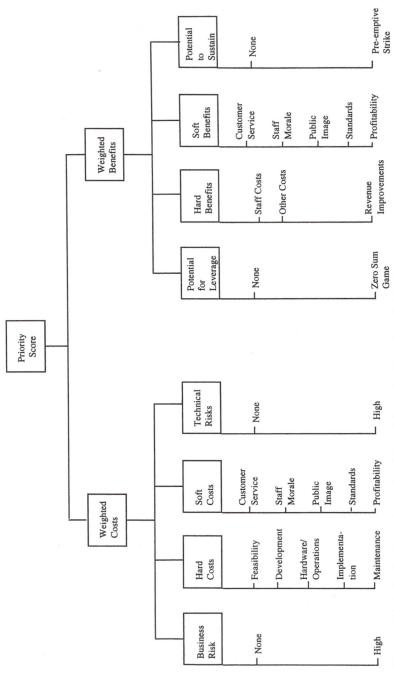

Figure 14.4 Evaluation scheme for determining priorities of candidate systems

'shaping' and the 'choosing' modes of SCA. Scheduling is in essence a sequence of 'commitment packages' called for in the SCA. The process was not conceptually difficult but was complex as we juggled with build sequences, resources available, and expenditure profile. This was carried out by the project team as a technical exercise.

The agreed systems strategy from the project was endorsed by the Board and implemented. Over a five year period the new systems were developed and introduced resulting in substantial, measured benefits. Further information about the Sainsbury's case can be found in Ormerod (1995, 1996a).

Could this Particular Combination of Approaches Be Used Again?

The choice of cognitive mapping, SSM and SCA, in that order, to implement Ackoff's interactive planning fitted the requirement of the project well. Although the methods were not integrated in any formal sense, the four methods did complement each other. This raises two questions. Why do these particular methods fit together well and could the same combination be used in other circumstances?

Cognitive mapping is a good place to start on a strategy exercise because it captures the way that key actors think about the business, its purpose, its activities and its competitive strategy. This is very important. These after all are the people who will have to agree any new strategy and implement it; any proposals must therefore be in terms that they can relate to and that acknowledges their understanding of the issues. They are also a vital source of information. In interviews key actors will divulge their knowledge and insight of the business based on years experience and engagement with the issues. Cognitive mapping allows participants to develop and play with and analyse different strategic options. However, it does not provide a model with which to question the processes of the business.

The rich pictures and conceptual models of SSM provide the tools for debating and developing options to create the vision required by interactive planning. Further, SSM provides a robust tool to support field investigation and observation of the operations of the business. The emphasis moves from interviewing senior actors and high level strategies to observing and understanding the physical and human activity systems of the business. This is where strategies have to be implemented; this is where they have to make a difference. Both cognitive mapping and SSM result in suggestions for improvement. SCA assumes that plenty of options exist to be shaped, evaluated and selected. Once they do exist SCA helps provide closure.

Cognitive mapping, SSM and SCA thus complement each other in helping to implement interactive planning. There seemed to be every reason to take this particular combination of methods as a starting point for future strategy studies. An account of how this worked out at the Palabora copper mine can be found in Ormerod (1998) and at the Richards Bay dredging and refining operation in Ormerod (1996b). The choice of methods for a project can be greatly influenced by the previous experience of the project's designers (often the consultant). Hence a 'strand of practice' develops. While many consultants (investigators, analysts, change agents) have got into the habit of using one particular method to support their interventions and others chose one from several, after Sainsbury's I got into the habit of using several different approaches together in one intervention. Thus in approaching the PowerGen project I would be expecting to use several methods, particularly ones I had used before.

Business Process Re-engineering at PowerGen

Martin Neil, manager of the IT support Unit at RTZ (now Rio Tinto), on hearing my description of the Sainsbury's project, decided that a similar approach would help RTZ mines develop their information systems strategy. The collaboration that followed included the projects at Palabora and Richards Bay referred to above. Martin and I were now part of the same 'strand of practice'. After he left RTZ and joined PowerGen he was keen to instigate a similarly participative process. The opportunity arose towards the end of 1993 when it was agreed that an IS strategy would be developed for the UK Electricity Division. Martin suggested that we worked together on the project.

Making some initial inquiries we discovered that the Corporate Planning Department was about to launch a benchmarking exercise. We suggested the two projects should be merged. This made sense because at the heart of our IS strategy project we intended that a task force would analyse the business processes using SSM. Thus business process analysis was common to both projects as was the need to understand the business imperatives. Hence it was agreed that there would be one project. In discussion it also became clear that UK Electricity Division wanted to improve their processes before benchmarking them against outside organizations. We were therefore engaged not only in IS strategy development and benchmarking but also in business process re-design (BPR). No matter, BPR also requires process analysis and could easily be included.

The project was part of the drive to become the best electricity business in the world. The strategy of the UK Electricity business units was to continuously improve performance and radically rethink the way the business was operated. The project deliverables were specified to be:

- process descriptions to a consistent format and level for all key business processes;
- performance indicators at a business process level which are measurable in other similar processes in other industries and which enable measurement of process improvement;
- a prioritized list of business improvement initiatives;

- proposals for the next phase of benchmarking including likely external partners and options for co-ordination;
- an IS strategy consisting of the big picture of IS for UK Electricity Division and a prioritized list of IS initiatives that were large or crossed Unit boundaries.

We determined that we needed to engender the project with the same ethos of earlier projects; we needed to build enthusiastic, creative and empowered teams that had been so successful at Sainsbury's and RTZ. The project was named the Business Improvement Project (BIP).

The Design of the Intervention

There were a number of fixed points for the project. The deliverables were specified as was the overall duration. The senior management team, unlike Sainsbury's, did not want to be collectively involved in the project. (This desired lack of involvement would have to be challenged if the project was to succeed. In fact, the constraint was overcome later in the project.)

The outline of the benchmarking exercise had already been designed with dates, locations, and participants already chosen by the time I started. One of the consequences was that the task force syndicates would be run serially rather than in parallel as in previous projects. Thus the first syndicate would investigate the first business unit, Pool Operations (see Figure 14.5 for the overall business process model), over a three-week period. Then after a week's break the second syndicate would be set away to investigate Fuel Strategy and Supply Department. There were four business units treated this way with a fifth, Generation, treated rather differently because they had already started benchmarking power stations.

The process design thus differed from Sainsbury's in that whereas at Sainsbury's the syndicates of the task force worked in parallel for two days per week over an extended period, at PowerGen each syndicate was to be dedicated to the project full-time for three weeks. To ensure that a cross-functional view was taken each syndicate was drawn from several business units and each syndicate was encouraged to follow the processes beyond the boundaries of the area of the business they were investigating. The activities for each syndicate were planned as follows:

Week prior to start: The project team (4 PowerGen managers including Martin Neil and myself) would work on the process analysis of the business unit to be analysed and its context. The idea being to give the teams a flying start by giving them our rough version, which they could change and improve. Because the investigations were conducted in series rather than in parallel we could do this for each syndicate. In fact previous consultants had already produced some business process maps we could reuse.

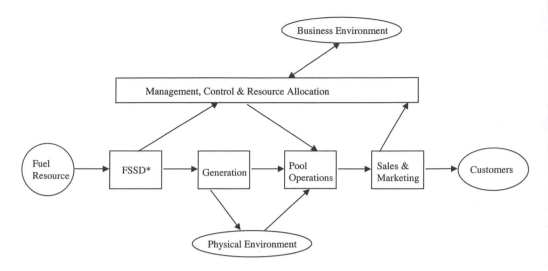

* Fuel Strategy and Supply Department

Figure 14.5 The UK Electricity business model

Week 1: On the Monday of the first week the 'foundation seminar' would be held. The task force syndicate would be introduced to the objectives of the project, the challenge they were being given, the scope of their investigation (which had previously been agreed with the relevant business unit manager), and the project deliverables. They would be introduced to some systems ideas and asked to draw a plan of interviews. For the remaining four days of the week their task would be to conduct interviews in order to 'understand the business'. They would be encouraged to look wider than the business unit in order to identify cross-business improvements and opportunities.

Week 2: On the Monday of the second week the 'process analysis seminar' would be held. The participants would practice the definition and analysis of processes in order to identify improvements, specify benchmarks, and assess the role of IT. For the remainder of the week they would continue their investigations and analysis.

Week 3: The task force syndicate would work together to complete their analysis, confirm the feasibility and desirability of their proposals and prepare a presentation for the General Manager and the other senior managers (members of UKEMT, the UK Electricity Management Team).

Week 4: The syndicate makes its presentation. During this week the project team prepares for the next syndicate.

I anticipated spending two days per week preparing and facilitating key workshops for the duration of the project. The project plan was relatively simple but presented a number of challenges to the project team:

(i)   could the stated requirement for an approach that fostered radical thinking be met;
(ii)   could account be taken of all the many other initiatives underway (numerous process analysis, benchmarking, and systems projects);
(iii) how would the results of the project be pulled together; and
(iv)   how would the senior management team be persuaded to get to grips with the issues.

The last two challenges would have to be dealt with once the project was underway; the first two could, in part, be tackled in the detailed design of the task force activities, including the choice of appropriate methods.

The Choice of Methods

The methods I selected to be central to the BIP project were:

- the interactive planning approach of Ackoff to create a forward looking dynamic which is exciting and fun;
- soft system methodology (SSM) to support the process analysis;
- systems thinking as a stimulus for creative thought by the task force syndicates;
- the viable systems model (VSM) to help the syndicates analyse the business processes;
- strategic choice approach (SCA) for the evaluation of the business process redesign opportunities and the shaping of the strategy.

These central methods were enriched by the use of other methods, such as the six thinking hats of de Bono (1985) and analysis of the five forces of Porter (1985). Interactive planning was chosen as the overarching approach because it had been found in the previous projects to create the framework for encouraging participants to become engaged in an energetic and enthusiastic way. New methods to formalize process analysis were becoming available in the wake of the growing interest in business process re-engineering (for instance, the IDEF approach). On examination these provided useful standards of documentation but little by way of additional insight. SSM was a natural choice for a process-based analysis as it had been used at RTZ for just this purpose with some success. It also was decided to make more explicit use of systems concepts given the importance of understanding the electricity supply system as a whole and PowerGen's part in it. Concepts such as reliability, survivability and recursion seemed likely to be important. At Palabora and Richards Bay the emphasis had been placed on the operational level of the business on the belief that the greatest value would be obtained from IT by applying it to low value repetitive tasks. Use had been made of feedback and feedforward control concepts to identify opportunities for monitoring, controlling, scheduling, and planning operational activities. In the case of PowerGen the emphasis was to be on the central activities rather than operations at the power stations.

SSM includes a simple representation of a systems control mechanism (plan-measure-control). However, the more comprehensive approach embodied in the VSM would provide an opportunity to explore the balance between control, co-ordination and audit activities. It would also ensure that an informed debate occurred between those engaged in controlling activities and those engaged in monitoring the environment and inter-acting with the corporate level. I also judged that the well-qualified PowerGen managers would engage with and benefit from the more sophisticated concepts involved. Finally, SCA was chosen to assist with the process of shaping the decision and obtaining agree-ment in the face of uncertainty. Past experience had shown that such support was both necessary and effective.

The methods chosen were those that had been found to work previously in Sainsbury's and RTZ with the addition of systems thinking and the VSM. I chose to introduce the VSM because I considered it insightful, relevant and likely to be within the capacity of the participants. However, cognitive mapping was not used. In part this was because the strategic issues were already well articulated and known, and in part because of the lack of initial involvement of the key senior managers. Even so, maps could have been used to capture aspects of interviews, but in this case they weren't. On reflection, a deeper analysis of the way that individual actors thought about their strategies and operations may have paid dividends later in the difficult debates that ensued when trying to reach a consensus.

The overall approach is set out in Figure 14.6. The 'box', referred to in the figure, is the sub-system derived from the business process model (see Figure 14.5) that is to be

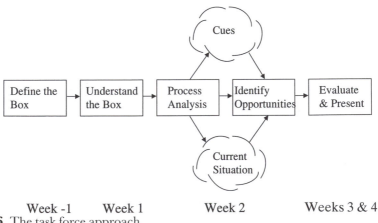

Figure 14.6 The task force approach

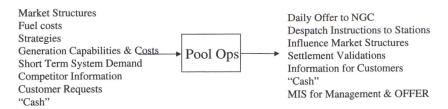

Objective: to meet revenue, market and pricing objectives determined
by the strategy at minimum cost to PowerGen

Constraints: Grid Code, Pool Rules, Environmental Compliance Policy
Competition Law Policy, Plant and Fuel Availability, Plant
Flexibility, Systems Constraints

Quality: Market Share, Price, Reliability

Figure 14.7 Box definition for Pool Operations

investigated by the task force. The task forces would also be encouraged to look beyond their box. The 'cues' in Figure 14.6 are obtained from reported successes in improving business process by redesign and the application of IT, captured in mini case studies. Throughout the workshops, systems ideas (for instance, the concepts of recursion, sub-systems and control) would be introduced and the participants would have the opportunity to question and practice the approach. The business model shown in Figure 14.5 is treated as a high level conceptual diagram (in SSM terms). Prior to the work-shops the objectives of the business unit (the box) would be agreed between the Manager and the project team in the form of a modified root definition (in SSM terms) referred to as box analysis. For example Figure 14.7, shows the starting point for the first task force, Pool Operations. The task force would then debate and modify the elements of the box analysis.

At the centre of the analysis by the task force, a process analysis (opening up the box) would be conducted, based on the conceptual models of SSM. Having conducted interviews and gathered some data, participants would work on a map of existing pro-cesses prepared by the project team. The project team would prepare the process map prior to the workshop partly to save time, but also to make sure that use is made of recent process analyses conducted in other initiatives. This would have the advantage of ease of communication (the process diagrams were familiar to the senior managers and some task force members), continuity with previous exercises, and momentum (the project builds on past efforts rather than reinventing them). These process maps are flatter (less recursive, in other words, fewer levels with each level containing many activities) than is normal for conceptual models in SSM. They would also represent the current processes rather than systems thinking. For example Figure 14.8 shows the project team's attempt to map the current activities for the second task force, Fuel

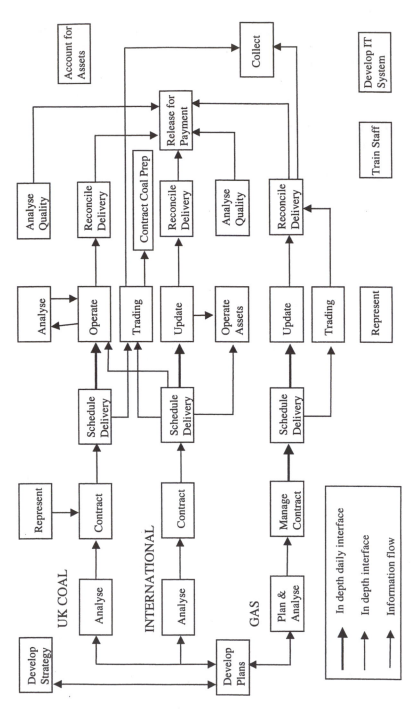

Figure 14.8 Process diagram for fuel strategy and supply department (FSSD) activities

Strategy and Supply Department, FSSD. Once the task force was happy with the representation of the current processes, they could analyse them using the results of the interviews, applying the VSM and following the processes into other business units.

The use of VSM was to be very simple. Each process was labelled by the task force members as either Systems 1(operations), Systems 2 (co-ordination), Systems 3 (control), Systems 3* (audit), Systems 4 (intelligence), or Systems 5 (policy) according to the VSM notation. Thus in Figure 14.8 the processes Develop Strategy and Develop Plans would be denoted Systems 4, the processes Analyse, Contract and Schedule Delivery would be Systems 3 and the processes Operate and Trading would be Systems 1, and so on. The pattern of activities could then be studied. For instance, for the fourth task force, Sales and Marketing, the processes were aggregated as shown in Figure 14.9 and participants could concentrate on the effectiveness on the operational and control mechanisms in turn.

The task force syndicate would then seek to identify and specify more effective processes both within and across existing organizational boundaries using the cues to suggest new ways of doing things and examining the people and systems support involved. By comparison of the new conceptual maps with the current process maps they would identify opportunities for improvement. These are captured in Candidate Improvement Sheets an example of which is shown in Figure 14.10; by comparing the processes generically with those in other industries they would produce benchmarks, and; by examining the key information requirements, they would identify the priorities for an information systems strategy. The intention was that SCA would be used to help

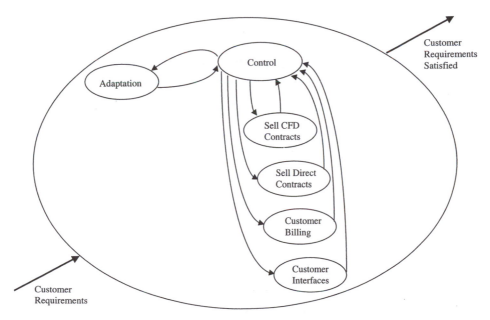

Figure 14.9 Process map – current sales and marketing

Candidate Improvement Sheet	**Title:** Integrate Gas **Author:** BIPT **Date:** 1/3/94

Number PO 15	Title: Integrate Gas Across the Business	? Process Redesign . . . Yes ? Process Efficiency . . ? IS Support . . . .

Description: To integrate Energy Resources, Gas Supply & Trading, and Gas Generation with a separate Pool Ops. Because PowerGen is effectively operating three separate entities into the pool, regulatory control can be limited

Quantified Benefits: Reduced regulatory exposure. Reduced overheads. Closer integration of Gas Generation, purchase vs sale decisions Make £50 m? minus £10 m (Pool Ops loss)	**Risks:** Missed opportunity to optimise between UK coal, gas and International
Future Potential: Buy Kinetica and spin off into separate company?	**Feasibility:** Energy Resources?

Figure 14.10 Candidate improvement sheet

to agree the way forward and obtain commitment; it was not clear at this point how final agreement would be obtained, nor who would be involved.

As in previous projects the approach adopted in the workshops was 'learning by examples', in this case examples based on each business unit. For instance, to understand one part of the analysis the participants would be asked to work in groups to analyse a given process in terms of its sub-processes. The answers from the groups would then be compared with each other and with the prior attempt of the project team. The prior attempt ensured that the project team gained familiarity with at least part of the business process and allowed them to test the approach. More importantly the task force syndicate would get a flying start with their analysis, working from the word go on the problem they faced. A road map, shown in Figure 14.11, was drawn up to help the task force syndicate members find their way through the approach. The numbers in each box indicates the worksheet(s) to support each activity.

Evolution of the Project

At the very first workshop the project manager from the Electricity Division's corporate planning department revealed the latest strategic thinking. The preferred scenario showed a demand shortfall in a couple of years time. One of the conclusions was that the Electricity Division needed to reduce its headquarters' cost base. The point was underlined by the fact that the Electricity Division had only been allocated offices for 200 staff

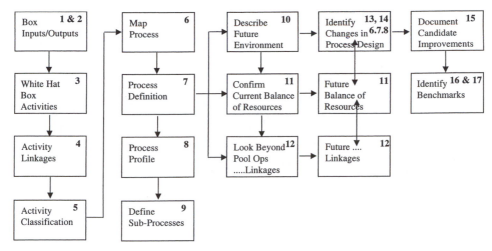

Figure 14.11 Task force road map

in the new headquarters building about to be occupied; the Division currently had 300 headquarters staff. The project was now crucial not only for the future of the company but also for near term financial performance. This meant that the senior managers were seeing the project as an opportunity to downsize. The project was now about business process redesign, benchmarking, IS strategy and downsizing. However, there was no need to change the project process and methods; it was a question of emphasis. It was more important than ever to ensure that the senior managers on the UK electricity management team (UKEMT) should engage with the ideas generated by the task force. Their earlier resistance to become involved was overcome by a workshop held after the first syndicate had finished their analysis.

The workshop took the form of a role-play, which brought home to UKEMT members the relationships between strategy, processes, organisational structure and staff numbers required. The management team were asked to act as consultants to Richard Branson, who wanted to start a new company, Virgin Power. Initially, they were asked to design an organization and specify the manning requirements for a company consisting of a single power station. Subsequently the brief was expanded to include more power stations of different operational characteristics. Gradually the complexity of Virgin Power grew towards that of PowerGen itself but the organization they came up with was simpler and fewer people were required to run it. This gave much food for thought. As a result it was agreed that an integration team would be set up, drawn from task force members. They would shape and evaluate the ideas coming out of the task force investigations. The members of UKEMT also agreed to get much more fully en-gaged and to consider the results in a series of workshops. The revised project plan is shown in Figure 14.12.

It was now possible to deploy the strategic choice approach (SCA) to shape and evaluate the strategic options. The number of issues were such that the shaping and design of

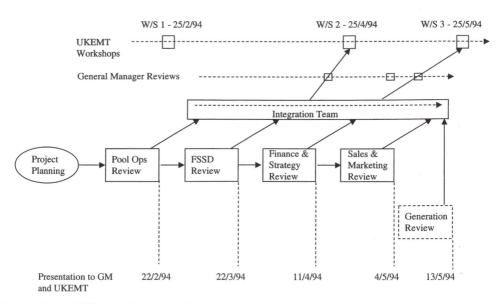

Figure 14.12 BIP overall project plan

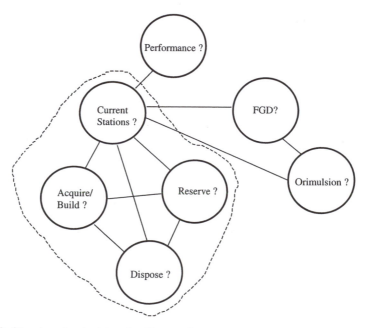

Figure 14.13 Shaping the decision for Generation

decision schemes had to be done for different parts of the business and then considered together. For instance, Figure 14.13 shows the shaping stage in the Generation domain, while Figure 14.14 shows some of the decision schemes in the Pool Operations domain. This brought some clarity to the decision making process, which was nevertheless very

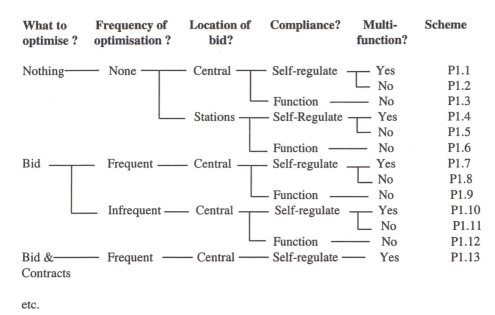

Figure 14.14 Pool Operations decision schemes

etc.

complex. The complexity and the fact that the changes being suggested would involve some ceding of power by some senior managers meant that agreement was difficult to achieve in open forum. The General Manager, head of UKED and sponsor of the project, decided to broker the final agreement individually with his management team. As a result some things were agreed for immediate action and others were deferred (in effect a commitment package was agreed).

Initially benefits were obtained from redesigning some operational processes and changing the IS strategy (particularly the cancellation of some major projects). After two years additional benefits followed the implementation of the suggested change in organizational structure. Further details of the PowerGen case can be found in Ormerod (1999).

Lessons Learnt From the Cases

In both cases it was possible to use both 'hard' and 'soft' methods to good effect. In designing the intervention process one is seldom confronted with a blank sheet of paper. The eight key factors that need to be taken into account are:

1. *The transformation to be achieved by the project:* Defined deliverables should include intangible outcomes such as learning, ownership and commitment as well as the more tangible outcomes such as options, strategies and recommendations. An appreciation of the organizational context will be required.

2. *The fixed points or constraints:* What are the constraints such as time available, deadlines, consulting cost, management time, and geographical location.
3. *The scope of the project:* Closely linked to deliverables and constraints, the scope of the project may limit the subject to be covered or that part of the organization that is to be the focus of attention.
4. *Involvement of interested and relevant parties:* Closely linked to the scope is the need to involve certain actors, groups or representatives of groups. Who needs to be involved and in what capacity? Some people can be canvassed for their views others need to be involved in the decision-making process.
5. *The nature of evidence:* What evidence and arguments are those involved in the decision-making process likely to find convincing?
6. *The ethos of the project:* Is this to be a careful analysis bringing expertise to bear or is it to be visionary and fun? Can it be both?
7. *The expertise and knowledge:* What expertise can both consultants and participants bring to the project? Which experts should be consulted and how much weight given to their advice?
8. *Competence:* Which approaches are the consultants confident of deploying? What are the competencies of the participants in engaging in such approaches?

When choosing the methods to deploy the first factor, the transformation, and the last factor, competence, are the most important. When trying to work out a suitable intervention design it is useful to be able to call on a number of approaches or parts of approaches. It may well be that one approach is sufficient, as in the hands of an expert a single approach can be adapted to suit many circumstances. In the cases described above and other projects I have displayed a preference for using different methods for different phases of the process; I like to play to their strengths. It certainly works. The prospect of using several unfamiliar approaches at once can be daunting. One approach is to always try to introduce one novel method each time you do a new project. Soon the list of familiar methods will grow, you will develop your own 'strand of practice'. Choosing the appropriate methods will get easier. Managing a successful change project in a complex organizational setting is never going to be an easy task. It requires determination, insight, organizational savvy and some luck. The availability of tried and tested approaches to call on and to use at will certainly helps. Using more than one approach enables the methodological support to be tailored to the particular requirement of the assignment in hand.

References

Ackoff, R.L. (1979). 'The future of operational research is past', *J. Opl Res. Soc.*, **30**, 93–104.
Ackoff, R.L. (1979). 'Resurrecting the future of operational research', *J. Opl Res. Soc.*, **30**, 189–99.
Corbett, C.J., Overmeer, J.A.M., and van Wassenhove, L.N. (1993). 'Strands of practice in OR (the practitioner's dilemma)', *Eur. J. Opl. Res.*, **41**, 625–40.

De Bono, E. (1985). *Conflicts: A Better Way to Resolve Them, Six Thinking Hats*, Penguin, London.

Ormerod, R.J. (1995). 'Putting soft OR methods to work: information systems strategy development at Sainsbury's', *J. Opl. Res. Soc.*, **46**, 277–93.

Ormerod, R.J. (1996a). 'Information systems strategy development at Sainsbury's Supermarkets using "soft" OR', *Interfaces*, **26**, 102–30.

Ormerod, R.J. (1996b). 'Putting soft OR to work: information systems strategy development at Richards Bay', *J. Opl. Res. Soc.*, **47**, 1083–97.

Ormerod, R.J. (1998). 'Putting soft OR to work: information systems strategy development at Palabora', *Omega, Int. J. Mgmt. Sci.*, **26**, 78–98.

Ormerod, R.J. (1999). 'Putting soft OR to work: the business improvement project at PowerGen', *Eur. J. Opl. Res.*, **118**, 1–29

Porter, M.E. (1985). *Competitive Advantage: Creating and Sustaining Superior Advantage*, Free Press, New York.

15 *Diverse Unity: Looking Inward and Outward*

John Mingers and Jonathan Rosenhead

This book has presented a range of different methodologies for structuring problems and decisions as well as the idea of combining them together through multimethodology. Each has been described both in general (in terms of aspiration, terminology, method, and process), and in application. In this final chapter we would like to draw some of the threads together by looking inwards at contrasts and congruencies among the methods, and outwards towards other related methods, areas of application and future directions of development and research.

Contrasts and Congruencies

There are some evident contrasts between the methodologies described in earlier chapters – they take different situations as their fields of application, and handle them in differing ways. These contrasts often appear large to authors, as they read and react to each other's work. They will, however, seem less significant to the reader than certain overriding similarities between the methods described – similarities which are in fact even greater than might appear, as the authors have been encouraged to concentrate on the more distinctive aspects of their respective approaches in order to avoid too much overlap. In this section we will try to draw out these common features behind the diversity of methods.

Points of Focus

Certain of the methodologies have a concentration on particular types of decision or problem situations, while others make few assumptions about the internal structure of situations for which they can be of use. In the latter category it is reasonable to place Strategic Options Development and Analysis (SODA), Soft Systems Methodology (SSM), and Strategic Choice. Yet in another sense each of the methods does provide a general problem structuring facility. Each deploys a repertoire of methods, any one of which may (or may not) be applied at some point in the course of a study. Many of them are quite eclectic in their willingness to take other approaches under their wings.

Though most of the methodologies have origins in operational research, they have tended to move away in varying degrees from the simple decision orientation of traditional OR. Thus, in the case of Drama Theory, decisions are of central concern. But they do not feature as alternatives to be assessed against each other. The focus is rather on helping to improve decision making by analysing the quite complex interactive *process* through which decisions emerge.

SODA shares this emphasis on process but, despite its OR pedigree, employs a technique which is not predominantly decision focused. This technique, cognitive mapping, centres as much on identifying organizational goals as it does on decision options. This contrasts with the approach of Strategic Choice and Robustness Analysis, whose emphasis is (more conventionally in an OR sense) on the choice between candidate decisions. Preferences, values, rankings, and the like do, of course, feature – but as means of comparing or excluding various decisions options rather than as subjects of equivalent status.

SSM makes a further contrast. Emerging from the somewhat different background of the systems approach, and indeed system design, the concern is more with how systems could work better, than with what decisions to take. The very word 'decision' is strikingly absent from the account Peter Checkland provides of it – we get no nearer than 'systemically desirable and culturally feasible changes'.

Such differences in origin and formulation do not detract from the overall homogeneity of the approaches. SSM and SODA will serve as an example. Despite their distinct theoretical bases, in systems thinking and in social psychology respectively, they are widely perceived as closely aligned in style and purpose – indeed their principal authors have played down any incompatibility (Checkland, 1985; Eden, 1985).

Products, Process, and Complexity

Another, related, way of understanding the diversity within the unity of these methodologies is to consider their orientation towards either visible or invisible products, to borrow a concept from Strategic Choice. For most of the approaches – SSM, SODA and Drama Theory – the outputs are skewed to a greater or lesser extent towards the invisible end of the spectrum. Though recommended actions and policy changes – the visible products – can be expected to emerge, they do so largely as an indirect result of the core methodology. The more direct effect is on the outlooks, perceptions, and appreciative judgements of the participants. These are the invisible products of the application of the methodology. With Strategic Choice and Robustness, recommendations as to action are generated more directly in the process of applying the methodology. The relative prominence of visible products in these cases is, in fact, a fairly logical consequence of their explicit focus on the act of commitment to decision.

It can be argued, perhaps, that there is a significant cleavage in the types of problem situation addressed by the problem structuring methodologies. In one case the problem situation is problematic principally because of lack of clarity or communication about objectives, purposes, 'what business we are in', etc. In such situations, methods whose products are largely invisible – interaction facilitated, understanding shared – are both necessary and sufficient. SODA and SSM seem to fall largely within this category.

In other cases, however, the problem situation may embrace very considerable degrees of complexity, which are not easy for decision makers to assimilate. For difficulties arising principally from complexity, it can be argued that a more elaborate technique is needed. Such techniques need bear little resemblance to the algorithms of the orthodox paradigm. With no remit to search for the unique optimum, they can avoid baroque impenetrability. Technique is required, simply, to structure and reduce complexity to a point where the decision process can appropriate it. The participants in that process may then feel able to act on the resulting understanding. Alternatively, the provisional understanding may provoke a refocusing of the problem, which may in turn benefit from further analytic effort.

At the strategic level, complexity arises less from sheer number of options than from interactions between different decision makers and from compounded uncertainties. However, these two sources of complexity produce different challenges to technique, which are reflected in particular problem structuring methodologies. The technical aspects of Drama Theory take as their subject matter the multiple possibilities of conflict and cooperation between at least semi-autonomous decision-makers, as well as their accompanying dimensions of emotion and apparently irrational behaviour. For Strategic Choice and Robustness Analysis, technique is used to engage with the complex interactions between possible combinations of interventions in the system under study, and the uncertainties which surround them. In each of these cases, the higher level of formal technique and of visible outputs represents, not a question of taste or of random variation, but a response to a different category of problematic situation.

If juggling with complexities presents difficulties for the individual, it is still less feasible in a group situation. Yet working with groups is a common characteristic of the methodologies described in this book. Some of the methods can certainly be used with or by an individual working alone, and the user-friendly software that has emerged for Strategic Choice (STRAD) and SODA (Decision Explorer), can enable individuals to use the approaches in isolation. However, this is seen as a supplement to, rather than a substitute for, group working.

Robustness Analysis is the approach least predicated on working with groups – though its transparency of method makes it easily accessible to non-specialists. By contrast, many of the developed methods (and a sizeable chunk of the technology) of SSM, SODA, and Strategic Choice would be rendered irrelevant in working with an individual decision-maker. The workshop format is the norm. It is worth noting that of these three, Strategic Choice is distinctive in aiming to 'structure complexity' rather than 'clarify objectives'. The provision of a general-purpose methodology, whose structuring of complexity can be adopted by lay groups and used in progressing their own understanding, represents a very considerable achievement.

Group Facilitation

The characteristically group nature of the decision processes which PSMs aim to assist has implications for the way in which the consultant who uses one of these methods will need to work. There is an essential contrast here with the use of traditional modelling methods. In these, the modeller extracts information from individuals, data-bases etc; then operates the technical aspects of the model in 'the backroom', without the involvement of any client; and then interprets, or perhaps 'sells', the implications of the model outputs to the client. The role performed is that of *analyst*.

As explained in Chapter 1, and exemplified throughout this book, PSMs need to be simple enough to be used, in part or whole, in direct contact with a group of relevant stakeholders. The consultant therefore has a double job – to operate the various stages of the method, while simultaneously organizing the group discussion that the method provokes and assists (Eden, 1990). This more elaborated role in the group context may be designated that of *facilitator*.

The facilitator is a disinterested party who designs and manages a workshop process (Huxham and Cropper, 1994). The facilitator is quite different from a meeting chair, who has a defined task, an agenda, and authority to resolve conflicts and rule on due process. S/he is not even a group leader, who may operate in a less structured format, but still has a personal interest in the nature of the outcome of the meeting. The facilitator has no interest in the outcome, and no authority to impose decisions. The authority of the facilitator arises only from the perception of the group that they are being helped constructively to make progress with their problem. To perform this role, the facilitator needs to be trusted by all participants, and so cannot be a 'player' in the situation which the group is concerned to change (Phillips and Phillips, 1993).

The job of the facilitator is extremely demanding, requiring as it does attention both to problem content and group process. It is advantageous to have two facilitators, one specializing in process and the other in content, though not exclusively (Ackermann, 1996). If support software is being used, one of the facilitators may input the emerging model to the computer in real time. The advantage of this is that the model is ready at any point for computer manipulation or display. The negative aspect is that one of the facilitators will tend to lose contact with the group.

Ackermann (1996), Phillips and Phillips (1993) and Vennix (1996) give full and essentially complementary accounts of how facilitation must work if it is to be effective. The general attitude of the facilitator must be of supporting others to get the work done; of inquiring – asking questions rather than making statements or giving answers; and of authenticity – no tricks, power games or manipulation. But beyond these generalities there are a range of do's and don'ts that both experience and theory have shown to make the difference between a well and a not-so-well facilitated workshop.

The facilitator's job starts well before the workshop itself. There will usually be a key contact (sometimes a small group) who is responsible for the workshop taking place at all. It is important that that this contact is given a full briefing in advance of how the workshop will operate and what it can be expected to achieve. In return, the facilitator needs to take the opportunity to gain a broad understanding of the organization (or organizations), and of the nexus of issues within which the subject area of the workshop is located.

Jointly the facilitator and the contact need to agree the makeup of the workshop – ensuring that key players are not omitted, but that the group stays a reasonable size. The size of group that can be managed varies somewhat between methods, but 8 to 10 usually works well. Members should be asked to commit themselves to attend throughout the workshop, or series of workshops if that is anticipated. A location away from the workplace should be agreed, and the facilitator should view it in advance to make sure that it is physically suitable for the method that will be used – e.g., accessible wall-space for flip charts. If there is a series of workshops, the facilitator and contact should meet in between to discuss progress, and to agree the broad approach for the next one.

The advantages of a workshop situation – that the knowledge and judgement brought to the room by the participants can be surfaced, and that any commitments entered in to bear the real assent of those present – can only be realized if all participate fully in the dialogue. Therefore it is the job of the facilitator to make it feel safe for all to express their views as fully and openly as possible. Outside the workshop room there will be inequalities of position, but participants must be treated with scrupulous equality during the proceedings. A member expressing apparently unpopular views or minority perspectives may need to be protected; for example, the facilitator can act as a lightning conductor, by intervening with 'I don't see why that is such a bad idea'. Reticent participants may need to be encouraged to express views, and certainly space should be made in the flow when they do show that they have something they wish to say.

There are of course potential problems caused by the dominant talker or the seemingly endless rambler. Rather than comment overtly on their behaviour, the facilitator must look for a non-obtrusive opportunity to steer back to the main topic currently being addressed, or to invite other members for their views on some aspect of what has been said.

Keeping on track without interfering with the spontaneity and creativity of the group frequently requires a strategy of purposeful *non*-intervention. Nevertheless there are a variety of types of intervention that are helpful if used with restraint:

• asking for clarification – in cases of possible ambiguity it is dangerous to underestimate the potential for miscommunication
• asking difficult or obvious questions – to confirm that underlying assumptions are shared
• making summarizing statements – may reveal or dispel obscurities or confusion
• reflecting back – 'you seem to have been saying…' can help to crystallize a common advance in understanding
• handing back from a new perspective – invites but does not compel participants to see a new meaning in what they have been saying

- reminding the group of their purpose, and inviting them to re-address it
- summarizing, and inviting participants to evaluate, the group's progress
- pacing the task – redirecting the group into a new type of activity, either because diminishing returns have set in, or with an eye on the clock.

You will observe that none of these interventions involves either contributing substantive knowledge or offering opinions about the subject under discussion. Some facilitators hold the view that, where they do have relevant knowledge or they gain insight from the problem structuring work itself, they should contribute substantively to the group discussions. However, many though not all subscribe to the view that to do this would undercut the special position of the facilitator as a neutral who can be trusted by all to perform the process manager role without bias. This is not to say that the facilitator should not have relevant substantive knowledge of the industry sector, the public service, the specific issue. Indeed without it s/he will often fail to understand the flow of debate, and so be unable to shape it constructively. Equally it is a real handicap not to understand in advance the relationships, including power and politics, between the participants *outside* the workshop. This can, for example, enable the facilitator to steer away from areas that are likely to provoke unproductive confrontation.

Potential conflict is always a factor in a workshop. It can arise from pre-existing interpersonal relations, or incompatible personal styles, but also from the diversity of interests represented. Overt conflict can be constructive, if it surfaces important issues that would otherwise lie submerged. It goes without saying that too much conflict can be highly disruptive. At least as dangerous, however, is premature concurrence of ideas, what Janis has termed 'groupthink'. For each member there will be a tension between what s/he sees as desirable, and the wish to be accepted into the group. Managing this tension, and the anxieties which go with it, is one of the facilitator's task. Probably the environment should be at least slightly uncomfortable if the group is to be productive. If there is too much agreement, the facilitator may wish to promote some controversy, perhaps under the guise of devil's advocate.

To carry out these tasks effectively on behalf of the group requires the facilitator to be both an active listener and a keen observer. What people say is important, but the symbolic as well as the overt content can be highly significant. After all, some things are difficult to say directly, and may be implied only obliquely – low expectations of support from senior management, for example. The facilitator may also gain insights into how best to help the group forward by reflecting on things *not* said, which may identify constraints so automatically accepted as not to need voicing.

The skilled facilitator will also pick up on non-verbal communication. Bodily posture can reveal whether a member is deeply engaged in the ongoing process, or sceptical. A fleeting facial expression may indicate opposition or disquiet which is not voiced – which is better surfaced by a question than left to nag. The facilitator also needs to monitor the mood of the group, in order to judge whether anxieties (when will we stop for lunch? *or* where is all this leading to?) are interfering with progress and need to be allayed.

Learning from Other Methods

Chapter 12 has provided short summaries of a number of additional methods. These are approaches, growing out of the OR and systems traditions, which construct models in order to assist organizational decision making. We have explained previously why we feel that they fall (just) outside the main scope of this book.

There are a very large number of other methods to help groups make progress with their problems, but which do not use models to represent the problematic situation. We pick out below two significant families of such methods. One is a set of methods that are designed to work participatively with larger groups; the other are approaches that have emerged in the specific context of development planning. Their resemblance to certain aspects of PSMs raises questions of what mutual lessons might be learnt, or what opportunities might be opened up by their use in combination.

Large Group Interventions

PSMs are designed to work with medium size groups – larger than a standard conversation but smaller than a public meeting. This size limitation (12 people is quite difficult to manage because of the pressure on 'air time' and on the facilitator's attentiveness, and 15 is definitely a crowd) excludes PSMs from use where larger numbers need to participate. The recent proliferation of methods designed specifically for the large group situation (though without use of models) presents an intriguing challenge to PSMs. Indeed, Bryson and Anderson (2000) have provided a useful comparative study of several of these methods including SODA and Strategic Choice.

One well established approach of this kind is the Nominal Group Technique (NGT) (Delbecq, 1975). It has found considerable use in Community Operational Research – which we will discuss shortly. NGT was developed in situations of public consultation where a group of essentially arbitrary individuals, perhaps local inhabitants, would meet to raise views and ideas. The primary requirement is for a non-threatening method that would ensure everyone felt able to express themselves and that all ideas were genuinely considered. The method involves round-robin generation of ideas, brief but non-judgemental explanations/discussions of each, and then anonymous voting to create an agreed agenda for detailed discussion. Thus NGT encourages the participation of less assertive members, and allows issues to be put in order of priority.

A new generation of large group intervention methods (Bunker and Alban, 1997; Pratt, Gordon and Plamping, 1999) have emerged more recently through the interplay of social psychology, psychoanalysis and systems theory. Although they have longer historical roots, it was only in the 1990s that their use became more common and their forms more diverse.

Participants may number from a few dozen up to a few hundred. The different forms of these events are all designed to allow all participants to have a voice, and to provide time to nurture relationships and establish genuine dialogue. Their purpose is to enable participants to explore possibilities, identify problems and find solutions. The underlying principle has been described as 'getting the whole system in the room', in order to achieve organisational change. The apparent contradiction between the attempt to encompass the whole system and the aspiration to real dialogue is managed by locating most of the work in small unfacilitated groups, but linked through facilitated large group sessions.

Just a few of these methods can be described here:

i) *Open Space Technology* was developed almost accidentally when an academic conference was deliberately started with no programme, no agenda, and no committee (Owen, 1992). Eighty five people sat in a circle and organized a 3-day programme in two hours. The main emphasis in self-organizing such complexity is on individual commitment, participation and fun! Participants are challenged to find issues of importance within themselves, and are invited to form groups to discuss them. There are four principles: i) Whoever comes are the right people; ii) Whatever happens is the only thing that could have happened; iii) Whenever it starts is the right time; and iv) When its over its over. And one law: The Law of Two Feet – if at any time you find yourself in a place where you are neither learning nor contributing then get on your feet and move somewhere else, to another group or even to the bar! The overall effect of these is to heighten productivity, commitment, and creativity whilst lessening tension and conflict.

ii) A *Future Search* conference brings together at one time and in the same room everyone (or at least representatives of all stakeholders) who has an interest in the issue to be discussed (Weisbord, 1987, 1992; Weisbord and Janoff, 1995). It is particularly suitable for complex systems issues, and for 70–80 participants. (If larger numbers need to be involved, several conferences can be held in parallel.) By contrast with Open Space, it is a design tightly choreographed over two or more days. The core work of the conference is carried out at round tables each with eight chairs. Each table seats a microcosm of the community, crossing levels and functions, but members spend much of their time working at flip-charts on the wall. At the end of each session reports back are made by roving microphone. Different sessions focus on history, current trends, and what people feel 'proud' or 'sorry' about in relation to the conference theme, before moving on to develop possible future scenarios. Common themes across the scenarios are integrated into an aspirational common future which is 'common ground' between the participants, and the action consequences which flow from it.

iii) *Team Syntegrity* (Beer, 1994; Holmberg, 1997) is a complex and sophisticated procedure for debating a range of connected issues among a potentially large (say 30) group of knowledgeable people. This could be within or between organizations, or a research network or local community. The method is based around the geometrical shape of polyhedra such as the icosahedron that is used to structure the participants into groups discussing related issues. The method has three stages – the 'problem jostle' where a large number of suggested issues are reduced to an agreed set; the 'topic auction' where participants organize themselves into discussion groups, each participant being both a member of some groups and an observer of others; and the 'outcome resolve' where several rounds of discussion and inter-communication occur. The result is a set of agreed Final Statements of Importance. Beware – a complete syntegration session will take two to three days!

Methods like these have some evident similarities with PSMs, and some clear differences. Both approaches aim to liberate creative thought by bringing together diverse experiences, knowledge bases and perspectives. Both aim to generate collaborative action towards a desired future. PSMs support this process by appropriate modelling, while large scale events provide at most a structured series of questions to assist interaction within and between groups. On the other hand, the output of a successful large scale intervention will have the assent of the entire community of stakeholders. The agreement generated by PSMs, in contrast, carries no comparable legitimation. It remains the property of the (relatively small) group who were present and will need to be explained and 'sold' to a larger audience. There thus appears to be a potential for both practices to learn and borrow from each others' methods.

Participatory Development Planning Methods

Third world development planning has been through a paradigm shift between a traditional approach and a more participatory alternative which mirrors that of operational research. The alternative approach has developed a number of methods with interesting parallels with PSMs, as well as some crucial differences. It may be instructive for the future development and practice of both participative development planning methods and of PSMs to explore the possible synergies between them.

The traditional approach to development planning concentrated on economic growth. Under the auspices of national governments and international agencies, professionals followed a top-down, prescriptive approach in formulating plans which largely excluded the participation of the intended beneficiaries (Bendeck, 2001). Gradually the ineffectiveness of this approach in actually delivering change became clear, and a view arose of development planning as a cooperative process involving a plurality of actors throughout society to identify strategies for guiding social change (Sagasti, 1988). According to Chambers (1997) this shift if taken seriously entails decentralization of the decision-making process, clients becoming partners, a move to bottom-up planning, controlled clients being substituted by empowered clients, and power shifting to local people.

A bewildering array of methods appropriate to this alternative view have been developed, with (*see* Cornwall, Guijt and Welbourn, 1993) three to five letter acronyms ranging from AEA to TFT. (For a general account of development planning methods, see Mikkelsen (1995), and Pratt and Loizos (1992).) The most widely used of these, inspired by Chambers, are Rapid Rural Appraisal (RRA) and its successor Participative Rural Appraisal (PRA) – though these names are now misleading as there have been many application in urban areas, and even in developed countries (including the British health service).

RRA aims to build up a picture of a local community over a short period of time, perhaps ten days. Rather than sitting in offices in the capital city or even further afield, multi-disciplinary teams descend on the area in question and collect information from the widest possible range of data sources. These data sources include not only government statistics and research reports, and maps and aerial photographs, but also the views of 'key informants'. These are, for example, local professionals, opinion formers and centres of gossip (perhaps a café or a hairdressers). The idea is to avoid the 'tyranny of quantification', and to 'triangulate' – that is, to view the situation from the perspective of a variety of different data sources, investigators, disciplines. The team reviews progress each evening, and can re-target its efforts.

Although RRA acknowledges the importance of involving the local community, the speedy arrival and departure of the professional team obviously militates against this, and also against the local sustainability of any initiatives agreed on. PRA attempts to overcome this difficulty with a more even-paced approach, and a commitment to 'handing over the stick' – that is giving control of the project to local people, respecting their knowledge and capabilities, and avoiding attitudes of professional superiority. Behaviour changes are necessary to achieve this. But there are also methods which help to make the local ownership of a study feasible.

Such standard methods as semi-structured interviews, group interviews with homogeneous membership to encourage openness (often called focus groups), and informal workshops for brainstorming or problem solving, are among those used by PRA for eliciting and collating information. Other methods (Mikkelsen, 1995; Bendeck, 2001) include:

- ranking exercises – these are used to secure an individual's or a group's preferences, priorities, opinions, expectations or beliefs. One common example is wealth ranking of local households (in order to identify poorer households for targeting). 'Card sorting' may be used to distinguish different categories, with the informants providing their own criteria for 'sameness'. Alternatively, locally available materials (seeds, stones) may be used as counters for matrix ranking. This allows informants, for example, to score a number of possible crops in terms of each of a number of attributes – cash generation, energy giving, storability, water requirement, etc.
- role playing – this is particularly useful for sensitive issues. It enables participants to express their view of aspects of life which might otherwise be hard to discuss, and to articulate the feelings aroused in them. This elicits comments and discussions from those watching. (This method has also been used in community OR, to be discussed below.)

- maps and diagrams – there are a wide range of simple schematic devices which present information in a readily understandable visual form (Conway, 1989). Resource maps display the location of natural resources. Seasonal diagrams show the changes that occur in residents' lives over an annual cycle. Other diagrams show the amount of time spent on different activities. All of these are prepared by community members themselves. Transects (cross-sections of an area based on systematic walks and observation) increase mutual understanding in the community, and between them and the professionals, about the general characteristics of their environment. Venn (or 'chapati') diagrams indicate social groupings and institutions, and their overlap, with perceived importance represented by size.

There are evident parallels between this alternative development planning paradigm, and that of operational research. By contrast with their respective orthodoxies, both are characterized by (Bendeck, 2001):

i) process similarities – work with groups, clients as active participants, down-playing of professional expertise, iterative learning, ownership of process and outcome; and
ii) technique similarities – reduced data requirements, diversity of tools, diagrammatic representations, accessibility and transparency.

Both Bendeck (2001) and Fassolo (1997) have observed and commented on this goodness of fit, and White and Taket (1997) have proposed a framework for their joint use. However as yet the possibility of symbiosis has been little exploited. It at least possible *both* that PSMs could learn from PRA's quite remarkable repertoire of low-tech methods, *and* that PRA and similar approaches could benefit from the addition of model-based methods linking action to consequence, which they currently lack.

Some Areas of Application

The principal concern of this book has been to introduce the reader to a range of methods. Practical applications have featured, in the main, simply as illustrations of particular methods. In this section we provide two illustrative examples of application areas where PSMs have made a concentrated contribution.

Information Systems

A major area of application, particularly for SSM (Stowell, 1995; Checkland and Holwell, 1998), has been that of designing information systems (IS). For many years information systems design was dominated by technical concerns. It was seen as essentially computerizing some process that already occurred manually and the IS design methodologies were largely concerned to develop efficient technological solutions to problems that were assumed to be clear and well-defined. This worked reasonably well for very basic operations such as payroll and transactions processing but a series of major IS disasters has demonstrated the failure of this approach in more ambitious applications (Poulymenakou and Holmes, 1996). To list just a few: in 1994 the London Ambulance Service scrapped a major (£10m) system for controlling ambulances (Beynon Davies, 1995). When it was first put into operation it performed so disastrously, endangering several lives, that it was never used again. Similar total failures occurred with the London Stock Exchange's Taurus system (£75m), a UK government system for the unemployed (£48m), and, as we write, another government system for controlling immigration.

A variety of reasons for these failures have been identified:

- Traditional IS methodologies are geared primarily towards the technological aspects of the design. They focus on data, data flows, and the system's functions thus concentrating only on technical solutions to what may be complex organizational and communicational issues.
- They are often oriented towards reproducing existing processes or else they assume that users can specify clearly what they would like the system to do. In practice there is no reason to assume that current practices are effective, or are appropriate for simply computerizing. Generally users will not be able to clearly visualize how a new system might work or how the task itself could be re-engineered. Users only come to *discover* what they want through participating in the design process (Markus and Keil, 1994).
- There is often a dislocation in thought and language between the IS analysts, who think about the technical characteristics of the system, and the users who are concerned with business tasks and objectives. Analysts need to be able to see the world through the eyes of the users.
- It is often assumed that a clear and comprehensive specification can be developed at the start and that this is then taken off and constructed by the developers. The reality is that many decisions should only be taken as the project develops with the continual participation of the users.
- Finally, of course, the construction of significant new organizational systems is as much a political process as it is a purely rational one (Robey and Markus, 1988).

These difficulties provide an ideal opportunity for PSMs, and SSM has been used extensively in a variety of ways (Mingers, 1995). To our knowledge other methods have not been taken up, but there would certainly seem to be scope for, say, cognitive mapping.

With SSM, the simplest approach perhaps is to use it as a front-end to a more traditional, harder systems design methodology. SSM is used in its own right to structure a debate about necessary business activities. Once this is agreed, the conceptual model can be used to define the information necessary to carry out these activities. This then forms the requirements analysis to be fed into the system design process. A more sophisticated approach is to make SSM the overall methodology for the project as a whole, in order to maintain participation and commitment, but to embed a hard method within it for the detailed design work. At a higher level, with strategic information systems, SSM can be used as part of the process of formulating the organisation's strategy out of which may stem requirements for several information systems (Galliers, 1993). Checkland's chapter within this book is an example, as is work by Ormerod (1995).

Community OR

Just as there was, from the 1960's at least, a traditional approach to modelling, so also there was a traditional clientele for this analytic work. They were, almost exclusively, relatively powerful organizations organized internally with a top-down chain of command (Rosenhead, 1986). Community Operational Research is the alternative practice of working with disadvantaged groups. In Britain the Operational Research Society set up in 1987 a unit, initially at Northern College outside Barnsley, to work with this different clientele. Such client groups, it was decided, should:

- exist to protect or advance the interests of their members;
- possess scant physical or financial resources;
- have no articulated management hierarchy;
- operate internally through consensus or democracy.

This initiative has generated a very considerable body of experience of modelling work for and with grass-roots organizations, not all of it carried out by the unit, and not all in Britain. Work has been carried out, for example, for tenants and residents groups, for parent teacher associations, for single issue protest groups, for voluntary organizations, for a community re-development bid, for a feminist collective, and for an anti-poverty alliance. (See Ritchie, Taket and Bryant, 1994; Mar Molinero, 1988; Thunhurst et al., 1992; Thunhurst and Ritchie, 1992; Bowen, 1995; Rosenhead and White, 1996).

A considerable proportion of the reported work has made use of PSMs. Thus, in a collection of masters student projects (Bowen, 1995), 20 out of 40 applications of specific methods were described as 'softer' approaches, and 14 of these 20 were of methods described in this book. This is a far higher proportion than one would expect to find in a collection of non-community projects. Taket and White (1997) take the particular suitability of PSMs (or *Issue* Structuring Methods as they prefer to call them) for work with community groups as the starting point for their discussion.

It is easy to see why this 'fit' between community OR and PSMs should appear

natural. Community groups' predicaments are likely to be 'wicked' rather than tame –
since tame problems concern the disposition of resources under the organization's
control, and they have few of these. Members of disadvantaged groups can also be seen
as the ultimate 'laypersons' in relation to modelling work. Through their employment
(and unemployment), and their education, few will have been exposed to the experience
of analytically-supported problem solving. Indeed they may have developed a healthy
distrust of experts, who usually seem to work for the organizations who are the source of
their problems. Transparent methods and a process under their own control are more
likely to gain their trust.

Recalling Table 1.3 from Chapter 1, the bottom-up nature of the PSM approach
does seems particularly appropriate to community OR, and this was indeed the case
advanced in the first edition of this book. However the argument was perhaps oversimplified, and roles clearly do exist for both PSMs and traditional modelling approaches
to work with community groups. After all, 20 out of 40 cases in Bowen (1995) were *not* of
softer methods.

Rosenhead (1993) proposed a four-way breakdown of possible types of community
OR projects, as shown in Table 15.1. Two of the categories indicate a potential for more
traditional analysis. One is concerned with the internal workings of the organization.
Even though the resources are small compared with those of powerful organizations,
issues concerning the rostering of staff (whether paid or voluntary), the definition of
information requirements, the managing of cash flow may still present difficulties to
organizations representing the disadvantaged. The second type of opportunity for a
conventional analytic approach is externally focused. This is where the community
organization needs to persuade external bodies. A business plan may need to be prepared to support a grant application. Or a private or public agency's proposal may need
to be subject to criticism from a community perspective – for example at a public
enquiry. In situations of these kinds, planning or counter-planning will need to be cast in
terms of an unambiguous problem definition.

It is where there are differences or ambiguities which need to be surfaced that PSMs
come into their own. Internally, this can occur where members of the organization disagree about priorities or strategic directions. Community organizations depend for their
strength on the cohesion of their members. Disarray will lead to loss of membership, and
the attrition of their already limited strength. PSMs' participative nature coupled with

Table 15.1 – Problem/method classification for community
operational research

Focus	Field	Indicated Methods
internal	physiological resolution of differences	problem solving problem structuring
external	strategy persuasion	problem structuring problem solving

an explicit treatment of alternative perspectives can facilitate the process of attitudinal shift and mutual accommodation through which such organizations move forward.

Taking an external focus, there is another class of problems concerned with how to manoeuvre in a volatile and possibly hostile world. Given their limited influence over their environment, community organizations need to position themselves so as to avoid vulnerability to the multiple uncertainties that beset them. They may also need to reach understandings with other, perhaps more powerful, organizations. There is a need, therefore, for the organization both to understand its strategic position and to negotiate based on that understanding. There are PSMs which can help to analyse situations in these terms, and in a participatory mode that assists group ownership.

It follows from this discussion that methodological pragmatism should be the order of the day, as Thunhurst (1987) advocated, when working with community clients. Nevertheless it also evident that community OR offers a particularly rich scope for the application of PSMs.

Research Issues

The first edition of this book summarized the state of the art of Problem Structuring Methods at the end of the 1980s. There has been much development since then – hence the justification for this substantially revised second edition. But this volume too can at best provide a 'freeze-frame' portrait of what is in fact a fast moving subject. It is therefore worth considering, as we do below, some possible future directions of development. These are, in a sense, loose ends: issues which have arisen in the development and discussion of PSMs to date. It cannot aspire to be comprehensive or predictive. Rather, this section suggests some areas which look worthy of further exploration and development.

Some such issues have already arisen in the fourteen preceding chapters. Many of these are specific to individual methods. We are concerned here with those that have a relevance wider than a particular PSM. These include:

- What are the problems of working with a multi-organisational group, rather than within a unitary organization, and how can they be mitigated?
- How difficult is it for individual consultants to work across paradigms?
- Which combinations of methods are the most effective and fruitful, and how should methods best be split up and then linked together?
- What is the balance, in working with larger project teams, between the advantage of a wider skill pool, and the costs of communication and indeed miscommunication?
- How can PSMs learn from participative development planning methods, and from methods for large-scale interventions, and/or extend PSM's range of application through joint working?

- To what extent can the types of community group problem for which PSMs are advantageous be specified?
- To what extent can PSMs deal with situations characterized by significant power differentials either within an organization or between organizations?

Two further potential areas for research and development which have not been explicitly raised before will be outlined below.

The Virtual Organisation

Generally, PSMs encourage group participation in decision making and they have all developed on the premise that these interactions will be face-to-face. However, with the development of video conferencing and the internet such exchanges will increasingly be virtual. What effects will this have on problem structuring? Whilst such technologies have obvious benefits, their disembodied nature clearly limits the quality and depth of the conversations that they can support. One piece of research (Rocco and Warglien, 1995) compared experimentally face-to-face with electronically-mediated decision-making in a Prisoner's Dilemma type situation. The general findings were that the electronic groups found it much harder to establish cooperation through group cohesion – all the face-to-face groups established stable, high-return patterns of behaviour, whilst none of the electronic groups did. But there was evidence that the electronic groups were better at pure, calculative, problem-solving. Whilst this is only one, small-scale, study its interesting results point to the need for much more research on the effects of increasing disembodiment.

Another development is that of multimedia or hypermedia systems that synthesize a variety of different modes of interaction, for example, traditional computer displays, sound, photos, videos, simulations, and also allow access to be structured by, rather than imposed upon, the user. *Theseus*, developed by Harnden and Stringer (1993) is an interesting example. This is a generic system for generating different learning environments. It sees the computer not as a *tool* with predefined functions, but as a *medium* of linked multimedia objects within which users can actively explore particular domains, generating their own paths and links, and in the process altering the underlying connectivity of the mediabase. The quality of experience of the user is enhanced by the use of dramatic (e.g., computer-gaming and theatre) and aesthetic effects in order to generate greater engagement and participation.

Managing Change – the Social and Political Context

Almost by definition problem structuring methods' primary purpose is to assist in the process of bringing about (beneficial) change within organizations even if, as is often the case with SSM, this is only learning and better understanding rather than organizational restructuring. However, there is an enormous literature under the rubric of the 'management of change', including much empirical evidence, that testifies adequately to the inertia and resistance to change that characterizes many organizational contexts (Collins, 1998). Indeed it would be strange if this were not the case, for any significant change is likely to create as many victims as beneficiaries and may well challenge established structures of power and influence.

Given this, it is somewhat surprising that in general the methods covered here do not really draw upon this material in a significant way. Cognitive mapping is founded in a psychological theory – Kelly's construct theory – but does not seem to bring this explicitly into play in action. SSM has been enhanced with Analyses 1,2,3 that cover the social and political aspects of a situation but these are quite superficial and idiosyncratic. Drama Theory stresses the importance of emotion in conflict situations but does not develop this theoretically. There is, surely, much to be gained by both sides here. PSMs need to learn from the change management literature both in terms of the psychology of individual development and learning, and at the social level of power and organizational culture. Conversely change management itself, in its practical and applied aspects, can make more use of successful methods such as SSM and SODA.

Coda

For the past 30 years and more, and especially over the last 10, Problem Structuring Methods have demonstrated their capability to extend the reach of model-based analysis. Classes of problem previously thought to be the domain of other systematic approaches or none are so no longer. Even so the potential for their use still far outstrips their application to date. This is a challenge, and an opportunity.

References

Ackermann, F. (1996). 'Participants' perceptions on the role of facilitators using Group Decision Support Systems', *Group Decision and Negotiation*, **5**, 93–112.

Beer, S. (1994). *Beyond Dispute: the Invention of Team Syntegrity*, John Wiley & Sons, Ltd, Chichester.

Bendeck, M. (2001). *Problem structuring methods for development: a conceptual clarification, with an application to participative health services planning in Mexico*. Doctoral thesis, London School of Economics, London.

Beynon Davies, P. (1995). 'Information systems "failure": The case of the London ambulance service's computer aided despatch project', *Eur. J. Inform. Syst.*, **4**(3), 171–84.

Bowen, K. (1995). *In at the Deep End: MSc student projects in community operational research*, Community Operational Research Unit, Northern College, Barnsley.

Bryson, J. and Anderson, S. (2000). 'Applying large-group interaction methods in the planning and implementation of major change efforts', *Public Administration Review*, **60**, 143–62.

Bunker, B.B. and Alban, B.T. (1997). *Large Group Interventions: Engaging the Whole System for Rapid Change*, Jossey-Bass, San Francisco.

Chambers, R. (Ed.) (1997). *Whose Reality Counts?: Putting the Last First*, Intermediate Technology Publications, London.

Checkland, P. (1985). 'Some reflections on the Henley Conference 1985', *J Opl Res Soc.*, **36**, 854–5.

Checkland, P. and Holwell, S. (1998). *Information, Systems and Information Systems: Making Sense of the Field*, John Wiley & Sons, Ltd, Chichester.

Collins, D. (1998). *Organizational Change: Sociological Perspectives*. Routledge, London.

Conway, G. (1989). 'Diagrams for farmers', in *Farmer First: Farmer Innovation and Agricultural Research* (Eds. R. Chambers, A. Pacey, and L.A. Thrupp), pp. 77–86, Intermediate Technology Publications, London. (Cited by Bendeck, 2001)

Cornwall, A., Guijt, I., and Welbourn, A. (1993). Acknowledging process: challenges for agricultural research and extension methodology, IDS Discussion Paper 333, Institute of Development Studies, University of Sussex, Brighton. (Cited by Mikkelsen, 1995).

Delbecq, A. (1975). *Group Techniques for Program Planning: a Guide to Nominal Group and Delphi*, Scott Foresman, Glenview, Ill.

Eden, C. (1985). 'Perishing thoughts about systems thinking in action', *J. Opl Res. Soc.*, **36**, 860–61.

Eden, C. (1990). 'The unfolding nature of group decision support – two dimensions of skill', in *Tackling Strategic Problems: the role of group decision support* (Eds. C. Eden and J. Radford), pp. 48–52, Sage, London.

Fassolo, B. (1997). What is the scope for adding model-based participatory methods to the repertoire of development planners? Masters paper, Department of Operational Research, London School of Economics, London.

Galliers, R. (1993). 'Towards a flexible information architecture: integrating business strategies, information systems strategies and business process redesign', *J. of Information Systems*, **3**, 199–213.

Harnden, R. and Stringer, R. (1993). 'Theseus – the evolution of a hypermedium', *Cybernetics and Systems*, **24**, 255–80.

Holmberg, S. (1997). 'Team Syntegrity assessment', *Systems Practice*, **10**, 241–54.

Huxham, C. and Cropper, S. (1994). 'From many to one – and back: an exploration of some components of facilitation', *Omega*, **22**, 1–11.

Mar Molinero, C. (1988). 'Schools in Southampton: a quantitative approach to school location, closure and staffing', *J. Opl Res. Soc.*, **39**, 339–50.

Markus, L. and Keil, M. (1994). 'If we build it, they will come: designing information systems that people want to use', *Sloan Management Review*, Summer.

Mikkelsen, B. (1995). *Methods for Development Work and Research*, Sage, New Delhi.

Mingers, J. (1995). 'Using Soft Systems Methodology in the design of information systems', in *Information Systems Provision: The Contribution of Soft Systems Methodology* (Ed. F. Stowell), pp. 18–50, McGraw-Hill, London.

Ormerod, R. (1995). 'Putting soft OR methods to work: information systems strategy development at Sainsbury's', *Journal of the Operational Research Society*, **46**(3), 277–93.

Owen, H. (1992). *Open Space Technology: a User's Guide*, Abbott, Potomac, Md.

Phillips, L.D. and Phillips, M.C. (1993). 'Facilitated work groups: theory and practice', *J. Opl Res. Soc.*, **44**, 533–49.

Poulymenakou, A. and Holmes, A. (1996). 'A contingency framework for the investigation of information systems failure', *European J. Information Systems*, **5**(1), 34–46.

Pratt, B. and Loizos, P. (1992). *Choosing Research Methods: Data Collection for Development Workers*, Oxfam, Oxford.

Pratt, J., Gordon, P., and Plamping, D. (1999). *Working Whole Systems: Putting Theory into Practice in Organisations*, Kings Fund, London.

Ritchie, C., Taket, A., and Bryant, J. (Eds.) (1994). *Community Works: 26 Case Studies Showing Community Operational Research in Action*, PAVIC Publications, Sheffield.

Robey, D. and Markus, L. (1988). 'Rituals in information system design', in *Readings in Information Systems: a Managerial Perspective* (Eds. J. Wetherbie, V. Dock, and S. Mandell), West.

Rocco, E. and Warglien, M. (1995). Computer mediated communication and the emergence of 'electronic opportunism'. Venice, Dipartimento di Economia e Direzione Aziendale, Universita degli Studi di Venezia.

Rosenhead, J. (1986). 'Custom and practice', *J. Opl Res. Soc.*, **37**, 335–43.

Rosenhead, J. (1993). 'Enabling analysis: across the developmental divide', *Systems Practice*, **6**, 117–38.

Rosenhead, J. and White, L. (1996). 'Nuclear Fusion: some linked case studies in community operational research', *J. Opl Res. Soc.*, **47**, 479–89.

Sagasti, F. (1988). 'National development planning in turbulent times: new approaches and criteria for institutional design', *World Development*, **16**, 431–48.

Stowell, F., (Ed.) (1995). *Information Systems Provision: the Contribution of Soft Systems Methodology*. London, McGraw Hill.

Taket, A. and White, L. (1997). 'Wanted dead OR alive – ways of using problem-structuring methods in community OR', *Int. Trans. Opl Res.*, **4**, 99–108.

Thunhurst, C. (1987). 'Doing OR with the community', *Dragon*, **2**, 143–53.

Thunhurst, C., Ritchie, C., Friend, J., and Booker, P. (1992) 'Housing in the Dearne Valley: doing community OR with the Thurnscoe Tenants Housing Cooperative Part 1: the involvement of the Community OR Unit', *J. Opl Res. Soc.*, **43**, 81–94.

Thunhurst, C. and Ritchie, C. (1992). 'Housing in the Dearne Valley: doing community OR with the Thurnscoe Tenants Housing Cooperative Part 2: an evaluation', *J. Opl Res. Soc.*, **43**, 677–90.

Vennix, J.A.M. (1996). *Group Model Building: Facilitating Team Learning Using System Dynamics*, John Wiley & Sons, Ltd, Chichester.

Weisbord, M.R. (1987). *Productive Workplaces: Organising and Managing for Dignity, Meaning, and Community*, Jossey-Bass, San Francisco.

Weisbord, M.R. (1992) *Discovering Common Ground*, Berrett-Koehler, San Francisco.

Weisbord, M.R. and Janoff, S. (1995). *Future Search*, Berrett-Koehler, San Francisco

White, L. and Taket, A. (1997). 'Beyond appraisal: participatory appraisal of needs and the development of action', *Omega*, **25**, 523–34.

Index

academic OR 7
acceptable options, robustness analysis 190–223
Ackerman, F. vii, 10, 21–41, 43–60, 243, 340
Ackoff, R.L. 3, 4–5, 7, 10, 303, 314–17, 321, 325
acquisitions, drama theory 249–65
action orientations 24–40, 45–59, 67–88,
    97–112
action phase, intervention processes 292–308,
    313–34
action research projects, SCA 115, 171–9
action stage, SSM 71–88
activity models, SSM 71–2, 77–88, 97–112, 312–34
actors, SSM 75–88, 101–12
agendas, workshops 145–6
AIDA see analysis of interconnected decision areas
analyses
    intervention processes 292–308, 313–34
    SCA 131, 152, 157, 170, 175–6
    SSM 73–4, 353
analysis concepts, new paradigms 1–19
analysis of interconnected decision areas (AIDA) 131,
    157–77
analytic hierarchy process xv
Anderson, S. 343
Anglo-French Concorde project 61, 65–6
appreciation phase, intervention processes 292–308,
    313–34
Arnoff, E.L. 10
Ashby, W.R. 40, 268
assessment phase, intervention processes 292–308,
    313–34

BAC see British Aircraft Corporation
BAe 264
balance windows, SCA 136–7
Beer, S. 270, 274, 300, 344
Bell Telephone Laboratories 61–2
Belton, V. 284–6
Bendeck, M. 345–7
Bennett, P. vii, 2, 3, 225–48
Best, G. 198, 202
Blair, T. 264
Bombardier 10
bottom-up approaches 11, 345, 350
Bowen, K. 349–50
BPR see business process reengineering
Branson, R. 331
briefing materials, confrontation analysis 246–7
British Aircraft Corporation (BAC) 65–6, 86

Brocklesby, J. 293
Bryant, J. vii, 225–48
Bryson, J. 343
build-up stage, drama theory 231–47
business process reengineering (BPR), PowerGen 322–34

capta concepts 99, 111
cards, drama theory 232–65
Casar, A. 68
case studies xiv, xvi
    cognitive maps 43–59, 315–34
    drama theory 242, 249–65
    M&As 249–65
    Marintec case study 121–49
    multimethodology concepts 303–4, 311–35
    NAO 43–59
    National Health Service 91–112
    Netherlands 115–16, 120–1, 151–80
    OMT 44–59
    PowerGen 303–4, 311–35
    robustness analysis 209–23
    Sainsbury's 303–4, 311–34
    SCA 115–16, 120–49, 151–80, 315–34
    SODA 39–40, 43–59
    SSM 87, 88, 91–112, 315–34
CASE tools 300
CATWOE concepts 74–88, 101–12, 300
causal loop diagrams (CLDs) 279–84, 289
Cause Maps 40
Chambers, R. 345–6
changes
    BPR 322–34
    drama theory 240–7, 253
    resistance factors 353
    social/political contexts 352–3
    SSM stages 71–88, 101–12
    uncertainty contrasts 183
Checkland, P. viii, 3, 6–7, 10, 61–89, 91–113, 294, 338,
    347, 349
chicken game 226–30, 238–9, 253
Churchman, C.W. 3, 10
Clarke, S. 92, 96–112
CLDs see causal loop diagrams
client systems 345
    SODA 22, 43–59
    SSM 73
    wicked problems 13, 350
clustering issues, cognitive maps 36–9, 49–59
co-ordination functions, VSM 271–6

cognitive maps xiv, 15, 23–59, 289–307, 315–34, 348, 353
   applications 43–59, 315–34, 348
   case studies 43–59, 315–34
   clustering issues 36–9, 49–59
   concepts 24–40, 353
   development methods 27–32
   examples 27–37, 43–59, 315–34
   interviews 30–2, 38, 44–59
   merged maps 32–40
   negative signs 28–9, 32
   size issues 29–30
   SODA 23–40, 43–59
   tails 28–39
cognitive psychology 77
cognitive theory 23–4
collaboration analysis *see* confrontation...
Collins, D. 353
commitment packages 142–9, 170–80, 187–206, 297
communications
   see also language...
   Habermas' three worlds 290–307
   non-verbal communications 342
   SCA 145–7
   SODA 23–40, 43–59
community groups, robustness analysis 222–3
community operational research 343, 349–51
comparative advantages, SCA 134–7, 167
comparison areas 119–20, 122–49, 157–80
comparison processes, SSM 71–88, 106–12
compatibility issues, SCA 127–49
competencies, multimethodologies 334
complexity issues 1, 4–9, 15–16, 268, 338–53
   disabling effects 36
   diverse unity considerations 338–53
   effects 1, 36, 40
   networks 1, 4–9, 15, 74, 115–49, 154–80
   representations 15–16
   SCA 115–49, 154–80
   SODA 23–40
compromises, drama theory 241–7
computers
   see also information technology
   future prospects 352
   software 26, 27, 36–9, 45–59, 125–49, 286, 339
Concorde 61, 65–6
conflicts xv, 18, 48, 316, 341–2
   drama theory 225–65, 353
   resolutions 242–7, 341–2
confrontation analysis 232–65
   see also drama theory
   briefing materials 246–7
   concepts 232–48
   M&As 249–65
   modelling processes 243–7
   usage 243–7
congruencies, methods 337–55
construct theory 23–6
consulting practices, SODA 23–40, 43–59

contexts 304
   PSMs 14–17
   SODA 23–6
controls
   SSM 77–88, 102–12
   VSM 272–6
Conway, G. 347
cooperation issues xv, 352
   dilemmas 236–65
   drama theory 225–65, 352
   virtual organizations 352
Corbett, C. 7
Cornwall, A. 345
corporate problems 7–9, 21–41
counterintuitive behaviours, system dynamics 276–84
Crichton, C. 115
critical systems heuristics (CSH) 300–6
critiques, paradigms 3–9
Cropper, S. 340
CSH *see* critical systems heuristics
cultural issues, SSM 69, 71–2, 75, 86, 353
customers, SSM 75–88, 101–12
cybernetics 268–9, 276
cyclic processes
   SCA 133–49, 152–80
   SODA 38–9
   SSM 71–2, 86–8

Dando, M.R. 2, 3
data
   concepts 98–9, 111, 293, 348
   demands 11, 34–6, 44–59, 314, 346–8
de Bono, E. 325
de Jong, A. 154
de Neufville, R. 12, 66
DE *see* Decision Explorer
debility concepts 194–8
deceit responses, drama theory 242–7
decentralization issues 345–6
deciding phase, robustness analysis 204–6
decision analysis xiv, 284–7, 305
decision areas, concepts 121–6, 154–7
decision conferencing, xiv, 284–7
Decision Explorer (DE) software 26, 27, 36, 45–59, 339
decision graphs 122–49, 154–80
decision links 122–49
decision making
   complementary models 118–20
   concepts 186–7
   drama theory 225–47, 338–55
   multimethodology concepts xiv, xvi, 283–4, 289–335
   new analysis paradigms 1–19
   planning contrasts 186–7
   robustness analysis xiv-xvi, 11–12, 181–223
   SCA 115–49, 151–80
decision packages, robustness analysis 189–91
decision processes 12–18
decision schemes, SCA 129–49, 160–80

decision support, drama theory 245–7
decomposed methodologies 299–300
Delbecq, A. 343
DELPHI approach 185, 202, 304–5
design issues 5, 62–3, 118–20, 126–49, 157–80, 205–6, 274, 294–306
deterrence dilemmas, drama theory 238–47, 257–65
development planning methods 343, 345–7, 351–2
diagrams 15, 17, 347
   see also maps
dichotomy, problems 4–6, 10–12, 18
dilemmas
   drama theory 230–65
   implications 236–43
   six dilemmas 236–65
directed graphs 27
diverse unity issues
   concepts 337–55
   focus points 337–8, 350–1
   groups 339–53
   other methods 343–7
   process 338–53
   research considerations 351–3
Dixit, A. 251
dominance analyses, SCA 167
drama theory xiv-xvi, 12, 15, 225–65, 293, 338–55
   see also confrontation analysis
   applications 242, 249–65
   basics 230–2
   cards 232–65
   case studies 242, 249–65
   changes 240–7, 253
   compromises 241–7
   concepts 225, 230–47, 353
   conflicts 225–65, 353
   cooperation issues 225–65, 352
   deceit responses 242–7
   decision support 245–7
   dilemmas 230–65
   diverse unity issues 338–55
   examples 233–40, 242, 249–65
   fallback 231–47, 255–65
   final state theorem 242–7
   futures 232–47, 255–65
   irreversible moves 241–7, 261–5
   Jerusalem taxi-driver story 251
   M&As 249–65
   modelling processes 243–7
   positions 232–65
   practicalities 234–6
   preferences 226–47, 255–65
   resolutions 242–7
   revenge issues 241–7, 261–5
   six dilemmas 236–43
   structure issues 230–47
   terminologies 245
   threatened futures 232–47, 255–65

dynamics
   SCA 118–20, 152, 159, 172–3, 276–84
   SD xiv, 26, 39, 276–84, 289, 305

Economist 264
Eden, C. viii, 3, 10, 21–41, 43–60, 243, 338, 340
effectiveness issues, SSM 78–88, 101–6
efficacy issues, SSM 78–88, 101–6
efficiency issues, SSM 78–88, 101–6
emergent properties 68
Emery, F.E. 183
engineers, projects 61–7
enquiring processes, SSM 70, 88
environmental issues 351
   SCA 116–39, 148–9, 154–80
   SSM 75–88, 101–12
   system dynamics 276–84
   turbulent environments 183–4
   uncertainties 116–39
   VSM xiv, 267–76, 297–307
EQUITY software 286
Espejo, R. 274
evaluations 181
   SSM 68–88
Evans, P.B. 230
exploring phase, robustness analysis 204–6

facilitators 13–14, 21–40, 45–6, 91–112, 120–49, 284–7, 340–53
   see also workshops
fallback, drama theory 231–47, 255–65
Fassolo, B. 347
feedback loops 268
   SCA 119–20
   system dynamics 276–84
filtered information concepts 99, 111, 268–9
final state theorem, drama theory 242–7
finding-out processes, SSM 71–4, 99–112
flexibility issues
   costs 206
   robustness analysis 187–223
Flood, R.L. 3
focus groups 59
focus points, diverse unity issues 337–8, 350–1
focus windows, SCA 125–49
forecasts, futures 184–6, 191–2, 263–4
Forrester, J. 276
French, S. 284
Friend, J. ix, 10, 115–49, 151, 182, 221
future PSM prospects 351–3
future scenarios 17, 85, 140–5, 154–80, 182–206, 232–65, 305
future search conferences 344

game theory 225–47, 250–65, 293
gor tonking example, SSM 81–3
graphs 15, 27, 122–49, 154–80, 347
Great Wall of China 61
Griffiths, R. 94
Group Explorer software 26, 36

group maps 40
groups
    see also teams; workshops
    development planning methods 343, 345–7, 351–2
    diverse unity issues 339–53
    large group interventions 343–5
    PSMs 1–2, 13–14, 267, 339–53
    robustness analysis 204–6, 339
    SCA 121–80, 339
    SODA 22–40, 45–59
Guardian 27

Habermas, J. 290–307
Hall, A.D. 61
hard systems 6–8, 10–11, 14, 63–7, 87–8, 289–309,
    319–34, 348–50
    see also operational research
Harnden, R. 274, 352
Harsanyi, J.C. 229
hedging tools 188
Hickling, A. ix, 115, 120–1, 145–8, 151–80
hierarchy concepts, systems 80
high ground problems 5
HIVIEW software 286
holistic thinkers 97, 108
Holmberg, S. 344
Holwell, S. 92, 98, 111, 347
Hoppe, R. 178
Hopwood, A.G. 8
Howard, N. ix-x, 225–65
human activity systems 69–88, 109, 290–1
Huxham, C. 340
Hypergame Analysis 12, 229

IB *see* issue-based models
idealized planning xv
ideas
    NGT 343–5
    SSM 67–88
IDEF approaches 325
incrementalism 184
individuals, SODA 23–40, 43–59
inducement dilemmas, drama theory 238–47, 257–65
influence diagrams 26, 39, 305
information
    concepts 98–9, 106–8, 111
    flows 65, 106–8, 346–7
information systems (IS)
    concepts 98–9, 111–12, 347–9
    disasters 348
    IT 108–9, 111–12, 348–9
    multimethodologies 312–34
    National Health Service 97–112
    PowerGen 322–34
    PSM applications 347–9
    Sainsbury's 312–34
    SSM 97–112, 347–9
    systems analysis concepts 63, 66, 347–9
information technology (IT)
    future prospects 352

IS 108–9, 111–12, 348–9
    software 26, 27, 36–9, 45–59, 125–49, 286, 339
innovations, transfers 116
inputs, transformation processes 74–88, 101–12, 334
intellectual resources system (IRS) 294–307
intelligence functions, VSM 272–6
Internet 352
intervention processes 290, 291–308, 311–35, 341–5
interviews 346
    multimethodologies 313–14
    SODA 30–2, 38, 44–59
irreversible moves, drama theory 241–7,
    261–5
IRS *see* intellectual resources system
IS *see* information systems
issue-based (IB) models 77, 101–2
IT *see* information technology

J. Sainsbury *see* Sainsbury's
Jackson, M. 3, 8, 299
Janoff, S. 344
Jerusalem taxi-driver story 251
Jessop, W.N. 115, 221
Journal of the Operational Research Society xiii
JOURNEY making methodology 21–2, 26–39
judgements 5–6, 9, 170

Keeney, R.L. 12
Keil, M. 348
Kelly, G.A. 23, 353
Keys, P. 3, 8, 299
knowledge concepts 98–9, 162
Kuhn, T. 2

Labour Party, cognitive maps 27–35
laddering up/down concepts 30–1
language uses 15–17, 23–9, 77, 290–1
    see also communications
large group interventions 343–5
Law of Requisite Variety 40, 268
learning systems 315–34, 343–7
    diverse unity issues 343–7
    open space technology concepts 344
    SCA 118–20, 152, 159, 172–3
    SSM 67–88, 91–112, 353
    system dynamics 276–84
Lee, A.M. 186
liquidity tools 187–8
Loizos, P. 346
London Ambulance Service 348
London Stock Exchange 348
LUMAS model 87, 91, 110–11

M&As *see* mergers and acquisitions
McLoughlin, J. 27, 29, 33
magical number 77, 80, 104
management issues
    see also changes
    concepts 67–8, 352–3
    drama theory 249–65

M&As 249–65
   multimethodologies 314–34
   NHS 94–112
   projects 61–7
   robustness analysis 217–19
   SCA 118–49
   SSM 67–88, 94–112
   VSM 268–76
management science *see* operational research
mapping methods, multimethodology concepts 295–9
maps 347
   cognitive maps xiv, 15, 23–59, 289–307, 315–34, 348, 353
   mind maps 26
Mar Molinero, C. 349
Marintec case study 121–49
Markus, L. 348
material world concepts 289, 290–307
MAUT *see* multi-attribute utility theory
MCDA *see* multi-criteria decision analysis
merged cognitive maps 32–40
mergers and acquisitions (M&As), drama theory 249–65
messes, problems 4–5, 21–40, 62
Metagame Analysis 12
methodologies
   see also multimethodology concepts
   concepts 87, 108–11, 289–309, 337–55
   definitions 289, 307–8
   robustness analysis 200–6, 221–3, 338–9
methods
   see also diverse unity issues
   concepts 87, 267–89, 307–8, 311–34, 337–55
   congruencies 337–55
   contrasts 337–55
   other methods 267–88, 343–7
   related methods 267–88, 343–7
Midgley, G. 8
Mikkelsen, B. 346
Miller, G. 77
Miller, R. 211, 220
mind maps 26
Mingers, J. x, 1–19, 267–309, 311, 313, 337–55, 348
mixed-motive games 226
modellers, roles 13–14, 22
modelling processes, confrontation analysis 243–7
modernism concepts 3–4
modes, robustness analysis 198–206
moments of truth, drama theory 231–47
monitoring and control systems, SSM 77–88, 102–12
moon landing 4, 62–3, 184–6
moon-ghetto metaphor 4
Morecroft, J. 283
Morgenstern, O. 225
multi-attribute utility theory (MAUT) 284–7
multi-criteria decision analysis (MCDA) 284–7
multi-future robustness issues 190–2, 197–206, 221–3
multi-stage models 229
multidimensional problems 289–91
multilateral analysis, drama theory 250
multimedia systems 352

multimethodology concepts xiv, xvi, 283–4, 289–335, 351
   applications 303–6, 311–35
   benefits 289–99
   case studies 303–4, 311–35
   definition 289
   design issues 294–303
   diverse unity issues 337–55
   examples 303–6, 311–35
   glossary 307–8
   Habermas' three worlds 290–307
   intervention processes 290, 291–308, 311–35
   mapping methods 295–9
   partitioned/decomposed methodologies 299–300
   processes 290, 291–308, 311–34
   reasons 289–94
   survey findings 304–6
   triangulation issues 290, 293–4
   types 308
Munro, I. 293, 304

Nalebuff, B. 251
National Audit Office (NAO) 43–59, 97
National Health Service 91–112, 184
nature, organizations 23–40
negative feedback concepts 276–8
negative signs, cognitive maps 28–9, 32
negotiations 12–14, 21–40, 239–65
Neil, M. 322–3
Netherlands
   case studies 115–16, 120–1, 151–80
   PSM applications 10
   SCA 115–16, 120–1, 151–80
networks, complexity issues 1, 4–9, 15, 74, 115–49, 154–80
nominal group technique (NGT) 343–5
non-verbal communications 342

objectivist stances 6–7, 16–17, 24, 63–4
official paradigms *see* traditional...
OMT *see* oval mapping technique
open space technology concepts 344
operational research (OR)
   characteristics 10–14, 222
   community operational research 343, 349–51
   concepts 2–3, 6–7, 63, 222, 338
   contrasts 10–15, 18
   hard systems 6–8, 10–11, 14, 63–7, 87–8, 289–309, 348–50
   movements xv-xvi
   remit 6–7, 8
   SODA 22, 38–9
   strategic choices 120
Operational Research Society of America (ORSA), code of conduct 2–3
Operational Research Society, UK 349
operational systems, SSM 77–88
operations
   multimethodology concepts 301–34
   VSM 269–76

opportunities 17, 107–8, 305, 353
options
    drama theory 232–65
    robustness analysis xiv–xvi, 11–12, 181–223
    SCA 126–49, 157–80
    scanning methods 16
OR *see* operational research
organizations
    community operational research 343,
        349–51
    innovation transfers 116
    nature 23–40
    purposes 25
    robustness analysis 187–206
    SCA 120, 146–9, 177
    SODA 23–40, 43–59
    SSM 68
    system dynamics 276–84, 305
    virtual organizations 352
    VSM 268–76, 297–307, 317–34
Ormerod, R. x, 10, 301, 311–35, 349
orphan analyses, clusters 53
ORSA *see* Operational Research Society of America
orthodox paradigms *see* traditional...
other methods 267–88, 343–7
outputs, transformation processes 74–88, 101–12,
    334
oval mapping technique (OMT) 40, 44–59
    see also cognitive maps
overview xiv–xvi
Owen, H. 344
owners, SSM 75–88, 101–12

paradigms 350
    see also traditional...
    analysis concepts 1–19
    characteristics 10–14, 308
    crises 2–3
    critiques 3–9
    definitions 308
    partitioned/decomposed methodologies 299–
        300
    prescriptions 10–14
Parston, G. 198, 202
participation 314–34, 343–7
    group development planning methods 343, 345–7,
        351–2
    SODA 36–9, 44–59
participative robustness analysis 203–6
participative rural appraisal (PRA) 346–7
partitioned methodologies 299–300
perceptions 197–206
    problems 14, 24, 66–88
    SSM 67–88, 91–112
personal world concepts 289, 290–307
PEST analysis 305
Phillips, L. 284–5, 340
Phillips, M.C. 340
pictures, rich pictures 73–4, 82–3, 290, 293, 297, 301–6,
    316–34

planning methods xv, 313–34
    concepts 186–7
    group development planning methods 343, 345–7,
        351–2
    Robustness Analysis 184–223
    uncertainty issues 184–206
pluralist approaches 8, 315–34, 351
policy sciences 3–4
political issues 289–90
    changes 352–3
    M&As 249–65
    SCA 115–49, 153–80
    SODA 21–40
    SSM 66, 73–4
Porter's five forces 304, 317, 325
positions, drama theory 232–65
positive feedback concepts 276–8
possibilities 17
Poulter, J. 92, 96–108
power dimensions 351–3
    SODA 22–40
    SSM 73–4
PowerGen 303–4, 311–35
PRA *see* participative rural appraisal
practical problems, technical problems 5–6, 10–11
pragmatic approaches 289–335, 351
Pratt, B. 346
preferences, drama theory 226–47, 255–65
prescriptions, paradigms 10–14
primary-task (PT) root definitions 77, 101–6, 109–11
prisoner's game 228–30, 236–9, 253, 352
probabilities 16–17, 120, 182–3
problem focus issues, SCA 124–49, 154–80
problem situations, SSM 71–4, 83–8, 91–112, 294–307
problem structuring methods (PSMs) xiii–xvi, 203–4,
    339–53
    applications 9–11, 347–53
    bottom-up approaches 11, 345, 350
    common features 12–18, 203–4, 267, 340
    community operational research 343, 349–51
    concepts 1–3, 9–18, 340, 347–53
    contexts 14–17, 304
    diverse unity issues 339–53
    future prospects 351–3
    groups 1–2, 13–14, 267, 339–53
    practical applications 9–11, 347–53
    research considerations 351–3
    structure and process 9–18
    tools 14–17
    virtual organizations 352
problems
    dichotomy 4–6, 10–12, 18
    messes 4–5, 62
    multimethodology concepts xiv, xvi, 283–4, 289–335,
        351
    new analysis paradigms 1–19
    perceptions 14, 24, 66
    system dynamics 278–84, 305
    tame problems 5, 10, 350
    well-put problems 10–12
    wicked problems 5, 11–14, 17–18, 350

problems solving concepts 6–7
process 338–53
    diverse unity issues 338–53
    multimethodology concepts 290, 291–308, 311–34
    PSMs 9–18
    SCA 120, 146–7, 177–8
    SODA 21–40, 338
    systems engineering 62–3
products
    diverse unity issues 338–53
    SCA 120, 146–7, 178–9
progress packages, SCA 142–9, 170–80, 187
projectors 54
projects
    concepts 61–2
    engineers 61–7
    management issues 61–7, 312–34
    SODA 32–40, 43–59
    steering committees 312–34
PSMs *see* problem structuring methods
PT *see* primary-task root definitions
purposeful activities, SSM 69–88, 98–112

RAND Corporation 4, 6, 63
ranking exercises 346
rapid rural appraisal (RRA) 346–7
rational comprehensive planning 184–6
Ravetz, J.R. 5–6, 10
RDs *see* root definitions
real world concepts, SSM 71–88, 98–9, 111–12, 300–6
reflective practices 97, 301–6
reformists 3
related methods 267–88, 343–7
relationships
    Habermas' three worlds 290–307
    SCA 117–39, 154–80, 221
    systemic nature 276–7
    uncertainties 117–39, 154–80
reliability issues, system dynamics 282–3
requisite models 13–14
research considerations, diverse unity issues 351–3
research programmes 64
resilience tools 188
resolutions, conflicts 242–7, 341–2
revenge issues, drama theory 241–7, 261–5
reviews, multimethodology concepts 301–6
revolutionaries 3
rich pictures, SSM 73–4, 82–3, 290, 293, 297, 301–6,
    316–34
Rio Tinto 322–3
risks, uncertainty issues 182–4
Ritchie, C. 349
Rittel, H.W.J. 3, 5, 10
Rivett, G. 93
robustness analysis xiv-xvi, 11–12, 181–223, 338–9
    applications 181–2, 209–23
    benefits 203
    case studies 209–23
    community groups 222–3
    concepts 181–207

debility concepts 194–8
deciding phase 204–6
definition 189–91
examples 192–206, 209–23
exploring phase 204–6
flexibility issues 187–206
groups 204–6, 339
methodologies 200–6, 221–3
mode 2 robustness 198–206
multi-future robustness issues 190–2, 197–206, 221–3
participative analysis 203–6
SCA 187, 221
screening phase 204–6
structuring phase 204–23
valuing phase 204–6, 221
workshops 204–6, 339
Rocco, E. 352
Rodriguez-Ulloa, R.A. 111
role playing methods 346–7
room layouts, SODA workshops 47, 57
root definitions (RDs) 15, 293–307
    CATWOE 74–88, 101–12, 300
    SSM 71–88, 102–12
Rosenhead, J. x-xi, xiii-xvi, 1–19, 181–223, 267–88,
    337–55
Royal Victoria Infirmary (RVI) 96–112
RRA *see* rapid rural appraisal
RTZ 322–3, 325
RVI *see* Royal Victoria Infirmary

Sainsbury's 10, 94, 303–4, 311–34
SAST *see* strategic assumption surface and testing
SCA *see* strategic choice approach
scenarios 17, 85, 140–5, 154–80, 182–206, 232–65, 305
Scholes, J. 10, 74, 82–3, 109, 111
Schon, D.A. 5, 6, 9, 15, 97
scientific paradigms, concepts 2–3
screening phase, robustness analysis 204–6
secondary problems, OR 7–8
Senge, P. 276
sequential decisions 186–7, 221
SFDs *see* stocks and flows diagrams
Shell 10, 186
shortlisting methods, SCA 133–7
Silverman, D. 24
six dilemmas, drama theory 236–65
Smyth, D.S. 74
social considerations 6–7, 11–14, 21–40, 289–307, 343–4
    changes 352–3
    SODA 21–40
    SSM 66–88
social world concepts 289, 290–307
SODA *see* strategic options development and analysis
soft systems 6, 11, 63–88, 109–12, 289–309, 312–34,
    348–51
soft systems methodology (SSM) xiv-xvi, 10–12, 22,
    61–113, 274, 289, 294–307, 312–53
    action stage 71–88
    analyses 73–4, 353
    applications 87, 88, 91–112, 315–34, 348–9

soft systems methodology (SSM) (*continued*)
assumptions 67–70
case studies 87, 88, 91–112, 315–34
CATWOE 74–88, 101–12, 300
change stage 71–88, 101–12
characteristics 67–70
comparison processes 71–88, 106–12
concepts 61–88, 109–12, 348–9
conceptual models 71–2, 77–88, 97–112, 293–307,
    321–34, 348–9
cyclic processes 71–2, 86–8
diverse unity issues 337–53
emergence 64–70
examples 74–7, 80–8, 91–112, 315–34
finding-out processes 71–4, 99–112
gor tonking example 81–3
IS 97–112, 347–9
learning systems 67–88, 91–112, 353
LUMAS model 87, 91, 110–11
National Health Service 91–112
nature 87, 109
problem situations 71–4, 83–8, 91–112, 294–307
rich pictures 73–4, 82–3, 290, 293, 297, 301–6,
    316–34
root definitions 71–88, 102–12, 293–307
stages 67, 70–88
systems engineering 61–7, 87–8, 91
transformation processes 74–88, 101–12, 334
software 26, 27, 36–9, 45–59, 125–49, 286, 339
solution space concepts 16
SOSM *see* system of systems methodologies
specifications, engineers 62–3
spreadsheets, SODA 39
SSM *see* soft systems methodology
Stafford, J.H. 66
steering committees 312–34
Sterman, J. 277, 283
Stewart, T.J. 284–7
stocks and flows diagrams (SFDs) 280–4
Stowell, F. 347
STRAD software 125–49, 339
strategic assumption surface and testing (SAST) xv,
    315–16
strategic choice approach (SCA) xiv-xv, 10–12, 22, 37,
    115–80, 187, 221, 293, 297–307, 315–55
applications 115–16, 120–49, 151–80, 315–34
case studies 115–16, 120–49, 151–80, 315–34
choosing mode 119–20, 137–49, 167–80, 297, 301–6,
    314–34
commitment packages 142–9, 170–80, 187, 297
comparing mode 119–20, 132–49, 157–80
concepts 115–49, 175–80
continuous developments 147–9
designing mode 118–20, 126–31, 138–49, 157–80,
    297
distinguishing features 145–7
diverse unity issues 337–55
dynamics 118–20, 152, 159, 172–3, 276–84
emphases 145–7
examples 115–16, 120–49, 151–80, 315–34

Marintec case study 121–49
origins 115–16
robustness analysis 187, 221
shaping mode 118–20, 121–6, 137–49, 154–80
STRAD software 125–49, 339
tools 120–1, 176
workshops 121–80, 339
strategic management maps 29–30, 32–40
strategic options development and analysis (SODA) xiv-
    xvi, 10, 12, 21–41, 43–60, 297, 337–55
    see also cognitive maps
applications 39–40, 43–59, 353
case studies 39–40, 43–59
concepts 21–41, 353
context 23–6
cyclic processes 38–9
developments 21–2, 32–40
difficulties 39–40
diverse unity issues 337–55
framework 23–6
NAO 43–59
OR 22, 38–9
perspectives 23–6
principles 21–41
projects 32–40, 43–59
software 26, 27, 36–9, 45–59, 339
summary 39–40
workshops 36–9, 46–59
stratified order concepts 80
Stringer, R. 352
structure issues
    drama theory 230–47
    game theory 226
    PSMs 9–18
    robustness analysis 203–6, 211–15
    SCA 115–39
    systems 68, 77–88
structured problems 7–8, 63–5
structuring phase, robustness analysis 204–23
subjectivist stances 6–7, 14, 17, 23
surveys, multimethodology concepts 301–6
swampy messes 5, 6, 15–16
SWOT analysis 305
syntegrity procedures, teams 344–5
System Dynamics (SD) xiv, 26, 39, 276–84, 289, 305
    applications 283–4
    CLDs 279–84, 289
    concepts 276–84
    principles 276–7
    processes 277–84
system of systems methodologies (SOSM) 8–9
systemic nature, relationships 276–7
systems xiii-xvi, 4–6, 23–40
    see also information...
    concepts 68–9, 77–8, 88
    hard systems 6–8, 10–11, 14, 63–7, 87–8, 289–309,
        319–34, 348–50
    hierarchy concepts 80
    larger group interventions 343–4
    robustness analysis 200–6, 221–3

SODA 23–40, 43–59
soft systems 6, 11, 61–88, 109–12, 289–309, 312–34, 348–51
SSM xiv-xvi, 10–12, 22, 61–89, 91–113, 274, 289, 294–307, 312–53
structures 68, 77–88
VSM xiv, 267–76, 297–307, 317–34
systems analysis concepts 63, 66, 347–9
systems engineering concepts 61–7, 87–8, 91

tails, cognitive maps 28–39
Taket, A. 347, 349
tame problems 5, 10, 350
task forces, multimethodologies 312–34
Tavistock Institute of Human Relations 115
teams
    see also groups
    syntegrity procedures 344–5
technical problems
    practical problems 5–6, 10–11
    SCA 115
techniques, concepts 307–8, 339
technologies
    see also information...
    SCA 120, 146–9, 176–7
    SODA 23–40, 43–59
    virtual organizations 352
Thatcher, M. 219, 241
Theory of Personal Constructs (Kelly) 23, 353
threat dilemmas, drama theory 232–5, 238–47, 255–65
threatened futures, drama theory 232–47, 255–65
threats 17, 232–47, 255–65
Thunhurst, C. 3, 10, 349, 351
Thurnscoe 10
time considerations 301–6
    robustness analysis 189
    SCA 118–49, 154–6, 171–9
Tolman, E.C. 26
Tomlinson, R. 13
tools
    PSMs 14–17
    SCA 120–1, 176
Tower Hamlets 10
trade unions, cognitive maps 27–35
traditional paradigms 3–9, 21, 338, 350
    see also paradigms
    contrasts 10–15, 18, 350
    modellers 13–14
transformation processes, SSM 74–88, 101–12, 334
transparency issues xv, 15–16, 222–3, 267, 350
triangulation issues 290, 293–4
Trist, E.L. 183
trumpet of uncertainty 183–4
trust considerations 30–1, 236–47, 258–65
turbulent environments 183–4

UK *see* United Kingdom
Ulrich, W. 300

uncertainty issues xv, 1, 10–11
    categories 116–18
    change contrasts 183
    concepts 8, 16–17
    effects 1, 8, 16–17
    OR 8
    planning methods 184–206
    robustness analysis xiv-xvi, 11–12, 181–223
    SCA 115–49, 154–80, 167–80
    trumpet of uncertainty 183–4
unilateral analysis, drama theory 249–50, 258, 261
United Kingdom (UK)
    Operational Research Society 349
    ORSA 2–3
United States of America (USA) 2–3, 4, 7
unstructured problems 7–9, 63–5
urban planning issues 3–4
USA *see* United States of America
utility scales 226

validation issues, system dynamics 282–3
values
    SCA 117–39, 154–80, 221
    uncertainties 117–39, 154–80
valuing phase, robustness analysis 204–6, 221
Van Wassenhove, L. 7
Venn diagrams 347
Vennix, J.A.M. 340
viable system model (VSM) xiv, 267–76, 297–307, 317–34
    applications 274–6, 317–34
    concepts 267–76
    principles 268–9
video conferences 352
Virgin Power 331
virtual organizations 352
vision 313–34
Von Neumann, J. 225
VSM *see* viable system model

Wagner, H.M. 63
Warglien, M. 352
Webber, M.M. 3
Webster, C. 92–3
Weiner, N 268
Weisbord, M.R. 344
well-put problems 10–12
Weltanschauungen concepts 69, 71, 75, 86, 92, 294
Weston, J. 264
White, L. 347, 349
Whorf, B. 26
wicked problems, concepts 5, 11–14, 17–18, 350
wide-band group decision support systems 13, 22
Williams, T. 10
Wong, H.-Y. 204
word-and-arrow diagrams 26

working environments
    SCA 116–39
    uncertainties 116–39
workshops 339–53
    see also groups
    agendas 145–6
    conflicts 341–2
    decision conferencing xiv, 284–7
    diverse unity issues 339–53

    MCDA 285–7
    robustness analysis 204–6
    SCA 121–80, 339
    SODA 36–9, 46–59
worldview concepts 69, 83, 92, 98–112

zero-sum games 226